OLIVIER MESSIAEN

ROUTLEDGE MUSIC BIBLIOGRAPHIES

SERIES EDITOR: BRAD EDEN

COMPOSERS

Isaac Albéniz (1998)
Walter A. Clark

C. P. E. Bach (2002)
Doris Bosworth Powers

Samuel Barber (2001)
Wayne C. Wentzel

Béla Bartók,
2nd Edition (1997)
Elliott Antokoletz

Vincenzo Bellini (2002)
Stephen A. Willier

Alban Berg (1996)
Bryan R. Simms

Leonard Bernstein (2001)
Paul F. Laird

Johannes Brahms (2003)
Heather Platt

Benjamin Britten (1996)
Peter J. Hodgson

William Byrd,
2nd Edition (2005)
Richard Turbet

Elliott Carter (2000)
John L. Link

Carlos Chávez (1998)
Robert Parker

Frédéric Chopin (1999)
William Smialek

Aaron Copland (2001)
Marta Robertson and
Robin Armstrong

Frederick Delius (2005)
Mary L. Huisman

Gaetano Donizetti (2000)
James P. Cassaro

Edward Elgar (1993)
Christopher Kent

Gabriel Fauré (1999)
Edward R. Phillips

Christoph Willibald Gluck,
2nd Edition (2003)
Patricia Howard

G.F. Handel,
2nd Edition (2004)
Mary Ann Parker

Paul Hindemith (2005)
Stephen Luttman

Charles Ives (2002)
Gayle Sherwood

Scott Joplin (1998)
Nancy R. Ping-Robbins

Zoltán Kodály (1998)
Mícheál Houlahan and
Philip Tacka

Franz Liszt, 2nd Edition
(2004)
Michael Saffle

Guillaume de Machaut (1995)
Lawrence Earp

Felix Mendelssohn Bartholdy
(2001)
John Michael Cooper

Giovanni Pierluigi da
Palestrina (2001)
Clara Marvin

Giacomo Puccini (1999)
Linda B. Fairtile

Maurice Ravel (2004)
Stephen Zank

Gioachino Rossini (2002)
Denise P. Gallo

Camille Saint-Saëns (2003)
Timothy S. Flynn

Alessandro and Domenico
Scarlatti (1993)
Carole F. Vidali

Heinrich Schenker (2003)
Benjamin Ayotte

Alexander Scriabin (2004)
Ellon D. Carpenter

Jean Sibelius (1998)
Glenda D. Goss

Giuseppe Verdi (1998)
Gregory Harwood

Tomás Luis de Victoria (1998)
Eugene Casjen Cramer

Richard Wagner (2002)
Michael Saffle

Adrian Willaert (2004)
David Michael Kidger

GENRES

American Music
Librarianship (2005)
Carol June Bradley

Central European Folk Music
(1996)
Philip V. Bohlman

Chamber Music,
2nd Edition (2002)
John H. Baron

Church and Worship Music
(2005)
Avery T. Sharp and James
Michael Floyd

Concerto (2006)
Stephen D. Lindeman

Ethnomusicology (2003)
Jennifer C. Post

Jazz Scholarship and
Pedagogy,
3rd Edition (2005)
Eddie S. Meadows

Music in Canada (1997)
Carl Morey

OLIVIER MESSIAEN
A RESEARCH AND INFORMATION GUIDE

VINCENT P. BENITEZ

ROUTLEDGE MUSIC BIBLIOGRAPHIES

Routledge
Taylor & Francis Group

LONDON AND NEW YORK

First published 2008
by Routledge

Published 2014 by Routledge
2 Park Square, Milton Park, Abingdon, Oxfordshire OX14 4RN
711 Third Avenue, New York, NY 10017

First issued in paperback 2014

Routledge is an imprint of the Taylor and Francis Group, an informa business

© 2008 Taylor & Francis

Typeset in Times New Roman by
Taylor & Francis Books

Library of Congress Cataloging in Publication Data
A catalog record has been requested for this book

ISBN 978-0-415-97372-4 (hbk)
ISBN 978-1-138-87025-3 (pbk)
ISBN 978-0-203-93558-3 (ebk)

This book is dedicated to my wife,
Esther Ann Wingfield Benitez,
for all her love and patience

Contents

Preface

PURPOSE AND SCOPE OF THE VOLUME

Since his death in 1992, Olivier Messiaen has increasingly been recognized as one of the major composers of the twentieth century. His music continues to be played and studied throughout the world. Messiaen also distinguished himself as a teacher at the Paris Conservatoire from 1941 to 1978, with William Albright, Jean Barraqué, George Benjamin, Pierre Boulez, Alexander Goehr, Karel Goeyvaerts, Tristan Murail, Karlheinz Stockhausen, and Iannis Xenakis numbering among his pupils. At l'Église de la Sainte-Trinité in Paris, one of the city's more prominent churches, Messiaen served as titular organist from 1931 to 1991. He was an avid collector of birdsongs throughout his life and incorporated them into his music. Indeed, Messiaen's knowledge of birdcalls was substantial, approaching that of professional ornithologists.

Interest in Messiaen and his music has been growing for several decades. Numerous primary sources are available, such as interviews and lectures, didactic treatises, commentaries on his works, articles and reviews for journals and essay collections, and prefaces to the books and music of others. Likewise, numerous musicological studies dealing with Messiaen's life and work have been published in several different languages. Many conferences, festivals, and concerts devoted solely to his music have taken place, and recordings of his works are numerous, all reflecting his international stature as a composer. In this technological age, information on Messiaen can be found on the Internet. Interestingly, no extensive annotated bibliography has ever been published that organizes this massive amount of data. The present volume, *Olivier Messiaen: A Research and Information Guide*, is intended to fill this important need.

In a word, *Olivier Messiaen: A Research and Information Guide* presents the reader with the most significant and helpful resources on Messiaen published between 1930 and 2007. Most of the entries are in English, French, and German, reflecting the significance of Messiaen scholarship in the United Kingdom, United States, France, Austria, and Germany. With regard to primary sources, the book attempts to be as comprehensive as possible, listing most of Messiaen's interviews and writings with an eye to offering a "biography in documents." The book, out of necessity, includes only those secondary resources that are considered to be the more consequential examples of Messiaen scholarship. An introductory chapter offers a short biography of Messiaen, a consideration of his musical style and works, and a discussion of Messiaen studies. Chapters 2 and 3 concentrate on the primary literature organized around the following categories: (1) manuscript collections; (2) articles and reviews; (3) pedagogical works; (4) lectures and librettos; (5) prefaces; (6) interviews; (7) correspondence; and (8) documentaries and filmed performances. Chapters 4 through 9, the body of the book, focus on the secondary literature, namely: (1) biographical and stylistic studies; (2) topical examinations; (3) discussions of particular works; (4) accounts of Messiaen in works devoted to other topics; (5) reviews of books and significant performances of Messiaen's music; and (6) examinations of source materials on the Internet. A list of works and a selected discography conclude the book.

Each chapter begins with a paragraph that outlines the general content and scope of its citations. Primary sources are generally listed in chronological order to emphasize the historical development of Messiaen's work. Interviews are listed in alphabetical order for ease of reference, with English translations accompanying them in reverse chronological order, so that the reader is presented with the latest translations. Secondary sources are listed in alphabetical order according to their particular categories, with entries by the same author usually listed in reverse chronological order. For secondary sources in a foreign language, references are almost always made to the original publication, with English translations listed immediately thereafter.

Each citation is assigned a unique sequence number and is identified by the following information as appropriate for books and articles: (1) author(s); (2) title; (3) editor(s); (4) translator(s); (5) publication information; and (6) ISBN, ISSN, and Library of Congress call numbers, which are confirmed through either the book's Copyright Information Page, the On-line Catalogue of the Library of Congress, or that of Indiana University (IUCAT). In certain instances, ISBN numbers are included for both hardback and paperback editions. Some citations of books and articles do not contain ISBN, ISSN, and/or Library of Congress call numbers due to their foreign derivation or to a lack of confirmation. Pagination is usually not included for references to multi-volume books. Multiple citations to essay collections are identified by author(s), titles of both the article and essay collection, and a reference to the essay collection's sequence number.

Capitalization practices for titles in French deserve comment. Messiaen's capitalization in the titles of his works is inconsistent. He apparently capitalized any word that had religious significance for him, such as "temps" in *Quatuor pour la fin du Temps*. In this volume, Messiaen's preferences in capitalization are respected despite any discrepancies that may result. With respect to books and articles, the convention of capitalizing the first word as well as the first noun is followed, even in subtitles, except in some cases where the original capitalization of an article or book is retained in order to respect an author's or editor's practice.

Annotations provide an overview of a source, describe its analytical methodology, point out key concepts, and highlight musical compositions under consideration. Moreover, they may include comparisons with related items. When the subject matter merits a lengthier discussion, annotations offer more detailed information in order to better acquaint the reader with the source and its significance for Messiaen. Annotations are normally based on the latest editions. Significant published reviews are listed at the end of selected annotations and collectively in chapter 8.

Through its annotations, the book attempts to point out which items are indispensable in the Messiaen literature for both the advanced student and experienced researcher. Although the critical evaluation of a source could prejudice a reader's opinion, it was deemed necessary in certain instances to make distinctions between sources of sufficiently high or low quality, given the abundance of secondary materials in the Messiaen literature and the unfortunate errors and misunderstandings about the composer and his music that have often cropped up. In other instances, annotations convey a more objective tone, leaving it up to the reader to judge a source's quality.

SELECTION CRITERIA

Sources have been included based on the following criteria:

1 Primary sources, such as manuscript collections, writings, didactic treatises, lectures, prefaces, interviews, correspondence, and documentaries.
2 Translations of primary sources.
3 Entire books, monographs, and essay collections devoted to Messiaen.
4 Articles devoted to Messiaen in scholarly journals.
5 Short essays or essays of marginal research value that are on topics on which relatively little has been written.
6 Essays of marginal research value by famous authors (e.g., Ned Rorem).
7 Noteworthy Ph.D. dissertations, selected high quality doctoral documents, and master's theses on Messiaen from various North American and British universities.
8 Significant discussions of Messiaen within sources devoted to other topics, such as articles, essays in collections, books, music history and music theory textbooks (geared to the advanced student), dissertations, dictionaries, and encyclopedias.
9 Selected reviews of books, essay collections, monographs, treatises, world premieres, and significant performances of Messiaen's works. As a rule, these reviews are not annotated.
10 Web sites devoted to Messiaen, including competitions, conferences, and festivals.

Sources have been excluded based on the following criteria:

1 Sources written in less common languages, such as Danish, Dutch, Finnish, Hebrew, Hungarian, Japanese, Norwegian, Polish, Russian, and Slovenian. Due to the selective nature of this research guide, Italian and Spanish are also excluded. However, some representative entries in Italian are included because of their significance to the Messiaen literature.
2 Liner notes by Messiaen for recordings, which are duplicated in the primary and secondary literature.
3 Reviews of published editions.
4 Reviews of recordings.
5 With a few exceptions, newspaper and magazine articles.
6 Conference presentations.
7 Honors theses.

Acknowledgments

I want to thank a number of people who provided me with advice and assistance during the writing of this book. I am particularly grateful to Nigel Simeone, Professor of Historical Musicology at the University of Sheffield, United Kingdom, for his assistance in supplying me with invaluable information regarding a number of primary-source items, as well as other materials that were not readily available. His generosity in sharing his special knowledge of Messiaen has made this book a stronger research tool in many ways. I am deeply in his debt. Sincere thanks are due to Randal Baier, Associate Professor and Multimedia, Fine and Performing Arts Librarian and former colleague at Eastern Michigan University, for his advice on bibliographic matters, and David Lasocki, Head of Reference Services at the William and Gayle Cook Music Library, Indiana University, for his help in securing different sources for my examination. Sincere acknowledgment should be made to a number of people who provided me with information or sources regarding their scholarly work either on or involving Messiaen: Stephen Broad; Christopher Dingle; Wai-Ling Cheong; Bridget F. Conrad; Robert Fallon; Jon Gillock; Stephen Hopkins; Peter Hill; and Andrew Shenton. Special thanks go out to Malcolm Ball for providing me with access to various audio and video materials on Messiaen that were not readily available. I want to thank Eric Isaacson, Benito Rivera, Joseph N. Straus, and Donald Wilson for their assistance during the initial stages of this project. To the library staffs at Bowling Green State University, Eastern Michigan University, and the Pennsylvania State University, I express my gratitude for their help in securing many sources. I am grateful to my colleagues at the Pennsylvania State University, particularly Professors Marylène Dosse and Maureen Carr, for their assistance and moral support during the writing of this book.

I am also pleased to thank Malcolm Crowthers for granting me permission to use his photograph of Messiaen wearing a scarf knitted by Yvonne Loriod-Messiaen taken outside La Trinité in 1982 to grace the cover of this book.

To Père Jean-Rodolphe Kars, former concert pianist and currently a chaplain at the Shrine of Paray-le-Monial, France, I must express my gratitude for his encouragement of my research on the life and music of Messiaen.

Finally, I should like to extend my deepest appreciation and profound gratitude to my wife, Esther Ann Wingfield Benitez. She encouraged me during every phase of the writing of this book and helped me with numerous practical matters associated with the project. I owe her so much.

1

Olivier Messiaen: Life, Musical Style and Works, and Studies

In order to provide a background for this annotated bibliography on Messiaen, chapter 1 considers his life and music and surveys related biographical, analytical, and stylistic studies, offering a picture of the current state of Messiaen research.

A SKETCH OF MESSIAEN'S LIFE

Note: the following biography is indebted to Peter Hill and Nigel Simeone's account of Messiaen's life in *Messiaen* (item 210).

Born on 10 December 1908 in Avignon, France, to the poetess Cécile Sauvage (1883–1927) and the well-known translator of English authors Pierre Messiaen (1883–1957), Olivier Eugène Prosper Charles Messiaen grew up in a cultured literary home. When his father was called up for military service during World War I, Messiaen moved with his family to Grenoble where he was brought up largely by his mother. She influenced him deeply, especially through her cycle of poems *L'Âme en bourgeon* ("The Budding Soul"), which not only was addressed to him during her pregnancy but also predicted that he would be a musician. At this time he was introduced to the fairy tales of Madame d'Aulnoy (1650–1705) and the plays of Shakespeare. He regularly staged and performed Shakespeare plays all by himself for his brother Alain. While living in Grenoble, Messiaen was impressed by nearby mountain landscapes, which would influence him for the rest of his life.

At the age of eight, Messiaen began to teach himself how to play the piano and compose. One of his first compositions was a piano piece inspired by Tennyson's *La Dame de Shalott*. Messiaen became acquainted with the operatic scores of Berlioz, Gluck, Mozart, and Wagner, which he received as childhood gifts, along with the music of Debussy and Ravel. Besides quietly reading Gluck's *Orphée* on a park bench in Grenoble, Messiaen was playing operatic scores on his uncle's piano, singing all of the principal roles. As a self-taught pianist he made remarkable progress, as evidenced by his ability to play Debussy's *Estampes* and Ravel's *Gaspard de la nuit*.

Once Messiaen's father was released from the French Army in 1918, he secured a teaching appointment at the Lycée Clemenceau in Nantes, to where the family moved. It was there at the age of ten (or perhaps eleven— see Hill and Simeone [item 210], 15–16) that Messiaen was given a copy of the vocal score of Debussy's *Pelléas et Mélisande* by Jean (or Jehan) de Gibon, his harmony teacher. The gift was a catalyst for determining Messiaen's eventual career as a musician. In 1919, Pierre Messiaen obtained a new teaching appointment at the Lycée Charlemagne in Paris. The Messiaen family moved to the capital from Nantes at which time Messiaen entered the Paris Conservatoire.

Although records at the Paris Conservatoire show Messiaen's official enrollment as beginning in 1920, Messiaen has always claimed that he started there in 1919. This is entirely plausible since he most likely audited classes before he was officially enrolled. After a decade of studying at the Paris Conservatoire, Messiaen earned second prizes in harmony and piano accompaniment (1924), and first prizes in piano accompaniment (1925), fugue (1926), organ and improvisation (1929), music history (1929), and composition (1930). Among his teachers were (1) Georges Falkenberg, piano; (2) Jean Gallon, harmony; (3) Noël Gallon, private lessons in harmony and counterpoint (for ten years); (4) César Abel Estyle, piano accompaniment; (5) Georges Caussade, fugue; (6) Charles-Marie Widor and Paul Dukas, composition; (7) Marcel Dupré, organ and improvisation; (8) Maurice Emmanuel, music history; and (9) Joseph Baggers, timpani and percussion.

In 1931, Messiaen left the Paris Conservatoire and assumed the post of titular organist at the Église de la Sainte-Trinité. He distinguished himself as a composer-organist in the 1930s through a series of theologically oriented works for different media. As evinced by his interview with journalist José Bruyr immediately after his appointment at La Trinité (see item 155), Messiaen was by now a staunch Roman Catholic, and his faith already had an important bearing on his musical outlook. On 22 June 1932, Messiaen married the composer-violinist Louise Justine ("Claire") Delbos (1906–59), to whom he dedicated his song cycle *Poèmes pour Mi* ("Mi" was Messiaen's nickname for Claire) in 1936. Their son Pascal was born in 1937, inspiring another song cycle *Chants de Terre et de Ciel* a year later. In 1932, Messiaen most likely began teaching at the École Normale de Musique, and in 1936, at the Schola Cantorum. With Yves Baudrier, Daniel-Lesur, and André Jolivet, Messiaen founded the group La Jeune France in 1936. Taking their cue from a title once used by Berlioz, La Jeune France strove for freedom, passion, sensuality, and youthfulness in their works, distancing themselves from the neoclassicism of the time. The group was active in Paris between 1936 and 1939, as well as during the German Occupation of France.

After France declared war on Germany on 3 September 1939, Messiaen was called up for military service. In an article he wrote for the journal *L'Orgue* in the early part of 1940 that featured French organists writing about their life in the armed forces (item 52), Messiaen provided a description of military life. He complained about the chores he had to do, preferring instead to focus on music. To make his situation more tolerable, he would read a few pages of his pocket scores of Beethoven's symphonies, Ravel's *Ma Mère l'Oye*, Stravinsky's *Les Noces*, and Honegger's *Horace victorieux* every night. In May 1940, Messiaen was among the thousands of French soldiers taken prisoner when the German army rolled through France. He was sent to Stalag VIII A, a prisoner-of-war-camp at Görlitz in Silesia. While in captivity, he composed the *Quatuor pour la fin du Temps* and premiered the work, along with fellow performers Henri Akoka, Jean Le Boulaire, and Étienne Pasquier, on 15 January 1941.

After his release by the Germans in 1941, Messiaen was appointed to teach harmony at the Paris Conservatoire. He began to attract gifted pupils and was subsequently giving private group lessons in musical analysis between 1943 and 1947 at the home of Guy-Bernard Delapierre (see items 257 and 320). Delapierre, an Egyptologist and composer of film scores whom Messiaen met while in captivity, lived at 24 rue Visconti, which had once been the home of the dramatist Jean Racine (1639–99), hence the meeting place of Messiaen's unofficial analysis classes had historical significance. In 1944, Messiaen wrote the *Technique de mon langage musical*, which he dedicated to Delapierre. At this time, Claire Delbos's health began to deteriorate, resulting in her eventually entering a nursing home at La Varenne in 1953, where she died in 1959. Meanwhile, Messiaen's musical and personal attentions were now focused on the pianist Yvonne Loriod, which resulted in several consequential works for or involving piano, such as *Visions de l'Amen* (1943), *Vingt Regards sur l'Enfant-Jésus* (1944), and *Trois petites Liturgies de la Présence Divine* (1944). Following these works were three based on the Tristan legend: *Harawi* (1945), the *Turangalîla-Symphonie* (1946–48), and *Cinq Rechants* (1948–49). Although not lovers while Claire Delbos was still alive (both were staunch Roman Catholics), Messiaen and his young muse finally married in 1961.

In 1947, Messiaen was appointed to teach a special class in musical analysis at the Paris Conservatoire. Subsequent years saw teaching engagements in Budapest (1947), Tanglewood (1949), Darmstadt (1949–51), and Saarbrücken (1953). In 1966, Messiaen was appointed to teach composition at the Paris Conservatoire. During his long tenure there, he taught pupils from around the world and achieved a stature as a composer-teacher equaled only by Schoenberg in the twentieth century. Messiaen enjoyed teaching immensely, but had to retire in 1978 at the age of 70.

Messiaen's teaching activities influenced his work as a composer in the late 1940s and early 50s. With experimental works such as *Cantéyodjayâ* (1949), *Quatre Études de rythme* (1949–50), *Messe de la Pentecôte* (1950), and *Livre d'orgue* (1951–52) that included innovative approaches to serialism, it seemed that Messiaen wanted to keep up with the musical scene of post-War Europe. However, in the 1950s, while not abandoning the serial techniques that he was developing, nor his modal practices, Messiaen turned to birdsong as a chief source for his compositional inspiration, producing three avian-inspired works in close succession—*Réveil des oiseaux* (1953), *Oiseaux exotiques* (1955–56) and *Catalogue d'oiseaux* (1956–58).

Upon the death of his first wife Claire Delbos in 1959 and his marriage to Yvonne Loriod in 1961, Messiaen experienced new bursts of creativity in the 1960s with several works flowing from his pen. One can discern a return to overtly theological subjects in the *Couleurs de la Cité céleste* (1963) after avian-inspired works, and the emergence of a monumental style in *Et exspecto resurrectionem mortuorum* (1964) and *La Transfiguration de Nôtre-Seigneur Jésus-Christ* (1965–69), which would continue into the 1970s and 80s with *Des canyons aux étoiles* (1971–74), *Saint François d'Assise* (1975–83), and the *Livre du Saint Sacrement* (1984). Beginning with *Petites esquisses d'oiseaux* (1985) and ending with *Concert à quatre* (1992), Messiaen, at one point convinced that he could no longer write music after *Saint François*, found new life as a composer by changing his style to one that emphasized simplicity and understatement rather than the colossal and monumental.

In the 1970s and 80s, Messiaen was acclaimed internationally as a composer. Those decades saw him and Yvonne Loriod-Messiaen traveling worldwide to give concerts and lectures, participate in festivals honoring him and his music, and notate birdsong, among other activities. Of course, during this time Messiaen received numerous commissions at which he was hard at work. However, various conditions, illnesses, and mishaps associated with old age began to take their toll: Messiaen became increasingly less mobile in the late 1980s and early 90s. His health began to decline. His acute back pain, attributed previously to arthritis, was diagnosed in February 1992 as stemming from cancer. On 21 April 1992, Messiaen was admitted to the Beaujon Hospital in Clichy to have an operation on his spine. In the early evening of April 27, he began coughing up blood and died soon afterwards. He was buried in the churchyard of Saint-Théoffrey, a short distance from his home in Petichet, in the French Alps.

A SURVEY OF MESSIAEN'S MUSICAL STYLE AND WORKS

In an interview with Claude Samuel, Messiaen stated that his music juxtaposes three fundamental themes: (1) the theological truths of the Roman Catholic faith, (2) human love as exemplified by the legend of Tristan and Iseult, and (3) nature as represented by birdsongs (*Olivier Messiaen: Music and Color: Conversations with Claude Samuel* [item 176], 20–21, 30–34.). All of these themes are, moreover, manifestations of God's presence in the world. Messiaen also mentions that his music includes sophisticated rhythmic techniques involving Greek metric patterns, Hindu rhythms (*deçi-tâlas*), rhythmic characters, nonretrogradable rhythms, and symmetrical permutations, along with an approach to pitch governed by sound-color relationships derived from his colored-hearing synesthesia. His works for various media testify to the inventiveness of these compositional techniques. While basic to his musical style, the list of techniques mentioned in the interview with Samuel, however, is not complete.

To comprehend Messiaen's music is to go beyond the catalogues of compositional techniques that he often mentions in interviews and lectures and find those common threads that connect them. The following discussion will consider those threads, examining each one in turn, beginning with the three theological poles around which Messiaen's music revolves.

Many of Messiaen's works, particularly those written for the organ, are religious in nature. Surprisingly, only a minority are actually designed for use in the liturgy (e.g., *Messe de la Pentecôte*). The majority of them are intended as liturgical acts of praise for the concert hall. With pieces such as the *Trois petites Liturgies*, *La Transfiguration de Nôtre-Seigneur Jésus-Christ*, *Des canyons aux étoiles*, and *Saint François d'Assise*, Messiaen removed the artificial barriers separating sacred from secular by transporting the Catholic liturgy into places for which it was not originally meant.

In Messiaen's treatment of the Tristan legend, human love is regarded as transcending the human body and mind to mirror divine love. The three works that comprise the Tristan trilogy, *Harawi*, the *Turangalîla-Symphonie*, and *Cinq Rechants*, are related only in spirit, with no narrative continuity tying them together. In music and text, the song cycle *Harawi* incorporates Peruvian melodies that present surrealistic images related to love and death. Besides containing passages of love music that push the boundaries of good taste, the *Turangalîla-Symphonie* is a summation of Messiaen's musical style up to 1948, with its multiple textural layers and rhythmic speculations. *Cinq Rechants* for unaccompanied chorus takes its musical inspiration from *Le Printemps* by Claude Le Jeune (1528/30–1600). It is a sequence of verse-refrain forms, in which a wide variety of musical effects is achieved through the interleaving of a French text with one in a pseudo-Hindu language, spoken syllables, and humming.

Nature in the form of birdsong holds a prominent place in Messiaen's compositional aesthetic. The decade of the 1950s saw Messiaen collecting birdsong in specially designed music-manuscript notebooks known as *cahiers*. These intense activities resulted not only in a series of avian-inspired works in the 1950s but also in the prevalence of birdsong in his musical language and religious symbolism ever since. Messiaen insisted on the accuracy of his avian transcriptions, making adjustments only for the micro-intervals and extremely fast speeds of birdsong. Yet, he often incorporated aspects of his musical style into his finished bird music. His beliefs about birds were medieval in tone. As reflected in *Saint François d'Assise*, Messiaen considered birds as possessing extraordinary gifts bestowed by God, such as their colorful plumage, abilities to sing and fly, and their instinct for migration. They are, in essence, the Earth's equivalent to Angels. Many works from the 1960s to 80s include birdsong as a prominent component, such as *Chronochromie* (1960), *Des canyons aux étoiles, Saint François d'Assise,* and *Un Vitrail et des oiseaux* (1986), among others.

Early in his career, Messiaen treated the individual attributes of sound as separately composable elements. This led to a compositional style, codi-fied in the *Technique de mon langage musical*, that emphasized the separa-tion of musical parameters. Of these parameters rhythm garnered the most attention in Messiaen's compositional speculations. Messiaen believed that rhythm should be inspired by nature, where movements are free and unequal. Through the juxtaposition of long and short note values, one could achieve, according to Messiaen, a truly rhythmic music that avoided the equal divisions and square repetitions of classical music. Thus Messiaen focused on a small note value (such as a sixteenth note) and its free multi-plication to generate his rhythmic sequences, moving consequently to an ametrical conception of music. Whether employing Greek metric patterns, Hindu *deçi-tâlas*, rhythmic characters derived from his analysis of Stravinsky's *Danse sacrale*, nonretrogradable rhythms, added values, or permutational techniques, Messiaen's rhythmic successions are characterized by both complex and flexible qualities, vastly different, in a word, from the rhythmic successions of metrical music.

The first work to include these rhythmic innovations was the organ cycle *La Nativité du Seigneur* (1935). Messiaen's rhythmic procedures devel-oped along increasingly serial lines in works such as the *Quatuor pour la fin du Temps* (1940–41), *Vingt Regards sur l'Enfant-Jésus, Turangalîla-Symphonie, Cantéyodjayâ, Quatre Études de rythme, Messe de la Pentecôte,* and *Livre d'orgue,* reaching an apex in *Chronochromie* with the technique of sym-metrical permutations. Although he continued to employ these rhythmic techniques in works of the 1960s and beyond, Messiaen did not stop searching for new rhythmic innovations. In the "Sermon to the Birds" from *Saint François d'Assise,* different instruments play simultaneously in and out of tempo, generating a chaos that was for Messiaen characteristic of nature.

The "charm of impossibilities" is a compositional aesthetic that domi-nated Messiaen's work as a composer. It is associated with certain pitch and rhythmic constructs that are forced into closed circuits because of their structural symmetries, evoking a magical charm as a result. Messiaen's nonretrogradable rhythms and symmetrical permutations reflect the charm of impossibilities in the rhythmic domain, as the former technique involves a series of durations that exhibits the same order of values both forwards and backwards, while the latter technique features rhythmic schemes in which a rhythmic series is permutated cyclically until the original series is restored.

The modes of limited transposition typify the charm of impossibilities in the pitch domain. They consist of seven symmetrical pitch collections that reproduce their original pitch contents after being transposed a certain number of times. This reduces the number of distinct forms from twelve to some smaller value, hence the designation "limited transposition." The modes were the earliest elements of Messiaen's harmonic vocabulary to develop. As a student, Messiaen was encouraged to explore unconventional modalities by his organ teacher, Marcel Dupré (1886–1971). By the late 1920s, he was already using his modal system in works such as *Le Banquet céleste* for organ (1928) and the *Préludes* for piano (1928–29).

The modes are also important components of Messiaen's approach to sound-color relationships. Each transposition of a mode evokes a specific color association in his synesthesia. Moreover, Messiaen treats the modes in his music, as well as specially invented chords not derived from the modes, as if they were complementary colors on a canvas, juxtaposing them so that they can enhance one another, just like a painter who enhances one color in a picture by juxtaposing it with its complement. Because of Messiaen's emphasis on color in his music, triadically based sonorities can be sounded alongside the most dissonant harmonies, a procedure characteristic of many of the later works from *La Transfiguration de Nôtre-Seigneur Jésus-Christ* to *Éclairs sur l'Au-Delà* (1988–92).

An acoustical corollary to complementary colors in Messiaen's sound-color aesthetic is the phenomenon of natural resonance. Put briefly, natural resonance involves adding notes, which represent artificial harmonics, to a given pitch structure in order to modify its timbre. The effects of natural resonance have been compared to the complementary fringe effects one experiences when staring at a given color on a white background for a long time. In both instances there are coloristic halos surrounding each entity. Messiaen has described his magnum opus *Saint François d'Assise* as containing all of his sound-color harmonies.

A DISCUSSION OF MESSIAEN STUDIES PAST AND PRESENT

The following discussion will assess the current state of Messiaen research by surveying the secondary literature of the last thirty years, focusing on books in English, French, and German. It will conclude by offering suggestions for future scholarly inquiry. Given Messiaen's stature as a composer, "it is surprising that he has not been accorded the same degree of attention [by scholars] as, for example, Igor Stravinsky." (Andrew Shenton, "The

Unspoken Word: Olivier Messiaen's 'Langage Communicable'" (item 222), 7.) Despite numerous studies on Messiaen's life and work, much more work needs to be done.

Because Messiaen discussed his music at great length in various media, Messiaen research has tended to stay fairly close to his ideas about himself and his music, preferring not to challenge his position as the music's "most authoritative voice." Recent scholarship, however, has begun to dispute Messiaen's picture of his life and work, dispelling myths and uncovering new insights about him and his music. While a majority of scholars have produced general biographical-stylistic accounts of Messiaen's life and work, others are pursuing more specialized topics, such as Messiaen's life and musical activities before he became an international celebrity, his colored-hearing synesthesia, musical aesthetics, and approaches to musical time, pitch structure, and timbre.

Robert Sherlaw Johnson's survey of Messiaen's music and compositional style is by far the best comprehensive study of the composer in English during the past thirty years (*Messiaen*, item 213). Messiaen indicated that Johnson's book was the most thorough account of his music. Johnson identifies Messiaen's approaches to harmony and rhythm, and his ability to integrate earlier procedures with newer ideas, as key elements that distinguish the composer's work in the twentieth century. In his book on Messiaen (*Olivier Messiaen and the Music of Time*, item 208), Paul Griffiths attempts to comprehend the composer's manipulation of musical time in order to understand his compositional style. Since he views Messiaen's music as being conceived in terms of individual events lacking larger musical contexts, Griffiths compares pitch relationships in Messiaen's compositions with those in tonal music in order to characterize the composer's approaches to melody and harmony.

Harry Halbreich's study of Messiaen's life and works is the most significant French-language source on the composer (*Olivier Messiaen*, item 209). He presents a comprehensive discussion of the composer's pitch language, particularly with respect to Messiaen's later harmonic vocabulary. Halbreich includes several chords in his discussion that are not addressed in the *Technique de mon langage musical* (item 88) or by other Messiaen authors. In 1988, Theo Hirsbrunner completed a study of Messiaen's life and creative work (*Olivier Messiaen: Leben und Werk*, item 211). In addition to outlining Messiaen's career and addressing his compositional techniques, Hirsbrunner compares Messiaen's music with that of Boulez, Ravel, and Wagner in three separate sections.

Two collections of English-language essays on Messiaen in the 1990s exhibit a broad range of inquiry directed at various aspects of the composer's musical life. As a whole, neither collection strays far from Messiaen's opinions of his music. The eighteen essays in *The Messiaen Companion* (item 240) not only address specific compositions but also provide more information regarding Messiaen's religious motivations, bird music, and activities as a teacher. The eleven essays in *Messiaen's Language of Mystical Love* (item 236) cover diverse aspects of Messiaen's world, especially the humanistic basis of his teaching, the link between mathematics and theology underlying his musical approach, compositional techniques governed by self-imposed limitations, and the celebratory nature of his subject matter.

Finally, three foreign-language essay collections on Messiaen should be mentioned, namely, *Olivier Messiaen, homme de foi: Regard sur son œuvre d'orgue* (item 238), *Portrait(s) d'Olivier Messiaen* (item 241), and *Olivier Messiaen: La Cité céleste–Das himmlische Jerusalem: Über Leben und Werk des französischen Komponisten* (item 248). Although these collections consider familiar topics, they also examine less familiar ones, such as the specific theological elements that drive Messiaen's music, or his critical reception in post-war Germany.

In recent years, scholars have begun to focus more on the historical aspects of Messiaen's life and work. What they have uncovered is changing our view of Messiaen. In their biography of the composer (*Messiaen*, item 210), Peter Hill and Nigel Simeone were granted unprecedented access to Messiaen's archive by his widow, Yvonne Loriod-Messiaen. They provide fascinating new information about Messiaen's professional and personal life. Another important volume, despite its shortcomings, is Rebecca Rischin's *For the End of Time: The Story of the Messiaen Quartet* (item 486). Rischin dispels several myths about the *Quatuor pour la fin du Temps*, particularly regarding cellist Étienne Pasquier having only three strings on his instrument at the work's premiere, or that there were thousands of prisoners in an auditorium that could only seat about 400.

In perusing this volume, the reader will become acquainted with current research being produced by Messiaen scholars. But as stated earlier, much more work needs to be done, especially concerning Messiaen's harmonic language, serial techniques, approaches to musical time, incorporation of birdsong or plainchant into his music, the role of improvisation in his work as a composer, the use of color in his music, or the various phases of Messiaen's life, particularly the earlier years when he was forming friendships and professional relationships in the 1930s.

The state of Messiaen research is changing. As will be evident in this research guide, scholars are presently addressing topics that have been neglected in the past. With interest in Messiaen's music looming larger as time passes, it is hoped that this book will serve as a springboard for both the advanced student and experienced scholar in their study of one of the most complex and creative musicians of the twentieth century.

Listed below are descriptions of Messiaen bibliographies in chronological order. With the exception of Simeone's catalogue of Messiaen's music, none of the bibliographies is comprehensive in scope.

MESSIAEN BIBLIOGRAPHIES

1. Zinke-Bianchini, Virginie. *Olivier Messiaen: Compositeur de musique et rythmicien: Notice biographique: Catalogue détaillé des œuvres éditées.* Paris: L'Émancipatrice, 1949. 18 p. ML 134.M54 Z5.

   Contains a chronology of Messiaen's life followed by a detailed catalogue of his published works through 1949. The catalogue is arranged according to the following categories: (1) piano, (2) chamber music, (3) voice and piano, (4) chorus, (5) organ, (6) orchestra, and (7) didactic treatises. Also includes a list of recordings, primarily by Yvonne Loriod, dating from 1947 to 1949. At the end of the catalogue (p. 18) is a note stating that Zinke-Bianchini's work was "approved by Messiaen."

2. Evans, Adrian C. "Olivier Messiaen in the Surrealist Context: A Bibliography." *Brio* (Spring 1974) 2–11; (Autumn 1974): 25–35. ISSN: 0007–0173.

   A two-part bibliography. Part 1 lays out how the information is arranged and disseminated. It features a list of works by genre. Included with each piece are listings of relevant articles and recordings. Part 2 opens with an essay that relates Messiaen's musical output to surrealism. Characterizes Messiaen's musical development as comprising three distinct periods: *developmental* (1917–36), *consolidatory* (1937–49), and *transmutational* (1949 to the present [1974]). The first two periods are linked with a *microscopic* phase, and the last with a *macroscopic*. Two modes of thought are present from the outset that are said to be in conflict, the *egocentric*, which is characterized as a desire "to penetrate the inner recesses of experience," and the *deocentric*, which is described as a desire "to inhabit and function in a mystical universe." The conflict represents, in a word, the "age-old confrontation of microcosm and macrocosm." Part 2 concludes with a bibliography arranged according to: (1) Catalogues; (2) Biography and General Surveys—Books, Articles; (3) Influences—Debussy, Dukas, and Stravinsky; (4) La Jeune France; (5) Pupils; (6) Technique—Books, Articles; (7) Birdsong; (8) Other Writings by Messiaen—Prefaces, Articles; and (9) General Record Review Articles.

3. Urwin, Ray W. "Olivier Messiaen: A Bibliography." *The American Organist* 13 (December 1979): 50–51. ISSN: 0164–3150.

   A bibliography compiled at Yale University while Urwin was working on his M.A. thesis on the later organ works of Messiaen (see item 401). Attempts to be as comprehensive as possible by including sources that were unavailable for examination. Arranged according to books, and articles, lectures, and letters.

4. Urwin, Ray W. "Messiaen Bibliography." *The American Organist* 18 (January 1984): 54–55. ISSN: 0164–3150.

An update of Urwin's bibliography published in *The American Organist* in December 1979 (item 3). Includes articles, books, dissertations, and theses, with some annotated. Sources not limited to organ music.

5. Morris, Dr. David, comp. *Olivier Messiaen: A Comparative Bibliography of Material in the English Language.* Ulster: University of Ulster, 1991. x, 59 p. ISBN: 187120657X.

Designed for university students and researchers to help them locate articles and books on Messiaen. Attempts to cover all the major articles on Messiaen published in English. Notes the omissions of this bibliography, particularly articles in American journals, general history books, and dictionaries. In the book's layout, articles are listed in chronological order, preceded by a list of sections from similarly arranged monographs. Book titles are abbreviated and are accompanied by chapter numbers or headings. Journal titles are also abbreviated. The bibliography is arranged according to twelve general areas: (1) Short Biographies and Histories; (2) Introduction to Style; (3) Birdsong; (4) Colour; (5) Modes of Limited Transposition; (6) Rhythm; (7) Religion and Symbolism; (8) Messiaen and Debussy; (9) The Piano Music; (10) The Organ Music; (11) Messiaen's Place in History; and (12) Miscellaneous. Contains discussions of Messiaen's life and musical language.

6. Simeone, Nigel. *Olivier Messiaen: A Bibliographical Catalogue of Messiaen's Works.* Musikbibliographische Arbeiten, vol. 14. Tutzing: Hans Schneider, 1998. xix, 249 p. ISBN: 3795209471.

In this catalogue, Simeone arranges Messiaen's music and writings according to "Published Works" (pp. 1–184), "Unpublished Works" (pp. 185–96), and "Shorter Writings" (pp. 197–202). All three lists progress chronologically. For each entry in the main part of the book, Simeone provides the title, date of composition, scoring, dedication or superscription, and first or earliest known performances. For first editions, he supplies the publisher, edition, collation, plate number(s), date of publication, wrappers, format, engraver, and printer. At the end of each entry, Simeone gives additional relevant information in order to provide the reader with a richer context for the source. Under "Published Works" Simeone lists didactic treatises such as the *Vingt leçons d'harmonie* (1939),

Technique de mon langage musical (1942), and the *Traité de rythme, de couleur, et d'ornithologie* (1949–92), and the Brussels, Notre Dame, and Kyoto conference booklets, as well as Messiaen's commentaries on Mozart's twenty-two piano concertos, under "Shorter Writings." Appendix 1 includes reviews in *Le Courrier musical* and *Le Ménestrel* of Messiaen's early works from 1930–39, while Appendix 2 is a list of printing records of Messiaen's music by his publishers Durand, Alphonse Leduc, and Universal. Contains a bibliography and index of works. An excellent research tool.

Reviews: Theo Hirsbrunner, *Dissonanz* 66 (November 2000): 55; David Morris, *MLA Notes* 57/1 (September 2000): 116.

2

Primary Sources I: Collections, Articles and Reviews, Pedagogical Works, and Lectures and Librettos

The citations in this chapter constitute significant primary sources on Messiaen. They include information about fair copies of works, compositional sketches, birdsong notebooks, program notes, and correspondence found at various institutions and libraries. The citations likewise include many of Messiaen's articles and reviews, pedagogical works, and lectures and librettos. The annotations in this and the following chapter are detailed, revealing a "biography of Messiaen" in documents.

COLLECTIONS

(I would like to thank Nigel Simeone for his advice and assistance on collections of Messiaen's autograph music and prose manuscripts.)

7. New York. James Fuld Music Collection. The Pierpont Morgan Library, New York City.

Contains a program for a concert played by Messiaen on 20 December 1945 at Saint Mark's Church, London, for the *Huitième Concert Spirituel*. Messiaen played *La Nativité du Seigneur* in its entirety for the second time in London. Also contains an autograph letter dated Paris, 14 November 1964, from Messiaen to an unidentified person. Having been named a "Grand Officier de l'Ordre de Mérite" in June 1964, Messiaen was looking for a sponsor who possessed the "Grand Croix of the Légion d'Honneur." Planned acquisitions by the Pierpont Morgan Library, Department of Music Manuscripts and Books.

8. New York. Mary Flagler Cary Music Collection. The Pierpont Morgan Library, New York City.

   Contains an autograph manuscript dated Paris, 26 June 1943, of responses to a questionnaire sent by S.I.A.M.F., and an undated autograph manuscript (1949?) of a descriptive commentary of *Cinq Rechants*.

9. New York. Morgan Collection. The Pierpont Morgan Library, New York City.

   Contains an autograph letter dated Paris, 4 June 1942, to Comte Étienne de Beaumont (1883–1956). Messiaen thanks the Count for a check of 1,000 francs, mentions that he will not forget their musical project for the winter, and expresses his gratitude to the Count for writing Dr. Piertzig (*sic* [Piersig]) on his behalf.

10. Paris. Messiaen Archives. Fondation Olivier Messiaen, Paris, France.

    The most significant collection of primary documents associated with Messiaen, unparalleled in content. Yet, despite its paramount importance, the collection has not been catalogued due to the foundation's private ownership. According to a private communication from Jessica Meuriot, artistic coordinator of the Fondation Messiaen, the foundation is undergoing reorganization and information about the archives' contents might be available in the future. Thus, there is currently no listing of the foundation's holdings either in print or online to which scholars can turn for possible areas of research. To examine any of the materials found in the Messiaen Archives requires, moreover, special permission. What follows is a general description of its contents taken from p. 402 of Hill and Simeone's book, *Messiaen* (item 210):

    (1) Messiaen's diaries from 1939 to 1992
    (2) Autograph sketches and drafts of some works
    (3) Photocopies of autograph manuscripts
    (4) Letters to Messiaen sometimes with copies of his replies
    (5) Articles by Messiaen (in manuscripts and typescripts)
    (6) Speeches and scripts by Messiaen (in manuscripts and typescripts)
    (7) Commentaries by Messiaen on his music (in manuscripts and typescripts)
    (8) Informal working notes, records of meetings and telephone conversations, and other manuscript documents
    (9) Books and articles about Messiaen
    (10) Concert programs
    (11) Other documents including posters, Conservatoire certificates, and miscellaneous papers

(12) Photographs

(13) Typed transcriptions of passages from Messiaen's diaries by Yvonne-Loriod Messiaen with her annotations ("Olivier Messiaen: Relevé des concerts, des classes et des évènements de la vie d'Olivier Messiaen notées au jour le jour sur ses agendas depuis 1939")

11. Paris. Bibliothèque Nationale de France, Département de la Musique, Paris, France.

Contains a significant variety of source materials (see Hill and Simeone, *Messiaen* [item 210], 402):

(1) Autograph manuscripts of *Saint François d'Assise*, the complete *Quatre Études de rythme, and the Traité de rythme, de couleur, et d'ornithologie (1949–1992)*

(2) Sketches of *Visions de l'Amen* (one leaf)

(3) Approximately 200 birdsong notebooks (cahiers de notation des chants d'oiseaux). The birdsong notebooks are still the property of Yvonne Loriod-Messiaen, who has put them "en dépôt" at the Bibliothèque Nationale. They are largely inaccessible at the moment (private communication from Nigel Simeone)

(4) Letters from Messiaen to Claude Arrieu, Nadia Boulanger, André Cœuroy, Denise Tual and others about the Concerts de la Pléiade

12. Washington, D.C. The Music Division of the Library of Congress. Washington, D.C.

Includes the autograph manuscript of the *Turangalîla-Symphonie*, and correspondence with both Serge Koussevitzky and the Koussevitzky Foundation (1936–49), and Leonard Bernstein (1949–63).

ARTICLES, ESSAYS IN COLLECTED EDITIONS, REVIEWS, AND OTHER MATERIALS BY MESSIAEN

Certain articles, essays, and reviews by Messiaen, especially those dating from 1936–39, could not be accessed through normal library channels despite every effort to obtain them. For the sake of comprehensiveness, they are listed below without annotations. The reader is referred to Stephen Broad's dissertation, "Recontextualising Messiaen's Early Career" (item 206), for transcriptions of articles and reviews from 1936–39 (see Appendix 1, pp. 4–74).

13. Messiaen, Olivier. "L'Ascension: Quatre méditations symphoniques par Olivier Messiaen." *Le Monde musical* (28 February 1935): 48–49.

Unsigned article by Messiaen on the orchestral version of *L'Ascension*. Mentions how tonality is enriched by the modes of limited transposition and how they bring new color to both melody and harmony. Includes a descriptive commentary of each movement and reproductions of musical examples in Messiaen's facsimile.

14. Messiaen, Olivier. "L'Émotion, la sincerité, de l'œuvre musicale." Paris: n.p., 1936 (see Hill and Simeone, *Messiaen* [item 210], 403).

15. Messiaen, Olivier. *"La Nativité du Seigneur*, neuf méditations pour orgue, d'Olivier Messiaen.*" Tablettes de la Schola Cantorum* (January-February 1936), unpaginated (2 pp.).

16. Messiaen, Olivier. "Marcel Dupré: *Cours d'harmonie analytique.*" *Le Monde musical* (29 February 1936): 40.

A positive review of Dupré's harmony volume, lauding its high sense of professionalism. (In "Recontextualising Messiaen's Early Career" [item 206, Appendix 1, p. 43, n. 8], Broad provides the context for Messiaen's review in a translation of an undated letter from Messiaen to Dupré: I would like first of all to thank you for sending and kindly dedicating to me a copy of your *Cours d'harmonie analytique*. I was very touched to receive this little package from you. I have started to read it, and do not need to tell you of my admiration because I will shortly translate it elsewhere with more eloquence when I write an article for *Le Monde musical* on your "treatise.")

17. Messiaen, Olivier. "Maurice Le Boucher: *Enseignement du piano. Vingt morceaux manuscrits destiné à l'étude progressive de la lecture du piano.*" *Le Monde musical* (29 February 1936), 60.

A short review of a piano sight-reading book praising its music and pedagogical orientation. Messiaen regards the book as a helpful tool for beginners and teachers of sight reading.

18. Messiaen, Olivier. "La Transmutation des enthousiasmes." *La Page musicale* (16 April 1936): 1.

19. Messiaen, Olivier. *"La Nativité du Seigneur*. Neuf méditations pour orgue, d'après Messiaen.*" Le Monde musical* (30 April 1936): 123–24.

Although not signed by Messiaen, presumably by him. Notes the premiere of the work on 27 February 1936 at La Trinité with Daniel-Lesur, Jean Langlais, and Jean-Jacques Grunenwald each playing three movements. "Pillages" the preface to *La Nativité du Seigneur* in order to explain added values and the modes of limited transposition. (Because this article moves from the third person in the initial paragraph into the first person after that, and includes a sentence not found in the preface to *La Nativité*, Broad argues that this article is by Messiaen [item 206, Appendix 1, pp. 44–45, nn. 10 and 13]. He also notes how another article by Messiaen on *La*

Nativité [see item 15] quotes material from this article [item 206, Appendix 1, p. 69, n. 4], adding further credence to Messiaen's authorship.) Contains seven musical examples.

20. Messiaen, Olivier. "Récital Guy Lambert." *Le Monde musical* (30 April 1936): 124.

Positive review of a recital played by Guy Lambert. The program included music by Bach, Franck, Vierne, and Tournemire, with a piece by Mignan offered as an encore.

21. Messiaen, Olivier. "*Ariane et Barbe-bleue* [de Paul Dukas]." *La Revue musicale* 166 (May-June 1936): 79–86. ISSN: 0768–1593.

In an essay written on the occasion of Paul Dukas's death in 1935, Messiaen examines *Ariane et Barbe-bleue* (1907), the only opera written by his former composition teacher at the Paris Conservatoire. Messiaen interprets the character of Ariane as bringing forth the light of truth to the wives of Barbe-bleue, while attempting to convince the women to free themselves from the darkness symbolized by their husband. In the end she fails. In Messiaen's opinion, Dukas's view of Ariane as representing the truth found in all religions, philosophies, aesthetics, and civilizations, past, present, and future, points to the Christian view of Jesus as described in the Gospel of Saint John, who brings forth the light of God's truth to humankind.

Of great import to any study of sound-color relationships in Messiaen's music are his comments on the "precious jewels scene" in Act I. As the Nurse opens the first six doors for Ariane, colors emanating from six jewels (amethysts, sapphires, pearls, emeralds, rubies, and diamonds) emerge from the shadows. To set the scene musically, Dukas uses a series of variations on Ariane's theme, each with a particular orchestration, in B major, A-flat major, C major, D major, B-flat major, and F-sharp major that correspond, respectively, to the violet, blue, milky white, green, red, and diamond projected by the jewels. Hence for Messiaen, this passage, through its linkage of orchestration and tonality to the color of the stones, anticipates modern theories of sound-color relationships.

But more interestingly, Dukas's color associations for A-flat major through F-sharp major correspond closely to Messiaen's color associations for the same tonalities in his synesthesia. (In his synesthesia, Messiaen links the color of a tonality with the color of its tonic triad. That is why he associates the tonality of A-flat major with blue-violet, C major with white, D major with green, B-flat major with red, and F-sharp major with a "sparkling of all colors." (See: item 90, Olivier Messiaen, *Traité de rythme, de couleur, et d'ornithologie (1949–1992)*, vol. 7 passim; item 180, Almut Rößler, *Contributions to the Spiritual World of Olivier Messiaen: With Original Texts by the Composer*, 117–18; and item 429, Vincent P. Benitez, "Pitch Organization and Dramatic Design in *Saint François d'Assise* of Olivier Messiaen," 150–76.)

22. Messiaen, Olivier. "La Jeune France reconnaissante." *La Page musicale* (12 June 1936): 1.

23. Messiaen, Olivier. "Charles Tournemire: Précis d'exécution de registration et d'improvisation à l'orgue." *Le Monde musical* (30 June 1936): 186.

    Positive review of Tournemire's organ method book. Messiaen summarizes the contents of each chapter, citing the fourth chapter on the art of improvisation as the culmination of the treatise.

24. Messiaen, Olivier. "Récital d'orgue Jean de Middeleer." *Le Monde musical* (30 June 1936): 186.

    Positive review of an organ recital by Jean de Middeleer. Messiaen praises his performance of modern Belgian and French organ works for its precise execution, rhythmic strength, and overall virtuosity.

25. Messiaen, Olivier. "Éclairages de compositeurs." *La Page musicale* (29 November 1936): 1.

26. Messiaen, Olivier. "Musique religieuse." *La Page musicale* (5 February 1937): 1.

27. Messiaen, Olivier. "Derrière ou devant la porte? ... (Lettre ouverte à M. Eugène Berteaux)." *La Page musicale* (26 February 1937): 1.

28. Messiaen, Olivier. "Chronique de Paris [March 1937]." *La Sirène* (March 1937): 14–15.

29. Messiaen, Olivier. "Les Récitals d'orgue: Albert Beauchamp et Guy Lambert." *Le Monde musical* (31 March 1937): 74.

    Concert reviews of two recital programs at the organ of the Schola Cantorum and a festival dedicated to Alexandre Guilmant's organ music at La Trinité.

30. Messiaen, Olivier. "Chronique de Paris [April 1937]." *La Sirène* (April 1937): 22.

31. Messiaen, Olivier. "Billet Parisien: Réflexions sur le rythme." *La Sirène* (May 1937): 14.

32. Messiaen, Olivier. "Post Ludes Libres (Charles Tournemire)." *Le Monde musical* (31 May 1937): 138.

33. Messiaen, Olivier. "Billet Parisien [June 1937]." *La Sirène* (June 1937): 14.

34. Messiaen, Olivier. "Récital d'orgue Jeanne Baudy." *Le Monde musical* (June-July 1937): 174.

    A positive concert review of an organ recital played by Jeanne Baudy at Saint-Séverin, featuring the organ works of Bach, Franck, Liszt, Dupré, and Widor. Messiaen also praises the singing of vocal works by Dupré and Renée Philippart at the same concert.

35. Messiaen, Olivier. "Billet Parisien: Les Fêtes de la lumière." *La Sirène* (July 1937): 18–19.

36. Messiaen, Olivier. "Billet Parisien: Quatre Opéra-bouffes." *La Sirène* (September 1937): 11.

37. Messiaen, Olivier. "Billet Parisien: Un Festival Roussel." *La Sirène* (October 1937): 11.

38. Messiaen, Olivier. "Symphonie en mi majeur par Joseph Gilles." *Le Monde musical* (30 November 1937): 272.

    A review of a symphony for organ and orchestra by Joseph Gilles. Praises the work's classical style and writing for the organ.

39. Messiaen, Olivier. "Billet Parisien: Le Mana de Jolivet." *La Sirène* (December 1937): 8–10.

40. Messiaen, Olivier. "Billet Parisien [January 1938]." *La Syrinx* (January 1938): 19–20.

41. Messiaen, Olivier. "Billet Parisien: De la Procession Debussy-Ravel." *La Syrinx* (February 1938), 25–26.

42. Messiaen, Olivier. "Le Premier Livre d'orgue de Georges Migot." *La Revue musicale* 182 (March 1938): 228. ISSN: 0768–1593.

    A review by Messiaen of the *Premier Livre d'orgue* (published by Éditions Alphonse Leduc) by the French composer Georges Migot (1891–1976). After praising Migot's musical style, Messiaen discusses four of the more significant pieces in the collection, "Au Calvaire," "Bergerie à la crèche," "Antienne en musette," and "La Rosace."

43. Messiaen, Olivier. "Billet Parisien: Un Spectacle Darius Milhaud." *La Syrinx* (March 1938): 25–26.

    A review by Messiaen of a performance of *Pauvre Matelot* (1927) and the stage premiere of *Esther de Carpentras* (1925–27) by Darius Milhaud at the Opéra-Comique on 3 February 1938. Messiaen notes each work's dramatic plot and musical language and style, which includes a strong dose of polytonality. He praises the choreography created by Constantin Tcherkas for a ballet set to Milhaud's *Suite provençale* (1936) that concludes the performance of *Pauvre Matelot*, as well as Roger Désormière's conducting of *Esther de Carpentras*.

44. Messiaen, Olivier. "L'Orgue." *Le Monde musical* (31 March 1938): 84; Reprint, *Charles Tournemire (1870–1939)*, *L'Orgue: Cahiers et mémoires*, no. 41, p. 86. Paris: Association des Amis de l'orgue, 1989. 124 p. ML 410.T6847 C47 1989.

A review of Tournemire's *Sept Chorals-Poèmes pour les Sept Paroles du Christ en croix*, Migot's *Premier Livre d'orgue*, and Langlais's *Ave Maria* and *Ave Maris stella*. Messiaen mentions a scale (C-D-sharp-E-F-G-A-flat-B-C), which he says is of Indian origin, that Tournemire uses throughout the work in the manner of a leitmotif. Messiaen's discussion of Migot's *Premier Livre d'orgue* is an abridged version of the review he wrote for *La Revue musicale* (see item 42). In his examination of Langlais's *Ave Maria* and *Ave Maris stella*, Messiaen focuses on the use of contrapuntal techniques.

45. Messiaen, Olivier. "Billet Parisien: L'Orgue Mystique de Tournemire." *La Syrinx* (May 1938): 26–27.

A review of Charles Tournemire's *L'Orgue Mystique* (1932), a collection of 51 offices that incorporate plainchant melodies appropriate to each Sunday of the liturgical year. Messiaen comments upon the five compositional types—Prélude à l'Introit, Offertoire, Elévation, Communion, and Pièce terminale—linked with each office. He notes their relative lengths, relationships to the plainsong melodies with which they are associated, effects of organ registration, and allusions to the musical style of Debussy. Messiaen opines that the pieces of the Pièce terminale category reflect the summit of Tournemire's art because of their partially Gothic, partially modern, musical style.

46. Messiaen, Olivier. "Charles Kœchlin – Choral et Sonatine pour orgue." *Le Monde musical* (31 January 1939): 74.

A review of Kœchlin's *Choral et Sonatine* for organ describing the structure and style of the work.

47. Messiaen, Olivier. "Contre la Paresse." *La Page musicale* (17 March 1939): 1.

48. Messiaen, Olivier. "Autour d'une Œuvre d'orgue." *L'Art sacre* (April 1939): 123.

49. Messiaen, Olivier. "Autour d'une Parution." *Le Monde musical* (30 April 1939): 126.

A defense of *Chants de Terre et de Ciel* by Messiaen in light of the criticism that ensued after its premiere on 23 January 1939. Messiaen describes the work's religious nature and what he attempted to depict in different songs. He closes the article by justifying his musical language and the compositional techniques that drive it.

50. Messiaen, Olivier. "Le rythme chez Igor Stravinsky." *La Revue musicale* 191 (May 1939): 91–92. ISSN: 0768–1593.

In this article Messiaen outlines what he gleaned from his analysis of Stravinsky's use of rhythm. For Messiaen, the *Rite of Spring* and *The Wedding* (*Les Noces*) are Stravinsky's most significant works from a rhythmic point of view. Particularly important in this article is an early reference to rhythmic characters (*personnages rythmiques*). While he does not mention rhythmic characters by name, Messiaen points to Stravinsky's rhythmic procedures in the "Glorification of the Chosen One" and the "Sacrificial Dance" from the *Rite of Spring* as stemming from the Hindu *deçi-tâla simhavikrîdita*, which is divided into two rhythmic cells, one that progressively augments and diminishes by a basic value while the other stays the same.

51. Messiaen, Olivier. "De la musique sacrée." *Carrefour* 1/4 (June/July 1939): 75.

An essay on the nature and purpose of sacred music. Messiaen believes that true happiness is only achieved when man finds God through faith. It is faith that touches the heart of man, filling the emptiness of that heart with the abundant truth of God. If faith is going to lead man to God, then it must play a prominent role in the arts that focus on the aesthetic expression of beauty and truth. Since it is the most immaterial of the arts, capable of expressing the transcendent beauties and truths of God, music is considered to be an act of faith. Hence the best kind of music is one that focuses on sacred truth, for in doing so, music deals with a religious subject that is alive, namely God.

Messiaen discusses different topics related to sacred music. Not surprisingly, plainchant is extolled as fundamental to all religious composition. Messiaen then considers how the works of various composers relate to his arguments about sacred music. The B-minor Mass, Passions, and organ chorales of Bach are praised as monuments of faith. Wagner's *Parsifal* and Debussy's *Le martyre de Saint-Sébastien* are not considered as true acts of faith; rather, they have the appearance of religion. Finally, Tournemire's *l'Orgue mystique* is regarded as epitomizing the best sacred music of the late 1930s through its use of plainchant, Debussyian harmonies and poly-tonality, and rhythm.

Messiaen closes by advocating that music be rooted in faith, touching on all subjects without ceasing to touch God. He believes that a great artist and Christian will be needed to bring forth such a music, a statement probably referring to himself.

52. Messiaen, Olivier. Contribution to Miramon Fitz-James, "Les Amis de l'Orgue et la guerre." *L'Orgue*, nos. 40–41 (December-March 1939–40): 30–38. ISSN: 0030–5170.

An article devoted to the printing of letters from organists serving in the French military in 1939–40. Authors are identified by their initials, branch of service, and rank. Identified as "soldat pionnier d'infanterie O.M.," Messiaen writes about his life in the French army. He complains about the difficulty of doing both his military chores and thinking about music. To resolve his dilemma, he reads a few pages of his pocket scores each night, which included Beethoven's symphonies, Ravel's *Ma Mère l'Oye*, Stravinsky's *Les Noces*, and Honegger's *Horace victorieux*. Messiaen also talks about meeting the film composer Maurice Jaubert (1900–40—on 19 June 1940, Jaubert was mortally wounded at Azérailles, France and died several hours later) and his experiences playing the organ on different occasions. In particular, he notes how his fellow soldiers were not shocked by his avant-garde style improvisations, unlike "the pious Parisian ladies" who would not countenance them. Finally, Messiaen wonders whether he will ever be able to complete his then current organ work *Les Corps glorieux*.

53. Messiaen, Olivier. "*Quatuor pour la Fin du Temps.*" *Lumignon: Bimensuelle du Stalag VIIIA*, no. 1; 1 April 1941, 3–4. (I want to thank Nigel Simeone for providing me with a scan of this document from his private collection, "Nigel Simeone, private collection".)

In the first issue of the French-language camp newspaper of Stalag VIII A, Görlitz, Silesia, where he was imprisoned from 1940–41, Messiaen describes the composition and world premiere of the *Quatuor pour la fin du Temps*. He notes how the piece was inspired by the tenth chapter of the Book of Revelation where the Angel declares that there will be no more time, and how it was written for and played by the camp's prisoners. Messiaen attempts to reconstruct the commentaries that he provided before each movement during the work's first performance. What results can be considered an earlier version of the music's published preface. The sixth and eighth movements possess different titles: "Fanfare" instead of "Danse de la fureur, pour les sept trompettes," and "Deuxième louange à l'éternité de Jésus" instead of "Louange à l'Immortalité de Jésus." Significant historically to say the least.

54. Messiaen, Olivier. "Technique de mon langage musical." *Musique et radio* 33/386 (November 1942): 253–54.

55. Messiaen, Olivier. "Sur mon traité de composition." *Comœdia* (5 December 1942): 1, 4.

An explanation by Messiaen of the *Technique de mon langage musical* before its publication by Alphonse Leduc in 1944. After listing the chapters of the *Technique*, Messiaen discusses its organization. He begins his treatise with an examination of rhythm, the primary material of music and, according to him, the least understood. After dealing with rhythm, Messiaen proceeds to melody (which has primacy in music and is the principal goal of research) and form, indicating various techniques of melodic development along the way. Next come harmony and the modes of limited transposition. Here Messiaen discusses compositional techniques associated with his use of chords and the modes. He then argues how his compositional techniques are interconnected by pointing out various relationships between different chapters in the *Technique*: chapters six (polyrhythm) and nineteen (polymodality), chapters three (added values) and thirteen (added notes), and chapters five (nonretrogradable rhythms) and sixteen (modes of limited transposition). He closes the essay by mentioning his idea of the "charm of impossibilities": a non-technical listener not accustomed to his music will not keep track of all of its details; instead, that person will submit to the strange charm caused by limited transposition and the lack of retrogradation.

56. Messiaen, Olivier. "Querelle de la musique et de l'amour." *Volontés de ceux de la resistance* (16 May 1945): 1.

Prefaced by a short biography of Messiaen, presumably by Yves Baudrier ("Y. B."), this polemical essay by Messiaen addresses arguments raging in Paris in the 1940s about neoclassical music. He is decidedly against it. He longs for a musical innovator who will deliver everyone from the mechanistic qualities of neoclassicism by emphasizing love, particularly the divine type, in his music. (One must conclude that Messiaen is talking about himself.) Messiaen then laments how he has been placed in the middle of these arguments. He encourages his opponents to leave Stravinsky, Jolivet, and his enthusiastic students, such as Serge Nigg and Jean Martinet, alone and to await the appearance of this "musician of love."

57. Messiaen, Olivier. "Béla Bartók." *Images musicales* (19 October 1945): 4.

58. Messiaen, Olivier. "Le 2e Concerto de Béla Bartók." *Lumières de la ville* (18 December 1945): 25.

    A review of a performance at the Théâtre des Champs-Élysées on 15 November 1945 of Béla Bartók's Second Piano Concerto by the Orchestre National de la Radio, under the direction of Manuel Rosenthal with Yvonne Loriod as soloist. In the first half of the review, Messiaen comments upon the work, noting aspects of melody, harmony, texture, and timbre. In the second half of the review, he praises Loriod's performance, viewing it as extraordinary, considering the fact that she learned the concerto in eight days.

59. Messiaen, Olivier. "L'inspiration musicale." *Opéra* (19 December 1945): 10.

60. Messiaen, Olivier. "Réponses à une enquête: Olivier Messiaen, ou les harmonies poétiques et ingénieuses." *Contrepoints* 3 (March-April 1946): 73–75. Reprint, *La Revue musicale* 306–7 (1977): 35–37. ISSN: 0768–1593.

    A response to an inquiry by Fred Goldbeck, a French journalist, sent out to different French composers in the mid-1940s, querying them about their compositional poetics. Messiaen not only discusses his aesthetics and pitch and rhythmic techniques but also refers to the "Le Cas Messiaen" scandal that was embroiling him. (See Lilise Boswell-Kurc, "Olivier Messiaen's Religious War-time Works and their Controversial Reception in France [1941–46]," item 205, pp. 1–182.) He mentions how critics mocked him at the premiere of *Vingt Regards sur l'Enfant-Jésus* at the Salle Gaveau on 26 March 1945. While commenting on the piece, Messiaen addressed issues raised by the controversy, such as how his music is both theological and nonsensual in nature.

61. Messiaen, Olivier. "Concert Line Zilgien (Concert de La Revue musicale)." *La Revue musicale* 201 (September 1946): 267. ISSN: 0768–1593.

    A review by Messiaen of a concert of seventeenth and eighteenth-century French organ music played by Line Zilgien, Messiaen's deputy organist at La Trinité, on the Clicquot organ at Saint-Nicholas-des-Champs. (The date of the concert is not specified.) The concert also included vocal works from the same period sung by Gisèle Peyron. After discussing the challenges of playing this repertoire, Messiaen praised the performances of both Zilgien and Peyron.

62. Messiaen, Olivier. "Maurice Emmanuel: Ses 'trente chansons bourguignonnes.'" *La Revue musicale* 206 (1947): 107–8. ISSN: 0768–1593.

In this special issue of *La Revue musicale* devoted to his former music history professor at the Paris Conservatoire, Maurice Emmanuel (1862–1938), Messiaen summarizes the musical contents of his teacher's "Trente chansons bourguignonnes" (1913), a collection of thirty folksongs from the province of Beaune, after those collected by C. Bigarne, A. Bourgeois, and C. Masson, arranged for voice and piano. (Six songs were arranged later for choir and orchestra in 1914–15 and 1930–35; ten songs were arranged for voice and orchestra in 1914 and 1932–36.) He characterizes the collection from melodic, harmonic, and rhythmic vantage points. Besides admiring the modal qualities of the music, Messiaen notes Emmanuel's creative use of harmony in various settings, pointing out procedures reminiscent of Ravel and Debussy. He concludes the essay by mentioning how much Emmanuel had influenced him as a student. For Messiaen, when he had heard "Trente chansons bourguignonnes" at a festival devoted to Emmanuel's works in 1932, he was converted instantly to modal music. Fifteen years later while writing this article, his enthusiasm had not changed.

63. Messiaen, Olivier. "Notes de travail pour l'Accompagnement Musical de 'Matins du monde' à l'Église de la Trinité." In Roger Michael, *Matins du monde*, 109–12. Paris: Bordas, 1949. 121 p. ML 53.M6 M3 1949.

At La Trinité on 13 March 1948, Messiaen provided a musical accompaniment of organ improvisations for a performance of Roger Michael's "Les Matins du monde," an oratorio for spoken voices. Through an essay published in the first edition of the text in 1950, Messiaen explained how he devised the musical accompaniment. The essay is valuable for insights into his approach to improvisation, particularly the meticulous planning that went into an extemporized piece.

64. Messiaen, Olivier. "Orgue." La Trinité, May 1951, 3.

65. Messiaen, Olivier. "Hommage à un Maître disparu: Jean de Gibon." *Écho du Pays de Redon*, 26 January 1952.

66. Messiaen, Olivier. "La Nature, les chants d'oiseaux." *Guide de concert* 229 (3 April 1959): 1093–94.

67. Messiaen, Olivier. ["Hommage à Roger Désormière."] *Les Lettres françaises* 1001 (8 October – 6 November 1963): 11.

A tribute to Roger Désormière (1898–1963). When he was seventeen years old, Messiaen saw Désormière conduct for the first time at the Salle Gaveau. On the program was Stravinsky's *Rite of Spring*. Messiaen admired Désormière's interpretation of that piece, noting its rhythmic precision. He recollects fondly how Désormière conducted concerts for La Jeune France, the world premiere of his *Trois petites Liturgies de la Présence Divine*, and the French premiere of his *Turangalîla-Symphonie*. Indeed, Messiaen preferred Désormière's interpretation of the *Turangalîla-Symphonie* to that of Leonard Bernstein, who conducted the world premiere of the work a year earlier. Messiaen praises Désormière's ability as a flutist, composer, and conductor, and also singles him out as a champion of the music of Rameau, Berlioz, and Debussy. Messiaen closes his tribute by remembering the last two times he saw Désormière conduct, which was at the Théâtre des Champs-Élysées with the Orchestre National. Désormière's first program included Boulez's "Soleil des eaux," while the second one featured Stravinsky's "Petrouchka" and De Falla's "Tricorne." Messiaen states that he will never forget Désormière who, in Messiaen's youth, was both a friend to composers and a great conductor.

68. Messiaen Olivier. "Matière-lumière, espace-temps, son-couleur ... " *Prevues* 179 (January 1966): 39–41.

A rambling essay on the state of serial music in France. Messiaen begins by discussing the nature of musical language. In his opinion, it has never exhibited a break. Its continuity is based on principles of opposition and alternation as manifested by long and short durations, high and low pitches, strong and weak dynamics, short and sustained articulations, and thin and thick textures. Musical language as it exists in nature also includes the manipulation of harmonics in a sonority (a reference to the concept of natural resonance) as well as silence. Messiaen notes the penchant of musicians to classify music according to historical periods, countries of origin, types of texture (monophonic, polyphonic, heterophonic), methods of pitch organization (modal, tonal, serial), and approaches to rhythm and dynamics. But these categories present a false picture of what music is since they do not address the principles of alternation and opposition. Messiaen goes on to argue that serial music is not a break with the past but a union of the horizontal and vertical, as seen in the works of Webern and Boulez. But more and more, musicians are returning to natural phenomena and their imitation.

In the rest of the essay, Messiaen promotes his ideas about sound-color relationships and time and space as an alternative to serialism.

He mentions how the Swiss painter Charles Blanc-Gatti (his friend) suffered from a physiological synesthesia that allowed him to see colors when he heard music and how those experiences could be duplicated by taking mescaline, a drug known by the ancient Aztecs and Mayans. He then describes his own peculiar type of colored-hearing synesthesia.

The subject then switches to serialism. Messiaen states that if one interprets the word "serial" in a directional sense as in the strict unfolding of durations, pitches, dynamics, timbres, attacks, densities, and tempi, then this conception, although useful for post-Webernian serial composers in avoiding common sonorities and rhythms and employing "melodies-of-timbres" in orchestration, is now obsolete. Boulez has replaced the notion of a series with the more fecund ideas of homophony and heterophony, while younger composers such as Jean-Claude Eloy are researching timbres and durations. All in all, younger composers have dispensed with the word "serial" and its connection with academicism. They view Schoenberg, Berg, and Webern as precursors to Boulez. Messiaen closes his essay by speculating on musical trends of the last quarter of the twentieth century. But why play the prophet he asks? Messiaen exhorts everyone to be in an intellectual communion with light and the music of nature. Through transformed senses or a synthetic knowledge comparable to that possessed by angels, Messiaen encourages everyone to embrace the unknown unions of matter and light, space and time, and sound and color, for they are truly the new means of listening to music.

69. Messiaen, Olivier. "Absence et présence de Roger Désormière." In *Roger Désormière et son temps*: *Textes en hommage*, ed. Denise Mayer and Pierre Souvtchinsky, 127–33. Monaco: Éditions du Rocher, 1966. 189 p. ML 422. D42 M4.

Another tribute to Désormière by Messiaen. He lauds Désormière for his outstanding abilities as a flutist, composer, and conductor, as well as his support of French music both past and present. Messiaen singles out the extraordinary eclecticism of Désormière's choice of programs for his concerts and expresses his admiration for Désormière's performances of Debussy's *Pelléas et Mélisande* at the Opéra-Comique from 1946–49. Messiaen also notes how Désormière conducted the world premiere of the *Trois petites Liturgies de la Présence Divine* on 21 April 1945 and the French premiere of the *Turangalîla-Symphonie* on 25 July 1950. Finally, Messiaen discusses the bond shared by Désormière and Boulez as seen not only through "Déso's" (a nickname given to Désormière by a critic after he conducted the world premiere of Boulez's *Soleil des eaux*) support of Boulez's music but also through comparisons of Désormière and Boulez as conductors.

70. Messiaen, Olivier. "Hommage d'Olivier Messiaen aux artistes de l'orchestre." *L'Artiste musicien de Paris* 64/14 (1966): 15–17.

71. Messiaen, Olivier. "Notice sur la vie et les travaux de Jean Lurçat (1892–1966) par M. Olivier Messiaen lue à l'occasion de son installation comme membre de la section de musique: Séance du mercredi 15 mai 1968" (Paris: Institut de France, 1968): 7–16.

In December of 1967, Messiaen was elected to the newly created chair (decree number 67–778 of 23 August 1967) of the Académie des Beaux-Arts of the Institut de France. His installation took place on 15 May 1968. After being introduced at the meeting, Messiaen gave a speech honoring the life and work of the artist Jean Lurçat (1892–1966). Besides praising Lurçat's paintings and tapestries, Messiaen noted affinities between Lurçat's work and that of his own, declaring him to be a "great rhythmician of color."

72. Messiaen, Olivier. [Reminiscence of Suzanne Balguerie.] In *Hommage à Suzanne Balguerie*, 6. N.p.: Imprimerie d'Allier [1968?].

73. Messiaen, Olivier and J. Roy. "Olivier Messiaen." In *Dictionnaire de la musique: Les Hommes et leurs œuvres*, ed. Marc Honegger, 2:713. 2 vols. Paris: Bordas, 1970. ISBN: 204019973X. ML 100.D65.

In this dictionary article, Messiaen authors the biographical part and provides a selected list of works. J. Roy writes about Messiaen's musical style, noting how it defined itself through the successive acquisition and use of different musical elements and techniques.

74. Messiaen, Olivier. "Hommage à Marcel Dupré." *Le Courrier Musical de France* 35 (1971): 113. ISSN: 0011–0620.

A tribute by Messiaen to Marcel Dupré on the occasion of Dupré's death in 1971. Messiaen begins by recalling a ceremony at Saint-Sulpice on 7 May 1971 honoring Dupré when he was still alive. He then reflects upon Dupré's musical career as a performer, composer, and teacher, hailing him as the "Liszt of the organ."

75. Messiaen, Olivier. "Discours prononcés dans la séance publique tenue par l'Académie des Beaux-Arts le mercredi 23 mai 1973 pour la réception de M. Marc Saltet, élu membre de la section d'architecture en remplacement de M. Charles Lemaresquier" (Paris: Institut de France, 1973): 3–10.

In a ceremonial speech as president of the Académie des Beaux-Arts, Messiaen welcomes the recently elected Marc Saltet to the organization's seat in architecture made vacant by the death of its previous occupant, Charles Lemaresquier. Messiaen reviews Saltet's curriculum vitae, lauds his accomplishments as an architect, and mentions the time when Saltet invited him to come to Versailles and Trianon in order to hear their birds. He accepted and was delighted by what he had experienced during his visit.

76. Messiaen, Olivier. "Discours de M. Olivier Messiaen, Président, Institut de France, Académie des Beaux-Arts, séance publique annuelle du 14 novembre 1973" (Paris: Institut de France, 1973).

77. Messiaen, Olivier. "Les Grandes Orgues de l'église de la Sainte-Trinité à Paris." Paris: La Trinité, October 1980. (I want to thank Nigel Simeone for providing me with a photocopy of this document from his private collection, "Nigel Simeone, private collection").

A booklet by Messiaen tracing the history of the organ Cavaillé-Coll built for La Trinité in 1868. Messiaen describes the various restorations performed on the instrument through the years. While he insists that the timbres of the original stops of the Cavaillé-Coll organ were respected for restorations performed during his tenure as titular organist, he mentions how the organ was enriched through the addition of more mixture and reed stops, as well as how the organ, through its electrification, new combination generals, and three keyboards, was now capable of more frequent and varied changes of color. Yet, the most beautiful sounding stops remain those by Cavaillé-Coll. Messiaen compares the organ at La Trinité with other instruments in France and the United States, provides more observations about the organ's tonal characteristics, and supplies the instrument's specifications.

78. Messiaen, Olivier. "Évocation de Cécile Sauvage." *Annales de Haute-Provence* 50/291, 1er semestre (1981): 114–18. ISSN: 0240–4672.

A speech given by Messiaen on 23 July 1980 at a ceremony honoring his mother Cécile Sauvage in the city of Digne in Haute-Provence. On that occasion, the "Amis du Pays dignois" placed a plaque on the house at 17, avenue de Verdun, in which Sauvage had once lived from 1888–1907. The speech is a moving tribute by Messiaen to his mother. He both describes and praises her poetry. He closes the speech by reciting lines from *L'Âme en bourgeon*, a book of poems written while she was pregnant with him. For Messiaen, these poems had a profound influence on his life as a musician. The speech was subsequently published by the *Annales de Haute-Provence.*

79. Messiaen, Olivier. "Discours prononcés dans la séance publique tenue par l'Académie des Beaux-Arts présidée par M. Albert Decaris,

Président de l'Académie, le mercredi 2 mai 1984 pour la réception de M. Iannis Xenakis" (Paris: Académie des Beaux-Arts, 1984), 9–11. Reprinted in *Portrait(s) de Iannis Xenakis*, ed. François-Bernard Mâche, 83–86. Paris: Bibliothèque Nationale de France, 2001.

In May 1984, Messiaen served as the principal speaker for Xenakis's induction ceremony into the Académie des Beaux-Arts of the Institut de France. Messiaen recalls his first meeting with Xenakis at the Paris Conservatoire, in which he encouraged the Greek composer not to worry about studying harmony and counterpoint but to base his composing on his knowledge of mathematics and architecture. Messiaen closes his speech with a dithyramb, based on Stéphane Mallarmé's "Le Tombeau d'Edgar Poe," in honor of Xenakis.

80. Messiaen, Olivier. "Obstacles." In *20e siècle: Images de la musique française*, ed. Jean-Pierre Derrien, 168–72. Paris: SACEM et Papiers, 1986. 172 p. ML 270.5.A14 1986.

In this essay, Messiaen recounts four conflicts with his listening public that have intensified over the years. They are related to his conceptions of rhythm, color, birdsong, and faith. Messiaen's goal in this essay is to explain what these subjects mean to him. First, Messiaen states that most people mistakenly equate rhythm with the steady beat of a military march. On the contrary, rhythm for Messiaen is irregular, as evidenced by the waves of the sea or sound of the wind in nature. Messiaen recounts his study of rhythm after he left the Paris Conservatoire and explains some of his rhythmic techniques (e.g., nonretrogradable rhythms, rhythmic characters, and symmetrical permutations). Messiaen then discusses the role of sound-color relationships in his music within the context of listeners who hear sounds but see nothing. He elaborates on various associations between his harmonic language and the colors he experiences in his peculiar brand of synesthesia.

In like manner, Messiaen comments upon his use of birdsong in his music within the framework of listeners who are ignorant of them. Finally, Messiaen believes that his most vexing conflict with his listening public is in the area of religion. He is a devout Roman Catholic who has dedicated the majority of his works to expounding the mysteries of his faith. His listeners do not understand him because they are either atheists or indifferent to religion. Messiaen notes the scriptural writings and Christian authors that have influenced him the most. He then goes on to cite different works that best represent his religious views.

The ideas included in this article, along with the explanations of Messiaen's compositional techniques, can also be found in *Musique et couleur: Nouveaux entretiens avec Claude Samuel* (see item 175) and *Conférence de Kyoto* (see item 100), which are both contemporaneous with this essay.

81. Messiaen, Olivier. "L'intuition du premier jour." In *Éclats/Boulez*, ed. Claude Samuel with the collaboration of Jacqueline Muller, 6–7. Paris: Éditions du Centre Pompidou, 1986. 143 p. ISBN: 2858503427. ML 410.B773 S193 (IUCAT).

In this collection celebrating Pierre Boulez's sixtieth birthday and the tenth anniversary of IRCAM (*L'Institut de Recherche et Coordination Acoustique/Musique*), Messiaen recounts his first meeting with Boulez after a performance of his *Quatuor pour la fin du Temps* in the salons of Guy Bernard-Delapierre (ca. 1942), his interactions with Boulez as a student in his harmony class, and a conversation he had with Boulez while on a metro in Paris in which he predicted that Boulez would be a leading figure in the music of the future. Included on these two pages is an essay by Michel Fano (see item 613) describing his time as a student in Messiaen's analysis class at the Paris Conservatoire, in which Boulez came to analyze his *Deuxième Sonate* for piano (1948).

82. Messiaen, Olivier. "Analyse manuscrite de la *Messe Solennelle*." In Marie-Louise Jaquet-Langlais, *Jean Langlais (1907–1991): Ombre et Lumière*, 163. Paris: Éditions Combre, 1995.

Contains an analysis of Langlais's *Messe Solennelle* (1949) by Messiaen in his autograph manuscript, in which he examines each movement (Kyrie, Gloria, Sanctus, Agnus Dei). He remarks that the work is not extraordinarily difficult to perform, since all the vocal parts are doubled by the organ and the entrances of the choir are carefully prepared.

83. Messiaen, Olivier. "Message from Olivier Messiaen." *Contemporary Music Review* 17, part 4 (1998): 15. ISSN: 0749–4467.

A message from Messiaen to the Japanese composer Yoritsune Matsudaira (1907–2001) on the occasion of the latter's birthday. Published in an anonymous English translation, Messiaen expresses his appreciation for Matsudaira's music and transcriptions of Japanese music. He also conveys his gratitude to Matsudaira for championing his works in Japan and for his hospitality while visiting that country on different occasions.

84. Messiaen, Olivier. ["Tribute to Daniel-Lesur."] In Nigel Simeone, "Daniel-Lesur," *The Musical Times* 143/1881 (Winter 2002): 6–8. ISSN: 0027–4666.

In an essay on Daniel-Lesur on the occasion of his death on 2 July 2002, Simeone includes a speech given by Messiaen on 14 March 1990 in which he honored Daniel-Lesur at the Institut de France in Paris by presenting him with the award of "Grand Officier of the Légion d'Honneur." Simeone translated the speech from a typescript in Messiaen's private archives, reproducing it in the article by special permission of Yvonne Loriod-Messiaen. The speech is a warm and affectionate tribute to a longtime colleague and friend. Messiaen traces his association with Daniel-Lesur, noting his friend's many accomplishments.

PEDAGOGICAL WORKS

85. Messiaen, Olivier and others. *Vingt Leçons de Solfège Modernes dans les Sept clés.* Paris: Henry Lemoine, 1934. 54 p.

   Written in 1933, published with a copyright date of 1934. Five of the twenty pieces in this volume, geared to improving one's reading of clefs, are by Messiaen (see nos. 3, 8, 11, 14, and 18), with the remaining fifteen by Claude Arrieu (nos. 4, 10, and 16), Georges Dandelot (nos. 2, 5, 7, 12, 15, and 20), Georges Hugon (nos. 1, 6, 9, 13, and 17), and Marc Starominsky (no. 19).

86. Messiaen, Olivier. *Vingt Leçons d'Harmonie.* In French, English translation by Felix Aprahamian and German translation by Sieglinde Ahrens. Paris: Alphonse Leduc, 1951. 53 p. MT 50.M58 (IUCAT).

   The *Vingt Leçons d'Harmonie* was originally published in 1939. This edition of 1951 includes English and German translations by Felix Aprahamian and Sieglinde Ahrens, respectively, of Messiaen's preface and comments on the realization of each exercise.

   These four-part exercises (open score, using soprano, alto, tenor, and bass clefs) by Messiaen are conceived in the styles of selected composers from Monteverdi to Ravel in order to outline harmonic principles of the seventeenth through twentieth centuries. Figured bass has been supplied in each exercise in order to indicate the analysis for the student. Additional remarks are given to assist the student in analyzing more difficult passages. The *Vingt Leçons d'Harmonie* is indicative of Messiaen's work as a Professor of Harmony at the Paris Conservatoire from 1941 through 1947. There he emphasized the evolution of harmonic style from the seventeenth through twentieth centuries through the study of various masterworks. He often composed harmony exercises for his students to realize in the style of a given composer under discussion.

87. Messiaen, Olivier. *Les 22 concertos pour piano de Mozart.* With a preface by Jean-Victor Hocquard. Paris: Éditions Garamont Librairie Séguier, 1987. 99 p. ISBN: 2906284467. MT 130.M8 M3 1987.

Program notes by Messiaen for Yvonne Loriod-Messiaen's performances of Mozart's twenty-one piano concertos and the Concerto-Rondo (K. 382) with the Orchestre des Concerts Lamoureaux in Paris, between 7 November and 19 December 1964. Conductors included Pierre Boulez, Bruno Maderna, and Louis Martin. A preface by Jean-Victor Hocquard ("Le concerto pour piano dans l'Œuvre mozartienne") serves as a general introduction.

88. Messiaen, Olivier. *Technique de mon langage musical. Texte avec exemples musicaux.* Paris: Alphonse Leduc, 2000. 112 p. ISBN: 2856890547.

The *Technique de mon langage musical* was originally published in 1944 in two volumes, the first containing the text and the second musical examples (Olivier Messiaen, *Technique de mon langage musical*, 2 vols. [Paris: Alphonse Leduc, 1944]). This new edition was published in 2000 and features both text and musical examples in a single volume, which makes studying the *Technique* easier when compared to its original two-volume format. Translated editions of the *Technique* include one in English by John Satterfield, and in English and German by Satterfield and Sieglinde Ahrens, respectively (idem, *The Technique of My Musical Language*, trans. John Satterfield, 2 vols. [Paris: Alphonse Leduc, 1956]; idem, *Technique de mon langage musical*, in French, English translation by John Satterfield and German translation by Sieglinde Ahrens, 2 vols. [Paris: Alphonse Leduc, 1956–66]).

The *Technique* is not a theoretical treatise per se, but an inventory of Messiaen's compositional devices and techniques. Messiaen wrote the *Technique* in response to questions proposed by his students. While the book is useful for understanding Messiaen's earlier compositions spanning *Le Banquet céleste* (1928) to *Visions de l'Amen* (1943), it is out of date.

After an introduction and an initial chapter mentioning the "charm of impossibilities," the *Technique* focuses on the elements that compose Messiaen's approaches to rhythm, melody, form, and harmony. Hindu rhythms, added values, augmentation and diminution, retrogradable and nonretrogradable rhythms, polyrhythms, rhythmic pedals, and rhythmic notation are covered in chapters two through seven. Melody, including plainchant, Hindu ragas, birdsong, and techniques of melodic development, particularly *interversion*, is discussed in chapters eight through ten. Various formal types are then addressed in chapters eleven through twelve. Finally, added notes, invented chords, resonance effects, assorted chord connections, expansions of groups of notes, and the modes of limited transposition are dealt with in chapters thirteen through nineteen. A catalogue of Messiaen's music (up to 1942) concludes the treatise, with one to two stars awarded by the composer in order to indicate how characteristic a work is. In earlier editions of the *Technique*, both versions of the *L'Ascension* suite were not awarded any stars, suggesting that Messiaen regarded the work as uncharacteristic. In the present edition, both versions have inexplicably acquired two, suggesting that they are now quite characteristic.

Reviews: Christopher Dingle, "Messiaen and Ravel," *Tempo* 59/231 (January 2005): 61–62; Istvan Anhalt, *The Canadian Music Journal* 2 (Autumn 1957): 67, 69, 71; Elliott W. Galkin, *Notes* 14/4 (September 1957): 575–76; and Frederick Jacobi, "Messiaen's Language: Birds and Butterflies," *Modern Music* 23/3 (Summer 1946): 231–32.

89. Messiaen, Olivier. "Olivier Messiaen analyze ses Œuvres." In *Olivier Messiaen, homme de foi: Regard sur son Œuvre d'orgue* (item 238), 31–67.

A compilation of Messiaen's commentaries on his organ works, from *Le Banquet céleste* to *Livre du Saint Sacrement*, drawn from his published liner notes and scores. Also includes biblical citations associated with the organ works, various short paragraphs by Messiaen on matters of faith reproduced in his handwriting, and pictures supporting his views on faith.

90. Messiaen, Olivier. *Traité de rythme, de couleur, et d'ornithologie (1949–1992)*. 7 vols. Paris: Alphonse Leduc, 1994–2002. ISBN: 2856890474, 2856890482, 2856890490. MT 6.M59 T7 (IUCAT).

The *Traité de rythme, de couleur, et d'ornithologie (1949–1992)* was begun around 1948 and remained unpublished at the time of Messiaen's death in 1992. It is cumulative in nature, containing the most comprehensive account of Messiaen's compositional theories and practices, hence superseding the earlier *Technique de mon langage musical*. Yvonne Loriod-Messiaen followed Messiaen's directions scrupulously as she prepared the *Traité* for publication. It was published by Alphonse Leduc in seven volumes, with the last one appearing in 2002.

The *Traité* reflects thirty years of Messiaen's work as a teacher at the Paris Conservatoire. It centers on his ideas about rhythm. While there are detailed discussions of plainchant, birdsong, sound-color relationships, and various pieces by Messiaen and other composers in the *Traité*, rhythm underpins each discussion. Indeed, this emphasis on rhythm is demonstrated in the first three volumes. The first volume contains chapters on time, rhythm, Greek metric patterns, and Hindu rhythms. It includes analyses of the thirty-nine choruses from Claude Le Jeune's *Le Printemps* and excerpts from several works by Messiaen. The second volume features discussions of nonretrogradable rhythms, augmentation and diminution, rhythmic pedals and canons, and rhythmic characters. It contains analyses of Stravinsky's *Rite of Spring*, and Messiaen's *Turangalîla-Symphonie*, *Messe de la Pentecôte*, *Livre d'orgue*, and *Vingt Regards sur l'Enfant-Jésus*. The third volume covers symmetrical permutations and the technique of "hors tempo" where some birds, in the context of simultaneous birdsongs, sing outside of the established tempo. It includes analyses of *Chronochromie*, *Quatre Études de rythme*, *Livre d'orgue*, *Visions de l'Amen*, and *Harawi*.

The fourth volume deals with plainchant and melodic accentuation in Mozart and features analyses of Messiaen's *Messe de la Pentecôte* and Mozart's twenty-one piano concertos. The fifth volume, issued in two parts and edited by Yvonne Loriod-Messiaen, centers on birdsong and its use in Messiaen's music. Messiaen provides the origin and basic characteristics of each bird and analyzes their songs in terms of neumes and Greek metric patterns. *Sept Haïkaï* is analyzed in the sixth chapter. The sixth volume is devoted to Debussy and an examination of some of his works. Yvonne Loriod-Messiaen reconstructed some of the Debussy analyses from Messiaen's annotated scores. The seventh volume focuses on sound-color relationships with discussions of the modes of limited transposition and color chords (e.g., chords of transposed inversions on the same base note). It includes tables that list the modes and color chords along with their transpositional levels and color associations.

Reviews: Christopher Dingle, vol. 1, *Tempo* 192 (April 1995): 29–30, 32; vols. 2 and 3, *Tempo* 202 (October 1997): 25–26; vol. 4, *Tempo* 205 (July 1998): 26–27; vols. 5–7, *Tempo* 58/227 (January 2004): 41–46; and Jean Boivin, "*Le Traité de rythme, de couleur, et d'ornithologie d'Olivier Messiaen* (tomes I, II, III et IV) [Review of vols. 1–4]," *Circuit* 9/1 (1998): 17–26.

91. Baggech, Melody. "An English Translation of Olivier Messiaen's *Traité de Rythme, de Couleur, et d'Ornithologie*, Volume 1." D.M.A. document, University of Oklahoma, 1998. xv, 411 p.

An English translation of volume one of the *Traité de rythme* (item 90).

92. Messiaen, Olivier and Yvonne Loriod-Messiaen. *Ravel: Analyses des Œuvres pour Piano de Maurice Ravel.* Paris: Durand, 2003. 104 p. ISBN: 0634080369. MT 145.R19 M47 2003.

    This volume features Messiaen's analyses of Ravel's *Ma Mère l'Oye, Gaspard de la Nuit,* and *Le Tombeau de Couperin.* Yvonne Loriod-Messiaen reconstructed these analyses from both Messiaen's annotated scores and her memories of his analysis class at the Paris Conservatoire. They cover aspects of Ravel's musical style—form, melody, harmony, and rhythm. In keeping with his pedagogical approach, Messiaen points out similarities between Ravel's music and that of other composers or musical cultures. This book is highly recommended, for little is said about Ravel in the *Traité de rythme.*

    Reviews: Christopher Dingle, "Messiaen and Ravel," *Tempo* 59/231 (January 2005): 61–62.

LECTURES AND LIBRETTOS

Lectures

93. Messiaen, Olivier. *Conférence de Bruxelles.* With French, German, and English Texts. Paris: Alphonse Leduc, 1960. 14 p. ML 60.M587 C7.

    A lecture given by Messiaen at the Philips Pavilion in Brussels on 15 September 1958. Published in French with anonymous German and English translations. The lecture deals with Messiaen's philosophy of time, rhythmic techniques, and the inspiration he derived from nature, especially that from birdsong.

94. Messiaen, Olivier. "Vortrag in Brüssel." Translated by Heinz-Klaus Metzger. In *Musik-Konzepte 28: Olivier Messiaen* (item 243), 3–6.

    Heinz-Klaus Metzger's 1982 revision of the anonymous German translation of Messiaen's Brussels lecture published by Alphonse Leduc (see item 93). The revision is based on the original French text.

95. Messiaen, Olivier. "Musikalisches Glaubensbekenntnis." In *Melos* (item 242), 381–85.

    For its special issue honoring Messiaen on the occasion of his 50th birthday in 1958, *Melos* published, with the consent of Alphonse Leduc, an anonymous German translation of the composer's Brussels lecture. Leduc used the same translation in their trilingual edition of the lecture two years later (see item 93).

96. Messiaen, Olivier. *Conférence de Notre-Dame.* Translated into English by Timothy J. Tikker; translated into German by Almut Rößler. Paris: Alphonse Leduc, 2001. 31 p. ML 60.M565 (IUCAT).

In this lecture given on 4 December 1977, Messiaen reflects on how music may be adapted to the sacred through liturgical music, religious music, and colored music. His discussion of colored music is valuable because it supplies many of the central ideas behind his approach to sound-color relationships in his works.

97. Messiaen, Olivier. "Conférence de Notre-Dame." Translated by Timothy J. Tikker. In *Contributions to the Spiritual World of Olivier Messiaen: With Original Texts by the Composer* (item 180), 57–66.

English translation of Messiaen's Notre-Dame lecture (see item 96).

98. Messiaen, Olivier. "Conférence de Notre-Dame." Translated by Timothy J. Tikker. *The Diapason* 76/1 (January 1985): 10–11. ISSN: 0012–2378.

This English translation of Messiaen's Notre-Dame lecture is identical with that found in item 97. These translations differ in minor respects, however, with the translation of item 96.

99. Messiaen, Olivier. "La musique sacrée." Paris: Alphonse Leduc, 1977. 11 p.

The entire Notre-Dame lecture is reprinted here under the title "La musique sacrée" for a series entitled "Recherches et experiences spirituelles." Includes an introduction, along with an appreciation of Messiaen by an "arch-priest" (l'archiprêtre).

100. Messiaen, Olivier. *Conférence de Kyoto.* Translated into Japanese by Naoko Tamamura. Paris: Alphonse Leduc, 1988. 36 p. ML 410.M52 A2 (IUCAT).

A lecture given by Messiaen on 12 November 1985 in Kyoto in which he summarizes his musical language in light of four issues that have continually troubled him in his dealings with the public: (1) misperceptions about the nature of rhythm; (2) the linking of sound with color; (3) ignorance of birdsong among city dwellers; and (4) speaking about the Christian faith to non-believers. Thus, the lecture focuses on rhythm (Greek and Hindu rhythmic patterns, nonretrogradable rhythms, rhythmic characters, symmetrical permutations, open and closed fan techniques, and rhythmic serialization), sound-color relationships involving both the modes of limited transposition and nonmodal sonorities, birdsong, and religious music, closing with remarks on *Saint François d'Assise.* In French and Japanese.

Librettos

101. Messiaen, Olivier. *Saint François d'Assise (Scènes Franciscaines): Opéra en 3 actes et 8 tableaux: Poème et musique d'Olivier Messiaen.* Libretto. Paris: Alphonse Leduc, 1983. 54 p. ML 50.M57 S2.

    Libretto for Messiaen's opera *Saint François d'Assise.* In addition to the opera's text, this booklet includes a preface by Messiaen noting sources for the libretto, such as the *Fioretti, Considerations on the Stigmata,* and *Canticle of the Creatures*; information on the performers for the world premiere on 28 November 1983 in Paris, and directions for the wearing of costumes.

3

Primary Sources II: Prefaces to Works, Interviews, Published Correspondence, and Documentaries and Filmed Performances

This chapter is a continuation of the previous one. It includes prefaces to works, interviews (including selected ones with Yvonne Loriod-Messiaen), published correspondence, and documentaries and filmed performances. Included in this section are prefaces written by Yvonne Loriod-Messiaen and Olivier Latry for works published after Messiaen's death.

PREFACES TO WORKS, ARTICLES/SPECIAL ISSUES, AND BOOKS

Works by Messiaen

Opera

102. Messiaen, Olivier. *Saint François d'Assise (Scènes franciscaines): Opéra en 3 actes et 8 tableaux*. 8 vols. Paris: Alphonse Leduc, 1983, 1988–92. M 1500.M58 S2 Acts 1–3, Scenes 1–8 (IUCAT).

Each of the opera's tableaux includes a synopsis of its drama and a description (*Analyse*) of its musical-dramatic content. Messiaen discusses each tableau chronologically and points out important dramatic moments and the musical techniques he uses to reinforce them. Like many of the analytical commentaries that follow, while these descriptions provide valuable glimpses into Messiaen's compositional intentions, they are of limited use analytically because they indicate what but not why something is happening. Finally, contains descriptions of the costumes that each character wears during the tableau.

Orchestral Works

103. Messiaen, Olivier. *Les Offrandes oubliées: Méditation symphonique pour Orchestre.* Paris: Durand, 1931. M 1002.M5803 P.

    A religious introduction comprised of three stanzas, in which Messiaen describes the suffering of Jesus on the Cross, the sinfulness of humankind, and the spotless communion table upon which the Bread of Life and of Love is offered.

104. Messiaen, Olivier. *Le Tombeau resplendissant.* With a preface by Yvonne Loriod-Messiaen. Translated from the French by Joane Bennett. Paris: Durand, 1997.

    A preface by Yvonne Loriod-Messiaen that provides a backdrop to the piece—when it was composed and the circumstances surrounding its creation, namely how the death of Messiaen's mother Cécile Sauvage in 1927 was still felt in the piece, and how his subsequent stay with his paternal aunts restored his mental and physical health—as well as a summary of the piece's form and musical elements.

105. Messiaen, Olivier. *Réveil des oiseaux.* Paris: Durand, 1955. M 1010.M608 R4.

    In this preface, Messiaen states that there are only authentic birdsongs in *Réveil des oiseaux.* He advises performers to reproduce, as closely as possible, the mode of attack and timbre of the birds. Each bird is identified by name at its first appearance in the score below the instrument that represents it. Onomatopoeic suggestions, placed above the notes, are included to help performers find the desired timbres and attacks. The conductor should explain all of this to his or her musicians, as well as respect the music's metronome markings, performance suggestions placed at the bottoms of pages, and grand silences. Since the pianist must imitate the mode of singing of a large number of birds, he or she is advised to take early morning walks in the woods during the spring in order to become acquainted with the original models. Messiaen concludes his preface by describing the programmatic intent of the music, which focuses on a spring day that begins at midnight and ends at midday. He provides information as to which bird (and its associated instrumental timbre) is singing at midnight, at four o'clock in the morning, at sunrise, and so on.

106. Messiaen, Olivier. *Oiseaux exotiques.* Vienna: Universal, 1959/1995. M 1010.M608 O4 1995.

Contains two prefaces written by Messiaen. Published in French with anonymous German and English translations. In the first preface, Messiaen supplies information about the commissioning (Pierre Boulez for the Domaine Musical concerts at the Petit Théâtre Marigny, Paris), dates of composition (1955–56), first performance (10 March 1956, Petit Théâtre Marigny), and dedicatee (Yvonne Loriod) of *Oiseaux exotiques.* After suggesting how the instruments should be placed in a concert hall, Messiaen notes how tempi with metronome markings, the character of each birdsong, and fingerings and pedalings in the piano part are all meticulously indicated in the score, suggesting that performers should follow them. He also draws attention to how the conductor is provided with numerous footnotes to help him or her emphasize specific musical features and ensure acoustical balance. In the second preface, Messiaen lists the birdsongs, Hindu rhythms, and Greek metric patterns used in the piece. He also includes details regarding the colors, calls, and native habitats of some of the birds. Messiaen urges conductors and pianists to read the second preface carefully, for he believes that it can serve as an aid to a superior performance.

107. Messiaen, Olivier. *Chronochromie.* Paris: Alphonse Leduc, 1963. M 1045.M58 C5.

Contains two prefaces by Messiaen. In the first preface, Messiaen notes when *Chronochromie* was written (1959–60) and how it was the result of a commission from Heinrich Strobel and the Südwestfunk Orchestra. The temporal structure of the piece consists of thirty-two durations treated in symmetrical permutations. The melodic structure of the piece is based on birdsongs from France, Sweden, Japan, and Mexico. Messiaen emphasizes that the complex sounds and timbres of the piece color the music's durations. He describes the piece's form, which is an expansion of the strophe-antistrophe-epôde of the Greek triad. In the shorter second preface, Messiaen alerts conductors to the fact that all instruments are written as they will actually sound.

108. Messiaen, Olivier. *Sept Haïkaï: Esquisses japonaises.* Paris: Alphonse Leduc, 1966. M 1010.M608 H3.

A descriptive commentary of each of the seven pieces contained in the work. Mentions the different compositional techniques that occur during the course of a piece, such as the Indian rhythms dedicated to the three *Shakti* in the first and seventh movements.

Describes the landscapes associated with specific pieces, such as "Le parc de Nara et les lanternes de pierre," "Yamanaka-cadenza," and "Miyajima et le torii dans le mer." Notes the importance of sound-color relationships in "Miyajima." Lists the Japanese birds used in the work, describing the plumage, associated orchestral colors, and songs of most of them. Dedicated to Yvonne Loriod-Messiaen, Pierre Boulez, Fumi Yamaguchi, Seiji Ozawa, Yoritsuné Matsudaïra, Sadao Bekku and Mitsuaki Hayama, the ornithologist Hoshino, and the landscapes, music, and birds of Japan.

109. Messiaen, Olivier. *Couleurs de la Cité céleste.* Paris: Alphonse Leduc, 1966. M 985.M58 C8 (IUCAT).

Two prefaces by Messiaen. In the first one, he describes the important role color plays in the piece. It determines the form of the entire work to such an extent that all musical elements such as plainchant, Hindu rhythms and Greek metric patterns, the permutation of duration, and birdsongs are employed solely to enhance its expression. Messiaen also mentions how sound-color relationships symbolize God and the heavenly Jerusalem. The second preface contains more details about *Couleurs de la Cité céleste.* Messiaen not only lists the five quotations from the Book of Revelation that inspired the work (4:3, 8:6, 9:1, 21:11, and 21:19, 20) but also refers to rhythmic techniques, plainchant, and birdsongs used in the music.

110. Messiaen, Olivier. *Et exspecto resurrectionem mortuorum.* Paris: Alphonse Leduc, 1966. M 1245.M58 E9 (IUCAT).

Messiaen recounts the commissioning of the work by André Malraux, its composition and orchestration in 1964, and how it was scored for the vast spaces found in churches, cathedrals, the open air, or mountaintops. He mentions several powerful images that were in his mind as he was composing the piece: Mexican pyramids; ancient Egyptian temples and statuary; Romanesque and Gothic churches; texts on the resurrection by Saint Thomas Aquinas; and the French Alps. After discussing the piece's instrumentation, Messiaen provides an analysis of the composition. He examines each of the work's five movements, noting how different musical elements reinforce the meaning of each movement's scriptural text. Messiaen closes his preface with information on the first three performances of the work and a note to the conductor.

111. Messiaen, Olivier. *Des canyons aux étoiles.* Paris: Alphonse Leduc, 1978. M 1040.M575 C3.

Given the length of the work, a long preface is provided that includes an introduction and analytical notes on each of the work's twelve movements. Messiaen explains that the title deals with the soul's ascent from the canyons to the stars and beyond to the resurrected souls of Heaven, in order to glorify God and all of creation. Hence the work is primarily a religious one involving praise and contemplation, and secondarily a geological and astronomical one. The sound-colors of the piece contain all the colors of the rainbow, along with the blue of the Stellar's Jay and the red of Bryce Canyon. The birdsongs are mainly from Utah and the Hawaiian islands, and the sky is symbolized by Zion Park and the star Aldebaran. After mentioning the commissioning of the work by Ms. Alice Tully and the music's instrumentation (which includes wind and sand machines), Messiaen analyzes each movement.

112. Messiaen, Olivier. *Un Vitrail et des oiseaux*. Paris: Alphonse Leduc, 1992. M 947.M47 V5 1992.

After noting when *Un Vitrail et des oiseaux* was composed (1986), who commissioned it (Pierre Boulez for the Orchestre de l'Ensemble Intercontemporain), and its instrumentation, Messiaen outlines the piece's form and musical elements, particularly birdsongs.

113. Messiaen, Olivier. *La Ville d'En-Haut*. Paris: Alphonse Leduc, 1994. M 947.M55 V5 (IUCAT).

Short preface by Messiaen explaining the work's textual inspiration and musical content. The music is motivated by Colossians 3:1 and Revelation 21:2. It centers on glimpses of life after death. Messiaen describes the musical content of the work, especially its bird calls. The brass chorale symbolizes the glory of the heavenly Jerusalem; the birdsongs of the xylos (xylophone, xylorimba, and marimba), woodwinds, and piano the joy of the resurrected, assured of being near to Christ; and the ever-changing colors evoked by the music's chords represent the light from above.

114. Messiaen, Olivier. *Un Sourire*. Paris: Alphonse Leduc, 1994. M 1045. M58 S6 1994.

Short preface by Messiaen describing the composition of the work in 1989 at the request of Marek Janowski to honor the bicentenary of Mozart's death in 1991. Messiaen characterizes the work as containing a very simple melody played by the violins, alternating with an exotic birdsong played by the xylos (xylophone, xylorimba, bells, suspended cymbal), woodwinds, and brass. Messiaen notes that despite all of Mozart's sorrows, sufferings, hunger, cold, incomprehension, and the nearness of death, he never stopped smiling. This was likewise evident in his music. That is why Messiaen has titled his homage "A Smile."

115. Messiaen, Olivier. *Éclairs sur l'Au-Delà*. Paris: Alphonse Leduc, 1998. M 1045.M58 E3 1998.

Preface by Yvonne Loriod-Messiaen. She describes how the work resulted from a commission from the New York Philharmonic Orchestra for its 150th anniversary. The piece was written and orchestrated between 1987 and 1991. *Éclairs sur l'Au-Delà* is a series of meditations on life after death and the celestial Jerusalem, borrowing its texts primarily from the Book of Revelation, and secondarily from the Gospels of Saints John, Matthew, and Luke, the First Epistle of Saint John, and the Book of Daniel. Loriod-Messiaen notes the use of the Australian Superb Lyrebird's song in the piece and its religious significance for Messiaen. Moreover, in keeping with Messiaen's practice of listing all birdsongs used in a composition and including the names of birds in different languages, Loriod-Messiaen provides a list of the birds used in each movement. She also supplies the work's instrumentation. Most of Loriod-Messiaen's preface is devoted to analytical commentaries of each movement.

116. Messiaen, Olivier. *Concert à quatre*. Paris: Alphonse Leduc, 2003. M 1040.M575 C6 2004.

Preface by Yvonne Loriod-Messiaen describing the genesis of the work. Inspired by Mozart, Scarlatti, and Rameau, and conceived as a homage to Mstislav Rostropovich, Heinz Holliger, and Catherine Cantin. Composed in 1990 but left unfinished after Messiaen's death in 1992. Recounts how the work was completed. Includes analytical commentaries of each movement taken from Messiaen's notes. Finally, contains a list of birdsongs used in the movement in French, Latin, and English.

Chamber and Instrumental Works

117. Messiaen, Olivier. *Quatuor pour la Fin du Temps*. Paris: Durand, 1942. M 422.M48 Q3.

Preface to one of the greatest works of the twentieth century. Messiaen talks about the inspiration behind the music, Revelation 10:1–7, where the angel declares that there will be no more time, and the circumstances surrounding its composition. He refers to aspects of the work's musical language (e.g., modes of limited transposition and special rhythms) and explains the symbolism behind the use of eight movements in the *Quatuor*. Messiaen then comments on the musical and symbolic contents of each movement and outlines a theory of his rhythmic language. He closes the preface by giving advice to those who perform the work, encouraging them to adhere closely to what is notated in the score but not at the expense of a vibrant interpretation. For English translations of the preface, see Clyde Holloway, "The Organ Works of Olivier Messiaen and Their Importance in His Total *Oeuvre,*" pp. 479–86 (see item 212), and Rebecca Rischin, *For the End of Time: The Story of the Messiaen Quartet,* pp. 129–34 (see item 486).

Organ Works

118. Messiaen, Olivier. *Offrande au Saint-Sacrement.* Paris: Alphonse Leduc, 2001. M 11.M.

    In his preface, organist Olivier Latry states that the *Offrande au Saint-Sacrement* was discovered by Yvonne Loriod-Messiaen in 1997. Latry believes that the work dates from 1928 because its second theme bears some stylistic resemblances to themes found in *Le Banquet céleste.* In addition, Latry considers the piece's registration as being influenced by Tournemire. Includes an anonymous English translation of the preface.

119. Messiaen, Olivier. *Prélude.* Paris: Alphonse Leduc, 2002. M 11.M58 P8 (IUCAT).

    Latry states that the *Prélude,* like the *Offrande au Saint-Sacrement,* was discovered by Yvonne Loriod-Messiaen in 1997. He speculates that the work was written in late 1929, not only because of its stylistic similarities to the *Diptyque* but also because of the G4 required in the pedal part and A6 in the keyboard part, which were possible on an atypical organ possessed by the Paris Conservatoire during Messiaen's student days. Includes an anonymous English translation of the preface.

120. Messiaen, Olivier. *La Nativité du Seigneur.* 4 vols. Paris: Alphonse Leduc, 1936. M 11.M58 N2 (IUCAT).

    An important source for understanding Messiaen's earlier music. Messiaen discusses how *La Nativité du Seigneur* is treated from the vantage points of theology, the organ as an instrument, and compositional style. From the theological point of view, there are five ideas that deal with Christ and his incarnation and life on earth, the spiritual birth of Christians, characters associated with Christmas, and the maternity of the Virgin Mary. From the instrumental point of view, the organ is used with few registrational changes and an economy of timbres (e.g., reeds with few foundations). The pedal participates in the musical texture as an upper voice and is no longer limited to the bass. From the compositional point of view, five techniques are listed that are quintessentially Messiaen: (1) the modes of limited transposition; (2) enlarged pedals, embellishments, and appoggiaturas; (3) added value; (4) the progressive increase or decrease of intervals; and (5) the chord on the dominant. Modes 1–3 are discussed in detail, with characteristic harmonizations supplied for the second and third modes. Two fourth modes are mentioned, which are in actuality modes 6 and 4 of the later *Technique de mon langage musical*. They are characterized as uninteresting because they can be transposed six times, an overly large number of transpositions compared to modes 1–3 and thereby not in keeping with Messiaen's aesthetic of restriction.

Enlarged pedals, embellishments, and appoggiaturas refer to dissonant notes of like function being grouped together, in order to make them more perceptible in a post-tonal harmonic environment, while added values refer to the transformation of a rhythmic pattern through the addition of a short value (either by a dot, note, or rest) to one of its notes. The progressive increase or decrease of intervals anticipates Messiaen's technique of *agrandissement asymétrique* (asymmetrical enlargement), the pitch counterpart to *personnages rythmiques* (rhythmic characters). During several repetitions of a musical idea or passage, some notes are transposed up a half step, others are transposed down a half step, while others remain stationary. Finally, while the chord on the dominant is explained as containing all the notes of a major scale, it is in reality a V^{13} chord. It is shown with its inversions transposed so that they share the same bass note, which points to Messiaen's later chords of transposed inversions on the same bass note.

For English translations of the preface, see Irene Feddern, *Messiaen on Messiaen: The Composer Writes about His Works*, pp. 7–9 (item 121), and Clyde Holloway, "The Organ Works of Olivier Messiaen and Their Importance in His Total *Oeuvre*," 474–78 (item 212).

121. Feddern, Irene, trans. *Messiaen on Messiaen: The Composer Writes about His Works*. Bloomington, IN: Frangipani Press, 1986. 26 p. MT 145.M54 M54.

English translations of Messiaen's liner notes to his recordings of his organ works on the Ducretet-Thompson label (*Le Banquet céleste* [1928] through *Livre d'orgue* [1951–52]) and the preface to his organ work *La Nativité du Seigneur*. According to Feddern, translations are deliberately literal in order to retain the flavor of the original.

122. Messiaen, Olivier. *Méditations sur le mystère de la Sainte Trinité.* Paris: Alphonse Leduc, 1973. M 11.M58 M3 (IUCAT).

Messiaen opens his preface with an explanation of the *langage communicable,* a musical language developed for the *Méditations sur le mystère de la Sainte Trinité.* It consists of three basic elements: (1) a Roman alphabet in which each letter is assigned a fixed pitch, duration, and register, (2) a Latin-based system of grammatical cases, and (3) a set of leitmotifs. These elements are used to "translate" phrases from the *Summa theologiæ* of Saint Thomas Aquinas into music. The preface to the *Méditations* also includes Messiaen's commentaries on each piece's musical and symbolic contents.

123. Messiaen, Olivier. *Livre du Saint Sacrement.* Paris: Alphonse Leduc, 1989. M11.M.

Messiaen describes the organization of the eighteen pieces that comprise this organ collection. The first four pieces center on the adoration of the invisible Christ present in the Holy Eucharist. The next seven pieces recall the mysteries of Christ as seen through events in the life of Jesus, set out in chronological order. The last seven pieces prayerfully reflect on the mysteries of the Holy Eucharist. In the preface, Messiaen not only provides the textual basis of each piece but also describes musical elements and techniques used throughout most of the collection.

Piano Works

124. Messiaen, Olivier. *Visions de l'Amen.* Paris: Durand, 1950. M 214.M54 V5 1950 (IUCAT).

In this preface Messiaen, inspired by the Catholic writer Ernest Hello, explains that the work is based on the fourfold significance of the word "Amen," which deals respectively with the creative act, submission to the divine will, a desire for union with God, and acknowledgment of eternal consummation. He depicts the various meanings of "Amen" through seven "musical visions." What follows next in the preface is a description of the musical techniques used in each piece. Messiaen points out that he utilizes stylized birdsong in the fifth piece, "Amen des Anges, des Saints, du chant des oiseaux," and suggests that the rainbow of colors described in the Apocalypse is imitated in the last, "Amen de la Consommation." Messiaen closes the preface by explaining how his rhythmic techniques are indicated in the score.

125. Messiaen, Olivier. *Vingt Regards sur l'Enfant-Jésus.* Paris: Durand, 1947. M 25.M47 V5 (IUCAT).

In this preface, Messiaen writes about the symbolism, theological influences, and principal themes of *Vingt Regards sur l'Enfant-Jésus.* The piece deals with a series of contemplations of the infant Jesus in the manger by different theological and immaterial entities, as well as human beings. It also includes movements inspired by theological concepts and events, poetry, and the visual arts. Messiaen cites the work of Dom Columba Marmion ("Le Christ dans ses mystères") and Maurice Toesca ("Les Douze Regards") as influencing *Vingt Regards,* since both authors have written of similar contemplations by the shepherds, the angels, the Virgin Mary, and God the Father. Messiaen expanded their ideas by adding more contemplations to *Vingt Regards.* At the end of the preface, he attaches commentaries that are probably similar to those he read aloud before each of the movements played by Yvonne Loriod at the work's premiere (Salle Gaveau, Paris, 26 March 1945).

126. Messiaen, Olivier. *Mode de valeurs et d'intensités.* Nouvelle édition avec analyse du compositeur. Paris: Durand, 2000. M 25.M58 E84 2000 (IUCAT).

     In the preface to this new edition of *Mode de valeurs et d'intensités,* Messiaen explains the precompositional quasi-serial scheme that is employed in the piece. The scheme or "mode" consists of 36 pitches, 24 durations, 12 attacks, and 7 dynamics. The mode is divided melodically into three twelve-note series that are associated, respectively, with three durational series that increase chromatically. Each pitch and duration is associated with separate dynamic and articulation marks. Unlike the preface to the first edition, which only contained an explanation of the above-mentioned modal scheme, this preface also includes an analysis of the work similar to that found in the third volume of the *Traité de rythme* (see item 90). Accompanied by an anonymous English translation.

127. Messiaen, Olivier. *Catalogue d'oiseaux.* 7 vols. Paris: Alphonse Leduc, 1964. M 25.M58 C23 (IUCAT).

     In his introduction, Messiaen provides the dates of composition for the *Catalogue d'oiseaux* (October 1956 to 1 September 1958). To prepare for the composition of these pieces, Messiaen remarks how necessary it was for him to travel and stay repeatedly in different parts of the world, in order to notate the songs of each bird. He maintains that memories dating back several hours or years were reawakened due to the precision of his notation. The work is dedicated to his avian models and Yvonne Loriod. There are thirteen movements in the *Catalogue d'oiseaux* divided among seven volumes. Each volume lists the avian species found in the work. Messiaen provides each movement with a descriptive program of the bird and its natural habitat, laid out as a preface to the score. The following annotations summarize these prefaces.

Premier livre:

(1) *Le Chocard des Alpes* (Alpine Chough): Messiaen relates the strophe-antistrophe-epôde of the Greek triad to the mountains of the Dauphiny in the French Alps. Interspersed between these sections are the cries of the Alpine Chough and Raven, along with music devoted to the flight patterns of the Golden Eagle and Alpine Choughs, in couplets 1 and 2.

(2) *Le Loriot* (Golden Oriole): set in the early morning of June in the gardens and forests of the Charente district in southern France. The Golden Oriole's song is joined by the calls of the Wren, the Robin, Blackbird, Redstart, Song Thrush, two Garden Warblers, and Chiffchaff.

(3) *Le Merle bleu* (Blue Rock Thrush): begins along the cliffs overlooking the Mediterranean Sea in the Roussillon region of France, near the Spanish border, in June. Features vivid pictures of the marine environment. The Blue Rock Thrush sings in the heights, recalling Balinese music in its song. Its blue plumage contrasts with the blue of the sea. The Thekla Lark and the Herring Gull are also heard in the piece.

Deuxième livre:

(4) *Le Traquet Stapazin* (Black-Eared Wheateater): set in the Roussillon region of France in the moors and terraced vineyards at the end of June. Describes the Black-Eared Wheateater's appearance and song. Amidst descriptions of the scenery, other birdsongs are noted, namely that of the Ortolan Bunting, Spectacled Warbler, Herring Gull, Raven, and Goldfinch. Describes how time passes from 5:00 a.m. to 10:00 p.m. Refers to the sun as the red and gold disc rising from the sea and into the sky. More birdsongs are heard at 9:00 a.m., including the Orphean Warbler, Corn Bunting, Rock Bunting, Melodious Warbler, and Thekla Lark. Several Black-Eared Wheateaters then answer each other. Characterizes the sun as disappearing behind the mountains encircled in blood and gold. More birds sing: the Spectacled Warbler, Ortolan Bunting, Black-Eared Wheateater, and Herring Gull. At the end of the piece, the Spectacled Warbler's song is recalled.

Troisième livre:

(5) *La Chouette Hulotte* (Tawny Owl): describes the appearance of the Tawny Owl, whose voice evokes terror. Messiaen claims to have

heard it around 2:00 a.m. in the woods of Orgeval, of Saint-Germaine-en-Laye, and on the road from Petichet to Cholonge (Isère). Mentions the cries of the Little Owl and Long-Eared Owl, and the Tawny Owl again, which depict, when taken together, the sinister and frightening aspects of the night.

(6) *L'Alouette Lulu* (Wood Lark): set in the Great Pine Forest in the region of Forez at midnight. Involves a contrast between the chromatic and flowing descending runs of the Wood Lark heard high above the forest, opposed by the pungent tremolos of the Nightingale hidden in a bush.

Quatrième livre:

(7) *La Rousserolle Effarvatte* (Reed Warbler): based on the passing hours of the day, from midnight to 3:00 a.m. of the following day. Conceived in a circular manner where the second half repeats the events from the first half but in reverse order. Set in the swamps of the Sologne district. Although the Reed Warbler is the predominant songster, the music involves the songs of nineteen different species of birds, along with the sounds of other creatures that inhabit the swamps (such as frogs). But of all the birdsongs, those of the Warbler family dominate the music. The songs build to a peak at noon, signaled by the insect chirping of the Grasshopper Warbler. At nine o'clock in the evening, the sun sets, bathed in warm colors, on the pond of irises, while the Bittern emits a resonant and terrifying trumpet-like sound. At three o'clock in the morning, the Reed Warbler sings a long solo. The piece concludes with a recollection of the pond music and the call of the Bittern.

Cinquième livre:

(8) *L'Alouette Calandrelle* (Short-Toed Lark): set in the arid and rocky Crau wilderness of the Provence region in July, from 2:00 to 6:00 in the afternoon. Song of the Short-Toed Lark punctuated by the dry and monotonous percussion of the Cicadas. The Kestrel's warning is heard, then the Short-Toed Lark in two-part counterpoint with the Crested Lark. At 6:00 p.m., the Skylark delivers a song while soaring above. It is answered by the Quail and its call. The piece concludes with a reminiscence of the Short-Toed Lark's song.

(9) *La Bouscarle* (Cetti's Warbler): takes place along the river bank of the Charente region in late April. The piece includes numerous birdsongs, second only to *La Rousserolle Effarvatte*. The two principal birds are the Cetti's Warbler and the Kingfisher. Reflections of

the trees grace the river's surface. At the end of the piece, the flight of the Kingfisher, in which the bird exposes its colorful plumage to the sun, is followed by silence and then one last call from the Cetti's Warbler.

Sixième livre:

(10) *Le Merle de roche* (Rock Thrush): the setting is the cliffs and rocks of the Cirque de Mourèze in the Héralt region in May. Begins at night. The Eagle Owl sings, the female responding. At dawn, the Jackdaws sound their various cries followed by the Black Redstart. The Rock Thrush then sings its song from ten in the morning to five in the afternoon. The Black Redstart takes up its calls again followed by the Jackdaws, which signals the end of dusk. It is night once again, and the Eagle Owl sings, bringing about shadow and terror.

Septième livre:

(11) *La Buse variable* (Buzzard): as in the first piece, set in the mountains of the Dauphiny, along Lake Laffrey and described in terms of its form. Consists of an introduction, three couplets, and a coda. Within this formal scheme, the Buzzard sounds its call while flying. It eventually descends. Various birds, including the Buzzard, sound their cries. A violent struggle occurs between six Carrion Crows and the Buzzard for the same prey. The bystanding Red-Backed Shrike sounds its alarm, followed by the Whitethroat's strophes and the Mistlethrush's refrain. The Buzzard sounds its call again as it takes off, slowly soaring up.

(12) *Le Traquet rieur* (Black Wheateater): like *Le Traquet Stapazin*, this setting is in the Mediterranean coast of the Roussillon region of France. Messiaen describes a beautiful sunny morning in May, with a rocky cliff, moors, and a blue sea silvered by the sun providing a backdrop for the birdsongs in this piece. The Black Wheateater's songs are juxtaposed with those of the Blue Rock Thrush, Herring Gull, Swifts, Black-Eared Wheateater, and Spectacled Warbler, along with joyful impressions of the blue sea.

(13) *Le Courlis cendré* (Curlew): set in the Île d'Ouessant in the Finistère region, off the coast of Brittainy. On Pern Point, the Curlew sounds its solo, evoking the desolation of seascapes. On Feunteun-Velen Point, all the avian calls of the seashore are followed by more songs. Fog and night gradually cover the sea. The piece reaches a climax with the sound of the light-house foghorn. The music closes with the song of the Curlew followed by the sound of the surf.

128. Messiaen, Olivier. *Prélude* (1964). Edited by Yvonne Loriod-Messiaen. Paris: Durand, 2000. M25.M.

     Short preface presumably by Yvonne Loriod-Messiaen accompanied by an anonymous English translation. Discusses the form of the work.

129. Messiaen, Olivier. *La Fauvette des jardins*. Paris: Alphonse Leduc, 1972. M 25.M58 F4 (IUCAT).

     Like the Reed Warbler (*La Rousserolle Effarvatte*) from the *Catalogue d'oiseaux*, this piece is based on the passing hours of the day, beginning after dark between the end of June and the beginning of July, to 9:00 p.m. of the following night. It is set in the Dauphiny mountains, along Lake Laffrey and the foot of the mountain of the Gran Serre in Petichet, Isère. Messiaen describes the environment of the eighteen French birds who sing in this piece in vivid, coloristic detail. The Garden Warbler's song seems to make time stand still. As is customary with Messiaen, the birdsongs in this piece are all listed in several languages.

130. Messiaen, Olivier. *Petites esquisses d'oiseaux*. Paris: Alphonse Leduc, 1988. M 25.M.

     Describes the six pieces found in this collection as both simultaneously similar and different. They are similar in harmonic style because of their changing sound-colors, brought about by the use of the chords of transposed inversions (which predominate), chords of contracted resonance, and chords of total chromaticism. Because each bird has its own proper aesthetic, the pieces differ in their melodic and rhythmic contents. Written in 1985 and dedicated to Yvonne Loriod-Messiaen.

Vocal Works

131. Messiaen, Olivier. *Trois petites Liturgies de la Présence Divine*. Paris: Durand, 1952. M 2101.5.M.

     In an undated preface, Messiaen recounts when *Trois petites Liturgies* was composed, and the circumstances of its world premiere at the Concerts de la Pléiade in Paris at the Salle de l'Ancien Conservatoire on 21 April 1945. He goes on to describe other performances of the work through 1963, particularly one occurring on 20 September 1957 at the Scuola grande di San Rocco, Venice, where Stravinsky and the future Pope John XXIII, Cardinal Roncalli, were present. Messiaen devotes the rest of the preface to an analytical description of the three-movement work, noting its formal structures, themes, birdsongs, compositional devices, and textual sources. In an additional section entitled "Musical Examples," Messiaen provides detailed descriptions of the color associations of the modes of limited transposition used in the work. This section seems to originate from an even later date than that suggested by his recounting of the work's performances: not only does it include color associations that correspond closely with those Messiaen described in the 1960s and 70s, but also a published signature that closed many of his later writings (see Wai-Ling Cheong, "Messiaen's Triadic Colouration: Modes as Interversion" [item 323], 58).

132. Messiaen, Olivier. *Chant des Déportés*. Paris: Alphonse Leduc, 1998. M 1530.M594 C4 1998 fol.

According to the uncredited information in the score, Henry Barraud, Director of Music of Radio France, commissioned Messiaen in 1945 to compose a work honoring the liberation of prisoners from German concentration camps. After its premiere in November 1945, *Chant des Déportés* was placed in the Radio France library, where it remained for 46 years—for his part, Messiaen thought the work to be lost. In an interview conducted in October 1991, Messiaen expressed regrets regarding the apparent loss of *Chant des Déportés*. The interviewer promised to look for the score, which he subsequently located in the Radio France library. He sent a photocopy of the score to Messiaen, who was delighted by the work's rediscovery. Includes an English translation.

133. Messiaen, Olivier. *Cinq Rechants*. Paris: Éditions Salabert, 1949. M 1586.M.

Contains a performance note by Messiaen. He explains the significance of the music's complex meters and diamond-shaped notes. He encourages singers to perform the durations exactly and to pronounce the pseudo-Hindu language as written. Finally, Messiaen states that since love governs the work, it is entirely sufficient to guide the singers in interpreting the piece.

134. Messiaen, Olivier. *La Transfiguration de Nôtre-Seigneur Jésus-Christ*. Paris: Alphonse Leduc, 1972. M 2000.M58 T7 (fol.).

Contains performance notes for the percussionists, a Latin pronunciation guide for the singers, a list of performances between 1969 and 1972, and diagrams of how concerts in Paris, London, and Strasbourg were set up. States when the composition was written and describes its textual sources, formal design, and instrumentation. Brief commentaries on each piece follow, in which religious texts and their theological significance are described, as well as the musical techniques used. The prefatory material concludes with the work's Latin texts accompanied by their French translations.

Electronic Works

135. Messiaen, Olivier. *Fête des belles eaux*. Paris: Alphonse Leduc, 2003. M 685.M.

     Messiaen describes the circumstances surrounding the composition of the *Fête des belles eaux* for the Paris Exposition ("Exposition Internationale des Arts et des Techniques appliqués à la Vie Moderne") in 1937. The city of Paris organized a festival of sound, water, and light along the banks of the Seine River, accompanied by works commissioned from twenty composers. One of them was Messiaen's *Fête des belles eaux*. While his colleagues opted for more traditional performing forces, Messiaen chose a sextet of Ondes Martenot, which he believed was a fabulous choice, considering how the music was to be amplified by loudspeakers placed on all the buildings along the Seine. He remarks how the form and timings of the music were imposed upon him according to the changing displays of water and light. Quoting the Gospel of Saint John (4:14), he views the music accompanying the jets of water shooting up to a great height as a symbol of divine grace and eternity.

Works by Others

136. Messiaen, Olivier. Preface to *Mana: 6 pièces pour piano*, by André Jolivet. Paris: Éditions Costallat, 1946. M 25.J75 M3 (IUCAT).

     Messiaen begins his introduction by discussing the stylistic use of rhythm, melody, harmony, pitch registers, texture, and silence in *Mana*. He then turns his attention to musical themes and how they shape each piece. Messiaen's text is translated into English by Pierre Messiaen, the composer's father, and Rollo Myers. The translation is marred by typographical errors.

137. Messiaen, Olivier. Preface to *Pulsations: Rythmes à frapper*, by Jean-Michel Bardez. 2 vols. Paris: Éditions Rideau Rouge, 1976.

     A short preface by Messiaen in his own script praising the pedagogy of Bardez's book on rhythm. He believes that it will greatly benefit young students of solfège.

138. Messiaen, Olivier. Preface to *Flûtes au present: Traité des techniques contemporaines sur les flûtes traversières à l'usage des compositeurs et*

des flûtistes, by Pierre-Yves Artaud and Gérard Geay. Paris: Éditions Jobert & Éditions musicales transatlantiques, 1980. 131 p. MT 340.A77 1980.

In this preface Messiaen describes the contents of a flute method book that deals with special effects and techniques used in contemporary music. He states that because one of the authors is the flutist Pierre-Yves Artaud, the book is geared toward professional performers. He believes that *Flûtes au present* will benefit both performers and composers alike, as well as contribute to the notation and technique of the flute.

139. Messiaen, Olivier. Preface to *Dichrostachys: Pièces pour orgue,* by Francine Guiberteau. Paris: Éditions M. Combre, 1983.

In this preface reproduced in his own cursive script, Messiaen characterizes Guiberteau's *Dichrostachys* as excellent music and well written for the organ. He appreciates her employment of liturgical themes, as well as how the music responds to the text from the *Dialogue des Carmélites* by Georges Bernanos that inspired it.

140. Messiaen, Olivier. Preface to *Musique à chanter pour les classes de formation musicale,* by Jean-Paul Holstein, Pierre-Yves Level, and Alain Louvier, 9 vols. Paris: Alphonse Leduc, 1983–86.

Not examined.

141. Messiaen, Olivier. Preface to *Variations pour piano (ut dièse mineur): Deux mélodies,* by Denis Joly. Saint-Étienne: Académie Musicologique du Forez, 1987. M 3.1.J64 M5 1987.

In another preface published in his own cursive script, Messiaen writes that Denis Joly, deceased at the time this preface was written, was a fellow student in Jean Gallon's harmony class at the Paris Conservatoire. They would often discuss music after class, solidifying their friendship as a result, which lasted over fifty years. Messiaen declares that Joly left posterity several precious works, three of which are included in this publication. The *Variations pour piano* are dedicated to Paul Dukas, who was both Messiaen and Joly's composition teacher (Messiaen also mentions that he and Joly both studied organ with Marcel Dupré). Messiaen praises the *Variations,* opining that Dukas would have appreciated their beauty, pianistic writing, and means of expression. He also maintains that all those who perform the *Variations* or the two songs set to texts by Laurent Tailhade will only wish that Joly, a fine musician who was apparently preoccupied with his duties as Director of the Paris Conservatoire, had composed more. (Messiaen is incorrect by stating that one of the texts is by Arthur Rimbaud, for the publication labels both texts as being written by Tailhade.)

142. Messiaen, Olivier. Preface to *Technique de l'onde éléctronique, type Martenot: Volume 1: Le Clavier,* by Jeanne Loriod (3 vols.). Paris: Alphonse Leduc, 1987. MT 724.L67 1987.

In this preface dating from May 1982 that is accompanied by an anonymous English translation, Messiaen discusses the historical context, construction, timbral possibilities, and seven principal models of the Ondes Martenot. He praises Jeanne Loriod's method book for its exhaustive coverage of the instrument's playing techniques and timbres. He notes that the Ondes Martenot's conceivable types of attacks far exceed those of conventional instruments. He also discusses the instrument's different models, singling out how the fifth and seventh inspired various works by Honegger, Jolivet, Varèse, Landowski, Murail, and himself.

Articles/Special Issues

143. Messiaen, Olivier. "Préface [to 'Experiences musicales (musiques concrètes, électronique, exotiques)']." *La Revue musicale* 244 (1959): 5–6. ISSN: 0768–1593.

An overview by Messiaen of the state of *musique concrète* in 1959. For him, *musique concrète* changed, signaled by its new name, *recherches musicales*. While its sonic materials remained the same, *musique concrète* was transformed by more methodical approaches to composition, the notation of scores, less reliance on chance, and the compositions of the inventor of *musique concrète*, Pierre Schaeffer. In addition to Schaeffer, Messiaen mentions Iannis Xenakis, Luc Ferrari, and François Mache as the music's other notable proponents. He also notes how exciting it is to follow a *musique concrète* score while listening to it.

144. Messiaen, Olivier. Preface to "Étude comparée des langages harmoniques de Fauré et de Debussy," by Françoise Gervais. *La Revue musicale* 272 (1971): 7–8. ISSN: 0768–1593.

Messiaen praises Gervais's study of the harmonic languages of Fauré and Debussy, regarding it as an important contribution to the science of musical analysis. He appreciates how Gervais sheds more light on the spirit and technique of these two composers by comparing their music with that of past (recent or distant) and present epochs. He believes that Gervais's work possesses real didactic value and would greatly benefit not only students in conservatories, particularly analysts, harmonists, and composers, but musicologists as well.

145. Messiaen, Olivier. [Preface to "L'Itinéraire."] *La Revue musicale* 421–24 (1991): 7. ISSN: 0768–1593.

In this extract from a 1974 interview conducted by Frantz Walter used as an introductory essay to this quadruple issue of *La Revue musicale*, Messiaen expresses his support for the "Itinéraire" movement as represented by the contemporary music group "L'Itinéraire" in France. For him, it represents the future for young composers. It transcends the cerebral qualities of past aesthetic movements, such as serialism, by emphasizing the sincere and beautiful in art.

Books

146. Messiaen, Olivier. Preface to *Chansons folkloriques françaises au Canada: Leur langue musicale*, Marguérite Béclard d'Harcourt and Raoul d'Harcourt, eds. Quebec: Presses Universitaires Laval, 1956. x, 449 p. M 1678.H3 C5.

In his preface to this anthology of Canadian folksongs, Messiaen states that he will concentrate on the folksongs themselves and not on the outstanding work of the anthology's editors, Marguérite Béclard d'Harcourt and Raoul d'Harcourt, who had previously collaborated on a collection of Peruvian folksongs from which Messiaen had borrowed a number of melodies for *Harawi*. For Messiaen, Canadian folksongs are derived from French folksongs, with the former being more strongly modal in quality than the latter. Messiaen then addresses these modal qualities, stating that many of the anthology's folksongs belong to either the Dorian ("mode de *ré*"), Mixolydian ("mode de *sol*"), or Lydian ("mode de *fa*") modes.

147. Messiaen, Olivier. Preface to *La Prophétie musicale dans l'histoire de l'humanité*, by Albert Roustit. Roanne: Horvath, 1970. 259 p. ML 3849.R79.

An unusual preface to say the least. Messiaen suggests that one might be astonished to find him, a Catholic, writing a preface for a book by Roustit, a Protestant. They often disagreed on musical and spiritual matters, but Messiaen was impressed by Roustit's thesis and evidence that the history of music mirrors that of humankind and biblical prophecies. He encourages all interested persons to read the volume in order to prepare themselves for the terrible events (e.g., the appearance of the Antichrist) that will precede the end of time and space and one's entrance into eternity.

148. Messiaen, Olivier. Preface to *La Prophétie musicale dans l'histoire de l'humanité*, by Albert Roustit. Translated from the French as *Prophecy in Music: Prophetic Parallels in Musical History*, by Dr. John A. Green. Paris: l'Imprimerie D.K. Paris Vè, 1975. 290 p.

English translation of item 147.

149. Messiaen, Olivier. Forward to *Marcel Dupré Raconte*, by Marcel Dupré. Paris: Éditions Bornemann, 1972. Translated from the French and edited by Ralph Kneeream as *Marcel Dupré (1886–1971): Recollections*. Melville, NY: Belwin-Mills Publishing Corp., 1975. 169 p. ML 410.D947 A33.

Messiaen wrote this foreword specifically for the English translation of *Marcel Dupré Raconte*. He reminisces affectionately about his former organ teacher at the Paris Conservatoire, taking note of how four photographs found in the book evoke memories of Dupré as both man and musician.

150. Messiaen, Olivier. [Introduction.] *La Recherche Artistique présente hommage à Olivier Messiaen* (item 247), 3. Idem. [Introduction to the Programme Booklet for Paris, 1978.] In Almut Rößler, *Contributions to the Spiritual World of Olivier Messiaen* (item 180), 9–10. Idem. "Les recherches scientifiques." In *Olivier Messiaen: Das Orgelwerk* (item 250), 1. Idem. "La rencontre avec un Autre." In *Olivier Messiaen, homme de foi* (item 238), 5.

A short essay in Messiaen's handwriting that outlines his ideas on the meaning of faith. Published originally as an untitled introduction to *La Recherche Artistique présente hommage à Olivier Messiaen* in 1978, it was also included in Almut Rößler's *Contributions to the Spiritual World of Olivier Messiaen* followed by an English translation, *Olivier Messiaen: Das Orgelwerk* as "Les recherches scientifiques" (drawn from the essay's opening three words), and *Olivier Messiaen, homme de foi* as "La rencontre avec un Autre."

For Messiaen, faith is the sole reality. To grasp it fully, one must meet God by passing through death and resurrection, exiting, in other words, the temporal world. Music can prepare a person for this journey by means of its capacity to conduct a perpetual dialogue between space and time, and sound and color, which leads to a unification of these elements. The musician who grasps this fundamental principle can achieve a foretaste of eternity. Messiaen also explains what music signifies to him by paraphrasing Saint Thomas Aquinas ("La musique nous porte à Dieu", "par défaut de vérité," jusqu'au jour où Lui-même nous éblouira, "par excès de vérité." Music carries us to God "by an absence of truth," until the day when He Himself will dazzle us "by an excess of truth" [my translation]). He believes that music, despite its lack of truth, has the capacity to bring a person closer to God, who one day will reveal a superabundance of truth.

151. Messiaen Olivier. Preface ("Olivier Messiaen parle de Maurice Emmanuel") to *L'histoire de la langue musicale: Antiquité – Moyen Age*, by Maurice Emmanuel, vol. 1. Malakoff: Éditions Henri Laurens, 1981. ISBN: 2862680346.

In this preface, Messiaen recounts his music history studies with Maurice Emmanuel at the Paris Conservatoire, noting how Emmanuel's ideas on mode and rhythm oriented his compositional thought toward new musical approaches to sound. He also mentions pieces by Emmanuel that played a role in his musical formation: (1) *Sonatine sur des modes hindous* for piano, (2) the opera *Salamine*, and (3) *Trente chansons Bourguignonnes du Pays de Beaune* for either voice or chorus and piano. In particular, Messiaen expresses his admiration for Emmanuel's modal accompaniments to the *Trente chansons bourguignonnes*, believing that he captured the poetic spirit of each song. Messiaen encourages the reader of *L'histoire de la langue musicale* to read or listen to this collection of music in order to better understand the book's emphasis on doing away with bar lines and major tonalities and replacing them with Greek metric patterns and the modes of plainchant.

152. Messiaen, Olivier. [Preface.] In Anne Le Forestier, *Olivier Messiaen: L'Ascension*, Cahiers d'analyse et de formation musicale, 1:i. Paris: Alphonse Leduc, 1984.

Not examined.

153. Messiaen, Olivier. Preface to *L'Âme en bourgeon, by Cécile Sauvage*. Paris: Libraire Séguier Archaimbaud, 1987.

Not examined.

INTERVIEWS

(Interviews of Messiaen are listed in alphabetical order according to the interviewer's surname or Messiaen's name (when that is more appropriate), with accompanying translations following immediately thereafter. This is intended to make it easier for the reader to find a particular interview.)

Messiaen

154. Birkby, Arthur. "Interview with France's Noted Organist and Composer Olivier Messiaen." *Clavier* (April 1972): 18–24. ISSN: 0009–0854X.

A short interview of Messiaen conducted in his studio at the Paris Conservatoire before he had to teach a class. Although concerned primarily with various aspects of Messiaen's organ works and their performance, the interview explores Messiaen's ideas on time and space.

155. Bruyr, José. "Olivier Messiaen." In *L'Écran des musiciens, seconde série*, 124–31. Paris: José Corti, 1933.

An interview given by Messiaen in 1931 at the time of his appointment as *organiste titulaire* at La Trinité but published in 1933. (For a detailed examination of the interview, see Peter Hill and Nigel Simeone, *Messiaen* [item 210], 37–39. Hill and Simeone consider the interview "the most revealing of Messiaen's published conversations from his early years, with some valuable observations on musical trends of the time" [p. 37].) Bruyr (1889–1980) interviewed Messiaen at his home at 67 rue Rambuteau. Topics discussed included the influence of his mother, the poetess Cécile Sauvage, on his work as a musician; his childhood in Grenoble; his teachers in Paris; early works composed between 1928–31; compositional techniques and musical trends of the time, which prompted remarks by Messiaen on how tonality should be enriched, not destroyed, and on neoclassicism and the music of Ravel, Albert Roussel, and Stravinsky; the religious nature of Messiaen's works; and the importance of religion in his musical outlook. Highly recommended.

156. Cadieu, Martine. "Entretiens sur l'art actuel: Martine Cadieu avec Olivier Messiaen." *Les Lettres françaises*, 7–13 January 1965, 1 and 8.

An interview of Messiaen interspersed with commentary. Asks Messiaen for his thoughts on a variety of topics, such as the state of musical life in present-day France, the perception of compositional technique on the part of the listening public, electronic music, Goléa's three stylistic periods for Messiaen's œuvre, various composers, Hindu rhythms, plainchant, and birdsong.

157. Ernst, Karin. "Interview mit Olivier Messiaen." In *Der Beitrag Olivier Messiaens zur Orgelmusik des 20. Jahrhunderts* (item 229), 318–24. Also published in *Olivier Messiaen: Das Orgelwerk* (item 250), 8–14.

Conducted at the Paris Conservatoire on 24 October 1977. Focuses on Messiaen's work as an organist, organ music, and thoughts on organ building and contemporary organ composition. In this interview, Messiaen reflects upon the influences of Dupré and Tournemire in his life, his organ works (here Messiaen humorously refers to the *Diptyque* composed in 1930 as a sin of his youth [p. 321]), the problem of performing his organ music on instruments other than the one at La Trinité, and contemporary organ music in which he expresses his admiration not only for Ligeti's *Volumina* but also for that composer's music in general.

158. Gavoty, Bernard. "Qui êtes-vous, Olivier Messiaen." *Journal musical français* (6 April 1961). ISSN: 0449–2102.

Bernard Gavoty, the music critic of *Figaro*, interviewed Messiaen in February of 1961 prior to a performance of the *Trois petites Liturgies de la Présence Divine* at a Youth Music Concert in Paris. After dealing with various aspects of Messiaen's early life, the interview turns to the topics of rhythm and birdsong. Messiaen notes the importance of rhythm in his music and his intention to write a treatise on rhythm. He talks about his work with birdsong and describes how he notates it.

159. Gavoty, Bernard. "Who Are You Olivier Messiaen?" *Tempo* 58 (Summer 1961): 33–36. ISSN: 0040–2982.

English translation of Bernard Gavoty's interview of Messiaen conducted in February of 1961 (see item 158).

160. Gavoty, Bernard and Daniel[-]Lesur. *Pour ou contre la musique moderne?*. With a preface by Henry Barraud. Paris: Flammarion, 1957. 340 p. ML 197.G33.

Between 1 January 1954 and 2 July 1955, Gavoty and Daniel-Lesur explored the state of modern music, especially in France, through numerous interviews, which included one with Messiaen, in a series of radio broadcasts on Radiodiffusion Française. They published their inquiry two years later. In his interview, which the authors describe as a monologue, not a conversation, but one that is grand in scope, Messiaen discusses how he has tried to liberate rhythm from its traditional associations with measure, meter, and symmetry. He also elaborates on the role of religion in his approach to composition, professing to be a believer, not a mystic, who talks of the mysteries of his Roman Catholic faith. Messiaen concludes his interview by talking about his song texts and their ties to the work of surrealistic poets such as Paul Éluard and Pierre Reverdy. He maintains that his texts have no literary pretensions and are designed solely with the music in mind.

161. Gilly, Cécile and Claude Samuel, eds. "Les vertus de l'analyse." In *Acanthes An XV: Composer, enseigner, jouer la musique d'aujourd'-hui*. Paris: Éditions Van de Velde, 1991. ISBN: 2858681732.

An undated interview of Messiaen (conducted presumably by Claude Samuel. This interview is taken from a collection of essays published by the Acanthes Center. Founded in 1977 under the name "Sirius," Acanthes is devoted to the study and performance of contemporary music). Messiaen discusses his work as a teacher at the Paris Conservatoire and elements of his musical language, especially sound-color relationships and rhythm. Messiaen is also asked whether he knew any of the American composers who studied with Nadia Boulanger and whether he would recommend the study of harmony, counterpoint, and the classical repertoire to a young composer of today. He responds affirmatively to both questions, although with respect to the latter, he made an exception with the young Xenakis, encouraging the Greek composer to find his own "voice" through his knowledge of architecture and mathematics.

162. Glandaz, Olivier. "Olivier Messiaen et l'orgue." In *L'Orgue: Revue trimestrielle* 224 (item 246), 15–23.

Olivier Glandaz, a French organbuilder, talked regularly with Messiaen in the organ loft at La Trinité between two Sunday services during the composer's later years. In this essay, Glandaz discusses Messiaen's ideas about organ registration, activities as an improviser and liturgical musician, thoughts about organ building and design, and how the Cavaillé-Coll organ at La Trinité related to his compositional aesthetic. He intersperses his observations with that of the composer.

163. Glandaz, Olivier. "Olivier Messiaen's Views on the Organ." *The American Organist* 28/9 (September 1994): 5761. ISSN: 0164–3150.

An expanded version of item 162, translated into English. Messiaen did not care for historic organbuilding practices, believing them to produce copies suitable only for the performance of Bach and his contemporaries. Since he considered the organ to be an instrument of light capable of suggesting varied timbres, as well as continually evolving to meet the challenges of new repertoires, Messiaen preferred instruments with expanded tonal palettes. The article also includes Messiaen's thoughts on mechanical vs. electric action, additions to the Cavaillé-Coll organ at La Trinité during Messiaen's tenure there, and organ timbres, along with Glandaz's observations about Messiaen as both performer and improviser during concerts and church services held at La Trinité.

164. Goléa, Antoine. "Messiaen und der Glaube." In *Melos* (item 242), 397–99.

According to the preface, this article is a German translation (presumably by Goléa) of the second of a series of interviews with Messiaen that Goléa was about to bring out in a collection of interviews with the publisher Rocher in Monaco, which we know now to be *Rencontres avec Olivier Messiaen* (see item 165, pp. 33–42). In the interview, Messiaen discusses his Catholic beliefs and how they influenced his work as an organist and composer. He talks about his teachers, early childhood experiences, scriptural and liturgical texts, and the religious symbolism behind the "Offertoire" ("Les choses visibles et invisibles") from the *Messe de la Pentecôte*, and "Les Mains de l'abîme" and "Les Yeux dans les roues" from the *Livre d'orgue*.

165. Goléa, Antoine. *Rencontres avec Olivier Messiaen*. Paris-Genève: Slatkine, 1984. 281 p. ISBN: 2050002181. ML 410.M52 G64. (IUCAT).

This source consists of a dozen radio interviews of Messiaen conducted by Goléa on Radiodiffusion Française in 1958, and Goléa's observations about Messiaen's compositional aesthetics and music. The interviews deal primarily with Messiaen's works up to *Chronochromie* and the composer's thoughts about contemporary music. Goléa first considered interviewing Messiaen on French radio in 1953 while working as Messiaen's assistant in Darmstadt, where he served as a translator for the composer's analysis courses. It took another three years before Messiaen consented to Goléa's project. After the interviews were completed and subsequently edited, Goléa combined them with his observations and commentaries to form a book, which was published by René Julliard in 1961 with Messiaen's approval. For English translations of various excerpts, see Clyde Holloway, "The Organ Works of Olivier Messiaen and Their Importance in His Total *Oeuvre*" (item 212).

166. Guth, Paul. "Nébuleuses spirales, stalactites et stalagmites suggèrent des rythmes à Olivier Messiaen." *Le Figaro Littéraire* (February 14 1953): 4.

An interview that addresses different aspects of Messiaen's approach to rhythm. Guth interviews the composer after observing him teach at the Paris Conservatoire on Stravinsky's use of rhythmic characters in the "Danse sacrale" from the *Rite of Spring*. Topics covered include Hindu rhythms, arsis and thesis, anacrusis-accent-termination, added values, nonretrogradable rhythms, rhythmic canons, birdsong, and the composer's Tristan trilogy consisting of *Harawi*, the *Turangalîla-Symphonie*, and *Cinq Rechants*.

167. Lade, Günter. "Gespräch mit Olivier Messiaen." *Ars Organi* 36/4 (December 1988): 171–75. ISSN: 0004–2919.

A German translation of an interview conducted on 26 February 1987 while Messiaen was in Vienna to hear the Viennese premiere of his *Livre du Saint Sacrement* played by organist Thomas Daniel

Schlee at the Wiener Konzerthaus. In the conversation, Messiaen responds to several typical questions, such as those having to do with his early musical training, first attempts at composition, composers who influenced him, the role of the organ in his life, and the significance of the instrument at La Trinité for his organ music. However, we also get to hear Messiaen respond to a few atypical questions, such as those having to do with his relationships with Tournemire, a mentor whom he greatly admired; Widor, his first composition teacher, and Duruflé and Jehan Alain, both of whom he respected, although he felt Alain's music was closer to his in spirit. Other atypical questions center on Messiaen's thoughts on the future of the organ in the Catholic Church, where he expresses conservative views regarding the use of Latin (versus the vernacular) in the Mass and what constitutes good church music, and the role played by improvisation in his organ works.

168. Lade, Günter. "Gespräch mit Olivier Messiaen." *Ars Organi* 36/4 (December 1988): 171–75. Translated by Timothy Tikker as "A Conversation with Olivier Messiaen." *The American Organist* 34/7 (July 2000): 80–81. ISSN: 0164–3150.

English translation of Lade's interview (see item 167).

169. Lyon, Raymond. Entretien avec Olivier Messiaen. *Le Courrier musical de France* (1978): 126–32. ISSN: 0011–0620.

Interview of Messiaen on the occasion of his seventieth birthday that took place on 30 September 1978 at his residence on the rue Marcadet. According to Lyon, the printed interview is an exact transcription of the recorded conversation he had with Messiaen. Lyon wanted to discuss the opera (*Saint François d'Assise*) Messiaen was composing at the time, but Messiaen refused. Instead, they talked about Messiaen's childhood years, ornithology, religious beliefs, and sound-color relationships.

170. Marti, Jean-Christophe. "Entretien avec Olivier Messiaen." In *Saint François d'Assise* (item 425), 8–18.

An interview conducted in January 1992. Before querying Messiaen about his opera *Saint François d'Assise*, Marti asks him about stages in his career that he considered to be fundamental and compositions that he might prefer. Messiaen answers by maintaining that he has always liked *Trois petites Liturgies de la Présence Divine*. He talks about the controversy surrounding its world premiere, interspersing his remarks with thoughts about various composers and their music. Marti moves on by asking Messiaen questions about time and eternity, the Resurrection, and his musical language before tackling

Saint François. When discussing the opera, Messiaen explains its dramatic design and repertory of musical themes. He also notes the importance of birdsong in the sixth scene, *Le Prêche aux oiseaux.* At the end of the interview, Messiaen describes how inspiration returned to him in the form of the *Livre du Saint Sacrement* for organ after believing that he could no longer write music following *Saint François.* Reprinted as liner notes with English and German translations in *Saint François d'Assise (Scènes franciscaines)*; Arnold Schoenberg Chor and Hallé Orchestra, Kent Nagano, conductor; Deutsche Grammophon 445 176–2 (see item B.11).

171. Massin, Brigitte. *Olivier Messiaen: Une poétique du merveilleux.* Aix-en-Provence: Éditions Alinéa, 1989. 232 p. ISBN: 2904631771. ML 410.M595 M42 1989.

During the course of several interviews, focuses on Messiaen's religious faith and how it shaped his life and music. Attempts to gain a glimpse of how his creative mind worked and why it was linked intimately with his view of Christianity. Traverses several topics in five chapters, including the idea of the *merveilleux*, the marvelous and supernatural aspects of Messiaen's faith; his connection to the church as both composer and organist; poetry, astronomy, and theology; space and time; and a discussion of his works, which includes valuable information on *Saint François d'Assise.* Adds many comments throughout the interviews, such as describing Messiaen as a difficult person to interview, with answers seemingly prepared in advance (p. 19).

172. Meltzheim, Irène and Père Pascal Ide. "Le musicien de la joie: Entretien avec Olivier Messiaen: 60 années à la Trinité." *Du côté de la Trinité: Le journal de la paroisse* (March 1991): 1–2. (I would like to thank Nigel Simeone for providing me with a copy of this interview.)

An interview on the occasion of Messiaen's sixty years of service as titular organist at La Trinité. Messiaen talks about a variety of topics, such as: (1) his Cavaillé-Coll instrument; (2) the reciprocal relationship between his work as an improviser and composer; (3) the inspiration he receives from Hindu rhythms and birdsong; (4) the influence of the liturgical cycle and scriptural readings on his choice of organ registrations; (5) sound-color relationships; (6) the liturgical renewal movement and how plainchant can never be replaced; (7) how faith influences composing; (8) his last organ work, the *Livre du Saint Sacrement*; (9) the origins of his faith; and (10) how he regrets composing some purely technical and profane works. The source also contains separate short essays by Messiaen on the electrification of the organ at La Trinité and the four dramas (faith, birdsong, sound-color relationships, and rhythm) that have affected his work throughout his life.

173. Messiaen, Olivier. "Des paroles d'esprit: Entretien avec Olivier Messiaen." In *Charles de Gaulle*, ed. Michel Cazenave and Olivier Germain Thomas, 44–46. Cahiers de l'Herne, no. 21. Paris: L'Herne, 1973. 370 p. DC 373.G3 C498.

In this interview for a memorial volume dedicated to Charles de Gaulle, Messiaen voiced his admiration for a man whom he considered as a symbol of France. In explaining his reasons for signing a petition supporting de Gaulle's reelection in 1965, Messiaen recalled his days as a prisoner of war at Stalag VIII A in Silesia in which the very name of de Gaulle brought forth hope amidst despair. He regarded de Gaulle as more than just a political figure but someone who embodied France itself. In this respect, Messiaen compared de Gaulle to Joan of Arc. All in all, a rare instance in which the composer expressed his politics.

174. Messiaen, Olivier. *Entretien avec Claude Samuel*. In *Messiaen Edition*; various performers, including Olivier Messiaen and Yvonne Loriod-Messiaen, and ensembles; liner notes; Warner Classics 2564 62162–2, 2005; 18 CDs; 109–35 (translated into English by Stuart Walters).

Recorded in Messiaen's apartment in Paris in October 1988. Included on the eighteenth compact disc. Topics discussed include Messiaen's thoughts on his works, birdsong, sound-color relationships, the nature of religious music, his opera *Saint François d'Assise*, his teaching at the Paris Conservatoire, Boulez and Stockhausen, his love for Japan, and his celebrity around the world.

175. Messiaen, Olivier. *Musique et couleur: Nouveaux entretiens avec Claude Samuel*. Paris: Belfond, 1986. 311 p. ISBN: 2714417159. ML 410.M595 A3 1986.

In 1985 Messiaen once again agreed to collaborate with Claude Samuel—journalist, music critic, author, artistic director, and radio-television producer—by adding more conversations to the 1967 book *Entretiens avec Olivier Messiaen* (see item 181). What resulted was a revised and expanded version of that book, published in 1986 as *Musique et couleur: Nouveaux entretiens avec Claude Samuel*.

With the exception of the newer conversations and the insertion of new and updated material in the older ones, the content of *Musique et couleur* is remarkably similar to that of *Entretiens avec Olivier Messiaen*. The first two chapters ("A Lyrical Expectation" [pp. 13–18] and "Landmarks" [pp. 19–40]) deal with the foundations of

Messiaen's music (the poetic influence of his mother Cécile Sauvage, Shakespeare, Roman Catholicism, the Tristan myth, nature, and time and eternity) and thus correspond to the earlier book's first conversation. Chapter 3 ("From Technique to Emotion" [pp. 41–64]) likewise has a counterpart in the second conversation of the earlier book. It takes up the topics of sound-color relationships in Messiaen's music, the modes of limited transposition, and Messiaen's opinions on pitch organization in music, orchestration, and the Ondes Martenot. However, there are things not included in the earlier book, such as more information regarding Messiaen's favorite painters and his thoughts about artistic correspondences between different painters and composers.

Chapter 4 ("Of Sounds and Colors" [pp. 65–70]), a new conversation, is an in-depth look at the role of sound-color relationships in Messiaen's music. Chapters 5 ("In Search of Rhythm" [pp. 71–90]) and 6 ("My Birds" [pp. 91–106]) offer little change from their counterparts (conversations three and four) in the earlier book. They address, respectively, the subjects of Messiaen's approach to rhythm and fascination with birds. Chapters 7 ("The Orient Experience" [pp. 107–16]) and 9 ("An American Paradise" [pp. 169–90]), both new conversations, focus on Messiaen's travels to Japan and the United States and their impact on him as seen by the stylized use of Gagaku music in *Sept Haïkaï* and the Noh drama in *Saint François d'Assise*, and by the inspiration of Bryce Canyon, Utah for *Des canyons aux étoiles*. Finally, chapters 8 ("Trajectory" [pp. 117–68]), 10 ("Transmitted Knowledge" [pp. 191–208]), and 11 ("Contradictions of the Century" [pp. 209–26]), which correspond to conversations five through seven of the earlier book, cover many subjects, from Messiaen's opinions on various composers, to updated discussions of his music, and his reflections on his work as a teacher at the Paris Conservatoire.

Chapter 12 ("Saint Francis of Assisi" [pp. 227–76]) is the most significant new addition to the book because of its valuable discussion of Messiaen's opera, *Saint François d'Assise*. It takes a detailed look at the work by examining its genesis, structure, use of leitmotifs, orchestration, staging problems and solutions, and reception by the public. Chapter 13 ("Visited Lands" [pp. 277–86]), another new conversation, is a travelogue, beginning on 29 April 1985, that lists Messiaen's world-wide trips and triumphs.

176. Messiaen, Olivier. *Olivier Messiaen: Music and Color: Conversations with Claude Samuel*. Translated by E. Thomas Glasow. Portland, OR: Amadeus Press, 1994. 296 p. ISBN: 0931340675. ML 410.M595 A3 1994.

English translation of item 175. Not included in the original is an homage to Messiaen by Claude Samuel ("In Memoriam: Olivier Messiaen" [pp. 261–62]), and an updated discography (pp. 269–81) and bibliography (pp. 283–88).

Reviews: Vincent Benitez, *Indiana Theory Review* 17/2 (Fall 1996): 93–102; Christopher Dingle, *Tempo* 192 (April 1995): 29–30, 32.

177. Murray, Michael. "An Interview with Olivier Messiaen." *The Diapason* 70 (December 1978): 3, 5. ISSN: 0012–2378.

In November 1970, organist Michael Murray interviewed Messiaen in French on his syndicated broadcast series, "Conversations." Murray translated excerpts from that interview into English and published them in *The Diapason* in 1978. They cover several areas of Messiaen's life and work, such as his childhood in Grenoble, his days at the Paris Conservatoire, early compositions such as the *Préludes* for piano (1929) and *Les Offrandes oubliées* (1930), color, and birdsong. Particularly valuable in this interview are Messiaen's remarks about color and its role in his approach to composition.

178. Nichols, Roger. "Messiaen at 70: Roger Nichols Talks to the Composer, Who Is 70 on December 10." *Music and Musicians* 27/4 (December 1978): 20–23. ISSN: 0027–4232.

Nichols interviewed Messiaen on the occasion of his seventieth birthday. The interview contains candid and detailed responses from Messiaen to a variety of questions. In answering a question as to whether or not he has experienced a stylistic curve similar to that of Beethoven, Messiaen says no, because he has not renounced his past and has kept up with the latest musical trends through his role as a teacher at the Paris Conservatoire. As a result, he possesses a wealth of materials that is growing all of the time. Messiaen talks about Poulenc, Milhaud, and Honegger, as well as the hostile reactions he encountered in the press, which he attributes to him being a Catholic. He mentions how his work with birdsong has met with misunderstanding. But on the other hand, he takes pride in the fact that he is the only person who has really notated birdsong, pointing out that professional ornithologists are unable to do this. The most significant part of the interview deals with the subject of color. Here Messiaen not only traverses familiar territory but also reveals some aspects of the role of sound-relationships in his music that are infrequently mentioned in other interviews, such as a sound-complex having only one color (a complicated color or a simple one), or violent harmonies evoking red and gentle harmonies evoking blue.

179. Rößler, Almut. *Beiträge zur geistigen Welt Olivier Messiaens.* Duisburg: Gilles und Francke, 1984. 168 p. ISBN: 3921104874.

This volume focuses on the theology of Messiaen as seen through Almut Rößler's encounters with the composer as an interviewer, audience member while someone else posed questions to him, and interpreter of his organ works. It also contains various texts by Messiaen. Rößler translated all French texts into German with the assistance of Edgar Ries. Of interest are: a public discussion involving Messiaen on 7 December 1968 during the First Düsseldorf Messiaen Festival in chapter 2 (pp. 27–38); Messiaen's Erasmus Address on 25 June 1971 in Amsterdam in chapter 3 (pp. 39–48); a platform discussion involving Messiaen on 11 June 1972 in the Bach Hall of St. John's Church during the Second Düsseldorf Messiaen Festival in chapter 4 (pp. 50–59); two interviews of Messiaen by Rößler in Paris on 23 April 1979 and 16 December 1983 in chapters 6 (pp. 71–124) and 7 (pp. 126–54), respectively, the second interview coming on the heels of the world premiere of *Saint François d'Assise*; and Rößler's essay on rhythmic freedom in the performance of Messiaen's organ works in chapter 8 (pp. 155–62). In the book's translation (see item 180), this last chapter is augmented by two additional essays that are drawn from Rößler's appendix to Ingrid Hohlfeld-Ufer's volume, *Die musikalische Sprache Olivier Messiaens* (see item 505). One deals with general observations concerning the interpretation of Messiaen's organ works (pp. 145–57), and the other with the registration and interpretation of particular pieces (pp. 158–69).

180. Rößler, Almut. *Contributions to the Spiritual World of Olivier Messiaen: With Original Texts by the Composer.* Translated by Barbara Dagg, Nancy Poland, and Timothy Tikker. Duisburg: Gilles und Francke, 1986. 188 p. ISBN: 3921104998. ML 410.M595 B3813 1986.

English translation of item 179. Translations from the German (chaps. 1–4, 6–8, appendices, concluding remarks) by Barbara Dagg and Nancy Poland. Translation of the *Conférence de Notre-Dame* (chap. 5) from the French by Timothy Tikker.

Reviews: David Palmer, *The Diapason* 77/11 (November 1986): 6.

181. Samuel, Claude. *Entretiens avec Olivier Messiaen.* Paris: Belfond, 1967. 236 p. ML 410.M595 S3.

In 1967 at the invitation of Pierre Belfond, Messiaen agreed to collaborate with Claude Samuel on a set of seven conversations that were to be recorded. The conversations were published later that year as *Entretiens avec Olivier Messiaen* by Éditions Pierre Belfond.

These seven conversations provide a sketch not only of a complex human being but also that of an equally complex music. Conversation one (pp. 9–31) introduces many of the elements that form the foundation of Messiaen's music: (1) the poetic intuitions of his mother Cécile Sauvage that directed him toward music; (2) his reading of Shakespeare as a child; (3) Roman Catholicism, the Tristan myth, and nature as represented by birdsong; and (4) the dialectical opposition between time and eternity. In conversation two (pp. 35–61) Messiaen ruminates about the role of sound-color relationships in his music, his perception of color in the music of other composers, his compositional techniques, and assorted topics related to pitch organization in music, orchestration, and the Ondes Martenot. The next two conversations tackle big topics, with conversation three (pp. 65–91) focusing on Messiaen's rhythmic language and conversation four (pp. 95–118) addressing birdsong. In conversation five (pp. 121–74) Messiaen discusses composers who have influenced his approach to music, such as Mozart, Gluck, Wagner, Debussy, Ravel, Honegger, Milhaud, Rameau, Scarlatti, Chopin, and Albéniz. He closes conversation five by talking about his musical works through *Et exspecto resurrectionem mortuorum* (1964). Conversation six (pp. 177–98) explores Messiaen's relationship to the modern world, particularly his discomfort with it, and work as a teacher. Conversation seven (pp. 201–16) concludes the book by considering Messiaen's views on modern music.

Reviews: Bennitt Gardiner, "Dialogues with Messiaen," *Musical Events* (October 1967): 6–9.

182. Samuel, Claude. *Conversations with Olivier Messiaen*. Translated by Felix Aprahamian. London: Stainer and Bell, 1976. 140 p. ISBN: 0852493088. ML 410.M595 S33.

    English translation of item 181.

    Reviews: Arthur Lawrence, *The Diapason* 70 (December 1978): 4.

183. Samuel, Claude. *Permanences d'Olivier Messiaen: Dialogues et Commentaires*. Paris: Actes Sud, 1999. 484 p. ISBN: 2742723765. ML 410.M595 S35 1999.

    Reprints the "Musique et couleur" interviews from 1986 minus the last chapter, "Les domaines visités" (see item 175). Interspersed between the chapters are assorted materials that range from commentaries to a correspondence between Samuel and Messiaen from 1971–92. Updates the bibliography and discography from the 1986 publication.

184. Strobel, Heinrich. "[Gespräch mit] Olivier Messiaen." *Melos* 16, no. 4 (April 1949): 101–4.

An interview conducted on the occasion of the first performance of Messiaen's "Trois Tâla" (movements 3, 4, and 5 of the *Turangalîla-Symphonie*, selections sanctioned by Messiaen himself) in 1949 in Baden-Baden, Germany, by the Südwestfunkorchester conducted by André Cluytens. There Messiaen discussed his music and ideas with the editor of *Melos* (presumably Heinrich Strobel). The interview covers a variety of topics, from La Jeune France, rhythm, the modes of limited transposition, to discussions of Messiaen's works, concluding with a consideration of his new symphony (*Turangalîla-Symphonie*) that was going to be premiered later that year in Boston by the Boston Symphony Orchestra. Of note in this interview is Messiaen's discussion of his rhythmic device known as *personnages rythmiques* (rhythmic characters) that differs from his usual remarks where one rhythm augments at each repetition, another diminishes at each repetition, and the third rhythm stays the same. Instead, in addition to the three characters mentioned above, Messiaen states that there is a fourth one that augments and diminishes alternately with each repetition.

185. Walter, Edith. "Entretien-Dossier: Olivier Messiaen." *Harmonie* (November 1983): 14-25.

Interview of Messiaen on the occasion of the world premiere of *Saint François d'Assise* in Paris. Messiaen discusses the opera's background, dramatic design, music (especially sound-color relationships, rhythm, and birdsong), and staging at the Palais Garnier. The interview is followed by a summary of the opera's dramatic design by Messiaen (pp. 19–20) and extracts from his interviews with Antoine Goléa and Claude Samuel (see items 165 and 181, respectively).

186. Zimmerman, Heinrich. "Ein Gespräch mit Olivier Messiaen." *Musik und Kirche* 29 (1969): 38–39. ISSN: 0027–4771.

This article summarizes the public discussion with Messiaen that took place on 7 December 1968 on the stage in the Bach Hall of the Johanneskirche, Düsseldorf, during the First Düsseldorf Messiaen Festival celebrating his sixtieth birthday. Topics covered include the interpretative relevance of the biblical or liturgical quotations that Messiaen attached to his organ works, Teilhard de Chardin's possible influence on Messiaen, birdsong, Xenakis, Hindu rhythms, the modes of limited transposition, and jazz. Most of the discussion was transcribed for Almut Rößler's book, *Beiträge zur geistigen Welt*

Olivier Messiaens (pp. 27–38; see item 179), and translated into English by Barbara Dagg and Nancy Poland for Rößler's *Contributions to the Spiritual World of Olivier Messiaen* (pp. 27–37; see item 180).

Yvonne Loriod-Messiaen

187. Hill, Peter. "Interview with Yvonne Loriod-Messiaen." In *The Messiaen Companion* (item 240), 283–303.

On 9 January 1993 Peter Hill interviewed Yvonne Loriod-Messiaen at her apartment on the rue Marcadet in Paris. The conversation covered various topics. She discusses her compiling of the *Traité de rythme, de couleur, et d'ornithologie (1949–1992)* and the way in which Messiaen composed, a process that included numerous sketches. She also considers whether or not Messiaen wrote idiomatically for different instruments, and how his music should be performed. The conversation then focuses on Loriod-Messiaen herself: her childhood; early music study; studies at the Paris Conservatoire, which includes an account of her first encounter with Messiaen in the latter's harmony class; and descriptions of her fellow students. The conversation returns to the subject of Messiaen, namely regarding questions of fingering in his piano music, his difficult personal life, his experience as a prisoner of war during World War II, his piano music, his work with birdsong, *Saint François d'Assise*, *Éclairs sur l'Au-Delà*, and his legacy as a composer. Highly recommended.

188. Tüngler, Irene. "Yvonne Loriod[-Messiaen] interviewed by Irene Tüngler." In *Messiaen Edition*; various performers, including Olivier Messiaen and Yvonne Loriod-Messiaen, and ensembles; liner notes; Warner Classics 2564 62162–2, 2005; 18 CDs; 136–38 (translated into English by Stuart Spencer). (For a French text of the interview, see Irene Tüngler, "Interview with Yvonne Loriod[-Messiaen]," in Olivier Messiaen, *Trois petites Liturgies de la Présence Divine*; Orchestre National de France, Kent Nagano, conductor; Yvonne Loriod, piano; Jeanne Loriod, Ondes Martenot; liner notes; Erato 0630–12702–2, 1996; 16–18.)

Not on any of the collection's compact discs. Moreover, does not specify when or where the interview took place, although one could surmise the early to mid-1990s based on Loriod-Messiaen's remarks about Messiaen's death and preparing the *Traité de rythme, de couleur, et d'ornithologie (1949–1992)* for publication.

Despite its brevity, this interview traverses a wide terrain of subject matter. Tüngler asks Loriod-Messiaen about her husband as a person and if she was ever involved in his work as a composer. She responds by stating that Messiaen was an extrovert, contrary to biographies that describe him as the exact opposite, and that she was never involved in his compositions or work. Tüngler touches upon other topics, such as Loriod-Messiaen's understanding and appreciation of Messiaen's music, her predilections for other musical works, and her relationship with her husband. Loriod-Messiaen answers by noting how her grasp and admiration of Messiaen's music has increased over the years, especially since she has begun to put together the *Traité de rythme*. She confides to Tüngler that her favorite composers are Mozart and Messiaen. Finally, she mentions the "Le Cas Messiaen" affair of 1945 and states that her personal relationship with Messiaen was completely harmonious.

PUBLISHED CORRESPONDENCE AND DEDICATORY NOTES

189. Fauqet, Joël-Marie, ed. "Correspondance inédite: Lettres d'Olivier Messiaen à Charles Tournemire." In *Charles Tournemire (1870–1939)*, *L'Orgue: Cahiers et mémoires*, no. 41, 80–85. Paris: Association des Amis de l'orgue, 1989. 124 p. ML 410.T6847 C53 1989.

Contains twelve unpublished letters from Messiaen to Tournemire from 1930–33 that are in private archives. A revealing account of the relationship between the two musicians. Messiaen's letters address different topics, such as: (1) his comments about Tournemire's *l'Orgue mystique*; (2) events leading up to his appointment at La Trinité; (3) inviting Tournemire to the public dress rehearsal of *Les Offrandes oubliées* on 5 December 1931 at the Société des Concerts in order to glean his opinion about the work; (4) trying to congratulate Tournemire on the quality of some of his pieces from the *l'Orgue mystique* that were played by Dom Charles Letestu in the second half of his recital at Sainte-Clotilde on 14 December 1931; (5) Messiaen's thanks to Tournemire for his positive review of *Les Offrandes oubliées* in the *Le Courrier musical* of 15 December 1931; (6) Messiaen's suggestion that he and his (first) wife Claire Delbos come to Tournemire's home in order for her to play his *Thème et variations* for the older musician, and that Tournemire critique Messiaen's *Hymne au Saint-Sacrement*; and (7) Messiaen's comments about Tournemire's *Trois poèmes* pour orgue, op. 59, and his opinion that if modern musicians had Tournemire's faith, they, although not capable of matching Tournemire in musical quality, would definitely write better music.

190. Loriod-Messiaen, Yvonne, and Olivier Messiaen. *«Bien Cher Félix . . .»: Letters from Olivier Messiaen and Yvonne Loriod to Felix Aprahamian.* French and English Text. Edited and translated by Nigel Simeone. Cambridge: Mirage Press, 1998. 55 p. ISBN: 0953408701. ML 410.M52 A15 (IUCAT).

Contains the correspondence between Messiaen and his second wife, Yvonne Loriod-Messiaen, and Felix Aprahamian (1914–2005), a champion of Messiaen's music in England since the mid-1930s. This volume is especially valuable for its detailed information on Messiaen's visits to England and the first performances of several of his major works there from 1936–47, the decade before he achieved international stardom with the *Turangalîla-Symphonie* in 1949.

191. Wangermée, Robert, ed. *Paul Collaer: Correspondance avec des amis musiciens.* Liège: P. Mardaga, 1996. 479 p. ISBN: 2870096062. ML 423.C77 A4 1996.

Contains letters from Messiaen to Paul Collaer (1891–1989) during the 1940s (see pp. 371–72, 402–3, and 413). Messiaen thanks Collaer for an upcoming performance of the *Quatuor pour la fin du Temps* in Brussels, mentions the *Visions de l'Amen* (still in manuscript), confirms performance dates for several of his pieces for Belgian radio (I.N.R. [l'Institut national de Radiodiffusion]), and talks about going to the United States not only to teach at Tanglewood but also to arrange for the world premiere of the *Turangalîla-Symphonie* in Boston.

192. Loriod-Messiaen, Yvonne. "Lettre de Madame Yvonne Loriod-Messiaen." In *Olivier Messiaen, homme de foi: Regard sur son œuvre d'orgue* (item 238), 12.

A reproduction of a letter dated 22 October 1994 from Yvonne Loriod-Messiaen to Père Francis Kohn, curé of La Trinité, giving her consent to the Messiaen Festival (Intégrale de l'œuvre d'orgue d'Olivier Messiaen) that was to be held in March/April of 1995. She also asks the curé to thank the six organists (Jennifer Bate, Jon Gillock, Naji Hakim, Louis Thiry, Thomas Daniel Schlee, and Hans Ola-Ericsson) who were going to play Messiaen's complete organ works during the festival, Père Jean-Rodolphe Kars, and the rest of the festival's participants.

193. Loriod-Messiaen, Yvonne. "A Letter from Madame Yvonne Loriod-Messiaen." In *Celebration Messiaen: The Complete Works for Organ* (item 239): 12–13.

On p. 12, a reproduction of a testimonial to Jon Gillock from Yvonne Loriod-Messiaen dated 8 November 1998 on the occasion of his performing Messiaen's complete organ works in six concerts at the Riverside Church in New York in 1999. Loriod-Messiaen recounts the history of Gillock's relationship with Messiaen, praises his past performances of Messiaen's organ works, and expresses her gratitude to him for the feat he was about to undertake. Gillock provides an English translation of the letter on p. 13.

DOCUMENTARIES AND FILMED PERFORMANCES

194. Messiaen, Olivier. *Olivier Messiaen et les oiseaux*. A film by Denise R. Tual and Michel Fano. 80 min. SOFRACIMA, Denise Tual, and Fondation Royaumont, 1973. Videocassette.

A film by Denise Tual and Michel Fano offering a multifaceted portrait of Messiaen. Interviewed for the film are the composer, his wife Yvonne Loriod-Messiaen, and Iannis Xenakis. The film includes scenes of Messiaen recalling his childhood in Grenoble, transcribing birdsong, imitating birdcalls with Loriod-Messiaen playing them immediately on the piano, improvising on the organ at La Trinité, teaching on Debussy's *Pelléas et Mélisande* at the Paris Conservatoire (perhaps the most valuable part of the film), talking about the *Quatuor pour la fin du Temps*, and discussing sound-color relationships in his music. Works played during the film include: (1) *Trois petites Liturgies de la Présence Divine*; (2) *Et exspecto resurrectionem mortuorum*; (3) *Visions de l'Amen*; (4) *Quatuor pour la fin du Temps*; and (5) *Sept Haïkaï*. For a transcription of the class session at the Paris Conservatoire, see Jean Boivin, *La classe de Messiaen*, 214–23 (item 203). For an English translation of excerpts from the class session, see Vincent P. Benitez, "A Creative Legacy: Messiaen as Teacher of Analysis," 120–25, 128–29, 138–39 (item 411).

195. Messiaen, Olivier. *Olivier Messiaen: The Music of Faith*. Produced and directed by Alan Benson. 79 min. London Weekend Television/ Films for the Humanities & Sciences, 1985/2000. Videocassette, DVD. ML 410.M55 O556 2003 DVD.

Produced by London Weekend Television in 1985 for the British television program, "The South Bank Show." This documentary covers the life and music of Messiaen. It is narrated by the composer with an English translation heard over his voice. The documentary addresses his early life in Grenoble, particularly his relationship with his mother, Cécile Sauvage; his days as a student at the Paris Conservatoire; his Roman Catholic faith as seen through *La Transfiguration de Nôtre-Seigneur Jésus-Christ* and *Les Corps glorieux*; the influence of Debussy; his love of birdsong; the role of sound-color relationships and natural resonance in his approach to harmony; the circumstances surrounding the composition of the *Quatuor pour la fin du Temps*; his teaching at the Paris Conservatoire; his pivotal relationship with his student Yvonne Loriod, an acclaimed pianist who eventually became his second wife; and the *Turangalîla-Symphonie*. A valuable part of the documentary is the commentary by Messiaen's student George Benjamin. Highly recommended.

196. Messiaen, Olivier. *Les Leçons.* Directed by Olivier Mille. 60 min. Artline Productions, 1988. Videocassette.

In July 1987, Messiaen, along with Yvonne-Loriod Messiaen, participated in masterclasses given in Chartreuse de Villeneuve-lez-Avignon as a part of the Acanthes Center's annual month-long focus on the music of an important contemporary composer. Messiaen discusses the elements of his musical language and the role of faith in his compositional aesthetic. Features performances of Messiaen's music.

197. Messiaen, Olivier. *Quartet for the End of Time; Improvisations.* Directed by Georges Bessonnet. 82 min. G.B. Productions France/ Image Entertainment, 1991/1999. DVD. M424.M47 Q87 1999 DVD.

Contains three improvisations (ca. 25 minutes) on "Puer natus est nobis" (Unto us a child is born) performed by Messiaen on 21 October 1985 on the Cavaillé-Coll organ at La Trinité. They include: (1) "And the Shepherds See a Group of Angels in the Fields Who Are Singing, 'Glory to God in the Highest'"; (2) "And the Three Kings Had Seen the Star of the Christ in the East and Headed Toward Nazareth" ("Nazareth" is a mistake on Messiaen's part when he announced the textual basis of this improvisation; the "Three Kings" were headed, of course, to Bethlehem); and (3) "And as a Present, the Three Kings Gave Mary and Jesus Gold as Though to a King, and Incense as Though to a God, and Myrrh as Though to a Mortal Man." Includes shots of Messiaen playing at the organ console, and the organ case and loft. After the improvisations, *Le Quatuor Olivier Messiaen* (Alain Moglia, violin; Michel Arrignon, clarinet; Sonia Wieder-Atherton, cello; Jean-Claude Henriot, piano) performs the *Quatuor pour la fin du Temps* at the Vaulx de Cernay Abbey, recorded live on 30 November 1991.

198. Messiaen, Olivier. *Liturgie de cristal.* Directed by Olivier Mille. 57 min. Idéale Audience Internationale/Artline Productions, 2002. Videocassette.

Contains archival clips of Messiaen (from 1964 to 1987) discussing his compositional techniques, scenes from Denise Tual's *Messiaen et les oiseaux*, and filmed performances of excerpts from his works, including the 1998 Salzburg production of *Saint François d'Assise*, all brought together to create a self-portrait of the composer.

199. Messiaen, Olivier. *Messiaen: Quartet for the End of Time*. Directed by Astrid Wortelboer. 60 min. Amaya, 1993. Videocassette.

Not examined. Contains an interview of Messiaen by Leo Samana conducted in 1991 ("Entretien avec Olivier Messiaen").

4

Biographical and Stylistic Studies

This chapter focuses on general biographical and stylistic studies of Messiaen's music, as well as more specialized discussions. It also includes essay collections, program booklets, and special periodical issues devoted to Messiaen.

GENERAL STUDIES OF MESSIAEN'S LIFE AND MUSIC, STYLE, AND AESTHETICS

200. Arnault, Pascal and Nicolas Darbon. *Olivier Messiaen: Les sons impalpables du rêve.* With prefaces by Yvonne Loriod-Messiaen and Jacques Petit. 2d ed. Lillebonne: Millénaire III Éditions, 1999. 187 p. ML 410.M595 A86 1999.

A critical study of Messiaen and his work. Part I (pp. 9–50) is devoted to various biographical and stylistic elements that helped shape Messiaen's character and compositional aesthetics. Included in this section is information about his work as a teacher at the Paris Conservatoire from 1941–78. Part II (pp. 51–96) consists of analyses of selected keyboard works and music involving voice: (1) *Préludes* (1929); (2) *Vingt Regards sur l'Enfant-Jésus* (1944); (3) *Quatre Études de rythme* (1949–50); (4) *Livre d'orgue* (1951–52); (5) *Trois Mélodies* (1930); (6) *Cinq Rechants* (1948–49); (7) *Harawi* (1945); and (8) *Saint François d'Assise* (1975–83). Part III (pp. 97–172) examines Messiaen's ideas on rhythm, melody, and harmony in the *Technique de mon langage musical* (1944), as well as compositional techniques that postdate the *Technique*. Part III closes with an analysis of *Éclairs sur l'Au-Delà* (1988–92), which is deemed a synthesis of Messiaen's techniques.

201. Bell, Carla Huston. *Olivier Messiaen.* Boston: Twayne Publishers, 1984. 158 p. ISBN: 0805794573. ML 410.M595 B4 1984.

Derived from her dissertation of 1977 (see item 202), Bell's study examines ten representative works by Messiaen from 1929 to 1958, beginning with the "Chant d'extase dans un paysage triste" from the *Préludes* for piano, and ending with "La Chouette Hulotte" from the *Catalogue d'oiseaux,* in order to provide a better understanding not only of Messiaen's musical style but also of his position in twentieth-century music. Prefaces her analytical appraisal of Messiaen's work by considering his major influences as well as the components of his musical language.

202. Bell, Carla Huston. "A Structural and Stylistic Analysis of Representative Compositions of Olivier Messiaen." D.Ed. dissertation, Columbia University, 1977. v, 321 p.

Basis of Bell's 1984 publication (see item 201). The only substantive differences between the two studies are the pieces analyzed. The dissertation examines nine works as opposed to the ten of the book. Moreover, the dissertation considers "Pourquoi?" from *Trois Mélodies,* which is not discussed in the book, and, conversely, does not examine "La Vierge et l'Enfant," from *La Nativité du Seigneur,* or "Reprises par interversion," from the *Livre d'orgue,* which are discussed in the book.

203. Boivin, Jean. *La classe de Messiaen.* Paris: Christian Bourgeois, 1995. 482 p. ISBN: 2267012499. ML 410.M595 B65 1995.

The most important publication to date on Messiaen's work as a teacher. The book is divided into two parts. Part one (chaps. 1–3) documents the history of Messiaen's teaching activities in France, from his work at the École Normale de Musique and the Schola Cantorum in the 1930s to the Paris Conservatoire from 1941–78. Boivin provides a wealth of information on Messiaen's harmony class (1941–46), the private lessons he gave in musical analysis at the home of Guy-Bernard Delapierre, his rivalry with René Leibowitz, the controversy in the press known as "Le Cas Messiaen," and later classes in analysis (1947–66) and composition (1966–78). Part two (chaps. 4–6) looks at Messiaen's approach to musical analysis, attempts to reconstruct analyses made by Messiaen from notes taken by students, and reflects upon his teaching legacy. Of additional value in this book is a transcription of the only known footage of Messiaen teaching (on Debussy's *Pelléas at Mélisande*) at the Paris Conservatoire taken from Denise Tual and Michel Fano's documentary film *Messiaen et les oiseaux* (1973—see item 194. For an English translation of excerpts from this transcription, see Vincent P. Benitez, "A Creative Legacy: Messiaen as Teacher of Analysis," [item 411], 117–39, passim.), and two appendices, the first listing the names of all students who attended Messiaen's classes from 1941–78, noting their nationalities and status as a student or auditor, and the second listing the repertoire studied for most of those classes. Highly recommended.

Reviews: Jean-Michel Bardez, "*La classe de Messiaen* de Jean Boivin," *Circuit* 9/1 (1998): 27–40; Christopher Dingle, "*La classe de Messiaen* by Jean Boivin," *Tempo* 202 (October 1997): 25–26.

204. Boivin, Jean. "La classe de Messiaen: Historique, reconstitution, impact." Ph.D. dissertation, Université de Montréal, 1993. 790 p. ISBN: 0315957298.

Examines Messiaen's work as a teacher at the Paris Conservatoire from 1941–78. Discusses his pedagogy and influence on the numerous composers who studied with him, including several Canadians who were mostly from Québec. The foundation for Boivin's book, *La classe de Messiaen* (see item 203).

205. Boswell-Kurc, Lilise. "Olivier Messiaen's Religious War-time Works and their Controversial Reception in France (1941–46)." 2 vols. Ph.D. dissertation, New York University, 2001.

This dissertation examines "Le Cas Messiaen," the affair in the French press surrounding the reception of Messiaen's religious works during the mid-1940s. Part one (chaps. 1–4) introduces the affair and considers those elements behind the controversy. Part two (chaps. 5–7) surveys the three most criticized aspects associated with Messiaen's war-time music: the commentaries that accompanied his works, the overly systematic nature of the *Technique de mon langage musical*, and the dichotomy produced by the music's spiritual and sensual elements. An exhaustive study shedding new light on the affair, especially how it was brewing for a long time and how it was driven not by the music's characteristics but by extra-musical matters. Highly recommended.

206. Broad, Stephen. "Recontextualising Messiaen's Early Career." 2 vols. Ph.D. dissertation, University of Oxford, 2005.

Reevaluates Messiaen's early career and development. Challenges the idea that Messiaen was somehow divorced from the main artistic movements of the twentieth century. Reassesses Messiaen's early career by examining: (1) his biographical and musical positioning in his own writings; (2) his relationship with his immediate musical contemporaries; (3) the role of Claire Delbos; (4) his relationship to French musical tradition; and (5) his role in French aesthetic debates of the 1930s. Contains a valuable bibliography (although devoid of sources written by German authors) and four appendices that include, respectively, annotated transcriptions of the articles Messiaen wrote for various French journals between 1936–39, a catalogue of Messiaen's journalism from 1935–39, selected personalia, and Messiaen's records at the Paris Conservatoire. Well researched and highly informative. A valuable study that should grace the bookshelves of any serious Messiaen scholar.

207. Dingle, Christopher. *The Life of Messiaen*. Cambridge: Cambridge University Press, 2007. ISBN: 052163220X.

Not examined in time for publication. Published March 2007. The following description is derived from the Web site at Cambridge University Press (www.cambridge.org/catalogue/catalogue.asp?isbn= 052163220X): "Olivier Messiaen stands as one of the most influential composers of the twentieth century and among the foremost religious artists of any era. When he died in 1992, the prevailing image was of a deeply religious man whose only sources of inspiration were God and Nature, and of a composer whose music progressed along an entirely individual path, impervious to contemporaneous events and the whims both of his fellow artists and the critics. *The Life of Messiaen* paints a more nuanced picture of the man and the musician, peering behind Messiaen's public persona to examine the private difficulties and creative struggles that were the true backdrop to many of his greatest achievements. Based upon the latest research, including previously overlooked sources, this book provides an excellent introduction to Messiaen's life and work, presenting a fascinating new perspective of a man whose story is more remarkable than the myths surrounding it."

208. Griffiths, Paul. *Olivier Messiaen and the Music of Time*. Ithaca, NY: Cornell University Press, 1985. 274 p. ISBN: 0801418135. ML 410.M595 G7 1985.

Concentrates on Messiaen's manipulation of musical time in order to understand his compositional style. Characterizes the composer's approaches to melody, harmony, and rhythm in relation to tonal conventions, concluding that Messiaen had a penchant for repetitive forms that evoke stasis—an absence of goal-directed motion—in his music. Proposes that what underlies all of Messiaen's works is a conception of music in terms of individual events with no underlying contexts. Examines Messiaen's life and music chronologically, placing a greater weight on the earlier works in order to promote connections they have with later compositions. Includes a chronology of Messiaen's life and music (up to *Saint François d'Assise*) and a catalogue of his works.

Reviews: Arnold Whittall, *The Music Review* 46/3 (August 1985): 226–28.

209. Halbreich, Harry. *Olivier Messiaen*. Paris: Fayard/Fondation SACEM, 1980. 532 p. ISBN: 221300790X. ML 410.M595 H3.

One of the most significant secondary French-language sources on Messiaen written by a former pupil of the composer. Divided into four parts ("L'homme et son univers," "Le langage musical," "L'œuvre," "Messiaen parmi nous"), this study provides insights into Messiaen's life, faith, compositional aesthetics, music, and work as a teacher at the Paris Conservatoire. Of particular note are the discussions of Messiaen's harmonic vocabulary and sound-color relationships. Halbreich includes several chords in his discussion of Messiaen's harmony that are not addressed in the *Technique de mon langage musical* or by other Messiaen authors prior to the 1990s. Moreover, he was the first scholar to list the color associations suggested by specific modal transpositions in Messiaen's colored-hearing synesthesia. According to Hill and Simeone, this study was written under Messiaen's "watchful supervision" (Hill and Simeone [item 210], 1.).

210. Hill, Peter and Nigel Simeone. *Messiaen*. New Haven and London: Yale University Press, 2005. xii, 435 p. ISBN: 0300109075. ML 410.M595 H55 2005.

In their biography, Hill and Simeone go beyond the portrait of Messiaen that emerged from his interviews, lectures, and didactic treatises, as well as from books written about him and his music. Although Messiaen meticulously described the elements of his musical language, he said very little about what drove their use in a composition. He was equally reticent about any new works in progress and divulged few details about his private life. Because they were granted access to the composer's archive by Yvonne Loriod-Messiaen, Hill and Simeone reveal information about Messiaen hitherto unknown to the scholarly world. Through their examination of the correspondence, diaries, lecture notes, musical notebooks (*cahiers*), and compositional sketches found at the archive, they draw a fascinating picture of both Messiaen's work and domestic life. They are able to trace the development of his musical ideas, accordingly allowing them to provide information not only about the genesis of different works but his compositional process as well.

They were also able to find a lighter side to Messiaen's personality. Although he was a serious individual, he could be gregarious and not without a sense of humor. Hill and Simeone show, furthermore, the more difficult aspects of Messiaen's private life, such as his care of Claire Delbos, his first wife, and the physical suffering he endured in later years. The book is well annotated and includes numerous reproductions of photographs and documents, along with an impressive bibliography. Highly recommended.

Reviews: William R. Braun, *Opera News* 71/1 (July 2006): 64; M. Neil, *Choice* 43/8 (April 2006): 1413; Andrew Thomson, "All for Jesus," *Musical Times* 147/1894 (Spring 2006): 73–80; David Schiff, "Music for the End of Time," *The Nation* 282/6 (13 February 2006): 25–29; Ditlev Rindom, "Illuminating the Beyond: The Life and Work of Olivier Messiaen," *The Cambridge Quarterly* 35/2 (2006): 188–91; and Bruce R. Schueneman, *Library Journal* 130/16 (1 October 2005): 78.

211. Hirsbrunner, Theo. *Olivier Messiaen: Leben und Werk*. Laaber: Laaber-Verlag, 1988. 242 p. ISBN: 3890071392. ML 410.M595 H57 1988.

Not only surveys Messiaen's life and career as a composer and teacher but also interprets his music from different perspectives. Compares Messiaen's music with that of Boulez, Ravel, and Wagner in three separate sections. Also discusses Messiaen's music in relation to absolute music, modernism, the composer's *langage communicable*, and tonality and atonality. Closes the study with a section devoted to *Saint François d'Assise*, where general information about the opera's genesis, instrumental forces, and dramatic and musical designs is provided.

Reviews: Almut Rößler, *Musica* 43/2 (March/April 1989): 165–66; *Musik und Kirche* 58/6 (1988): 303–4.

212. Holloway, Clyde. "The Organ Works of Olivier Messiaen and Their Importance in His Total *Oeuvre*." D.S.M. document, Union Theological Seminary, 1974. v, 586 p.

Lengthy study dealing with Messiaen's organ works up to the *Méditations sur le mystère de la Sainte Trinité* in the context of his total output. Provides valuable information on aspects of Messiaen's compositional style, as found not only in his organ music but in his other music as well. Includes English translations of excerpts from Antoine Goléa's *Rencontres avec Olivier Messiaen* (see item 165), Claude Samuel's *Entretiens avec Olivier Messiaen* (see item 181), and Messiaen's prefaces to his organ works and the *Quatuor pour la fin du Temps*.

213. Johnson, Robert Sherlaw. *Messiaen*. Berkeley: University of California Press, 1989. 232 p. ISBN: 0520067347. ML 410.M595 J6 1989.

This survey of Messiaen's music and compositional style is one of the best in English. Johnson identifies Messiaen's approaches to harmony, color, and rhythm, and his ability to integrate earlier procedures with newer ideas as key elements that distinguish the composer's work in the twentieth century. While noting that Messiaen's works lie outside of the French tradition, Johnson regards the composer's compositions, especially those up to the mid-1940s, as being influenced by Debussy and Stravinsky. Valuable also in this tome are appendices that include the 120 *deçi-tâlas* in modern notation from the thirteenth-century North Indian music treatise *Samgîta-ratnâkara*, attributed to Sharngadeva (these *deçi-tâlas* were listed in Lavignac's *Encyclopédie de la musique* and available to Messiaen during his student days—see Joanny Grosset, "Inde: Histoire de la musique depuis l'origine jusqu'a nos jours," in *Encyclopédie de la musique et dictionnaire du conservatoire*, ed. Albert Lavignac and Lionel de la Laurencie, 11 vols. (Paris: Delagrave, 1913), I/1: 301–4), and an impressive list of bird names in French, Latin, and English and the works from 1953 to 1986 in which they appear.

Reviews: Paul Griffiths, "Deux Regards," *The Musical Times* 116/1592 (October 1975): 881–83; David Drew, *Times Literary Supplement*, 12 September 1975, 1030; and Dika Newlin, *Library Journal* 100/13 (July 1975): 1328.

214. Luchese, Diane. "Olivier Messiaen's Slow Music: Glimpses of Eternity in Time." Ph.D. dissertation, Northwestern University, 1998. viii, 196 p.

Considers some of the elements that distinguish Messiaen's slow music. Argues that the frequently applied descriptive term "static" is insufficient because it overlooks the music's progressive qualities. Views Messiaen's slow music as ultimately paradoxical, as impressions of the changelessness of eternity are combined with the forward directionality of linear time. Chapters one through four lay the groundwork for the study's analytical application in chapter five, which involves analyses of four Messiaen works that span the 1930s to 1980s.

215. Mari, Pierrette. *Olivier Messiaen: L'homme et son œuvre*. Paris: Éditions Seghers, 1965. 191 p. ML 410.M595 M4.

Explores Messiaen's life, compositional techniques, and music according to medium. The analytical examination of his works is far from detailed: no musical examples accompany any discussion.

Although it does provide valuable information on various aspects of Messiaen's life, the book contains statements not supported by documentation. For example, mode 5, which is not one of Messiaen's color modes, is described as evoking "gray-rose-green studded with gold" (p. 29). Finally, the book contains a catalogue of works up to *Et exspecto resurrectionem mortuorum* (1965), a bibliography of Messiaen's writings, and a selected discography.

216. Michaely, Aloyse. *Die Musik Olivier Messiaens: Untersuchungen zum Gesamtschaffen.* Hamburger Beiträge zur Musikwissenschaft: Sonderband. Hamburg: Verlag der Musikalienhandlung Karl Dieter Wagner, 1987. 841 p. ISBN: 3889790275. ML 410.M595 M5 1987.

An exhaustive examination of Messiaen's music spanning 841 pages. Interprets the music's theological content as determining every aspect of structure. Relies heavily on Messiaen's commentaries and writings to comprehend his work. Analyzes the composer's musical language in relation to his theological ideas regarding the Creation, the Holy Trinity, and Resurrection and Eternal Life. Of note is the author's insightful discussion of sound-color relationships (pp. 357–90). Includes an appendix that lists Messiaen's works according to genre, a selected bibliography, and indexes of names and compositions by Messiaen, respectively. Highly recommended.

Reviews: Almut Rößler, *Musica* 43/2 (March/April 1989): 166–67.

217. Muncy, Thomas R. "Messiaen's Influence on Post-War Serialism." M.M. thesis, North Texas State University, 1984. ix, 106 p.

Attempts to demonstrate how Messiaen's *Mode de valeurs et d'intensités* (1949) influenced the development of post-war serialism as exemplified by Boulez's *Structures Ia* and Stockhausen's *Kreuzspiel*, both composed in 1951. Begins by trying to show how the serial aspects of *Mode de valeurs* are anticipated in Messiaen's systematization of musical parameters, as shown both in the *Technique de mon langage musical* and works from the 1940s. The study then looks at the music of the so-called experimental period of 1949–51, which includes *Mode de valeurs*. Finally, the study concludes by examining the influence of *Mode de valeurs* on the compositional design and structure of both *Structures Ia* and *Kreuzspiel*.

218. Nichols, Roger. *Messiaen,* 2d ed. Oxford Studies of Composers, no. 13. London: Oxford University Press, 1986. 89 p. ISBN: 019315465X (hard); 0193154595 (paperback). ML 410.M595 N5 1986.

A concise examination of Messiaen's life and compositional style, covering music up to *Saint François d'Assise* (1975–83). Since it is part of the Oxford Studies of Composers series, this volume is short and descriptive, geared to providing an overview rather than a detailed examination of Messiaen's works and the compositional techniques that inform them.

Reviews (of the first edition): Arthur Lawrence, *The Diapason* 70 (December 1978): 4; Paul Griffiths, "Deux Regards," *The Musical Times* 116/1592 (October 1975): 881–83.

219. Périer, Alain. *Messiaen.* Paris: Solfèges/Seuil, 1979. 191 p. ISBN: 2020001454. ML 410. M595 P5.

A chronological life and works study written by one of Messiaen's former pupils. Because of its date, examines Messiaen's music through *Des canyons aux étoiles.* Contains many photographs that were not available in most biographies of the time. According to Hill and Simeone, this study, like Halbreich's tome, was written under Messiaen's "watchful supervision" (Hill and Simeone [item 210], 1.).

220. Rostand, Claude. *Olivier Messiaen.* Paris: Éditions Ventadour, 1957. 48 p. ML 410.M595 R7.

A book on Messiaen by a harsh critic of his music in the French press during the "Le Cas Messiaen" affair of the 1940s. Rostand later became a staunch advocate of Messiaen's music. He explained his change of heart in the September 1961 issue of *Le Figaro littéraire* ("Bataille pour *Chronochromie*"). As for Messiaen, he forgave Rostand for his scathing reviews. The book itself considers Messiaen's then present-day activities of the mid-1950s, the "Le Cas Messiaen" affair, his life, the psychology behind his art (that is, its connection to his Catholic faith), and his compositional techniques and music.

221. Shenton, Andrew David James. *Olivier Messiaen's System of Signs.* Aldershot, Hants, England, and Burlington, VT: Ashgate, 2008. ISBN: 978-0-7546-6168-9.

Forthcoming (2008). Below is an abstract of the book provided by the author:

"In *Olivier Messiaen's System of Signs*, Andrew Shenton demonstrates how Messiaen sought to refine his compositions to speak more clearly about the truths of the Catholic faith by developing a sophisticated system of signs in which aspects of music become direct signifiers for words and concepts. Using the *Méditations sur le mystère de la Sainte Trinité* as a case study, Shenton uses an interdisciplinary approach utilizing several key concepts from philosophy, aesthetics, linguistics, semiotics, cognition studies and hermeneutics as well as a detailed knowledge of Catholic theology to analyze both the music and the message. He also deals with issues of understanding, interpretation, exegesis, performance, authorial intent and the role of the listener for analysis of music which expresses a theology if not a spirituality that may not be our own."

222. Shenton, Andrew David James. "The Unspoken Word: Olivier Messiaen's 'Langage Communicable'." Ph.D. dissertation, Harvard University, 1998. xi, 343 p.

This dissertation scrutinizes Messiaen's *langage communicable* in order to highlight its conceptual richness and to make it more comprehensible. The study places the language in historical context by discussing the history of musical cryptography, emphasizing twentieth-century French developments in the field. It analyzes Messiaen's *langage communicable* from linguistic and cognitive perspectives, setting up hermeneutical examinations of pieces by Messiaen (*Méditations sur le mystère de la Sainte Trinité, Des canyons aux étoiles*, and *Livre du Saint Sacrement*) that include the language. Each of these pieces is situated contextually within a broader semiotic system. The dissertation concludes by considering questions of meaning in music and their relationships to the language.

223. Sholl, Robert Peter. "Olivier Messiaen and the Culture of Modernity." Ph.D. dissertation, King's College, University of London, 2003. 383 p.

Argues that Messiaen viewed himself as a self-professed "liberator of humanity," who combined both modernistic and religious elements in his music throughout his career in order to bring society closer to God. This viewpoint of Messiaen as a "religious modernist" is based upon supposed connections he had, by way of the music and aesthetics of Charles Tournemire, to a nineteenth-century French tradition of anti-modernist thought, seen primarily through the writings of Joséphin "Sâr' Péladan (1859–1918) and Joris-Karl Huysmans (1848–1907). The study is distinguished by an impressive command of historical, literary, and theological sources related to Messiaen, as well as by insightful perspectives as to their place in the composer's life and work. However, the study is also characterized by a dismissive attitude toward the Messiaen literature, especially involving the composer's writings, as it seeks to reveal a more interesting Messiaen than hitherto described. This laudable goal notwithstanding, which it only sometimes fulfills, the study is full of statements at odds with those by Messiaen, giving the impression that the composer either did not know what he was doing or deliberately obfuscated his agenda. Finally, the study does not set up musical-theoretical frameworks for its analytical viewpoints; instead, it analyzes musical elements in an ad hoc manner without due regard for building methodical arguments.

224. Von Gunden, Heidi Cecilia. "Timbre as Symbol in Selected Works of Olivier Messiaen." Ph.D. dissertation, University of California at San Diego, 1977. viii, 134 p.

Asserts that the reason Messiaen's music is frequently misunderstood is due to the disregard of its mystic symbolism. Maintains that his music exhibits unity through timbre techniques that serve as sonorous symbol. Surveys Messiaen's use of sonic symbols, particularly those suggested by two eschatological books, the *Tibetan Book of the Dead* and the *Apocalypse* or *Book of Revelation*. Examines five compositions (*Quatuor pour la fin du Temps*, *Messe de la Pentecôte*, *Couleurs de la Cité céleste*, *Et exspecto resurrectionem mortuorum*, and *La Transfiguration de Nôtre-Seigneur Jésus-Christ*) for evidence of the use of timbre as sonorous symbol, based upon their ties to the eschatological literature and their use of instrumentation.

SPECIALIZED DISCUSSIONS OF MESSIAEN'S MUSIC

225. Adams, Beverly Decker. "The Organ Compositions of Olivier Messiaen." Ph.D. dissertation, University of Utah, 1969. viii, 153 p.

Survey of Messiaen's organ works up to the *Verset pour la fête de la Dédicace* (1961) from formal, harmonic, melodic, and rhythmic vantage points. Contains brief biographical information on Messiaen and an explanation of his musical language.

226. Ahrens, Sieglinde, Möller, Hans-Dieter, and Almut Rößler. *Das Orgelwerk Messiaens.* Duisberg: Gilles & Francke Verlag, 1976. 96 p. ISBN: 3921104076. MT 145.M54 A4 1976.

An updated stylistic survey of Messiaen's organ works beginning with *Le Banquet céleste* (1928—for an explanation of the date of composition for *Le Banquet céleste*, see Appendix 1, nn. 2 and 16) and ending with *Méditations sur le mystère de la Sainte Trinité* (1969). In this multi-authored volume, Hans-Dieter Möller discusses Messiaen's organ works through *Les Corps glorieux*, Sieglinde Ahrens the *Messe de la Pentecôte* and the *Livre d'orgue*, and Almut Rößler the *Verset pour la fête de la Dédicace* and the *Méditations sur le mystère de la Sainte Trinité*. An earlier edition of this work from 1968 only included the discussions by Möller and Ahrens.

227. Davidson, Audrey Ekdahl. *Olivier Messiaen and the Tristan Myth.* Westport, CT: Praeger Publishers, 2001. x, 144 p. ISBN: 0275973409. ML 410.M595 D38 2001.

    A condensed and updated version of the author's dissertation on Messiaen's Tristan trilogy, *Harawi, Turangalîla-Symphonie*, and *Cinq Rechants* (see item 228). Chapter one ("The Composer and the Myth") places the trilogy within the context of Messiaen's work as a composer, emphasizing the influence of Wagner and his opera *Tristan und Isolde.* The next three chapters are devoted, respectively, to analyses of *Harawi, Turangalîla-Symphonie*, and *Cinq Rechants* (chapter two: "*Harawi: Song of Love and Death*"; chapter three: "*Turangalîla-symphonie*: The Cosmic Dimension of Love"; and chapter four: "*Cinq rechants*: The Lovers Fly Away"). Unlike the author's dissertation, there is no concluding chapter to the study.

    Reviews: Tim Sullivan, *Journal of Musicological Research* 22/1–2 (January-June 2003): 174–77; Haig Mardirosian, *The American Organist* 36/10 (October 2002): 85–86; and J. Behrens, *Choice* 39/11–12 (July/August 2002): 1970.

228. Davidson, Audrey Jean Ekdahl. "Olivier Messiaen's Tristan Trilogy: Time and Transcendence." 2 vols. Ph.D. dissertation, University of Minnesota, 1975. ii, 423 p.

    An examination of Messiaen's Tristan trilogy (*Harawi, Turangalîla-Symphonie*, and *Cinq Rechants*). The author views each piece as containing problems, primarily musical, that require resolution. Her methodology relies on techniques of literary explication, and an approach to musical analysis derived from Messiaen's *Technique de mon langage musical.* Chapter one provides a context for the trilogy within Messiaen's œuvre. The author notes the composer's debt to Wagner and his music drama *Tristan und Isolde.* Chapters two through four focus on *Harawi*, interpreting the cycle as falling into three large sections: (1) songs one through four, which deal with the fluctuation of mood and scene, (2) songs five through nine, which display a high degree of tension, and (3) songs ten through twelve, which view the experience of love as ennobling. Chapters five through six are devoted to the *Turangalîla-Symphonie*, which is analyzed as exhibiting a bipartite structure. Movements one through five comprise the first part of the work, with the first four movements functioning as a prelude to the fifth, the symphony's climax. Movements six through ten form the work's second part. They address the fulfillment of love, although they do not evince a sense of progression. Chapter seven deals with *Cinq Rechants.* The work is characterized by extreme speed, making it the shortest piece in the trilogy. For the author, the brevity of *Cinq Rechants* produces an "art nouveau triptych" in which one large central panel is flanked by two unequal panels. *Harawi* and *Cinq Rechants*, the two unequal panels, serve to introduce and conclude, respectively, Messiaen's modern approach to the question of myth in music. The *Turangalîla-Symphonie*, the central and largest panel, is the broadest in terms of its treatment of mythic and musical materials. *Cinq Rechants* is also distinguished symbolically by an emphasis on both time and space. The dissertation's last chapter not only summarizes the study's findings but also contextualizes the Tristan trilogy in relation to Messiaen's music of the 1950s to 60s.

229. Ernst, Karin. *Der Beitrag Olivier Messiaens zur Orgelmusik des 20. Jahrhunderts*. Hochschulsammlung Philosophie: Musikwissenschaft, Band 1. Freiburg: Hochschulverlag, 1980. 367 p. ISBN: 3810720100. ML 410.M595 E7 1980.

An examination of Messiaen's contributions to twentieth-century organ music. After an opening chapter on French organ music at the beginning of the twentieth century (pp. 12–30) and a second chapter on the significance of Indian music for Messiaen's organ works (pp. 31–68), considers the composer's organ music from the perspectives of rhythm, melody, harmony, and form. Chapter three (pp. 69–127) is a detailed study of rhythm in Messiaen's organ music, looking first at Messiaen's conception of rhythm and then examining how the organ works manifest its different stages of development. (This chapter is essentially a catalogue of Messiaen's rhythmic techniques.) Chapter four (pp. 128–54) is an investigation of melody in Messiaen's organ works that looks at favored intervals, melodic idioms, the influence of plainchant, and the use of register changes. Chapter five (pp. 155–202) is a study of harmony in Messiaen's organ music that considers the modes of limited transposition, aspects of impressionistic harmony, color, atonality, and twelve-tone techniques. Chapter six (pp. 203–51) looks at the formal principles governing Messiaen's organ music. The last two chapters involve, respectively, an analysis of the *Méditations sur le mystère de la Sainte Trinité* (pp. 252–70) and a discussion of Messiaen's relationship to organ music composed after 1960 (pp. 271–308). In its appendix, the book includes interviews with Messiaen (see item 157), Almut Rößler, Wolfgang Stockmeier, and Gerhard Zacher, as well as reproductions of letters from Pierre Boulez and Karlheinz Stockhausen to the author. This material is followed by an index that correlates the book's discussions with Messiaen's organ pieces, and a bibliography.

230. Hsu [Forte], Madeleine. *Olivier Messiaen, the Musical Mediator: A Study of the Influence of Liszt, Debussy, and Bartók*. Madison, NJ: Fairleigh Dickinson University Press, 1996. 183 p. ISBN: 0838635954. ML 410.M595 H8 1996.

Hsu analyzes Messiaen's *Préludes* for piano (1929) and "Regard de l'Esprit de joie" from the *Vingt Regards sur l'Enfant-Jésus* (1944) in order to show how these analyses contribute to the works' interpretation and performance. The author uses Jan La Rue's approach to analysis (SHMRG: sound, harmony, melody, rhythm, growth) in examining each piece (Jan La Rue, *Guidelines for Style Analysis* (New York: W. W. Norton, 1970). Hsu also discusses the stylistic influences of Liszt, Debussy, and Bartók on Messiaen, with a special consideration of important similarities and differences between the piano music of Messiaen and Bartók. (This discussion, entitled "Bartók: Messiaen's Master of Thought?," was also published in the *Journal of the American Liszt Society*; see item 279.) Finally, the author provides interpretative comments for each analyzed piece.

Reviews: Charles Timbrell, *The American Music Teacher* 47/3 (December 1997-January 1998): 69, 71.

231. Kemmelmeyer, Karl-Jürgen. *Die gedruckten Orgelwerke Olivier Messiaens bis zum "Verset pour la fête de la Dédicace": Eine strukturwissenschaftliche Darstellung*. Forschungsbeiträge zur Musikwissenschaft, Band 25; Veröffentlichungen zur theoretischen Musikwissenschaft, Band 4. 2 vols. Regensburg: Gustav Bosse Verlag, 1974. 233 p. (vol. 1). ISBN: 3764921080. ML 410.M595 K4.

Develops structural models and types to describe Messiaen's compositional techniques in *Le Banquet céleste* through *Verset pour la fête de la Dédicace*. Because Messiaen's rhythmic techniques center on a small durational value and its free multiplication, they lead to a conception of rhythm as consisting of absolute durational values that can be serialized. Characterizes Messiaen's compositional approach as involving the manipulation and development of smaller units in pitch and rhythm that generate larger structural blocks. States that a pitch series is normally employed in an improvisational manner rather than as a means of integrating pitches. Contains an excellent bibliography and Messiaen's liner notes from the Ducretet-Thomson recordings in an appendix.

232. Pozzi, Raffaele. *Il suono dell'estasi: Olivier Messiaen dal* Banquet céleste *alla* Turangalîla-symphonie. Lucca: Libreria Musicale Italiana, 2002. viii, 220 p. ISBN: 8870963152. ML 410.M595 P6 2002.

A stylistic study of Messiaen's music from *Le Banquet céleste* through the *Turangalîla-Symphonie*. The book is divided into four parts followed by an appendix and other supplementary materials. The introduction ("La musica come simbole: Un profilo dell'estetica di Olivier Messiaen") provides a profile of Messiaen's compositional aesthetics. Chapter one ("L'Âme en bourgeon") considers his formative years as a composer through *L'Ascension* for orchestra (1933). Chapter two ("Ritmi di terra e di cielo") is an examination of the new musical style that emerged from *La Nativité du Seigneur* (1935) and *Les Corps glorieux* (1939). Chapter three ("Apocalissi, visioni, mitologie") concentrates on the music of the 1940s, from the *Quatuor pour la fin du Temps* (1940–41) through *Cinq Rechants* (1948–49). (Although it concludes with *Cinq Rechants*, which seems to contradict the book's title, chapter three devotes more attention to the *Turangalîla-Symphonie*.) The appendix contains tables of the modes of limited transposition, Greek meters, the 120 deci-tâlas of Sharngadeva, and special chords used by Messiaen in the 1930s and 40s. The book also includes Messiaen's song texts, a chronology of his life and works, a catalogue of his music, and a selected bibliography.

233. Reverdy, Michèle. *L'œuvre pour orchestre d'Olivier Messiaen.* Paris: Alphonse Leduc, 1988. 183 p. ISBN: 2856890385. MT 130.M37 R5 1988.

A chronological survey of Messiaen's orchestral music by one of his students. Although it identifies the compositional techniques used in each piece, the book does not speculate as to why they are used. In many ways, the book's discussions of Messiaen's music resemble those by the composer himself. The book includes a list of non-traditional orchestral instruments in their chronological order of appearance in Messiaen's music (pp. 177–79), and a glossary of his compositional devices and harmonic elements (pp. 180–81).

234. Reverdy, Michèle. *L'œuvre pour piano d'Olivier Messiaen.* Paris: Alphonse Leduc, 1978. 100 p. ISBN: 2856890040. MT 145.M54 R5.

A chronological survey of Messiaen's piano music up to *La Fauvette des jardins* (1970). Includes an opening chapter on Messiaen's musical language. Like the author's volume on Messiaen's orchestral music, this book explains what is happening musically in each piece but not why. The book does receive, however, a glowing commendation from Messiaen (Michèle Reverdy, *L'œuvre pour orchestre d'Olivier Messiaen*, [item 233], 3). He regards it as accurate from rhythmic and harmonic perspectives, and its study of form as its most original aspect.

235. Waumsley, Stuart. *The Organ Music of Olivier Messiaen.* 2d ed. Paris: Alphonse Leduc, 1975. 56 p. MT 145.M54 W4 1975.

A stylistic examination of Messiaen's organ music up to *Méditations sur le mystère de la Sainte Trinité* (1969). Based on the author's thesis at Birmingham University and updated from a previous edition of 1968. The only published English-language study devoted to Messiaen's organ works. Includes a summary of Messiaen's musical language followed by a chronological discussion of the organ music.

ESSAY COLLECTIONS, PROGRAM BOOKLETS, AND SPECIAL PERIODICAL ISSUES DEVOTED TO MESSIAEN

236. Bruhn, Siglind, ed. *Messiaen's Language of Mystical Love.* Studies in Contemporary Music and Culture, ed. Joseph Auner, vol. 1. New York: Garland Publishing, Inc., 1998. ix, 271 p. ISBN: 0815327471. ML 410.M595 M49 1998.

Arranged into four parts, this collection of eleven essays deals with diverse aspects of Messiaen's musical language. Part one explores the roles humanism, mathematics, and theology play in his work as a teacher and composer in order to introduce Messiaen the person. Part two not only examines the relationship between Messiaen's aesthetic of the "charm of impossibilities" and his compositional techniques but also surveys his approach to rhythm. Part three examines celebratory aspects of Messiaen's music as reflected through the theology of Saint Thomas Aquinas, Franciscan spirituality, and birdsong. Finally, part four delves into poetic, linguistic, and structural aspects of Messiaen's music. For individual entries, see items 264, 295, 327, 339, 352, 361, 413, 439, 446, 535, and 561.

Reviews: Vincent P. Benitez, *MLA Notes* 56/2 (December 1999): 424–26.

237. Dingle, Christopher and Nigel Simeone, eds. *Olivier Messiaen: Music, Art and Literature.* Aldershot, Hants, England, and Burlington, VT: Ashgate, 2007. ISBN: 9780754652971 (hardback); 9780754652977 (paperback).

Not examined. Forthcoming. According to information provided by Ashgate, this collection of essays evaluates Messiaen's position in the twentieth century. It attempts to counter common misconceptions associated with Messiaen in order to reveal more about the man and his music.

238. Église de la Trinité. *Olivier Messiaen, homme de foi: Regard sur son œuvre d'orgue.* Paris: Trinité Média Communication, 1995. 104 p.

Arising from the "Festival Messiaen" held at La Trinité in 1995, these essays explore the compositional and theological aspects of Messiaen's organ music along with various other facets of his work. The essays are organized into three categories: (1) "Le Festival Messiaen à l'Église de la Trinité: L'intégrale de l'œuvre d'orgue," (2) "Splendeur des Mystères: L'alliance de l'art et de la foi," and (3) "Hommage à Olivier Messiaen." The volume also includes a facsimile of an essay by Messiaen in his own handwriting on the meaning of faith, a glossary of technical terms, and a short bibliography. A must read for anyone desiring a better understanding of the role of faith in Messiaen's life and work. For individual entries, see items 89, 150, 192, 254, 281, 283, 284, 293, 302, 368, 384, 386, 387, 388, 389, 391, 393, 415, 416, 420, and 484.

239. Gillock, Jon. *Celebration Messiaen: The Complete Works for Organ.* Special Program Book in Honor of the Ninetieth Anniversary of the Birth of Olivier Messiaen. Edited by Madame Francine Matiffa. New York: The Riverside Church in the City of New York, 1999. 56 p.

This "Celebration Messiaen Booklet" was compiled by organist Jon Gillock to accompany his series of six concerts at the Riverside Church in New York in 1999, where he played the complete organ works of Messiaen in honor of the ninetieth anniversary of the composer's birth. The booklet contains several items authored by Gillock, namely a biography of Messiaen, an article on his organ music, an essay on his thoughts about the organ, and programs notes for each concert. The booklet also includes a reproduction of a letter from Yvonne Loriod-Messiaen to Gillock accompanied by Gillock's English translation. Beautifully illustrated with numerous photographs. For individual entries, see items 193, 274, 381, 382, and 383.

240. Hill, Peter, ed. *The Messiaen Companion.* Portland, OR: Amadeus Press, 1995. 581 p. ISBN: 0931340950 (hardback); 0931340942 (paperback). ML 410.M595 M48 1995.

The first to appear after Messiaen's death in 1992, this study contains eighteen essays, an appendix listing the organ specifications at La Trinité, a chronology of Messiaen's music, and a selected discography. The essays are arranged into three parts—part one, Interlude, and part two, using the *Turangalîla-Symphonie* (1946–48) as a convenient means to divide Messiaen's output into two parts. Part one opens with an essay devoted to the composer's musical language and is followed by four essays that consider Messiaen's music to 1948 by performance medium: (1) organ; (2) piano; (3) vocal; and (4) instrumental. The Interlude contains five essays on various topics (color, theology, birdsong, and teaching) that underlie Messiaen's work as a musician, along with an interview of Yvonne Loriod-Messiaen. Part two contains seven essays, with the last four devoted to examinations of *La Transfiguration de Nôtre-Seigneur Jésus-Christ, Des canyons aux étoiles, Saint François d'Assise*, and *Éclairs sur l'Au-Delà*. For individual entries, see items 187, 277, 287, 319, 347, 366, 373, 375, 376, 394, 402, 404, 405, 412, 414, 418, 435, 470, 474, 482, and 591.

Reviews: Richard D. Burbank, *MLA Notes* 53/1 (September 1996): 76–77; David Palmer, *The Diapason* 87/2 (February 1996): 8–9; and Julian Anderson, "Writ Small," *The Musical Times* 136 (August 1995): 434–35.

241. Massip, Catherine, ed. *Portrait(s) d'Olivier Messiaen*. With a preface by Jean Favier. Paris: Bibliothèque Nationale de France, 1996. 175 p. ISBN: 2717719857. ML 410.M595 P59 1996.

This collection of essays was published on the occasion of the "Hommage à Olivier Messiaen" exhibition that took place at the Bibliothèque Nationale de France, galerie Colbert, from 26 September to 17 November 1996. It contains six essays that examine Messiaen's life, understanding of theology, ideas on rhythm and color, connection with birdsong, writing for the piano, and opera, *Saint François d'Assise*. The collection is illustrated with numerous photographs and reproductions of documents, including autograph manuscripts of Messiaen's music and birdsong notebooks. It also contains a list of Messiaen's published works, lists of the honors and prizes Messiaen received, and a selected bibliography. Highly recommended. For individual entries, see items 280, 286, 343, 367, 408, and 431.

242. [Special Messiaen Edition.] *Melos* 25/12 (December 1958): 381–99.

Special issue honoring Messiaen on the occasion of his 50th birthday in 1958. Contains a German translation of the text of his speech at the Brussels International Exhibition, on 15 September 1958; an homage to Messiaen from many of his former students; an essay on Messiaen's life, influences, and musical techniques by Claude Rostand; and a German translation of an interview with Messiaen by Antoine Goléa. For individual entries, see items 95, 164, 297, and 423.

243. Metzger, Heinz-Klaus, and Rainer Riehn, ed. *Musik-Konzepte 28: Olivier Messiaen*. Munich: Edition Text + Kritik, 1982. 128 p. ISBN: 3883771317. ML 410.M54 O54 1982.

An issue devoted to Messiaen in a periodical that focuses on individual composers. Contents include: (1) a revised German translation of Messiaen's lecture at the Brussels International Exposition in 1958; (2) an examination of the "abyss" in Messiaen's works; (3) an essay devoted to Messiaen's relationship to new music after 1945 as seen through his association with non-Western musical systems and aesthetics; (4) a discussion of Messiaen's birdsong style and an analysis of the first movement of *Cinq Rechants*; and (5) analyses of *Livre d'orgue* and *Oiseaux exotiques*. Contains a list of works, bibliography, and a short discography compiled by Rainer Riehn. For individual essays, see items 94, 289, 313, 461, 516, and 584.

244. "Olivier Messiaen: 70th Anniversary." *Music: The AGO-RCCO Magazine* 12/12 (December 1978). ISSN: 0027–4208.

A special issue devoted to Messiaen on the occasion of his seventieth birthday on 10 December 1978. Includes: (1) an article on how a Christmas communion service at the Downtown United Presbyterian Church in Rochester, New York was built around *La Nativité du Seigneur*; (2) a comparison of the 1934 and 1960 editions of *Le Banquet céleste*; (3) a discussion of Messiaen's musical language; (4) an examination of Messiaen's organ registrations and how to adapt them to non-French instruments; and (5) translations of the liner notes from the Ducretet-Thomson recordings of Messiaen's organ music, along with the prefaces to *La Nativité du Seigneur* and *Méditations sur le mystère de la Sainte Trinité*, as a way to describe his compositional aesthetic. For individual entries, see items 342, 385, 396, 490, and 497.

245. "Olivier Messiaen: 80th Anniversary." *The Diapason* 79 (December 1988). ISSN: 0012–2378.

A special issue devoted to Messiaen on the occasion of his eightieth birthday on 10 December 1988. Contains (1) a birthday tribute, (2) an essay on *Méditations sur le mystère de la Sainte Trinité*, and (3) an examination of the organs associated with his music. For individual entries, see items 397, 400, and 518.

246. Sabatier, François et al. ["Tributes to Olivier Messiaen."] *L'Orgue: Revue trimestrielle* 224 (September/December 1992): 5–54. ISSN: 0030–5170.

A special issue honoring Messiaen's work as an organist. Includes essays that examine: (1) the man and the organist; (2) his approach to organ registration, work as an improviser and liturgical musician, ideas about organ building and design, and the importance of the Cavaillé-Coll organ at La Trinité in his compositional aesthetic;

(3) the *Livre du Saint Sacrement*; (4) his ideas about religion and its influence on his music; (5) recordings of his organ works; and (6) the unpublished letters of Bérenger de Miramon Fitz-James to Norbert Dufourcq from 1926–48, which mention Messiaen beginning in 1930. For individual entries, see items 162, 291, 300, 377, 399, and 526.

247. Samuel, Claude, artistic director. *La Recherche Artistique présente hommage à Olivier Messiaen*. Paris: La Recherche Artistique, November-December 1978. 110 p. ML 410.M52 R42 (IUCAT).

Program booklet associated with the concerts in France honoring Messiaen on the occasion of his seventieth birthday in 1978. Contains an untitled introduction by Messiaen on his view of faith published in his own handwriting, an essay by Claude Samuel on Messiaen ("Olivier Messiaen ou la multiplicité transcendée"), a list of the concerts in France celebrating Messiaen's music, an essay on Messiaen's work as a teacher in his own words ("Olivier Messiaen: Pedagogue de notre Temps"), and commentaries on Messiaen's music from *Le Banquet céleste* to *Des canyons aux étoiles*, taken primarily from his liner notes to recordings and/or prefaces to his works ("Olivier Messiaen analyse ses œuvres"), although there is one essay by Alain Michel on *La Transfiguration de Nôtre-Seigneur Jésus-Christ* ("La Transfiguration et la Beauté: d'Olivier Messiaen à Urs von Balthasar") that was included at Messiaen's request. At the end of each commentary is a list of dates and locations where that particular work was being performed in France. For individual entries not duplicated elsewhere, see items 150, 303, and 592.

248. Schlee, Thomas Daniel and Dietrich Kämpfer, ed. *Olivier Messiaen: La Cité céleste—Das himmlische Jerusalem: Über Leben und Werk des französischen Komponisten*. With a foreword by Hermann Josef Schuster. Köln: Wienand Verlag, 1998. 239 p. ISBN: 387909585X. ML 141.C64 M476 1998.

A collection of essays inspired by Messiaen's significant influence on the compositional thought and music of modern times. Published in 1998 to accompany a traveling exhibition on Messiaen's life and music. Organized by the Guardini Stiftung, the exhibition was held at the Akademie der Künste, Berlin, and eight other European cities. Provides a rich and varied profile of Messiaen. Includes papers by Claude Samuel, Père Jean-Rodolphe Kars, Elmar Budde, former students of Messiaen, and Chong-Hui Choe-Thomas. Also contains excerpts of interviews with Messiaen by Samuel (*Musique et Couleur* [item 175]) and Brigitte Massin (*Olivier Messiaen: Une poétique du merveilleux* [item 171]). Concludes with a long "life and works" section by Thomas Daniel Schlee. In its appendix, contains a glossary of selected pitch and rhythmic components of Messiaen's musical vocabulary. Beautifully illustrated. For individual entries not duplicated elsewhere, see items 260, 263, 282, 301, 305, and 424.

249. Sholl, Robert ed. *Messiaen Studies*. Cambridge Composer Series. Cambridge: Cambridge University Press, 2007. 296 p. ISBN-13: 9780521839815.

Not yet published. Available from November 2007. The following description is derived from the Web site at Cambridge University Press (www.cambridge.org/us/catalogue/catalogue.asp?isbn=0521839815): "The French composer Olivier Messiaen is one of the major figures of twentieth-century music. This collection of scholarly essays offers new cultural, historical, biographical and analytical perspectives on Messiaen's musical œuvre from 1941 to 1992. The volume includes: a fascinating snapshot of Messiaen's life in occupied France; a study of the Surrealist poetics of Messiaen's song cycle *Harawi*; a chapter on Messiaen's iconoclastic path to the avant-garde heritage that he bequeathed to his pupils; discussion on Messiaen's place in twentieth-century music; and detailed analysis of specific works, including his opera *Saint François d'Assise*. The chapters provide fresh insights on the origins, style and poetics of Messiaen's music, and therefore provide an inspiration and foundation for future scholarship. Reflecting and expanding upon the broad range of Messiaen's own interdisciplinary interests, the book will be of interest to students and scholars of music, art, literature and theology. Contributors include Nigel Simeone, Robert Sholl, Paul McNulty, Sander van Maas, Allen Forte, Jeremy Thurlow, Amy Bauer, Andrew Shenton, Stefan Keym, Robert Fallon, and Arnold Whittall."

250. Zahn, Dieter, and Angelika Hartmann, ed. *Olivier Messiaen: Das Orgelwerk*. Berlin: The Authors, 1991. 78 p.

A publication devoted to an examination of Messiaen's organ music. Includes: (1) a facsimile of Messiaen's handwritten essay on faith (originally published in 1978 as an untitled introduction to *La Recherche Artistique présente hommage à Olivier Messiaen* [see item 247]) accompanied by a German translation; (2) a chronology of Messiaen's life through 1978; (3) an anonymous German translation of Messiaen's lecture at the Brussels International Exposition on 15 September 1958 (see item 93); (4) a German translation of part of the conclusion of Messiaen's address upon his reception of the Erasmus Prize on 25 June 1971 in Amsterdam; (5) an interview with Messiaen conducted by Karin Ernst on 24 October 1977 in Paris (taken from Ernst's book *Der Beitrag Olivier Messiaens zur Orgel-musik des 20. Jahrhunderts* [see item 229]); (6) an essay on birdsong in Messiaen's music by Dieter Zahn; and (7) commentaries on Messiaen's organ music from *Le Banquet céleste* (1928) to *Livre du Saint Sacrement* (1984), drawn from the composer's prefaces to his organ works, liner notes, and other writings. For individual entries not duplicated elsewhere, see items 150 and 372.

251. "Zum 80. Geburtstag von Olivier Messiaen: Zu: 'Méditations sur le mystère de la Sainte Trinité' und zu 'Couleurs de la cité cèleste' [and 'Neumes Rythmiques']." *Musik und Bildung* 20/11 (November 1988). ISSN: 0027–4747.

A special issue celebrating Messiaen's eightieth birthday on 10 December 1988. Features analyses of *Méditations sur le mystère de la Sainte Trinité*, *Couleurs de la Cité cèleste*, and *Neumes rythmiques*. For individual entries, see items 464, 517, and 556.

GENERAL BIOGRAPHICAL, HISTORICAL, AND STYLISTIC DISCUSSIONS OF MESSIAEN AND HIS MUSIC IN ARTICLES AND ESSAYS IN COLLECTED EDITIONS

252. Anderson, Julian. "Olivier Messiaen (1908–92): An Appreciation." *The Musical Times* 133/1795 (September 1992): 449–51. ISSN: 0027–4666.

A tribute to Messiaen highlighting his life and work on the occasion of his death on 28 April 1992. Notes the contradictions associated with Messiaen as both a composer and person.

253. Angermann, Klaus. "Die Wollust der Ordnung: Messiaens constructive Sinnlichkeit." *Neue Zeitschrift für Musik* 149/9 (September 1988): 11–17. ISSN: 0170–8791.

Argues that the principles of order driving Messiaen's music are distinguished by an eclectic approach to composition and based upon a multi-dimensional concept of time. As models of these principles, cites different structural processes found in works of the 1940s to 80s. Sound-color relationships, linguistic structures, and religious elements are not only a part of these models but also are viewed metaphorically as a resonance structure, in which sensuous appeal and rational thought are reconciled through their interdependence. Also considers how Debussy, Wagner, Scriabin, Wyschnegradsky and colored-hearing synesthesia in general may have influenced Messiaen.

254. [Anonymous]. "Biographie d'Olivier Messiaen." In *Olivier Messiaen, homme de foi: Regard sur son œuvre d'orgue* (item 238), 14–15.

A short biographical sketch of Messiaen. Contains the usual highlights of his life and career, such as his birth in Avignon, childhood in Grenoble, studies at the Paris Conservatoire, organ position at La Trinité, association with La Jeune France, internment at a prisoner-of-war camp in Silesia during World War II, teaching post at the Paris Conservatoire, and the honors he garnered in his later years.

255. Armfelt, Nicholas. "Emotion in the Music of Messiaen." *The Musical Times* 106 (November 1965): 856–58. ISSN: 0027–4666.

Armfelt considers the emotive qualities of Messiaen's music through an examination of its most striking features. He views Messiaen's music as evoking intense statement rather than argument, an emotive quality that disturbs most critical listeners. Armfelt examines the relationship between Messiaen's compositional style and the various emotions associated with his music. He concludes his essay by stating that although listeners may not share Messiaen's religious beliefs, they can surely accept the fullness of its expression.

256. Beechey, Gwilym. "Christian Symbolism in Messiaen's Music." *Musical Opinion* 104/1242 (April 1981): 261–62. ISSN: 0027–4623.

A short article dealing with how Messiaen conveys Christian symbolism in his music. The study draws attention to Messiaen's harmonic and rhythmic practices, along with his use of plainsong, as the primary means he uses to express symbolic elements in his music. To illustrate its points, the article draws upon Messiaen's organ music up to *Méditations sur le mystère de la Sainte Trinité* (1969).

257. Bernard[-Delapierre], Guy. "Souvenirs sur Olivier Messiaen." *Formes et couleurs* (Lausanne: André Held), nos. 3–4 (1945): unpaginated (10 pp.).

An article of historical importance written by Guy Bernard-Delapierre, dedicatee of the *Technique de mon langage musical*, shortly after the premiere of the *Trois petites Liturgies de la Présence Divine* on 21 April 1945. He describes his first meeting with Messiaen while the two were being held captive by the German army in an open field near Toul, west of Nancy. He identifies Étienne Pasquier, the cellist of the Pasquier Trio, and Henri Akoka, a clarinetist, who were both going to participate in the historic performance of the *Quatuor pour la fin du Temps* approximately seven months later, as two people among a group of the composer's friends who tenderly deferred to

him. For his part, Messiaen seemed to transcend the difficult circumstances experienced by all of the prisoners in the camp. Bernard-Delapierre also provides information about Messiaen's ideas
on music, religion, and philosophy through conversations he had
with the composer while in captivity. Messiaen talked about how
Western music should be enriched by new modes and new rhythms,
and how he derived inspiration from plainsong and Hindu ragas.
The composer also discussed the role Christianity played in his
work, where both creator and creation were celebrated. Bernard-
Delapierre then describes his encounters with Messiaen after the
two were repatriated to Paris, such as hearing Messiaen and Marcelle Bunlet perform selections from *Poèmes pour Mi* and *Chants de
Terre et de Ciel* at his home on the rue Visconti, or Messiaen
improvise at La Trinité. But most importantly, he discusses the
reception of Messiaen's music, both positive and negative, at the
time. He describes the premiere of the *Trois petites Liturgies* as a
near-unanimous success, noting the approval of people like Jean
Cocteau, Francis Poulenc, and Arthur Honegger. Thus, his review,
in conjunction with many other favorable ones of the concert, tends
to dispel the myth that the music of the *Trois petites Liturgies* pre-
cipitated the "Le Cas Messiaen" affair, rather than a variety of
extra-musical matters (such as Messiaen's commentaries to his works)
as articulated by Lilise Boswell-Kurc in her dissertation on Messiaen's
war-time works (see item 205). Indeed, *Trois petites Liturgies* was
recognized at the time as a masterpiece by both press and public.

258. Borris, Siegfried. "Olivier Messiaen: Der pater gloriosus der Neuen
Musik." *Musica* 38/4 (July/August 1984): 331–35. ISSN: 0027–4518.

A stylistic overview of Messiaen's music. Discusses his compositional
techniques in relation to his musical works.

259. Bruhn, Siglind. "Religious Symbolism in the Music of Olivier Messiaen." *The American Journal of Semiotics* 13/1–4 (Fall 1996 [1998]):
277–309. ISSN: 0277–7126.

Notes that Messiaen's musical language remained uniform throughout his career due to his zeal for promoting his Catholic faith
through music. Views the three poles that Messiaen's music revolves
around (the theological truths of his Catholic faith, human love as
manifested by Tristan and Isolde, and nature as typified through
birdsong) as different manifestations of God's love. Believes that
within each pole are a variety of subtopics that reveal both the
consistency and richness of Messiaen's religious symbolism.
Explores the symbols related to each pole and their subtopics by
focusing on: (1) the symmetrical organization of tonal material as

expressions of God's perfection and love; (2) the symmetrical and dissymmetrical unfolding of rhythm to represent time and eternity; (3) congruency and incongruency in multi-layered passages and their relationship to time or the lack thereof; and (4) leitmotifs and themes and how they symbolize God's perfection. Examples are taken from *Vingt Regards sur l'Enfant-Jésus* (1944).

260. Budde, Elmar. "Vom Zauber des Unmöglichen: Zur geschichtlichen Voraussetzung des Komponierens von Farbklängen und Klangfarben in Werk Olivier Messiaens." In *Olivier Messiaen: La Cité céleste – Das himmlische Jerusalem: Über Leben und Werk des französischen Komponisten* (item 248), 21–27.

Uses Messiaen's ideas on sound-color relationships and the "charm of impossibilities" as the framework for a study of the correlation between time and color as a musical-immanent material problem from the nineteenth to early twentieth centuries. Looks at connections between sound and color as reflected in the thought and/or writings of E. T. A. Hoffmann, Schumann, Scriabin, Kandinsky, Schoenberg, and Adorno. Relates this historical survey to Messiaen's compositional aesthetic.

261. Chamfray, Claude. "Olivier Messiaen." *Le Courrier musical de France* 56 (4e trimestre 1976): 163–65.

A biography of Messiaen in the form of a three-column note card ("fiche"). From left to right, it lists important dates through 1975, Messiaen's age during those years, and his activities ranging from studies at the Paris Conservatoire to premieres of his works.

262. Charru, Philippe. "La théologie sonore d'Olivier Messiaen." *Études* (July-August 1996): 91–100. ISSN: 0014–1941.

Views Messiaen as a musical evangelist through the medium of his organ music. He sought to convey Christian truths through an instrument which was capable of supplying a great variety of timbres, prolonged sounds, pulsing rhythms, and extremely slow tempos that help to suspend musical time, hence expressing spiritual concepts that are indefinable.

263. Choe-Thomas, Chong-Hui. "Eine Kunst des modernen Europas? Vom 'Vogelhändler von Paris' zur 'Jahrhundertfigur': Zur Rezeption Olivier Messiaens in Deutschland." In *Olivier Messiaen: La Cité céleste – Das himmlische Jerusalem: Über Leben und Werk des französischen Komponisten* (item 248), 49–61.

An examination of Messiaen's critical reception by the German musical establishment. Describes Messiaen's initial encounter with

Germany as a prisoner-of-war in Stalag VIII A in Görlitz, Silesia, which resulted in the composition of the *Quatuor pour la fin du Temps*. Looks at Messiaen's teaching activities in Darmstadt and association with the festival for new music in Donaueschingen after World War II. Mentions the tremendous impact *Mode de valeurs et d'intensités* had on German musicians, particularly Stockhausen, and the impetus it gave to a new type of serial music. In the 1950s, Messiaen was hailed as one of the most important composers of new music by the German musical establishment. Messiaen was increasingly honored and recognized in Germany in the 1950s through 70s with birthday celebrations and festivals in his honor. Provides a detailed look at Messiaen's reception by the German press. Notes Messiaen's continued recognition in Germany in the 1980s.

264. Darbyshire, Ian. "Messiaen and the Representation of the Theological Illusion of Time." In *Messiaen's Language of Mystical Love* (item 236), 33–51.

Describes the dual character inherent in Messiaen's conception of music as a combination of the scientific and the supernatural. Focuses on Messiaen's representation of time, which is closely allied to spatial conceptions. Because of Messiaen's investigation of musical duration, compares the composer to a musical geometer who uses numbers to divide time just as a geometer uses numbers to divide space.

265. Dickinson, Peter. "Messiaen: Composer of Crisis." *Music and Musicians* 10 (October 1966): 26–30. ISSN: 0027-4232.

A stylistic survey of Messiaen's music. Divides the composer's output into three periods: (1) 1928–34, (2) 1935–48, and (3) 1948–66. Considers the junctures between periods as moments of crisis where Messiaen would turn to the organ or piano as a means to develop as a composer. States that his musical style is already evident in the first period. Examines the *Préludes* for piano (1929), noting Messiaen's use of melodies based on the tritone, the modes of limited transposition, added-sixth chords, polychordal textures, and ostinatos. The second period is characterized by an increasing interest in rhythm and emphasis on theological content, as seen through *La Nativité du Seigneur* (1935) and its use of added values, two ostinatos of different lengths set against each other, passages that feature stylized birdsong, and scriptural prefaces. (Missing in this examination is Messiaen's use of Hindu rhythmic patterns.) The third period is distinguished by an even stronger emphasis on rhythm and greater exploration of birdsong. Messiaen's increasing preoccupation with rhythm provoked a crisis at the end of the second period, which can be felt in *Cantéyodjayâ* (1949) and *Mode de valeurs et d'intensités* (1949) of the third period. In assessing Messiaen's position as a composer in 1966, the author argues that the tension between natural lyricism and rhythmic organization, which was quite evident in the music of the first and second periods, has been toned down in the works of the third. He concludes that what might assure Messiaen an historical place in the mid-twentieth century is less Catholic fervor and more technical integration in his music.

266. Dingle, Christopher. "Charm and Simplicity: Messiaen's final works." *Tempo* 192 (April 1995): 2–7. ISSN: 0040–2982.

Proposes that Messiaen changed his compositional style in the last years of his life, becoming a master of musical understatement after the composition of colossal works such as *La Transfiguration de Nôtre-Seigneur Jésus-Christ* and *Saint François d'Assise.* Surveys Messiaen's final works, starting with *Petites esquisses d'oiseaux* (1985) and concluding with *Concert à quatre* (1992). Special attention is given to *Éclairs sur l'Au- Delà* (1988–92) as an example of Messiaen's new approach to composition.

267. Flynn, George. "Olivier Messiaen: Mystical Composer." *The Christian Century*, 1 July 1992, 652–54.

A tribute to Messiaen on the occasion of his death in 1992. Describes the importance of Messiaen's Roman Catholic faith and interest in its more mystical aspects, and their influences on his music. Outlines the development of Messiaen's approaches to rhythm, harmony, and sound-color relationships, which characterize much of his music and shape its religious character. Looks at the "Quartet for the End of Time." Describes the influence Messiaen had on young composers and his younger colleagues in the 1940s and 50s and the international attention garnered by his music.

268. Forster, Max. "Das Meditative in der Musik Olivier Messiaens." *Musica sacra* 98/6 (1978): 344–54.

Examines the relationship between the musical and extra-musical in Messiaen's works that bear the title "Meditation," as in *La Nativité du Seigneur* and *Méditations sur le mystère de la Sainte Trinité.* Looks at "La Vierge et l'Enfant" from *La Nativité* and concludes that Messiaen created meditative music through the use of both traditional and nontraditional compositional techniques. By juxtaposing strict and free structures, Messiaen expressed different aspects of a theme necessary for the suggestion of meditative music.

269. Fowler, J. Roger. "An Introduction to the Music of Olivier Messiaen." *The Chesterian* (January 1954): 77–83.

As a response to Messiaen's increasing musical stature in post-war England, Fowler surveys the composer's life and music (up to the early 1950s due to the article's date) in order to further a better appreciation of Messiaen's work on the part of the English musical public. He discusses Messiaen's music chronologically, noting the components of the composer's aesthetics and musical language. The article contains some inaccurate statements (e.g., Messiaen born in Grenoble instead of Avignon [p. 78]) and does not provide sources for its quotations by Messiaen.

270. Freeman, Robin. "Trompette d'un Ange Secret: Olivier Messiaen and the Culture of Ecstasy." *Contemporary Music Review* 14/3–4 (1996): 81–125. ISSN: 0749–4467.

Freeman explores the relationship between Messiaen's cultural interests and music. To draw a picture of the composer's cultural profile, Freeman examines Messiaen's interests in art, literature, music, philosophy, poetry, and theology, with the goal of either supplementing or clarifying what Messiaen said in different interviews and lectures. According to Freeman, Messiaen might have been the last great figure in a nineteenth-century resurgence of Catholic art that reached its apogee after the Franco-Prussian war. By situating Messiaen's music in the culture from which it arose, Freeman believes that he presents a view of Messiaen that other scholars with more purely musical agendas may have been unaware.

271. Fulcher, Jane F. "The Politics of Transcendence: Ideology in the Music of Messiaen in the 1930s." *The Musical Quarterly* 86/3 (Fall 2002): 449–71. ISSN: 0027–4631.

Fulcher interprets the early music of Messiaen in political terms, by situating him and the rest of La Jeune France (Yves Baudrier, André Jolivet, and Daniel-Lesur) within the ideological-aesthetic clashes occurring in France in the mid-1930s. La Jeune France opposed the cultural ideals of both the political Left and Right. They strove for a new kind of cultural ideal, one based on a spirituality that was both universal and all-encompassing in its dimensions, a "politics of the spirit" that resembled the ideals of the nonconformist movement of French intellectuals, who sought a "third path" linking progressive Catholicism with politics and ideology. Thus for Fulcher, Messiaen was not a composer merely impelled by his Catholic faith, but one who turned to nonconformist ideals to guide his work. In the final analysis, Messiaen transcended religion and engaged political ideology, in short blurring the boundaries between the two, by composing a music that balanced innovation with French tradition.

272. Gautier, Jean-François. "Olivier Messiaen et ses eléves." *Le Spectacle du monde* 202 (January 1979): 107–10.

A tribute to Messiaen's impact as both composer and teacher on the musical world on the occasion of his seventieth birthday (10 December 1978). Notes the influences of Dukas, Debussy, the music of India, birdsong, and plainchant on his music and how they became a part of his pedagogical approach. Also mentions the significance of Messiaen's Catholic faith in his compositional aesthetic. Discusses the accomplishments of Messiaen's students, such as Boulez, Xenakis, Claude Ballif, and Pierre Henry.

273. Gavoty, Bernard. "Musique et mystique: Le 'Cas' Messiaen." *Les Études* (October 1945): 21–37.

In this article, Gavoty recognizes Messiaen's abilities as a composer. He likens the controversial reception of Messiaen's music in Paris in the mid-1940s, known as "Le Cas Messiaen," to other French controversies involving Dreyfuss and Wagner. However, Gavoty harshly criticizes Messiaen for his *Technique de mon langage musical*, which he found to be both erudite and irritating, and his notices and commentaries. He questions Messiaen's sincerity as a person and the profane atmosphere of his supposedly Christian music. (For more information on the "Le Cas Messiaen" affair, including discussions of the numerous articles and reviews written either criticizing or defending Messiaen, see item 205—Lilise Boswell-Kurc, "Olivier Messiaen's Religious War-time Works and their Controversial Reception in France [1941–46]".)

274. Gillock, Jon. "Olivier Messiaen: A Biographical Sketch." In *Celebration Messiaen: The Complete Works for Organ* (item 239): 4–7.

A sketch of Messiaen's life and works. Written by a former student and one of the best interpreters of his organ music. Besides highlighting major events, compositions, and performances, mentions the importance of theology, birdsong, and sound-color relationships in Messiaen's compositional world.

275. Goléa, Antoine. "Das Weltbild des Komponisten Olivier Messiaen." *Neue Zeitschrift für Musik* 130 (1969): 22–25. ISSN: 0170–8791.

An essay that attempts to describe Messiaen's view of life as reflected in his music. Believes that it is driven by a stress on a timeless universalism brought about by the deep spiritual unity of his musical language. Considers how that unity is conveyed musically. Concludes that Messiaen is not only an artist who strives for a physical and spiritual unity in his works, or a Catholic in the deepest sense of the word, or a bold pioneer in the fields of melody, harmony, and rhythm, but also an innovator who has enriched the actual sound of music through different textural and timbral means.

276. Griffiths, Paul. "Poèmes and Haïkaï: A Note on Messiaen's Development." *The Musical Times* 112 (September 1971): 851–52. ISSN: 0027–4666.

A reflection on the development of Messiaen's musical style during a twenty-five year period, spanning 1937 to 1962 using *Poèmes pour Mi* (1936) and *Sept Haïkaï* (1962) as stylistic yardsticks. After noting certain constant aspects of the composer's approach to composition, Griffiths distinguishes early Messiaen from later Messiaen through changes in compositional technique, concluding that the early music is motivated more by a mystical, surrealistic vision in which Messiaen personalizes his conception of God, whereas the later music is motivated more by a mystical, naturalistic vision in which Messiaen presents a more objective view of God, inviting the world to be filled with awe and joy.

277. Hill, Peter. "Introduction [to *The Messiaen Companion*]." In *The Messiaen Companion* (item 240), 1–11.

In this introduction to *The Messiaen Companion*, Hill looks at Messiaen's work as a musician in order to set the stage for the more detailed consideration taken up by the book's authors. He notes an adherence to a basic set of principles as Messiaen's most remarkable trait, producing works that exhibit a consistent musical language and technique regardless of their position in the composer's œuvre. To complete his picture of Messiaen, Hill discusses the composer's literary interests and religious faith and their impact on his music, preoccupation with time, musical life during the 1930s and 40s, interest in birdsong, and composition of massive works in the mid-1960s to mid-80s as an elder statesman of music.

278. Hirsbrunner, Theo. "Olivier Messiaen: '... sehr schwer einzuordnen!'." *Die Musikforschung* 42/3 (July/September 1989): 222–32. ISSN: 0027–4801.

Argues that the reason why Messiaen is so difficult to classify as a composer is because he incorporates non-Western elements into his musical language. In advancing this thesis, discusses Messiaen's serial techniques as found in "Mode de valeurs et d'intensités" from the *Quatre Études de rythme*, "La Chouette Hulotte" from *Catalogue d'oiseaux*, and "Les Stigmates" from *Saint François d'Assise*; the modes of limited transposition; and the *langage communicable*.

279. Hsu (Forte), Madeleine. "Bartók: Messiaen's Master of Thought?" *Journal of the American Liszt Society* 35 (January-June 1994): 61–86. ISSN: 0147–4413.

Investigates Bartók's influence on Messiaen. Documents Messiaen's admiration for Bartók, despite his downplaying of Bartók's importance as a twentieth-century composer. While exploring both significant similarities and differences between the two composers, emphasizes many traits that the two share in common. Drawn from chapter four of the author's monograph on Messiaen (see item 230—*Olivier Messiaen, the Musical Mediator: A Study of the Influence of Liszt, Debussy, and Bartók*), this article was published in advance of the monograph's publication in 1996.

280. Ide, le Père Pascal. "Olivier Messiaen théologien?" In *Portrait(s) d'Olivier Messiaen* (item 241), 39–46.

Père Pascal Ide, a doctor of philosophy and priest at La Trinité, proposes that Messiaen should be considered a theologian despite the fact that he did not write any theological works. Although Père Ide acknowledges the disquieting nature of his thesis, he believes that Messiaen merits the title. He notes how the majority of Messiaen's works celebrate the mysteries of the Christian faith. Even profane works such as the *Turangalîla-Symphonie* still have a religious connection as human love is but a reflection of divine love. Père Ide considers elements found in Messiaen's musical language, such as nonretrogradable rhythms or sound-color relationships, as evoking the transcendence of God. He also points out how Messiaen saw evidence of God in creation, as exemplified, for instance, by his *Des canyons aux étoiles*. In sum, Père Ide, quoting Harry Halbreich (see item 209), regards Messiaen as a harbinger of a great return to God that has characterized the end of the current millennium.

281. Ide, le Père Pascal. "Une rencontre décisive." In *Olivier Messiaen, homme de foi: Regard sur son œuvre d'orgue* (item 238), 76–79.

In this essay, Père Ide explores relationships between Messiaen and Saint Thomas Aquinas (1225–74). He examines their shared conceptions of God as being simple and joyous, approaches to theology, and similarities in spirit. In particular, Père Ide looks at how Messiaen and Aquinas both addressed theological subjects with a certain sense of detachment, how they could find Christian truth in unlikely sources, and how their theology embraced the horizontal and vertical aspects of the Cross.

282. Kars, Père Jean-Rodolphe. "Das Werk Olivier Messiaens und die katholische Liturgie." In *Olivier Messiaen: La Cité céleste—Das himmlische Jerusalem: Über Leben und Werk des französischen Komponisten* (item 248), 12–20.

A discussion of Messiaen's music as it relates to the Catholic liturgy. Père Kars looks at those works (primarily for organ) by Messiaen that either were designed for the liturgy or could easily play a role in it, as well as the more numerous compositions for the concert hall. In the latter case, the religious dimension is always present in a work's aesthetic orientation even if that piece manifests no obvious theological symbolism. In other words, these concert works are liturgical but in a broader sense of the term. Père Kars considers Messiaen's work as an organist and the sacramental and eschatological qualities of his music. As he examines Messiaen's musical language, Père Kars deems it necessary to continue to broaden the scope of what a liturgy means. He suggests that Messiaen's music evokes a cosmic liturgy, an ecstatic contemplation of the divine, a liturgy that knows no boundaries as it illuminates the mysteries of God through colored music.

283. Kars, Père Jean-Rodolphe. "Hommage à Olivier Messiaen." In *Olivier Messiaen, homme de foi: Regard sur son œuvre d'orgue* (item 238), 99.

An affectionate tribute by a former concert pianist turned priest who discusses Messiaen's spiritual impact upon him. Père Kars recounts his background—studies at the Paris Conservatoire, finalist at the Leeds International Piano Competition in 1967, first-prize winner at the First International Olivier Messiaen Piano Competition in 1968—that prepared him for his subsequent career as a concert pianist. In 1966 Père Kars began to study the piano music of Messiaen. He was fascinated by the music and passionate about the composer's accompanying commentaries. This led ultimately, in his opinion, to his conversion to Catholicism and vocation as a priest. In the final analysis, Père Kars considers Messiaen as his first spiritual father, as he and his music were used to bring Kars closer to God.

284. Lesur, Daniel- [Jean Yves]. "Hommage à Olivier Messiaen." In *Olivier Messiaen, homme de foi: Regard sur son œuvre d'orgue* (item 238), 89–90.

Daniel-Lesur reminisces about his association with Messiaen. He admired Messiaen as a composer, organist, and person. He fondly remembers the world premiere of *La Nativité du Seigneur* on 27 February 1936 when Messiaen, judging the piece to be too long and difficult for one organist to play, asked him to perform the work's first three movements (Jean Langlais played movements four through six, while Jean-Jacques Grunenwald played movements seven through nine). Daniel-Lesur also notes the delight he took in his intellectual interactions with Messiaen, and recalls the founding of La Jeune France of which he and Messiaen, along with Jolivet and Baudrier, were members.

285. Lyons, David Spence. "Olivier Messiaen." *Music in Education* 31/ 327 (September/October 1967): 567–70. ISSN: 0027–0433X.

Discusses Messiaen's work as a composer and teacher and tries to understand how he fits into the contemporary music scene of the mid-1960s. Contains some inaccuracies (e.g., the orchestral version of *L'Ascension* appearing after the organ version, not before; La Jeune France formed in 1931, not 1936).

286. Massip, Catherine, comp. "Regards sur Olivier Messiaen: Textes réunis par Catherine Massip." In *Portrait(s) d'Olivier Messiaen* (item 241), 7–38.

Presents a biographical sketch and portrait of Messiaen through various documents that include his program notes, prefaces, letters, and articles, as well as essays about Messiaen and his music by others. Contains many photographs of Messiaen throughout his career.

287. Mellers, Wilfrid. "Mysticism and Theology." In *The Messiaen Companion* (item 240), 220–33.

Mellers explores Messiaen's religious views and their impact on his music. He contrasts the religion of "Faustian" man with Messiaen's Catholicism. The former is a Protestant version of Christianity in which the ego and will are emphasized, while the latter exemplifies the Old Faith in which freedom from the ego and will is sought in order to find one's self. Mellers argues that from his earliest days, Messiaen sought to achieve such a release in his music through the use of a static harmonic language, which freed the sensory moment from any notion of a before and after. Mellers then links Messiaen's music with the early music of Satie and much of Debussy's music, claiming that these works can be characterized as mystical because of their lack of linear movement. The rest of the essay focuses on the *Quatuor pour la fin du Temps*, *Cinq Rechants*, and *Chronochromie*. In his examination of "Abîme des oiseaux," the third movement of the *Quatuor*, Mellers makes inaccurate statements regarding the use of microtonal pitches and Hindu ragas. In his discussion of *Chronochromie*, he notes the influence of rhythmic proportions inherent in nature and the music of Varèse on the work's composition. Mellers concludes by ruminating on whether or not Messiaen was a theosophical or theological composer, stating in the final analysis that he strove to embrace what Saint Thomas Aquinas considered to be the essence of God: bliss itself.

288. Messiaen, Alain. "Olivier Messiaen's 'Message'." *Musical Opinion* 103/1227 (January 1980): 133–34, 136. ISSN: 0027–4623.

An essay on Messiaen by his younger brother Alain (1912–90). Alain reminisces about the time when he and Olivier were children in Grenoble, especially when Olivier introduced him to Shakespeare, Maeterlinck, Calderon, and Ibsen. He surveys Olivier's life, musical style, and works through *La Transfiguration de Nôtre-Seigneur Jésus-Christ*.

289. Michaely, Aloyse. "L'Abîme: Das Bild des Abgrunds bei Olivier Messiaen." In *Musik-Konzepte 28: Olivier Messiaen* (item 243), 7–55.

Examines the symbol of the abyss in the music of Messiaen. Investigates its origins and theological connotations in the Bible and writings of the Early Church Fathers. Considers its place and meaning in Messiaen's compositional aesthetics and how it is represented musically in his works. Highly recommended.

290. Michaely, Aloyse. "Messiaens Trinitästraktate." *Musik und Kirche* 69/2 (March/April 1999): 90–98. ISSN: 0027–4771.

A consideration of the significance of the Trinity in Messiaen's music. Analyzes "Le Mystère de la Saint Trinité" from *Les Corps glorieux* and the fifth movement of the *Méditations sur le mystère de la Sainte Trinité*. Discusses how Messiaen uses musical techniques to depict the Persons of the Trinity.

291. Nardin, Paul. "Souvenirs." In *L'Orgue: Revue trimestrielle* 224 (item 246), 44–45.

A tribute to Messiaen that underscores the importance of his religious beliefs.

292. Nichols, Roger. "Boulez on Messiaen: Pierre Boulez in Conversation with Roger Nichols." *Organists' Review* 71/283 (1986): 167–70. ISSN: 0048–2161.

An interview in which Boulez comments on both his relationship to Messiaen as well as his former mentor's music. Boulez recounts his early studies with Messiaen as a harmony teacher, noting how Messiaen emphasized the evolution of harmonic style from the seventeenth through twentieth centuries in his classes, making links between different composers clear and comprehensible. Boulez then turns to the influence of the music of Asia on Messiaen, stating that in the final analysis, Messiaen absorbed such influences so completely that his music bears little resemblance to that of Asia. Finally, Boulez ruminates on various subjects, such as the influence of *Mode de valeurs et d'intensités* on the serial music scene of postwar Europe, Messiaen's penchant for using block forms, the premiere of the *Trois petites Liturgies de la Présence Divine* in 1945, conducting the tempi found in Messiaen's orchestral compositions, and Messiaen's foray into electronic music in 1952.

293. de Obaldia, René. "Hommage à Olivier Messiaen." In *Olivier Messiaen, homme de foi: Regard sur son œuvre d'orgue* (item 238), 93–95.

De Obaldia begins his tribute to Messiaen by discussing the composer's work as an organist at La Trinité during 1945–50. He then describes how he first met Messiaen before the war with Germany in 1940. At that time, de Obaldia was associated with literary circles that had aesthetic goals comparable to those espoused by La Jeune France, of which Messiaen was a member. There were meetings in Parisian salons where ideas were exchanged between writers and musicians desirous of new modes of expression. At one of those meetings, de Obaldia heard Messiaen improvise on a popular song of the day, "Les Gars de la Marine." Shortly after that, de Obaldia gave Messiaen a copy of one of his poems, "Action de Grâces," and a friendship began. De Obaldia then describes how he and Messiaen talked not only about music but literature as well. He found out that besides his taste for Shakespeare and the poetry of his mother Cécile Sauvage, Messiaen liked H. G. Wells, Robert Louis Stevenson, and Ernest Hello. De Obaldia concludes his essay by remarking how Messiaen continues to speak to the world through his music and how he encourages everyone to become children again in order to marvel at the world's beauty.

294. Petersen, Birger. "Musique théologique? Zur Analyse der Musik Olivier Messiaens." *Musik & Ästhetik* 8/31 (July 2004): 88–96. ISSN: 1432–9425.

Posits that Messiaen's music has been analyzed from either formal-compositional or theological-semantic perspectives. Notes that Stefan Keym's study of *Saint François d'Assise* (see item 442) attempts to synthesize the two viewpoints by focusing on color and time. Claims that Keym is not consistent in avoiding the semantical approaches he criticizes.

295. Peterson, Larry W. "Messiaen and Surrealism: A Study of His Poetry." In *Messiaen's Language of Mystical Love* (item 236), 215–24.

Explores the surrealist framework of the poetry Messiaen wrote for his art songs, *Trois petites Liturgies de la Présence Divine,* and *Cinq Rechants.* Not only uses the work of André Breton and Paul Éluard to define surrealism but also compares their work with that of Messiaen. Demonstrates how surrealist elements such as extravagant imagery, irrationality, and the "concept of the artistic relationship between the artist's work and his soul or inner self" are all present in Messiaen's poems.

296. Quénetain, Tanneguy de. "Messiaen: Poet of Nature." *Music and Musicians* 11/9 (May 1963): 8–12. ISSN: 0027–4232.

An overview of Messiaen's life and music through 1963. Looks at those factors that shaped his musical world, such as his exposure to Shakespeare as a child, his marriage to Claire Delbos, his association with La Jeune France, his internment as a prisoner of war in a Silesian stalag, his teaching post at the Paris Conservatoire where he met Yvonne Loriod, "Le Cas Messiaen," and his views on religion, which motivated him to study relationships between time and eternity as well as to commune with nature through birdsong. The article's biggest drawback is the lack of documentation for its quotes and many of its statements.

297. Rostand, Claude. "Messiaen erneuert die französische Musik." In *Melos* 25/12 (item 242), 393–96.

In his discussion of Messiaen's impact on French music, Rostand provides an overview of Messiaen's life and works, looks at his musical and literary influences, and surveys his musical techniques.

298. Rostand, Claude. "Olivier Messiaen." *Melos* 23 (October 1956): 284–86.

A short essay on Messiaen translated into German by Willi Reich. The essay's original publication is not specified. Rostand examines Messiaen's life and work through 1956. He surveys Messiaen's family background, student years at the Paris Conservatoire, and musical activities beginning in the 1930s. He then considers the role of religion in Messiaen's musical aesthetics as well as his compositional techniques.

299. Roy, Jean. "Olivier Messiaen." *Études* 371/1–2 (July/August 1989): 67–74. ISSN: 0014-1941.

A stylistic examination of Messiaen's music through *Saint François d'Assise.*

300. Sabatier, François. "Bérenger de Miramon Fitz-James et Olivier Messiaen." In *L'Orgue: Revue trimestrielle* 224 (item 246), 5–11.

Examines the unpublished correspondence between Bérenger de Miramon Fitz-James, founding president of Amis de l'Orgue and publisher of *L'Orgue*, and Norbert Dufourcq, noted musicologist and secretary of the society, from 1926–48. The letters contain references to Messiaen beginning in 1930 and ending in 1939.

301. Samuel, Claude. "Olivier Messiaen: Eine Würdigung." In *Olivier Messiaen: La Cité céleste – Das himmlische Jerusalem: Über Leben und Werk des französischen Komponisten* (item 248), 8–11.

In this tribute to Messiaen, Samuel draws a varied portrait of the composer by touching upon the contradictions that have characterized his life and work. The essay deals with a number of topics, including aspects of Messiaen's compositional process and musical style, his teaching at the Paris Conservatoire, his love of Japan and its people, the United States, the *Traité de rythme, de couleur, et d'ornithologie (1949–1992)*, and Schoenberg.

302. Samuel, Claude. "Hommage à Olivier Messiaen." In *Olivier Messiaen, homme de foi: Regard sur son œuvre d'orgue* (item 238), 84–85.

Ruminates about Messiaen and his position in contemporary music, arguing that the composer left a definite legacy in modern music despite listeners who could not fathom how such a religious person could be such a musical pioneer. For academics, Messiaen was an inoffensive eccentric, but to others, especially his former students, he was steeped in a world of musical innovation, sharing his ideas as both a composer and teacher. Although meeting Messiaen during his involvement with the first worldwide recording of the *Turangalîla-Symphonie* in the 1950s, Samuel got to know Messiaen better through later meetings and the two books of conversations completed in 1967 and 1986, respectively. During this time, Samuel was struck not only by the sincerity of Messiaen's faith but also by the sincere doubts the composer evinced toward each of his new works.

303. Samuel, Claude. "Olivier Messiaen ou la multiplicité transcendée." In *La Recherche Artistique présente hommage à Olivier Messiaen* (item 247), 6–10.

In this tribute Samuel recognizes Messiaen as one of the great composers of the twentieth century. He notes Messiaen's legacy as a teacher at the Paris Conservatoire where he attracted students from all over the world. Samuel considers Messiaen's creative work as revolving around the themes of: (1) nature; (2) sound-color relationships; (3) rhythm; (4) love; (5) and faith. In an age of doubt, suspicion, and despair, Samuel views Messiaen as a musician set apart, a man of faith conveying a different message.

304. Schlee, Thomas Daniel. "Olivier Messiaen: Musiker der Verkündigung." *Stimmen der Zeit* 220/11 (2002): 723–42. ISSN: 0039–1492.

     Regards the music of Messiaen as one of the most significant body of works composed in the twentieth century. Examines different spiritual and theological aspects of Messiaen's music. Looks at the importance of Messiaen's early years on his spiritual make-up, the influence of plainchant on his works, his theology as reflected in the *Conférence de Notre-Dame*, and various pieces from both musical and theological perspectives.

305. Schlee, Thomas Daniel. "La Cité céleste." In *Olivier Messiaen: La Cité céleste – Das himmlische Jerusalem: Über Leben und Werk des französischen Komponisten* (item 248), 64–233.

     A detailed and fascinating portrait of Messiaen that examines: (1) his association with the Paris Conservatoire as both student and teacher; (2) his childhood and adult years; (3) his religious beliefs; (4) birdsong; (5) sound-color relationships; (6) the music of the firmament; (7) the Tristan trilogy; (8) *Saint François d'Assise*; and (9) the *Quatuor pour la fin du Temps*. Accompanied by numerous photographs and facsimiles. Well worth the effort if you can read German.

306. Schlee, Thomas Daniel. "Hommage à Olivier Messiaen." *Österreichische Musikzeitschrift* 34/1 (January 1979): 28–40. ISSN: 0029–9316.

     Homage to Messiaen on the occasion of the composer's seventieth birthday from a former student and noted interpreter of his organ works. Schlee draws an affectionate portrait of Messiaen by using recollections from his student days at the Paris Conservatoire from 1977–78, anecdotal comments, and analytical and critical observations. He provides a biographical sketch of Messiaen, discusses his musical style, describes his teaching at the Paris Conservatoire, and talks about his work as an organist.

307. Schneider, Frank. "Olivier Messiaen oder die Botschaft der Liebe." *Beiträge zur Musikwissenschaft* 31/1 (1989): 39–49. ISSN: 0005–8106.

     Considers Messiaen as one of the most significant composers of the twentieth century. His compositional aesthetic is characterized by an inclusive approach to musical materials and intellectual thought. Messiaen has attempted to express divine love and redemption through his compositions. In this article, the author discusses these elements in relation to Messiaen's development as a composer.

308. Simeone, Nigel. "'Chez Messiaen, tout est prière': Messiaen's Appointment at the Trinité." *The Musical Times* 145/1889 (Winter 2004): 36–53. ISSN: 0027–4666.

Details the circumstances that led to Messiaen's appointment as organist titulaire at La Trinité in Paris, succeeding Charles Quef (1873–1931). Contains letters written by Marcel Dupré, Maurice Emmanuel, Charles Tournemire, and Charles-Marie Widor in support of Messiaen's application, as well as Messiaen's letters to Curé Hemmer, the parish priest of La Trinité, covering various issues related to his eventual appointment in 1931, including the Curé's reservations about Messiaen's playing of "dissonant" music when deputizing for Quef for two years. The rest of the article covers Messiaen's work at La Trinité after his appointment. The article is a must read for its valuable information about this often neglected aspect of Messiaen's life.

309. Simeone, Nigel. "Messiaen and the Concerts de la Pléiade: 'A Kind of Clandestine Revenge Against the Occupation.'" *Music and Letters* (November 2000): 551–69. ISSN: 0027–4224.

Simeone examines the genesis, rehearsal, performance, and reception of Messiaen's *Visions de l'Amen* and *Trois petites Liturgies de la Présence Divine* in light of the Concerts de la Pléiade for which they were composed. Before engaging in his examination, Simeone considers the origin of the Concerts de la Pléiade, examining the role film producer Denise Tual played in starting a concert series that was designed as an artistic resistance movement against the German Occupation of Paris during World War II, where performances of new or recent French music were banned. A must read for anyone interested in Messiaen's musical activities in the early 1940s.

310. Simeone, Nigel. "Messiaen in the 1930s: *Offrandes oubliées*." *The Musical Times* 141/1873 (Winter 2000): 33–41. ISSN: 0027–4666.

Examines Messiaen's professional and private life in the 1930s through: (1) a series of letters written by Messiaen to Claude Arrieu (1903–90); (2) three test pieces written by Messiaen as a faculty member at the École Normale de Musique that appeared in the musical supplements of *Le Monde musical*; and (3) three articles written by Messiaen published in *Le Monde musical*. Spanning the years 1929–41, although most date from 1931–34, the letters to Arrieu, who met Messiaen in Dukas's composition class at the Paris Conservatoire, reveal Messiaen's life as a young composer and teacher, husband and father, and dutiful citizen as seen by his military service Although two of Messiaen's test pieces were published later as a part of *Vingt Leçons de Solfège Modernes dans les Sept clés* by Henry Lemonie & Cie (*Solfège*—see item 85]) and *Vingt Leçons d'Harmonie* by Alphonse Leduc & Cie (*Chant donné*—see item 86), the third, *Morceau de Lecture à Vue* for piano, is heretofore unknown in the Messiaen literature. (According to Simeone [p. 40], Yvonne Loriod-Messiaen informed him that the piece will be published by Durand in the future. The author heard Peter Hill perform the piece on a concert at the Pennsylvania State University on 26 September 2006.) Finally, Simeone points out that two of the three articles by Messiaen are devoted to pieces the composer wrote or spoke little about (the orchestral version of *L'Ascension* and *Chants de Terre et de Ciel*), and that all three articles (the third focusing on *La Nativité du Seigneur*) were written when the pieces were relatively new.

311. Simeone, Nigel. "*Offrandes oubliées* 2: Messiaen, Boulanger and José Bruyr." *The Musical Times* 142/1874 (Spring 2001): 17–22. ISSN: 0027–4666.

In a follow-up article on Messiaen's early years (see item 310), Simeone investigates the sensitive relationship between Messiaen and Nadia Boulanger. Using surviving correspondence between the two housed in the Music Department of the Bibliothèque Nationale de France, he traces their various interactions, ranging from Messiaen seeking Boulanger's assistance in order to secure performances of his works to his participation or lack thereof as organist in memorial services for Boulanger's sister Lili and mother Raïssa at La Trinité, of which Nadia was a parishioner. Includes translated excerpts of an interview with Messiaen conducted in October 1931 by the Belgian poet and musicologist José Bruyr that Simeone incorporated into his biographical study of Messiaen (see items 155 and 210).

312. Stenzi, Jürg. "Das Rätsel Olivier Messiaen." *Österreichische Musikzeitschrift* 48/10–11 (October/November 1993): 536–42. ISSN: 0029–9316.

An examination of color, rhythm, and birdsong in the music of Messiaen.

313. Zeller, Hans Rudolf. "Messiaens kritische Universalität: Versuch über neue und 'außereuropäische' Musik." In *Musik-Konzepte 28: Olivier Messiaen* (item 243), 56–77.

Looks at the influence of non-Western musical systems and aesthetics in contemporary music and its impact on the music of Messiaen. Maintains that the aesthetic behind Messiaen's bird-inspired compositions of the 1950s is comparable to that of *musique concrète* (p. 74), because in both instances material is recorded and manipulated at a later point in time.

314. Zender, Hans. "Messiaens Aktualität: Das Haiku-Denken." *Beiträge zur Neuen Musik* 13 (1992): 46–48. ISSN: 0941–4711.

An examination of the relationship between Messiaen's compositional aesthetics and Japanese haiku.

5

Topical Studies

This chapter considers different aspects of Messiaen's music according to topics that reflect the work of Messiaen scholars. They range from analytical/theoretical studies to considerations of Messiaen's work as a teacher.

ANALYTICAL AND THEORETICAL STUDIES OF MESSIAEN'S MUSIC

315. Beirão, Christine Wassermann. "Olivier Messiaen: Un langage communicable: Eine 'kommunizierbare' Sprache." *Kirchenmusikalisches Jahrbuch* 84 (2000): 23–32. ISSN: 0075–6199.

     Messiaen has always mentioned how important the theological truths of the Roman Catholic faith were to his music. With this as a vantage point, the author surveys Messiaen's music and compositional techniques.

316. Benitez, Vincent P. "Messiaen as Improviser." *Dutch Journal of Music Theory* 13 (forthcoming, 2008).

     A discussion of the technical and theological aspects of Messiaen's approach to improvisation and how they influenced his work as a composer.

317. Benitez, Vincent P. "Aspects of Harmony in Messiaen's Later Music: An Examination of the Chords of Transposed Inversions on the Same Bass Note." *Journal of Musicological Research* 23/2 (April-June 2004): 187–226. ISSN: 0141–1896.

Studies Messiaen's approach to harmony in his later music of the 1960s to 1990s by examining the chords of transposed inversions on the same bass note. Places the chords of transposed inversions within Messiaen's more recent nonmodal harmonic vocabulary. Argues that they should be interpreted as chromatically enhanced triadic structures. Concludes the study by exploring how the chords of transposed inversions are used in musical passages, particularly in relation to the modes of limited transposition.

318. Bernard, Jonathan W. "Messiaen's Synaesthesia: The Correspondence between Color and Sound Structure in His Music." *Music Perception* 4/1 (Fall 1986): 41–68. ISSN: 0730–7829.

A consideration of what drives Messiaen's approach to sound-color relationships. Basing his study on the consistency of Messiaen's synesthetic responses as reflected in the modes of limited transposition, Bernard examines relationships between sound and color, developing a hierarchy of criteria—such as modal quality, spacing considerations, absolute pitch, and pitch-class set identity—that he believes are important in determining the color associations for musical passages. Although he is unable to answer many questions regarding sound-color relationships in Messiaen's music, Bernard is optimistic that they will be solved, in which case a theory of harmonic structure for Messiaen's music based on characteristic interval content and order could be developed. The article's only shortcoming is its tendency to regard passages from Messiaen's later works as possibly being modal when they are in fact based on known chords that lie outside of the composer's modal system, leading one to surmise that an incomplete picture of Messiaen's approach to sound-color relationships is being presented.

319. Bernard, Jonathan W. "Colour." In *The Messiaen Companion* (item 240), 203–19.

A continuation of Bernard's earlier study of color in Messiaen's music (see item 318). Although differing in certain respects—the article's examples are all new and the concept of *superimposition* (relating the vertical intervals of two sonorities) is omitted—this essay is similar to the earlier one.

320. Bernard-Delapierre, Guy. "La Musique: Olivier Messiaen." *Confluences* (June-July 1945): 551–56.

After noting recent performances of Messiaen's music and the controversy they aroused ("Le Cas Messiaen" [see items 205 and 273]), Bernard-Delapierre both considers and defends the elements of Messiaen's musical style, drawing from the *Technique de mon langage musical* in his discussion. He likewise defends Messiaen's religious beliefs, his desire to compose spiritual music, and his notices and commentaries. Despite the polemical nature of the article, it is a good exposition of Messiaen's compositional aesthetics of the 1940s.

321. Cheong, Wai-Ling. "Messiaen's Chord Tables: Ordering the Disordered." *Tempo* 57/226 (October 2003): 2–10. ISSN: 0040–2982.

An extension of Cheong's article in *Acta Musicologica* (see item 322). Using *Chronochromie* as a backdrop, the article examines the chord tables devised by Messiaen to illustrate: (1) his chords of transposed inversions on the same bass note; (2) his first and second chords of contracted resonance; (3) his revolving (or turning) chords; and (4) his chords of total chromaticism. Although it covers material found in the earlier article, this essay also explores other topics, such as Messiaen's motivations for setting up chord tables and what determined the pitch-class level for the first table of each chord type.

322. Cheong, Wai-Ling. "Rediscovering Messiaen's Invented Chords." *Acta Musicologica* 75/1 (2003): 85–105. ISSN: 0001–6241.

In this survey of Messiaen's invented chords that are not derived from the modes of limited transposition, Cheong considers four chord types: (1) the chords of transposed inversions on the same bass note; (2) the first and second chords of contracted resonance; (3) the revolving (or turning) chords; and (4) the chords of total chromaticism. Spurred by scholarly interest in Messiaen's account of his use of three of these chord types in *Chronochromie*, and relying on the first five volumes of the *Traité de rythme, de couleur, et d'ornithologie*, Cheong examines the structure and origins of these invented chords, noting Messiaen's inconsistent explanations of them in his interviews and writings, as well as how they appear without being named in early works such as *La Nativité du Seigneur* and in the *Technique de mon langage musical*. Does not deal with the sound-color associations of these chords.

323. Cheong, Wai-Ling. "Messiaen's Triadic Colouration: Modes as Interversion." *Music Analysis* 21/1 (March 2002): 53–84. ISSN: 0262–5245.

Examines the successions of chords devised by Messiaen to realize entire modes of limited transposition in strict order. Argues that they should not be considered as theoretical models but rather as practical means to engage a mode in Messiaen's music from both coloristic and permutational perspectives. Suggests that his quest for harmonic coloration is linked to linear and vertical reorderings of pitch.

324. Covington, Katherine Russell. "A Study of Textural Denseness in Selected Keyboard Works of Messiaen." M.M. thesis, Indiana University, 1971. 99 p.

Uses four keyboard works of Messiaen (*Cantéyodjayâ, Mode de valeurs et d'intensités, Messe de la Pentecôte,* and *Livre d'orgue*) to study textural density in music and its role in shaping a composition's structure. Outlines what components contribute to the density of a musical event and ranks their significance. Investigates the music by (1) surveying its structural aspects, (2) noting its changes of density according to the elements tabulated at the study's outset, and (3) determining a density value for each musical sound, which is explained in detail while describing each piece. Plots the textural density of musical excerpts on a graph in order to develop conclusions about Messiaen's use of density in his music. Notes that Messiaen delineates formal sections by means of changes in textural density. In order to unify sections, he uses the same density level and pattern of change when a section returns. To highlight motion toward a focal point, which generally occurs near the end of a movement, he increases both the density level and tempo of the music. Finally, looks at Messiaen's employment of planes of sound, which conveys an impression of depth.

325. Delaere, Mark. "Olivier Messiaen's Analysis Seminar and the Development of Post-War Serial Music." Translated by Richard Evans. *Music Analysis* 21/1 (March 2002): 35–51. ISSN: 0262–5245.

Deals with the impact of Messiaen's teaching on rhythm at the Paris Conservatoire on the theoretical thought and music of his students Boulez, Goeyvaerts, and Stockhausen, as a means to better gauge the composer's influence on the development of postwar serialism in Europe. Pays special attention to analytical notes made by Goeyvaerts on some twenty pieces during his studies with Messiaen at the Paris Conservatoire. Addresses the influence of Messiaen's approach to analysis on the work of these composers through Stravinsky's *Rite of Spring* and Mozart's Symphony in G Minor.

326. Drew, David. "Messiaen: A Provisional Study." *The Score* 10 (December 1954): 33–49; 13 (September 1955): 59–73; 14 (December 1955): 41–61.

Drew's three articles are the first substantive English-language study of Messiaen's music (because of their date, the articles cover only those works up to the early 1950s). In the first article, Drew provides a backdrop for his examination of Messiaen's works by surveying the composer's musical language and aesthetic. He notes the components of Messiaen's harmonic language—the modes of limited transposition, and chords resulting from either various kinds of superimposition or appoggiatura techniques—and approach to tonality where one tonal center tends to be emphasized for a considerable length of time, producing simultaneous states of tonal catalepsy and chord-to-chord motions at different levels of structure. Drew closes his survey by examining Messiaen's use of melody, especially how plainsong, Hindu music, and birdsong influence his melodic style, and rhythm, his primary preoccupation as a composer. In the second article, Drew discusses Messiaen's works, beginning with *Le Banquet céleste* for organ (1928) and concluding with *Visions de l'Amen* for two pianos (1943). He builds upon observations derived from his first article, noting Messiaen's use of chromatic modal harmony, tonal centers, static form, monody, and rhythm in his analyses. In the third article, Drew continues to look at *Visions de l'Amen*, moving on to *Vingt Regards sur l'Enfant-Jésus* (1944), *Quatre Études de rythme* (1949–50), *Messe de la Pentecôte* (1950), and *Livre d'orgue* (1951–52), closing with an examination of the *Turangalîla-Symphonie* (1946–48). He concludes by placing Messiaen's art within the context of twentieth-century music.

327. Fabbi, Roberto. "Theological Implications of Restrictions in Messiaen's Compositional Processes." In *Messiaen's Language of Mystical Love* (item 236), 55–84.

Explores how the idea of restriction is basic to Messiaen's musical language and characterizes its relationship to his faith. Examines Messiaen's compositional techniques related to pitch and rhythm, showing how they stem from his theology of restraint known as the "charm of impossibilities." Characterizes Messiaen's work as a longing for a truth that is both eternal and external. Since this longing involves death and resurrection, it is unattainable for the living and hence a "charm of a metaphysical impossibility." Yet, this longing is an "immanent and concrete aesthetic quality" of Messiaen's music which, as "it is incessantly compelled to re-become itself, incessantly recreates its *own* reality."

328. Fink, Monica. "Farb-Klänge und Klang-Farben im Werk von Olivier Messiaen." *Music in Art: International Journal for Music Iconography* 28/1–2 (Spring-Fall 2003): 163–72. ISSN: 1522-7464.

Discusses the pivotal role played by color in Messiaen's compositional approach and thinking. Looks at the modes of limited transposition and their color associations before examining various works, especially the *Préludes* for piano.

329. Forster, Max. *Technik modaler Komposition bei Olivier Messiaen.* Tübinger Beiträge zur Musikwissenschaft, ed. Georg von Dadelsen, vol. 4. Neuhausen-Stuttgart: Hänssler-Verlag, 1976. 148 p. ISBN: 3775102159. ML 410.M595 F7.

Views Messiaen's approach to composition as united by a modal system in which pitch and rhythm possess equal significance. The connection between the two parameters, which are in a "perfect analogy" based on their selection, grouping, and use in Messiaen's music, derives ultimately from his aesthetic of the "charm of impossibilities" where transpositional limitation and nonretrogradability are characteristic features. After outlining Messiaen's modal system as described in the *Technique de mon langage musical*, the author looks at pitch and rhythm in the composer's music in order to show how the dual meaning of "modus" works (as a means of selecting material that can be employed freely in a composition, and as a collection of material that cannot be changed when used). An examination of Messiaen's compositional techniques that is worth studying, especially chapter four (pp. 84–114) in which modal qualities of Messiaen's serial writing are investigated. Twelve-tone models are constructed according to how a mode of limited transposition is partitioned within the octave and then subjected to permutation in order to generate further models. Having established an analytical framework for modal twelve-tone rows, the author then analyzes "Reprises par interversions" and "Les Yeux dans les roues" from the *Livre d'orgue*, and *Mode de valeurs et d'intensités*. Closes the chapter with a discussion of row technique within a modal system where comparisons between Messiaen and Schoenberg are made.

330. Fremiot, Marcel. "Le rythme dans le langage d'Olivier Messiaen." *Polyphonie: Revue musicale trimestrielle* 2 (1948): 58–64.

Asserts that rhythm is the most important element in Messiaen's musical language, despite what the composer says about the primacy of melody in the *Technique de mon langage musical*. For the author, rhythm influences melody, harmony, and counterpoint in Messiaen's music. Surveys different rhythmic techniques from the 1930s and 40s, such as rhythmic pedals, rhythmic canons, augmentation and diminution, rhythmic cells, nonretrogradable rhythms, added values, prime numbers, Greek metric patterns, Hindu *deçitâlas*, and rhythms derived from birdsongs. Views Messiaen's rhythmic language as ametrical because it centers on a small duration and its free multiplication, which spawns rhythmic periods free of the constraints of traditional notions of beat or measure.

331. Gallatin, James A. "An Overview of the Compositional Methods in Representative Works of Olivier Messiaen." Ph.D. dissertation, University of Cincinnati, 1986. viii, 585 p.

Employs Allen Forte's ideas on pitch-class set theory to understand Messiaen's compositional techniques. Concludes that Messiaen's techniques are based upon those codified in the *Technique de mon langage musical*. To these techniques are added others, such as those derived from birdsong, symmetrical permutations, and the *langage communicable*, that develop them. Works analyzed in detail are selected from *Préludes* (1929), *Poèmes pour Mi* (1936), *Trois petites Liturgies de la Présence Divine* (1944), *Cinq Rechants* (1948–49), *Chronochromie* (1960), and the *Méditations sur le mystère de la Sainte Trinité* (1969).

332. Gárdonyi, Zsolt. "Olivier Messiaens Harmonik aus der Sicht der Orgelimprovisation." *Musik und Kirche* 63/4 (July/August 1993): 197–204. ISSN: 0024–4471.

Examines Messiaen's approach to harmony from the perspective of organ improvisation. Believes that a knowledge of Messiaen's improvisational practices can shed light on his complex musical notation. Looks at the origin of the chord of resonance in the harmonic series and how its registral realization as two different seventh chords not only lies comfortably underneath the fingers, but also makes seemingly difficult passages based on that chord more accessible as a result. In like manner, considers the harmonic possibilities of the second mode of limited transposition (that is, the octatonic collection) and how they are realized in Messiaen's organ and piano works.

333. Griffiths, Paul. "*Catalogue de couleurs:* Notes on Messiaen's Tone Colours on His 70th Birthday." *The Musical Times* 119 (December 1978): 1035–37. ISSN: 0027–4666.

Considers Messiaen's sound-color structures in an article celebrating the composer's seventieth birthday. Analyzing excerpts from *Sept Haïkaï* and *Couleurs de la Cité céleste* in which Messiaen links colors with specific chords, Griffiths tries to uncover how sound and color correspond in order to shed some light on Messiaen's approach to harmony.

334. Harris, Joseph E. "*Musique Colorée*: Synesthestic Correspondence in the Works of Olivier Messiaen." Ph.D. dissertation, University of Iowa, 2004. viii, 168 p.

This study attempts to quantify sound-color relationships in Messiaen's music, provide a method to ascertain unknown harmonic colorations, and demonstrate, through an analysis of "Apparition du Christ glorieux" from the *Éclairs sur l'Au-Delà*, how its findings lead to insights about the structure of Messiaen's music that might not be available through more conventional means. While the dissertation provides valuable information about synesthesia in general (i.e., synesthesia as an artistic metaphor in the late-nineteenth and early-twentieth centuries, modern theories of the etiology of idiopathic synesthesia, and criteria that can lead to the diagnosis of the condition), the methodology it proposes for the analysis of Messiaen's color chords, which is based upon the idea that a chord's pitch classes evoke individual colors, is problematic for two basic reasons that are worth noting here. First, the study ignores Messiaen's explanations of how sound is related to color in the *Conférence de Notre-Dame*, a curious omission in light of its heavy dependence on the composer's testimonies and writings: "It is childish to assign a color to each note. It is not isolated tones which produce colors, but chords, or better, complexes of tones. Each complex of tones has a well-defined color." (Olivier Messiaen, *Conférence de Notre-Dame*, [item 96], 11.) Thus it is the *interaction of notes* and *not the individual notes themselves* that produce colors in Messiaen's synesthesia. Second, although it has its analytical strengths, the methodology lacks precision now and then and leads to conclusions that run counter to the composer's ideas on natural resonance, which are closely allied to his ideas on color.

335. Healey, Gareth. "Messiaen and the Concept of 'Personnages.'" *Tempo* 58/230 (October 2004): 10–19. ISSN: 0040–2982.

In this article, Healey seeks to present a clearer picture of Messiaen's concept of "personnages" than that outlined by previous scholars. Drawing primarily from various analyses found in Messiaen's *Traité de rythme, de couleur, et d'ornithologie (1949–1992)*, and secondarily from the composer's conversations with Claude Samuel, Healey connects many of the dots lying behind the idea of "personnages" by showing its conceptual development as seen and employed by Messiaen, from its origins in Beethoven's Fifth Symphony, to its first substantial manifestation in Stravinsky's *Rite of Spring*, to its musical zenith in the *Turangalîla-Symphonie*. In his discussion, Healey does not limit the idea of "personnages" to rhythm ("personnages rythmiques") but extends it to melody and harmony ("personnages melodiques and harmoniques"), using a passage from the "Joie du sang des étoiles," the fifth movement of the *Turangalîla-Symphonie*, to illustrate his points.

336. Henstein, Robert John. "An Analysis of Three Song Cycles for Soprano and Piano by Olivier Messiaen." M.A. thesis, Kent State University, 1979. vi, 71 p.

Looks at Messiaen's use of melody, harmony, rhythm, and form in his song cycles for soprano and piano from the 1930s: *Trois Mélodies* (1930), *Poèmes pour Mi* (1936), and *Chants de Terre et de Ciel* (1938). Includes brief information on Messiaen's musical background and an overview of his compositional techniques up to 1939.

337. Hirsbrunner, Theo. "Ein neuer Begriff von der Zeit: Olivier Messiaens geistiges Vermächtnis." In *Von Richard Wagner bis Pierre Boulez: Essays*, 177–81. Wort und Musik: Salzburger Akademische Beiträge, no. 38. Anif, Austria: Müller-Speiser, 1997. 216 p. ISBN: 3851450485. ML 60.H66 1997 (IUCAT).

Argues that Messiaen redefined the concept of musical time through a rhythmic approach that emphasized the free multiplication of a small note value. Since rhythm no longer depends upon a divisive approach to meter, it is free to imitate the movements of nature, which are free and unequal. In a word, Messiaen approached rhythm in an ametrical fashion.

338. Ibáñez, Deborah Welsh. "Color, Timbre, and Resonance: Developments in Olivier Messiaen's Use of Percussion Between 1956–65." D.M.A. essay, University of Miami, 2005. vi, 100 p.

Investigates Messiaen's use of percussion in relation to his compositional techniques involving timbre, resonance, and textural color. Defines percussion groupings according to their timbral characteristics and how Messiaen combines them in his works. Focuses on the use of percussion in *Oiseaux exotiques*, *Chronochromie*, *Couleurs de la Cité céleste*, and *Et exspecto resurrectionem mortuorum*, and to a lesser extent, *Réveil des oiseaux* and *Des canyons aux étoiles*. Attempts to assist performers by providing more insights into Messiaen's percussion writing, in order to effect better performances of his music.

339. Johnson, Robert Sherlaw[-]. "Rhythmic Technique and Symbolism in the Music of Olivier Messiaen." In *Messiaen's Language of Mystical Love* (item 236), 121–39.

Traces the development of Messiaen's rhythmic techniques with a consideration of rhythm on a larger scale. Looks at the strategic role of silence in Messiaen's later music, as well as the religious character of his use of rhythm, from his early works to the first movement of *Des canyons aux étoiles* ("Le désert"). Much of the essay is derived from the author's book on Messiaen (see item 213).

340. Keym, Stefan. "Zum Zusammenhang zwischen Farben und Drei-klangskomponenten der 'speziellen Akkorde' Olivier Messiaens." *Musiktheorie* 19/3 (2004): 249–56. ISSN: 0177–4182.

   Short essay examining sound-color relationships in Messiaen's non-modal or special chords (e.g., the chords of transposed inversions on the same bass note, chord of total chromaticism, chords of con-tracted resonance [type 1], and turning chords). Links the colors evoked by these chords in Messiaen's colored-hearing synesthesia with their triadic components.

341. Krastewa, Iwanka. "Le langage rythmique d'Olivier Messiaen et la métrique ancienne grecque." *Schweizerische Musikzeitung/Revue musicale suisse* 112/2 (April/March 1972): 79–86.

   Considers the relationships between Messiaen's rhythmic language and ancient Greek meter. In order to avoid *isochronism* or rhythmic regularity, the ancient Greeks strove for the exact opposite by using varied rhythmic formulas in their metrical system. Messiaen bor-rowed this principle of irregularity by taking a *chronos protos* or small durational value and using it as a multipliable quantity to generate rhythmic sequences in his music. Irregularity in Messiaen's music can be found at different structural levels, such as within the measure, section, or work as a whole.

342. Landale, Susan. "Olivier Messiaen: Musical Language, Musical Image." In *Music: The AGO-RCCO Magazine* 12/12 (item 244), 36–39.

   Landale scrutinizes color and rhythm, two basic aspects of Mes-siaen's approach to composition, in order to achieve a better grasp of his music. In her discussion of color, she looks at Messiaen's melodic and harmonic devices (e.g., modes of limited transposition and their color associations) and musical forms stemming from melodic considerations. In her examination of rhythm, she reiterates much of what is already in the Messiaen literature (e.g., non-retrogradable rhythms, added values).

343. Louvier, Alain. "Olivier Messiaen, le rythme et la couleur." In *Por-trait(s) d'Olivier Messiaen* (item 241), 47–60.

   A survey of Messiaen's ideas on rhythm and sound-color relation-ships as seen through his teaching and music. The first two pages of the article duplicate the text of an earlier essay written in 1995 for *Olivier Messiaen, homme de foi* (see item 238). They serve to outline basic tenets of Messiaen's approach to rhythm (as experienced by Louvier in Messiaen's analysis class in 1965–66) before the article's discussion of its main topics. In his examination of Messiaen's ideas on rhythm, Louvier looks at many elements that comprise the composer's rhythmic aesthetic: (1) philosophical ideas about time and eternity; (2) a view of rhythm that encompasses all musical parameters; (3) Hindu *deçi-tâlas*; (4) Greek metric patterns; (5) irrational rhythms; (6) serialized durations; and (7) symmetrical permutations. In his discussion of Messiaen's ideas on sound-color relationships, Louvier considers the modes of limited transposition and the chords of transposed inversions on the same bass note. Louvier concludes his article by exploring how rhythm and sound-color relationships are synthesized in *Couleurs de la Cité céleste*.

344. Neidhöfer, Christoph. "A Theory of Harmony and Voice Leading for the Music of Olivier Messiaen." *Music Theory Spectrum* 27/1 (Spring 2005): 1–34. ISSN: 0195–6167.

Neidhöfer considers modal harmony and voice leading in the early music of Messiaen (1929–43). He presents a classification system for modal harmonies and voice-leading patterns based on their numbered position (*step class*) within the mode. He then examines registral lines in Messiaen's early music using his classification system, which, in his opinion, provides insights into the composer's contrapuntal and harmonic structures from modal, tonal, and mod-12 (pitch class) perspectives. Neidhöfer concludes his essay by examining harmonic and contrapuntal textures that involve different modes which are sounded either simultaneously or successively.

345. Nelson, David Lowell. "An Analysis of Olivier Messiaen's Chant Paraphrases." Ph.D. dissertation, Northwestern University, 1992. viii, 298 p.

A study of Messiaen's use of chant paraphrases from the *Lieber Usualis* and the *Lieber Gradualis* in five works written between the 1960s to 1980s. Each paraphrase is examined for its scoring, form, rhythm, metrical organization, melody, and harmony, and how these elements interact. Concludes that most chant settings become more complex as they unfold, exhibiting highly varied musical contents typical of Messiaen's approach to composition.

346. Peterson, Larry Wayne. "Messiaen and Rhythm: Theory and Practice." Ph.D. dissertation, University of North Carolina at Chapel Hill, 1973. xi, 239 p.

Peterson studies Messiaen's rhythmic techniques and compares them with historical approaches to rhythm, in order to underscore Messiaen's contributions to rhythmic theory. He illustrates these techniques by analyzing passages drawn from selected works. According to Peterson, Messiaen reviewed the author's analyses of his music.

347. Pople, Anthony. "Messiaen's Musical Language: An Introduction."
     In *The Messiaen Companion* (item 240), 15–50.

     A survey of Messiaen's musical language and style. Examines Mes-
     siaen's interest in modality, especially non-western types. Proceeds
     to aspects of the composer's melodic and harmonic language as seen
     through the *Technique de mon langage musical*, looking at the modes
     of limited transposition from different vantage points. Considers
     pitch relationships between the modes and common tonal harmo-
     nies by citing an example from the *Technique*, in which chords
     drawn from two different transpositions of mode 2 support domi-
     nant-seventh and tonic chords in the key of F-sharp major, respec-
     tively. Uses that example to facilitate a comparison between
     Messiaen and Stravinsky's use of modality. Characterizes Messiaen's
     approach to rhythm as ametrical, although acknowledges that there
     is both metrical and hypermetrical writing in his works. However,
     considers Messiaen's separation of pitch and rhythm, and that of
     other musical parameters, as a more important contribution to
     Western music than any of his rhythmic techniques. Finally, looks at
     Messiaen's fascination with self-imposed limitations on his approach
     to composition, sound-colors, numerical symbolism, extremes of
     tempo, and cyclic repetitions of pitch or rhythmic series. The essay's
     one major shortcoming is the failure to discuss Messiaen's non-
     modal chord types (chords of transposed inversions on the same
     bass note, the first and second chords of contracted resonance,
     turning chords, and the chords of total chromaticism), which are
     used extensively in his later music beginning in the 1950s.

348. Pozzi, Raffaele. "Note sulla genesi dei 'personaggi ritmici' nell'opera
     di Olivier Messiaen." *L'analisi musicale* (March 1991): 207–20.

     Examines the development of rhythmic characters in the music of
     Messiaen. Notes the origins of the compositional device in the
     music of Stravinsky, the Hindu rhythm *simhavikrîdita*, and Mes-
     siaen's techniques of development by elimination and amplification.
     Surveys the use of the rhythmic device in Messiaen's music of the
     1940s and early 1950s.

349. Roubet, Anne. "Harmonie, timbre, couleur: Modèles et analogies
     dans la pensée musicale d'Olivier Messiaen." *Analyse musicale*, no.
     48 (Sept 2003): 99–106. ISSN: 0295–3722.

     Using *Couleurs de la Cité céleste* as an emblematic example from
     Messiaen's complete œuvre, the author views the composer's use of
     color as primary, subsuming and subordinating harmony and
     timbre. Explores pitch and timbral elements in Messiaen's music

and what he said about them in the seventh volume of the *Traité de rythme, de couleur, et d'ornithologie*, and how they contribute to the religious symbolism of his music.

350. Salvi, Peter. "Harmonic Density in Messiaen." D.M.A. thesis, Cornell University, 1999. xi, 148 p.

Concentrates on how pitch is organized in Messiaen's music. Relates the composer's approach to pitch organization to the structural qualities of the chromatic aggregate. After examining the prominent events and total harmonic content of a work, compares that harmonic content to the work's formal design. Regards the completion of the chromatic aggregate as structurally significant in Messiaen's music.

351. Schweizer, Klaus. "'Dokumentarische' Materialien bei Olivier Messiaen. Zum 70. Geburtstag des Komponisten am 10. Dezember." *Melos/Neue Zeitschrift für Musik* 4/6 (1978): 477–85.

Examines how Messiaen assimilates pre-established musical materials such as plainchant melodies, given rhythmic patterns, and birdcalls into his music through changing accentuation. Believes that the reason Messiaen scarcely admits to how extensively he modifies these materials may be due to the fact that the use of pre-established materials is an important compositional impulse.

352. Shenton, Andrew. "Speaking with the Tongues of Men and of Angels: Messiaen's 'langage communicable'." In *Messiaen's Language of Mystical Love* (item 236), 225–45.

Examines Messiaen's *langage communicable*, a musico-linguistic system used in the *Méditations sur le mystère de la Sainte Trinité*, *Des canyons aux étoiles*, and the *Livre du Saint Sacrement*, both linguistically and musically, and situates it within the larger semiotic framework of the *Méditations*. Interprets the *langage communicable* within cognitive and theological contexts and stresses the complexity of Messiaen's semiotic system. By invoking Benjamin Lee Whorf's hypotheses and Steven Pinker's concept of *mentalese* ("a word used for the language of thought"), suggests that Messiaen's musical coding bypasses verbal constructions at the encoding and decoding stages.

353. Simundza, Mirjana. "Messiaen's Rhythmical Organisation and Classical Indian Theory of Rhythm (I)." *International Review of the Aesthetics and Sociology of Music* 18/1 (June 1987): 117–44. ISSN: 0351–5796.

Items 353 and 354 form a two-part essay that considers the rhythmic techniques Messiaen developed from his study of the Indian *deçi-tâlas* of the thirteenth-century Indian theorist Sharngadeva, as well as his use of South Indian rhythmic patterns in *Oiseaux exotiques*. After summarizing Messiaen's Indian-inspired rhythmic principles, the essay provides a table of the *deçi-tâlas* used by Messiaen, along with another table listing those compositions in which *deçi-tâlas* are employed. The *Quatuor pour la fin du Temps, Turangalîla-Symphonie*, and *Oiseaux exotiques* are then examined for their rhythmic organization. The essay concludes with a summary of the author's findings. Despite the clumsy English, this pair of articles is a valuable addition to the literature on Messiaen's rhythmic practice.

354. Simundza, Mirjana. "Messiaen's Rhythmical Organisation and Classical Indian Theory of Rhythm (II)." *International Review of the Aesthetics and Sociology of Music* 19/1 (June 1988): 53–73. ISSN: 0351–5796.

See item 353.

355. Street, Donald. "The Modes of Limited Transposition." *The Musical Times* 117/1604 (October 1976): 819–23. ISSN: 0027–4666.

Investigates the modes of limited transposition due to the growing popularity of Messiaen's music in England. After examining the structural qualities of the modes, undertakes a survey of how they were used by different composers in order to place them in an historical context.

356. Thissen, Paul. "Zahlensymbolik im Orgelwerk Messiaens." *Musica sacra* 109 (1989): 93–97. ISSN: 0179–0356X.

An examination of number symbolism in the organ works of Messiaen. Analyzes "Jésus accepte la souffrance" from *La Nativité du Seigneur*, and the "Offertoire" from the *Messe de la Pentecôte*.

357. Thissen, Paul. "Zahlensymbolik im Orgelwerk von Olivier Messiaen." *Kirchenmusikalisches Jahrbuch* 80 (1996): 115–31. ISSN: 0075–6199.

A longer and more developed version of the author's 1989 article found in item 356. Considers the symbolic import of numbers in Messiaen's compositional aesthetic. Investigates the relationship between numerological structure and theological content in "Jésus accepte la souffrance" from *La Nativité du Seigneur*, "Le Mystère de la Saint Trinité" from *Les Corps glorieux*, "Offertoire" from the *Messe de la Pentecôte*, and *Méditations sur le mystère de la Sainte Trinité*.

358. Trawick, Eleanor F. "Order, Progression, and Time in the Music of Messiaen." *Ex tempore* 9/2 (Summer 1999): 64–76. ISSN: 0276–6795.

After reviewing Messiaen's ideas about musical time, Trawick explores his use of rhythmic interversion and retrogression. Analyzes excerpts from the *Livre d'orgue*, *Cantéyodjayâ*, and "Île de feu II" from the *Quatre Études de rythme*.

359. Walker, Rosemary. "Modes and Pitch-Class Sets in Messiaen: A Brief Discussion of 'Première communion de la Vierge.'" *Music Analysis* 8, nos. 1–2 (1989): 159–68. ISSN: 0262–5245.

Uses pitch-class set theory to investigate "Première communion de la Vierge," the eleventh movement of *Vingt Regards sur l'Enfant-Jésus*. Focuses on modal and nonmodal pitch collections, hoping to relate the two and explain the "extra" pitches that are introduced at certain junctures in the piece. Concludes that Messiaen tends to use large pitch collections of cardinality seven and higher, and their subsets and supersets to represent the underlying control of one of the modes of limited transposition.

360. Williams, Graham. "The Theories of Olivier Messiaen: Their Origins and Their Application in His Piano Music." 2 vols. Ph.D. dissertation, University of Adelaide, 1978.

Investigates Messiaen's writings and their relationship to his piano music. Concentrates on the influences that were pivotal to his musical development. The study is organized into four parts. In chapters one through four, Messiaen's life and work are discussed. Chapters five through ten are devoted to theological, philosophical, and literary writings that influenced Messiaen, such as those by Saint Thomas Aquinas, Dom Columba Marmion, Plato, Aristotle, Henri Bergson, Cécile Sauvage, Paul Claudel, André Breton, and Paul Éluard. In chapters eleven through thirteen, Messiaen's musical language is explored with particular attention paid to rhythm. Chapters one through three of volume two consider Messiaen's piano music in term of its stylistic evolution. An exhaustive study that is highly recommended.

361. Wu, Jean Marie. "Mystical Symbols of Faith: Olivier Messiaen's Charm of Impossibilities." In *Messiaen's Language of Mystical Love* (item 236), 85–120.

Considers Messiaen's "charm of impossibilities" as manifested by his modes of limited transposition, nonretrogradable rhythms, and symmetrical permutations, and relates them to his theology. Analyzes modal color in "Le baiser de l'Enfant-Jésus" and nonretrogradability in the "Regard de l'Église d'amour," both from *Vingt Regards sur l'Enfant-Jésus*, and symmetrical permutations in *Chronochromie*.

BIRDSONG

362. Demuth, Norman. "Messiaen's Early Birds." *The Musical Times* 101/1412 (October 1960): 627–29. ISSN: 0027–4666.

    An article devoted to a discussion of *Réveil des oiseaux* (1953). Notes the originality of Messiaen's dawn chorus of thirty-seven birds, especially its contrived but inherently musical bird polyphony. Concludes that the piece is essentially a piano concerto based on the concertante principle, with cadenzas, as well as an orchestral transcription of a natural phenomenon.

363. Fallon, Robert Joseph. "Messiaen's Mimesis: The Language and Culture of the Bird Styles." Ph.D. dissertation, University of California at Berkeley, 2005. 329 p.

    Considers Messiaen's bird style from both musical and cultural vantage points. Argues that the composer's early music contains far more birdsongs than previously acknowledged. Demonstrates that Messiaen employed a sound recording to transcribe North American birdsongs in *Oiseaux exotiques* based upon research conducted at the Bibliothèque Nationale de France. With the aid of spectrograms, scrutinizes the accuracy of the transcriptions. Associates different meanings with different bird styles: joy amidst suffering in the "early style" (1929–48), peace and freedom during the Cold War in the "middle style" (1948–52), and divine wisdom in the "late style" (1952–56).

364. Henderson, Karen R. "A Study of the Use of Birdsong in the Compositions of Olivier Messiaen: What Is Musical about This Extra-Musical Connection?" M.M. thesis, University of Cincinnati College-Conservatory of Music, 1995. vii, 114 p.

    Delves into how Messiaen approached birdsong transcription and composition. To show the different stages in the development of Messiaen's birdsong technique, examines *Technique de mon langage musical*, "Liturgie de crystal" from the *Quatuor pour la fin du Temps*, "Chants d'oiseaux" from the *Livre d'orgue*, and "Le Merle bleu" from the *Catalogue d'oiseaux*. Maintains that although he came closer than any other composer with respect to the accuracy of his avian transcriptions, Messiaen was most interested in the structural possibilities of birdsong. He would take his experience of birdsong and then adapt it to his musical language. For Messiaen, birdsong represented a nonhuman, sonic world that he sought to make more comprehensible. It was a medium by which he could capture a glimpse of eternity.

365. Hold, Trevor. "Messiaen's Birds." *Music and Letters* 52 (April 1971): 113–22. ISSN: 0027–4224.

Explores the technique of birdsong in Messiaen's compositions, questioning the accuracy of the composer's transcriptions in the process. Challenges Messiaen's statement that he included only authentic birdsongs in *Réveil des oiseaux* (1953). Compares four of Messiaen's bird transcriptions with ones derived from a sound-spectrograph and phonograph recordings. While acknowledging that Messiaen captured certain traits of a bird's music, concludes that Messiaen's transcriptions should be viewed as "imaginative transmutations" rather than authentic reproductions.

366. Johnson, Robert Sherlaw. "Birdsong." In *The Messiaen Companion* (item 240), 249–65.

An examination of birdsong in the music of Messiaen. Johnson traces the development of birdsong in Messiaen's music, beginning with the composer's stylized uses of birdsong in the 1930s and 40s before moving on to his more realistic approaches in the 1950s and beyond where melodic intervals, pitch registers, and tempi are all altered to accommodate human performers. Johnson also explores the symbolism of birdsong along with its pitch structure and form. He makes insightful remarks regarding the pitch structure of Messiaen's avian melodies, noting the limits of pitch-class set theory as an analytical tool. Johnson attempts to develop formal criteria for the composer's avian-inspired pieces where there is little or no motivic repetition. His solution is to devise four formal categories (calls, short repetitive song patterns, varied song patterns, and long streams of "chattering" song), which he believes fulfill, through their interaction within a work, the requirements of form as demanded by the repetition and contrast of musical ideas.

367. Penot, Jacques. "Olivier Messiaen ornithologue." In *Portrait(s) d'Olivier Messiaen* (item 241), 61–74.

Considers Messiaen's preoccupation with birdsong. Describes the composer as an "ornithologue" rather than an "ornithologiste" based on Messiaen's use of that term to characterize his work. In Penot's opinion (see pp. 71–72), while both words are synonyms deriving from ornithological science, "ornithologue" is closer in meaning to the root word "logos" (which means knowledge or wisdom) from which "logique," "logue," or "logiste" derive. Accordingly, an "ornithologue" exhibits a more learned grasp of birds than an "ornithologiste," who, although highly adept, is more interested in knowing more about birds in order to protect them. Penot's essay duplicates much of his earlier effort for *Olivier Messiaen, homme de foi* (see item 368). That being said, he does expand upon that paper by elaborating upon Messiaen's association with Jacques Delamain, a famous French ornithologist, and noting the local ornithologists who assisted Messiaen during his different trips to notate birdsong.

368. Penot, Jacques. "Hommage à Olivier Messiaen." In *Olivier Messiaen, homme de foi: Regard sur son œuvre d'orgue* (item 238), 96–98.

Penot met Messiaen on the occasion of Messiaen and Yvonne Loriod's visit to the Réserve Naturelle de Camargue in 1959 (the year is incorrectly listed in the essay as 1949). At that time, Penot had no idea of Messiaen's notoriety as a musician. He notes that Messiaen appreciated the rigors of being an ornithologist: getting up early in the morning, going to bed late at night, or tolerating extreme temperatures in order to find birds and notate their songs. Messiaen would also secure, if necessary, the services of a local ornithologist to help him in his tasks. Penot describes Messiaen's approach to transcribing birdsong by quoting the composer. To wit, Messiaen would notate one part of a bird's song while simultaneously listening to another. Having Yvonne Loriod record these songs with a tape recorder allowed Messiaen to make a second, more accurate notation at home. However, he regarded the first notation done in the countryside as comporting to the variants found in nature and hence more artistic. Yet, Messiaen regarded the blending of the two notations as leading to a more accurate transcription. Penot concludes his essay by noting the impact Jacques Delamain had upon Messiaen.

369. Siohan, Robert. "Les Recherches d'Olivier Messiaen: Musique et ornithologie." *Le Monde* (3 February 1961). ISSN: 0026–9360.

A short article focusing on birdsong in Messiaen's music. Mentions various birds and their environments. Suggests that what underlies Messiaen's musical poetics is the imitation of nature.

370. Sooy, Julie A. "The Song of the Blackbird: Its Construction and Development in the Music of Olivier Messiaen." M.M. thesis, Bowling Green State University, 1994. 77 p.

Looks at the pitch and rhythmic content of the blackbird's song in eight compositions by Messiaen: (1) *Livre d'orgue*; (2) *Le Merle noir*; (3) *Réveil des oiseaux*; (4) *Chronochromie*; (5) *Catalogue d'oiseaux*; (6) *La Fauvette des jardins*; (7) *Méditations sur le mystère de la Sainte Trinité*; and (8) *Petites esquisses d'oiseaux*. Compares his representation of the blackbird's song with that found in nature. Investigates the use of intervals, tonal centers, modes of limited transposition, additive pitch processes, and pitch cells, along with rhythmic cells, ancient Greek metric patterns, and Hindu *deçi-tâlas*.

Concludes that while Messiaen's blackbird differs musically from the one found in nature, these differences do not diminish his artistry in depicting that bird's song in his music.

371. Tremblay, Gilles. "Oiseau-nature, Messiaen, musique." *Cahiers canadiens de musique* (Spring-Summer 1970): 15–40. ISSN: 0007–9634.

Investigates how Messiaen reproduces birdsong and nature in five works composed during the 1950–60s: (1) *Réveil des oiseaux*; (2) *Oiseaux exotiques*; (3) *Catalogue d'oiseaux*; (4) *Chronochromie*; and (5) *Sept Haïkaï*. Examines the challenges associated with notating birdsong and how Messiaen's approach to that subject evolved throughout his career. In each of the pieces under consideration, examines how Messiaen uses coloristic effects, instrumental timbres, and intricate notations to capture a bird's song and habitat.

372. Zahn, Dieter. "Vogelstimmen." In *Olivier Messiaen: Das Orgelwerk* (item 250), 15.

Characterizes Messiaen's avian-inspired music as evoking a sense of "freshness and fantasy." Notes his early connection to birdsong with the composition of the *Quatuor pour la fin du Temps* and the inclusion of a chapter on birdsong in the *Technique de mon langage musical*. Describes Messiaen's thoughts on the musical potential of birdsong. Mentions how Messiaen would transcribe birdsong first with a notepad and then later with the help of a tape recorder. Discusses the authenticity of Messiaen's avian transcriptions either for solo instruments or orchestra, noting how he approximated the "twilight of sound and noise" evoked by birds more effectively through the use of thicker textures in his later compositions.

INSTRUMENTAL, ORCHESTRAL, CHORAL, AND VOCAL MUSIC

373. Hayes, Malcolm. "Instrumental, Orchestral, and Choral Works to 1948." In *The Messiaen Companion* (item 240), 157–200.

Surveys Messiaen's instrumental, orchestral, and choral works from 1930 to 1948. Pieces examined are: *Les Offrandes oubliées* (1930); *Le Tombeau resplendissant* (1931); *Hymne au Saint-Sacrement* (1932); *Thème et variations* (1932); *L'Ascension* (1932–33); *Fête des belles eaux* (1937); *Quatuor pour la fin du Temps* (1940–41); *Trois petites Liturgies de la Présence Divine* (1944); *Turangalîla-Symphonie* (1946–48); and *Cinq Rechants* (1948–49). Considers musical influences, the circumstances under which a work was written, aspects of musical style, and the intersection between Messiaen's musical language and theology.

374. Hirsbrunner, Theo. "Die kleinen Orchesterformationen in Werken von Olivier Messiaen." *Das Orchester* 11 (November 1988): 1120–23.

   Discusses the handling of smaller instrumental ensembles within Messiaen's orchestral music. States that a key work in his approach to the orchestra was Stravinsky's *Rite of Spring* because of its instrumentation and use of rhythm. Messiaen was also influenced in his treatment of instruments by Milhaud's *L'Homme et son désir* and *La Création du monde*, and, less directly, Schoenberg's *Pierrot Lunaire*. Before analyzing two of Messiaen's works, *Couleurs de la Cité céleste* and *Et exspecto resurrectionem mortuorum*, looks at Boulez's *Le Marteau sans Maître* and *Éclat* in order to draw comparisons between the compositional developments of both teacher and student.

375. Manning, Jane. "The Songs and Song Cycles." In *The Messiaen Companion* (item 240), 105–56.

   A practical examination of Messiaen's songs and song cycles from a singer's perspective. Manning, an internationally known performer, considers *Trois Mélodies*, *La Mort du Nombre*, *Vocalise-étude*, *Poèmes pour Mi*, *Chants de Terre et de Ciel*, and *Harawi* with the goal of relating the dramatic and musical qualities of each piece to the interpretative challenges faced by singers.

376. Troup, Malcolm. "Orchestral Music of the 1950s and 1960s." In *The Messiaen Companion* (item 240), 392–447.

   This essay examines Messiaen's orchestral music from *Réveil des oiseaux* (1953) to *Et exspecto resurrectionem mortuorum* (1964). Asserts that these works are characterized by a deep attachment to birdsong, an exploration of sound-color harmonies, and a return to religion as evinced by plainsong adaptations. Notes that unlike previous works, Messiaen treats the orchestra as a collection of soloists, generating an "uncompromising linear polyphony" in the process. Often repeats technical information already noted by the composer in discussions of each piece. Concludes that Messiaen's preoccupation with timbre in these orchestral works influenced the timbral school of composition of the late twentieth century.

ORGAN MUSIC

377. Bonfils, Jean. "L'homme et l'organiste." In *L'Orgue: Revue trimestrielle* 224 (item 246), 12–14.

   A portrait of Messiaen as Christian, liturgical organist, and composer.

378. Bowyer, Kevin. "A Lateral Look at Messiaen: A Discourse in Bowerspeak on the Organ Music of Olivier Messiaen: With Anim-adversions on 'Things' in General." *The Organ* 73/287 (January 1994): 8–11.

A humorous dialogue on the subject of Messiaen's organ music between a "Wise Organist" and "Interested Person." The dialogue covers a lot of territory: (1) aspects of Messiaen's compositional style, (2) musical symbolism, (3) performance practice issues, (4) comparing Messiaen's organ works to one another, and (5) recommended recordings.

379. Crankshaw, Geoffrey. "Gillian Weir and Messiaen." *The Organ* 73/290 (October 1994): 147–48.

An interview of organist Gillian Weir in which she discusses Messiaen against the backdrop of her recordings of his organ music in 1994 (*Messiaen: Complete Organ Works*, Collins Classics 70312, 1994, 7 CDs). Weir talks about Messiaen's compositional style in relation to his organ music. Crankshaw describes Weir's recorded interpretations as outstanding, stating that she is in complete accord with Messiaen's creative vision for his music.

380. Demuth, Norman. "Messiaen and His Organ Music." *The Musical Times* 96/1346 (April 1955): 203–6. ISSN: 0027–4666.

Argues that to appreciate Messiaen's music more fully, one must understand his underlying mystical philosophy (i.e., theology), which is inextricably linked to his music. Regards Messiaen's mysticism as permeating his music. Considers the roles theology, birdsong, monodic textures, Hindu rhythms, harmony, and organ registration play in Messiaen's organ works from *Le Banquet céleste* (1928) to the *Livre d'orgue* (1951–52). Concludes that while Messiaen's organ music is original, and that it will take time to appreciate, studying it will not go unrewarded.

381. Gillock, Jon. "The Heritage and Legacy of Messiaen's Organ Music." In *Celebration Messiaen: The Complete Works for Organ* (item 239): 8–9.

This article on Messiaen's organ works is an English version of Gillock's earlier French essay written for *Olivier Messiaen, homme de foi: Regard sur son œuvre d'orgue* (see items 238 and 384). It differs, however, from its French counterpart by the inclusion of a chronology of Messiaen's organ works.

382. Gillock, Jon. "The Organ and Messiaen." In *Celebration Messiaen: The Complete Works for Organ* (item 239), 10.

Surveys Messiaen's thoughts on the organ as an instrument. After providing a brief history of the Cavaillé-Coll organ at La Trinité, looks at Messiaen's ideas on organ registration, the performance of his rhythms as well as the interpretation of his music in general, and tempo in his organ music. All of these statements are taken from Messiaen's conversations with the German organist Almut Rößler (see item 180).

383. Gillock, Jon. "Programme [sic] of Celebration Messiaen." In *Celebration Messiaen: The Complete Works for Organ* (item 239): 17–53.

Program notes by Gillock for his series of six concerts at the Riverside Church in New York in 1999 devoted to the organ music of Messiaen. For each piece, Gillock notes when it was composed and, most of the time, premiered; discusses its overall musical style; and describes the musical imagery and compositional techniques employed in the individual movements of large cycles. Of interest are Gillock's notes for Messiaen's posthumous organ works *Monodie*, *Offrande au Saint Sacrement*, and *Prélude* that have only recently come to light.

384. Gillock, Jon. "Originalité de l'œuvre d'orgue du point de vue musical et instrumental." In *Olivier Messiaen, homme de foi: Regard sur son œuvre d'orgue* (item 238), 27–30.

In this essay, Gillock notes the originality of the organ music of Messiaen from different perspectives. He considers Messiaen's organ works as the culmination of the French Romantic organ tradition exemplified by Franck, Widor, Vierne, Dupré, Tournemire, Duruflé, and Langlais. Gillock mentions the elements of Messiaen's musical language, claiming in the final analysis that the composer's music, influenced by plainchant, represents the summit of spiritual expression in the Roman Catholic faith. He views Messiaen, furthermore, as the Catholic counterpart to Bach. Gillock devotes the rest of his essay to Messiaen's innovative use of organ stops, employing several examples from the composer's works to illustrate his points.

385. Gillock, Jon, comp. and trans. "Messiaen's Organ Works: The Composer's Aesthetic and Analytical Notes." In *Music: The AGO-RCCO Magazine* 12/12 (item 244), 42–54.

Translates the liner notes from the Ducretet-Thomson recordings of Messiaen's organ music (*Le Banquet céleste* through *Livre d'orgue*) and the prefaces to *La Nativité du Seigneur* and *Méditations sur le mystère de la Sainte Trinité* as a way of presenting Messiaen's compositional aesthetic. Also includes remarks by Messiaen about his organ music from his 1967 conversations with Claude Samuel (in the translation by Felix Aprahamian—see Claude Samuel, *Conversations with Olivier Messiaen* [item 182], 2–3, 13–14, 16–17, 77–78, 80–81, 96) and his corrections to the printed scores that he pointed out to Jon Gillock when Gillock studied with him in Paris in the winter of 1977.

386. Glandaz, Olivier. "Olivier Messiaen et son instrument." In *Olivier Messiaen, homme de foi: Regard sur son œuvre d'orgue* (item 238), 81–82.

Considers Messiaen's ideas on the organ and organ registration. States that Messiaen made a break with tradition through his conception of the organ both as a vehicle for creation and as continually evolving. With respect to organ registration, color was paramount for Messiaen. He tended to use stops in a soloistic manner rather than combine them in related families as was the custom of his day. He was also opposed to the antiquarian movement in organ building. Although he was not hostile to instruments capable of playing Bach, Messiaen did not want organs limited to one or two repertoires. Moreover, he thought that antiquarian approaches to organ building adversely affected the sounds of reeds and foundations. After providing the registration of "Les Mains de l'Abîme" from the *Livre d'orgue* as a typical example of Messiaen's approach to organ registration, states that Messiaen achieved a whole array of coloristic effects from his organ at La Trinité. In the final analysis, artificial harmonics derived from mixture and mutation stops may lie at the core of Messiaen's search for color on the organ, since he not only was tempted to have other harmonics besides the commonly available fifths, thirds, or sevenths on his instrument but also viewed them as an integral part of the organ of the future.

387. Hakim, Naji. "Le Grand Orgue de l'église de la Trinité." In *Olivier Messiaen, homme de foi: Regard sur son œuvre d'orgue* (item 238), 80.

A short essay describing the Cavaillé-Coll organ during Messiaen's tenure as titular organist at La Trinité. The instrument has had a unique place in both the history of French organ building and music. Through modifications made to the original instrument as a result of his love for poetry and color, Messiaen played a pivotal role in determining the organ's aesthetic direction. Although he retained the organ's essential romantic sound by not altering its foundations and reeds, Messiaen expanded its sonorous potential by adding more mixtures and mutations. Thus the instrument was capable not only of grand tuttis and block registrations but also colorful combinations, such as the Positif's Quintaton 16' and Nazard 2 2/3', or the Grand Orgue's Clairon 4' and Plein Jeu IV.

Ultimately, the organ at La Trinité finds its best expression in the music that Messiaen wrote for it.

388. Halbreich, Harry. "Une théologie sonore: Par la connaissance vers l'Inconnaissable." In *Olivier Messiaen, homme de foi: Regard sur son œuvre d'orgue* (item 238), 21–26.

Because of their artistic and spiritual importance, considers Messiaen's organ works as not only unsurpassed in the twentieth century but also equaled only by the organ works of Bach in all of music. Compares the music of Messiaen with that of Bach from both musical and theological perspectives, emphasizing the characteristics that they have in common. Notes how both composers believed that all music was sacred and an act of worship. Concludes with a stylistic survey of Messiaen's organ works followed by a discussion of their relationships to the liturgical year, feasts of the dedication of churches, and the Holy Sacrament.

389. Kars, le Père Jean-Rodolphe. "Spiritualité de l'œuvre d'orgue de Messiaen." In *Olivier Messiaen, homme de foi: Regard sur son œuvre d'orgue* (item 238), 68–75.

A former concert pianist and first-prize winner of the 1968 Olivier Messiaen Piano Competition, Père Kars surveys the organ works of Messiaen according to their spiritual and theological themes. He notes that most of them are related to nearly all of the liturgical year—Christmas, Easter (the Passion and Resurrection), the Ascension, Pentecost, Trinity Sunday, the Holy Sacrament, All Saints' Day, Feast of the Dedication of Churches, and the Solemnity of Christ the King. Père Kars examines Messiaen's organ works according to the following categories, listed in their order of importance: (1) the Incarnation, Passion and Death, Resurrection, and Ascension of Jesus Christ; (2) the Holy Spirit; (3) God the Father; (4) the Holy Trinity; (5) the Holy Eucharist; (6) the Blessed Virgin Mary; (7) the Church; (8) the liturgy of the people of God; (9) the soul of the believer and his spiritual journey in grace to glory; (10) the invisible world, especially that of Angels; and (11) the glory of the invisible Church. He notes the theological significance of birdsong and the music of the stars in Messiaen's organ works as they foretell the resurrection of believers. Finally, Père Kars mentions two organ works that fall outside of any apparent spiritual category: "Reprises par interversion" and "Soixante-Quatre durées," both from the *Livre d'orgue*. Yet for Père Kars, they reflect a profound spiritual dimension, although more hidden: both pieces not only praise the God of time and space but also explore the relationships between time and eternity, leading Messiaen to the *Traité de rythme*. Highly recommended.

390. Klinda, Ferdinand. "Die Orgelwerke von Olivier Messiaen: Zum sechzigsten Geburtstag des Komponisten." *Musik und Kirche* 6 (November/December 1968): 263–69; 1 (January/February 1969): 10–12; 3 (May/June 1969): 106–14. ISSN: 0027–4771.

Stylistic consideration of Messiaen's organ music through the *Verset pour la fête de la Dédicace* published in three installments. Written in honor of Messiaen's sixtieth birthday in 1968. In part one, provides a biography of Messiaen, discusses his compositional style, and surveys his organ works. In part two, discusses Messiaen's organ music in relation to the modern organ and playing techniques. Considers his approaches to form, time, sound, structure, and playing within that aesthetic context. In part three, elaborates upon the issues raised in the second essay by detailing Messiaen's contributions to modern organ music. Considers stylistic elements found in the musical textures of manual and pedal parts, as well as how Messiaen handles registration, dynamics, agogic accent, articulation, and acoustics in his organ works.

391. Kohn, Père Francis. "Homme de foi et serviteur de Dieu." In *Olivier Messiaen, homme de foi: Regard sur son œuvre d'orgue* (item 238), 9–11.

A tribute to Messiaen as organist at La Trinité written on 1 November 1994 for the "Le Festival Messiaen à l'Église de la Trinité" in 1995. Père Francis Kohn, the last of the six curés who worked with Messiaen during his sixty-year tenure at La Trinité, notes the composer's dedication and faithfulness to his job as parish organist. He marveled at how Messiaen, a composer of international stature, could perform his duties with such humility. He also mentions special occasions on which the composer was honored by the church as well as Cardinal Lustiger of Paris. Kohn concludes his essay by noting the purpose of the "Le Festival Messiaen," which was simply not a homage to Messiaen but an intense exploration of the spiritual dimensions of his organ music.

392. Lee, John M. "The Earliest Organ Works of Olivier Messiaen: A Microcosm of Stylistic Transition." *The Diapason* 71 (February 1980): 6–7, 12–13. ISSN: 0012–2378.

Considers *Le Banquet céleste*, the *Diptyque*, and the *Apparition de l'Église éternelle* as part of the earliest phase of Messiaen's work as a composer. Although these pieces exhibit an eclecticism characteristic of a young composer seeking to express an individual style, the author believes that they are unique with respect to their integration of both old and new compositional techniques. Analyzes each composition from the vantage points of tonality, harmony, and form, with some attention paid to rhythm.

393. Lustiger, Cardinal Jean-Marie. "Musicien de l'invisible." In *Olivier Messiaen, homme de foi: Regard sur son œuvre d'orgue* (item 238), 7–8.

A short essay by Cardinal Jean-Marie Lustiger, Archbishop of Paris, on Messiaen's significance as a liturgical musician, written for the "Le Festival Messiaen à l'Église de la Trinité" in 1995. In Lustiger's view, Messiaen united Christian spirituality with musical art in his organ works, going beyond those considerations that might separate the two. He composed a music that not only illustrated his faith but also allowed one to penetrate into its deeper mysteries. Messiaen showed everyone how to progress along a spiritual path, inviting each person to submit to Christian truth in all its beauty.

394. Milsom, John. "Organ Music I." In *The Messiaen Companion* (item 240), 51–71.

Looks at the different technical procedures used by Messiaen in his early organ music from *Le Banquet céleste* (1928) to *Les Corps glorieux* (1939). Compares the aural experience of these works with their analytical apprehension. Notes the importance of timbre and sonority in Messiaen's organ music. Draws upon the composer's 1956 recordings of his organ works at La Trinité as a means to probe their sonorous nature.

395. Milsom, John. "Messiaen's Organ Music." *Gramophone* (December 1992): 31–32.

Milsom compares various interpretations of Messiaen's organ music to those recorded (in mono) by the composer in 1956, which were reissued by EMI in 1992 (*Messiaen par lui-meme: Organ Works*; see item B.6). He characterizes Messiaen's playing as imprecise rhythmically, and regards Messiaen's Cavaillé-Coll organ at La Trinité as contributing to the generally awful quality of sound found on the discs. Despite these misgivings, Milsom views Messiaen's interpretations as not only "spectacular and moving" but also superior to those by others. In assessing performances by other artists, Milsom looked for recordings that were both similar in spirit with and presented a creative alternative to those by Messiaen.

396. Otto, Theophil M. "Messiaen and the Baroque Organ: Notes on Purism and Pragmatism." In *Music: The AGO-RCCO Magazine* 12/12 (item 244), 40–41.

A discussion of Messiaen's organ registrations and how to realize them on instruments that bear little tonal resemblance to the composer's instrument at La Trinité in Paris. After exploring the relative merits of being a purist or pragmatist when registering Messiaen's organ works on non-French instruments, the author includes an English translation of Almut Rößler's essay about her experience with Messiaen when he was working out registrations for his organ music on the 1954 Beckerath organ at the Johanneskirche in Düsseldorf (see item 633). Rößler found Messiaen to be pragmatic in his approach to organ registration, concerned primarily with projecting the music clearly in a given acoustical setting.

397. Palmer, David. "Olivier Messiaen: A Tribute on His 80th Birthday." In *The Diapason* 79 (item 245), 10–11.

A birthday tribute on the occasion of Messiaen's eightieth birthday on 8 December 1988 that assesses his work, especially that for organ, and position as a composer in the late twentieth century. Palmer talks about many of the traits that characterize Messiaen's musical style.

398. Palmer, David. "Olivier Messiaen: A Biography." *The American Organist* 20/4 (April 1986): 65–71. ISSN: 0164–3150.

A short biography of Messiaen that provides context for the then upcoming world premiere of his *Livre du Saint Sacrement* (1984) on 1 July 1986 at the National Convention of the American Guild of Organists in Detroit. A typical biographical essay that outlines personal and musical events in Messiaen's life through 1986. Includes a chronological list of Messiaen's music (p. 71).

399. Roubinet, Michel. "À propos de la discographie d'Olivier Messiaen." In *L'Orgue: Revue trimestrielle* 224 (item 246), 46–54.

An annotated discography of the organ music of Messiaen. Includes recordings of the complete organ works by him, Louis Thiry, Jennifer Bate, and Hans-Ola Ericsson. Also includes recordings of selected works by Almut Rößler, Marie-Claire Alain, Susan Landale, Simon Preston, Rudolf Innig, Wolfgang Rübsam, Erik Boström, Kevin Bowyer, and Edgar Krapp. Provides the stoplist of the Cavaillé-Coll organ at La Trinité.

400. Tikker, Timothy J. "The Organs of Olivier Messiaen." *The Diapason* 79 (December 1988): 16–19; 80 (January 1989): 12–13; (February 1989): 10–13; (March 1989): 14–16. See item 245.

A four-part series that studies the organs associated with the music of Messiaen in order to bring forth a clearer picture of his approach to organ registration. Compares the registrations specified by Messiaen in his scores with the tonal resources of the instruments. Part one focuses on the history of the Cavaillé-Coll organ at La Trinité. It considers the relationships between the registrations of a particular organ work and the state of the Cavaillé-Coll organ at the time that work was composed. Part two examines other French organs associated with the music of Messiaen, such as the Cavaillé-Coll organ rebuilt by V. & F. Gonzales for the Palais de Chaillot in 1938. On that organ Messiaen premiered *Les Corps glorieux* on 15 April 1945. (While he acknowledges that the first performance of *Les Corps glorieux* took place on 15 November 1943 at La Trinité with the composer at the organ, Tikker argues that it was probably less public and hence less consequential compared to the performance at the Palais de Chaillot, because it took place during the German occupation of Paris [see p. 13, n. 31].) Also examined is the Jacquot-Lavergne organ at the Paris Conservatoire where the *Verset pour la fête de la Dédicace* was played for the 1961 organ *concours*. Part three looks at German organs: the E. F. Walcker organ associated with the world premiere of the *Livre d'orgue* at the Villa Berg, Stuttgart; and the von Beckerath tracker organ associated with the European and German premieres, respectively, of the *Méditations sur le mystère de la Sainte Trinité* and the *Livre du Saint Sacrement* at the Johanneskirche in Düsseldorf. Part four considers American organs, specifically the M. P. Möller organs associated with the world premieres of the *Méditations sur le mystère de la Sainte Trinité* and the *Livre du Saint Sacrement* in Washington, D.C. and Detroit, Michigan, respectively. Since the *Livre d'orgue*, all of Messiaen's organ works, except for the *Verset pour la fête de la Dédicace*, have seen their world premieres outside of France. But as the author notes, the registrations of these works show that they were intended for the Cavaillé-Coll organ at La Trinité. Although this article is geared toward professional organists with its discussions of organ construction, the tonal characteristics of individual stops and ensemble registrations, and French, German, and American schools of organ building, it is highly recommended.

401. Urwin, Ray. "The Late Organ Works of Olivier Messiaen." M.A. thesis, Yale University, 1978–79. 81 p.

     A study of the compositional innovations found in Messiaen's later organ music from *Les Corps glorieux* (1939) to the *Méditations sur le mystère de la Sainte Trinité* (1969), and their influence on contemporary organ composers such as William Albright, Charles Chaynes, Xavier Darasse, Bengt Hambraeus, André Jolivet, and Isang Yun.

402. Weir, Gillian. "Organ Music II." In *The Messiaen Companion* (item 240), 352–91.

     A performer's stylistic survey of Messiaen's later organ music from the *Messe de la Pentecôte* (1949–50) to the *Livre du Saint Sacrement*

(1984). In her discussion of the *Messe* and the *Livre d'orgue*, Weir focuses on Messiaen's rhythmic techniques (because of their importance in these works), presenting discussions of rhythmic characters, chromatic durations, permutation techniques, irrational values, nonretrogradable rhythms, serialized durations, and the free rhythm of birdsong. Weir then examines the *Verset pour la fête de la Dédicace*, a piece noted for its use of plainchant and birdsong, and issues related to the registration of Messiaen's organ music. She moves on to a consideration of Messiaen's last two organ cycles, the *Méditations sur le mystère de la Sainte Trinité* and the *Livre du Saint Sacrement*. In her discussion of the *Méditations*, Weir provides a thorough explanation of the composer's *langage communicable* and its rationale, in addition to noting aspects of his later musical style, which consists of intricately wrought musical textures that exude a grand simplicity. In the *Livre du Saint Sacrement*, she prefaces her survey of its movements by examining its theological plan, where the first four movements are associated with acts of adoration, the next seven describe events in the life of Christ, and the last seven focus on transubstantiation. Weir concludes her essay by recalling her encounters with Messiaen and reflecting on various aspects of the composer's organ music and how it should be performed.

PIANO MUSIC

403. Avery, James. "Olivier Messiaen: An Introduction to His Piano Music." *Contemporary Keyboard* 5 (August 1979): 36–42. ISSN: 0361–5820.

An introduction to Messiaen's piano works in which characteristic elements, such as the modes of limited transposition, *agrandissement asymétriques*, and nonretrogradable rhythms, are identified based primarily on an examination of "Regard de l'Esprit de joie" from *Vingt Regards sur l'Enfant-Jésus* (1944). Avery suggests ways to practice selected passages in "Regard de l'Esprit de joie," stating that these suggestions may be applied to other works. He also looks briefly at *Catalogue d'oiseaux* (1956–58) and *Modes de valeurs et d'intensités* (1949).

404. Hill, Peter. "Piano Music I." In *The Messiaen Companion* (item 240), 72–104.

Hill surveys Messiaen's early piano music from the *Préludes* to *Vingt Regards sur l'Enfant-Jésus*. He maintains that the *Préludes* owe little to Debussy; rather, they exhibit qualities characteristic of Messiaen, such as the suggestion of mysterious and tender moods, an acute sensitivity to harmony, and a strength of musical architecture. After a brief mention of the *Fantaisie burlesque, Pièce pour le Tombeau de Paul Dukas*, and *Rondeau*, Hill examines the *Visions de l'Amen*, the first of many pieces where the piano becomes the vehicle of Messiaen's grandest musical thoughts, where attention to detail gives way to a music epic in proportion and universal in expression. Hill concludes his essay by looking at *Vingt Regards sur l'Enfant-Jésus*, a piece which not only builds upon the model of *Visions de l'Amen* for its use of cyclic themes but also recaptures the tender intimacy of the *Préludes*.

405. Hill, Peter. "Piano Music II." In *The Messiaen Companion* (item 240), 307–51.

In this continuation of his earlier essay in *The Messiaen Companion* (see item 404), Hill examines Messiaen's later piano music from 1948–85. He offers insightful stylistic commentaries on each piece, tracing Messiaen's compositional odyssey from the pseudo-serial experiments first charted in *Cantéyodjayâ* and continued in *Quatre Études de rythme*, to the birdsong pieces of *Catalogue d'oiseaux, La Fauvette des jardins*, and *Petites esquisses d'oiseaux*. The essay's only shortcoming is its failure to explain the construction of Messiaen's later chord types, which would have enhanced the reader's appreciation of the composer's approach to harmony.

406. Hill, Peter. "For the Birds." *The Musical Times* 135/1819 (September 1994): 552–55. ISSN: 0027–4666.

After recently recording the complete piano works of Messiaen, Hill talks about performing the composer's music. His discussion includes frequent reminiscences of his studies with Messiaen. Hill mentions how Messiaen proclaimed that he was not a French impressionist, suggesting his dislike for any unnecessary blurring of the texture. In his approach to birdsong, Messiaen translated from rather than imitated nature, "inventing parallels or 'metaphors' which have their own purely musical integrity" (p. 552). Hill also remarks how the balancing of color and dynamic was Messiaen's ultimate criterion for virtuosity, and how the piano beginning in the 1940s served as a vehicle for Messiaen's thoughts and musical experimentation.

407. Lee, John Madison. "Harmony in the Solo Piano Works of Olivier Messiaen: The First Twenty Years." *College Music Symposium* 23 (1983): 65–80. ISSN: 0069–5696.

Investigates the harmonic structures found in Messiaen's solo piano works from the *Préludes* for piano (1929) through the *Quatre Études de rythme* (1949–50). Describes trends and consistencies of style among the pieces examined. The study also looks at melody, register, the spelling of chords, chord progression, and form when these factors are relevant to its interpretation of the composer's harmonic structures. In works from 1929 to 1944, the study notes: (1) Messiaen's use of tertian sonorities, particularly those with added notes; (2) the modes of limited transposition; (3) tonal ambiguities; (4) multiple superposition of tertian sonorities; (5) chord progressions that begin with tertian-based chords and move to less definitive ones; (6) occasional quartal structures; (7) harmonic planing; and (8) linear harmonies. As for the later works of 1949 to 1950, the study observes a variety of new techniques and harmonic structures not found in previous works, although in *Ile de feu I* and *II* there are techniques similar to those discussed in earlier compositions, such as the planing of untraditional harmonies, the superposition of quartal and quintal harmonies, the superposition of a nontertian chord over a tertian one, and the extended reiteration of a particular sonority.

408. Loriod-Messiaen, Yvonne. "Étude sur l'œuvre pianistique d'Olivier Messiaen." In *Portrait(s) d'Olivier Messiaen* (item 241), 75–160.

A performer's examination of the innovative textures found in Messiaen's piano music. Considers Messiaen to be the originator of contemporary writing for the piano because he used register in such a way that transcended the practice of previous composers. Notes how carefully Messiaen edited his piano scores, meticulously indicating how he wanted his music to be performed. Mentions the role of timbre in his approach to piano writing, a result of the many orchestral works he analyzed at the piano as a teacher at the Paris Conservatoire. Most of the article examines Messiaen's piano music in relation to extreme registers, distinctions between registers, geometric movements, fingering considerations, aspects of sonority, poetic style, rhythm, melodic interversions, and the treatment of chords, lines, and motifs.

409. Milsom, John. "Working with the Maître: Pianist Peter Hill Remembers Messiaen." *Gramophone* (September 1992): 20.

In this article, pianist Peter Hill recalls his studies with Messiaen while he was recording the composer's complete piano works. He remembers Messiaen as being open-minded regarding the performance of his music. In particular, Hill notes that Messiaen never showed the slightest inclination of turning him into a pseudo-Yvonne Loriod-Messiaen, preferring instead to encourage the development of his own musical insights. Hill offers a glimpse of

Messiaen's ideas on interpretation by recalling the composer's suggestions as to how the *Catalogue d'oiseaux* (1956–58) and *Vingt Regards sur l'Enfant-Jésus* (1944) should be played.

410. Pfaff, Timothy. "Keys to the Kingdom." *Piano Quarterly* (Summer 1992): 50–54. ISSN: 0031–9554.

A tribute to Messiaen on the occasion of his death on 28 April 1992 that includes a telephone interview of Messiaen student George Benjamin shortly after the composer's death. Most of the article focuses on Benjamin's discussion of Messiaen's organ and piano music. The article closes with another interview of Benjamin when he was artistic director of the San Francisco Symphony's "Wet Ink" Festival of new music in February 1992. Benjamin ruminates about the piano's role in his own approach to composing as well as its position in contemporary music of the late twentieth century.

MESSIAEN AS TEACHER

411. Benitez, Vincent P. "A Creative Legacy: Messiaen as Teacher of Analysis." *College Music Symposium* 40 (2000): 117–39. ISSN: 0069–5696.

Surveys Messiaen's work as teacher of analysis at the Paris Conservatoire. Examines his approaches to harmony, sound-color relationships, rhythm, melodic accentuation, and aesthetics. Includes an English translation of excerpts from Jean Boivin's transcription (see item 203—*La classe de Messiaen*) of the only known footage of Messiaen teaching (on Debussy's *Pelléas et Mélisande*) at the Paris Conservatoire, drawn from the 1973 documentary film, *Olivier Messiaen et les oiseaux*, produced by Denise Tual and Michel Fano (see item 194).

412. Benjamin, George. "Messiaen as Teacher: The Master of Harmony." In *The Messiaen Companion* (item 240), 268–73.

Benjamin recounts his experiences as a student in Messiaen's composition class at the Paris Conservatoire immediately before the composer retired in 1978. He found Messiaen to be a teacher who placed a great importance on developing a student's individuality; in other words, Messiaen did not want his students to be overly influenced by his music and ideas. Benjamin describes other attributes of Messiaen's pedagogy, such as his approach to harmonic analysis, where he stressed the development of certain chord types and their changing functions throughout music history as opposed to the study of harmonic levels, tension, and polyphony; the study of rhythm; the critiquing of student compositions in class; and the study of new instrumental techniques. All in all, a reverential portrait of Messiaen as a teacher.

413. Boivin, Jean. "Messiaen's Teaching at the Paris Conservatoire: A Humanist's Legacy." In *Messiaen's Language of Mystical Love* (item 236), 5–31.

Investigates Messiaen's teaching at the Paris Conservatoire as seen through the first three volumes of the *Traité de rythme, de couleur, et d'ornithologie (1949–1992)* and the recollections of his former students. Considers his personality, cultural refinement, faith, preoccupation with time and eternity, and ability to go beyond mere technique to the essence of creation.

414. Boulez, Pierre. "Messiaen as Teacher: The Power of Example." In *The Messiaen Companion* (item 240), 266–68. (This essay is a translation of a speech ["La toute puissance de l'exemple"] given on the occasion of Messiaen's seventieth birthday tribute at the Paris Opéra on 10 December 1978, following a performance of *Des canyons aux étoiles* by Yvonne Loriod-Messiaen and the Ensemble Inter-Contemporain directed by Boulez. The speech was first published in a collection of essays by Boulez entitled *Points de repère*, 2e éd. [Paris, 1980]. The present essay is taken from Martin Cooper's English translation of that volume, *Orientations: Collected Writings by Pierre Boulez* [see item 605].)

In this essay, Boulez considers the example Messiaen set as both a composer and teacher that inspired him to find himself as a musician. This kind of magic, as Boulez puts it, was accomplished not only by Messiaen's music but, more importantly, by the force of his personality and example. Boulez also discusses Messiaen's compositional legacy, one that includes liberating French music from the narrow confines of the "good taste" that dominated the aesthetic of France's musical past, and treating music as a universal phenomenon with no boundaries, which greatly enriched the older composer's powers of expression.

415. Castérède, Jacques. "Hommage à Olivier Messiaen." In *Olivier Messiaen, homme de foi: Regard sur son œuvre d'orgue* (item 238), 88.

Castérède was a student in Messiaen's analysis class at the Paris Conservatoire from 1949–52. He admired Messiaen's teaching, especially when the composer spoke about his own music. He recounts the time when Messiaen, during the course of analyzing the *Messe de la Pentecôte*, took seven or eight students to La Trinité to hear the music played on the instrument on which it was conceived.

After the passage of some thirty-five years, Castérède states that he can only now truly appreciate the significance of Messiaen's teaching and how much he learned.

416. Fano, Michel. "Hommage à Olivier Messiaen." In *Olivier Messiaen, homme de foi: Regard sur son œuvre d'orgue* (item 238), 87.

As a student at the Paris Conservatoire from 1949–51, Fano characterizes Messiaen's teaching of analysis as distinctly different from the dry academicism then prevalent at that institution. He notes how Messiaen taught with a passionate and generous spirit, fervently exploring uncharted musical territories and always guiding his students to find themselves as musicians. Fano was impressed, furthermore, by Messiaen's immense cultural education and knowledge of music when he taught in the classroom.

417. Goehr, Alexander. "The Messiaen Class." In *Finding the Key: Selected Writings of Alexander Goehr*, ed. Derrick Puffett, 42–57. London: Faber and Faber, 1998. xiii, 321 p. ISBN: 0571193102. ML 410.G563 A3 1998 (IUCAT).

An engaging account of Goehr's studies as a member of Messiaen's analysis class at the Paris Conservatoire from 1955 to 1956. Since Goehr maintains that his recollections are at odds with what has been written about Messiaen's class, the content of the essay goes beyond the typical reverent observations expressed by Messiaen's former students and explores intricate classroom dynamics between him and his pupils. From the outset, Goehr describes the tensions between Messiaen and his students, both French and foreign. Although the French students were highly accomplished musicians, they were largely ignorant of Messiaen's importance as a composer. Conversely, while less technically equipped, the foreign students, including Goehr, had come to Paris to study specifically with Messiaen, appreciating, in a word, his special talents. Goehr also discusses Messiaen's strengths and weaknesses as a teacher. Messiaen was at his best analyzing melody, relating music to literary and visual images, discussing Debussy by combining all of his musical interests in a unified manner, and, most importantly, lecturing on time and duration. On the other hand, Messiaen was a conservative teacher (not the revolutionary Goehr had envisioned) and at times bureaucratic. Following French tradition, Messiaen analyzed chordal structures individually with no regard for structural levels. In other words, all was surface. Highly recommended.

418. Hill, Peter. "Messiaen as Teacher: Messiaen on His Own Music." In *The Messiaen Companion* (item 240), 273–82.

Hill recalls his studies with Messiaen, which began in 1987, while he was recording the composer's complete piano music. He ruminates about what he learned regarding the interpretation of Messiaen's music as seen through the *Catalogue d'oiseaux* and *Vingt Regards sur l'Enfant-Jésus*. Hill notes the importance Messiaen placed on projecting the feeling of a piece; on balancing a principal line with its upper harmonic resonances, or the notes within a chord; on shaping virtuoso passages poetically; on rhythmic flexibility; and on exactness in pedaling. Reflecting on each of his sessions with Messiaen, Hill realized that the composer was actually helping him to develop his own interpretative ideas and insights.

419. Jolas, Betsy. "Milhaud, Messiaen: Maître et maître." In *Le Conservatoire de Paris: deux cents ans de pédagogie, 1795–1995*, ed. Anne Bongrain and Alain Poirier, with the collaboration of Marie-Hélène Coudroy-Saghaï, 371–77. Paris: Buchet-Chastel, 1999. 444 p. ISBN: 2283017742. MT 3.P2 C35 (IUCAT).

Darius Milhaud held the post of Professor of Composition at the Paris Conservatoire from 1949 to 1962. Messiaen held different posts, first as Professor of Harmony from 1941 to 1947, Analysis from 1947 to 1966, and Composition from 1966 to 1978. Jolas studied with both Milhaud and Messiaen, and praises the teaching of both musicians in this article.

420. Louvier, Alain. "Hommage à Olivier Messiaen." In *Olivier Messiaen, homme de foi: Regard sur son œuvre d'orgue* (item 238), 86.

Louvier was a member of Messiaen's analysis class at the Paris Conservatoire from 1965 to 1966, the last year in which Messiaen officially taught musical analysis before assuming his new duties as Professor of Composition in the fall of 1966. The topic that year was rhythm. Louvier describes Messiaen as possessing an inquisitive, universal spirit, likening him to Leonardo Da Vinci. Not only did he introduce his students to the musical thought of the Middle Ages, Antiquity, India, and Japan, Messiaen placed music in a new quadrivium comprised of mathematics, physics, cosmology, acoustics, physiology, poetry, philosophy, theories of movement, and color. Messiaen demystified the revolutionary aspects of recent music by demonstrating that their innovations in rhythm and timbre still could be traced to the work of great composers such as Mozart or Debussy. He taught his students how Debussy was a great rhythmician whose qualitative principles could be grasped in a quantitative manner. Finally, considered by many student composers as a master of Gregorian chant, Messiaen showed his students how the rhythmic principles of plainchant were still relevant to an understanding of twentieth-century music.

421. Rößler, Almut. "Olivier Messiaen als Lehrer: Ein Beitrag zum Prinzip der 'authentischen Interpretation'." *Musik und Kirche* 58/6 (1988): 285–89. ISSN: 0027–4771.

An internationally recognized performer of Messiaen's organ works who studied with the composer, Rößler describes qualities associated with Messiaen's teaching of organ interpretation, namely his (1) calm disposition, (2) strictness, (3) perfectionism, (4) faithfulness to the text, (5) approaches to rhythm and registration, and (6) imaginative handling of intellectual and theological subjects.

422. Schlee, Thomas Daniel. "Komponieren lehren und lernen: Olivier Messiaen (1908)." *Österreichische Musikzeitschrift* 42/12 (December 1987): 577–81.

Explores Messiaen's use of analysis of important musical works from all eras in his composition classes at the Paris Conservatoire, all in an effort to provide his students with a comprehensive education.

423. [Special Messiaen Edition.] "Hommage à Messiaen." In *Melos* 25/12 (item 242), 386–92.

Short essays by former students of Messiaen describing their interactions with him as a teacher. Contributors include Sieglinde Ahrens, Gilbert Amy, Jean Barraqué, Pierre Boulez, Jacques Charpentier, Raymond Depraz, Marcel Frémiot, Alexander Goehr, Karel Goeyvaerts, Yvette Grimaud, Yvonne Loriod, Jean-Louis Martinet, Serge Nigg, Jean-Jacques Normand, Makato Shinohara, Karlheinz Stockhausen, and Gilles Tremblay.

424. Stockhausen, Karlheinz et al. "Messiaen ist ein glühender Schmelztiegel: Zeitgenössische Zeugnisse über Messiaen." In *Olivier Messiaen: La Cité céleste – Das himmlische Jerusalem: Über Leben und Werk des französischen Komponisten* (item 248), 29–33.

Short tributes to Messiaen as a teacher by former students Karlheinz Stockhausen, Pierre Boulez, Iannis Xenakis, and Nguyen Thien Dao. Two of the tributes are reprinted from earlier publications. Stockhausen's contribution is a reprint of his 1958 essay for *Melos* (see item 423), and Boulez's essays ("Eine Klasse und ihre Schimären" ["A Class and Its Fantasies"] and "Rückblick" ["Retrospective"]) were published elsewhere, most notably in *Points de repère* (see item 604). Dao's text ("Über Messiaen") was written in 1979 (with no indication of publication), while Xenakis's tribute ("Über Messiaen") seems to be the only essay written specifically for this occasion.

6

Studies of Particular Works

This chapter contains sources that focus on individual works of Messiaen. They include analytical-theoretical studies, biographical considerations, performers' examinations, and stylistic discussions. They are arranged according to the following genres: (1) opera; (2) orchestral works; (3) chamber and instrumental works; (4) organ works; (5) piano works; (6) vocal and choral works; and (7) electronic works.

OPERA

Saint François d'Assise

425. L'Avant-Scène Opéra. *Saint François d'Assise: Messiaen.* Special Bilingual Program Book of the Salzburg Festival. Paris: L'Avant-Scène Opéra, Opéra d'aujourd'hui, no. 4, 1992. 125 p.

Issued in 1992 as a special program book on *Saint François d'Assise* by the Salzburg Festival in conjunction with performances of the opera in that city, this source, in both French and German, includes: (1) an introduction by Pierre Boulez ("Messiaen: Profil perdu," pp. 3–7); (2) Messiaen's last interview (see item 170—Entretien avec Olivier Messiaen," pp. 8–30) with Jean-Christophe Marti in January 1992; (3) a synopsis of the opera by Messiaen taken from the published score of *Saint François d'Assise* ("Argument," pp. 36–39); (4) a complete libretto with musical-dramatic commentary by Harry Halbreich ("Livret français intégral/Analyse musicale," pp. 41–101); (5) a listing of the opera's musical themes in Messiaen's autograph manuscript ("Thèmes musicaux," pp. 102–5); (6) an interview with José Van Dam on singing the title role ("Chanter le rôle-titre," pp. 116–19); and (7) various essays by René de Obaldia ("Séraphique Messiaen," pp. 32–35), Adolf Holl ("Réflexions sur François d'Assise," pp. 106–11), Jean-François Labie ("Ne vous procurez ni or ni argent," pp. 112–15), and Peter Sellars ("Pierre de touche," pp. 120–21). Contains a list of performances (complete as well as selected scenes) and a bibliography.

426. L'Avant-Scène Opéra. *Saint François d'Assise*. Paris: L'Avant-Scène Opéra, no. 223, 2004. 112 p. ISBN: 2843852021.

An updated version of item 425. In French only. New features include: (1) an introduction ("Points de repère," pp. 3–9) and glossary of Messiaen's musical terminology ("Glossaire," pp. 47–49) by Hélène Cao; (2) the inclusion of musical examples (presumably by Cao) with Harry Halbreich's 1992 musical-dramatic commentary on *Saint François d'Assise* ("Commentaire musical," pp. 14–45); and (3) essays by Gérard Condé ("La lumière luit dans les ténèbres . . . ," pp. 62–64) and Pierre Flinois ("Saint François d'Assise à la scène," pp. 70–77 [describes performances of *Saint François* from 1983 to 2004]; and "Discographie," pp. 78–81). Concludes with a history of the opera's performances (pp. 82–83) and an expanded bibliography (pp. 84–85) prepared by Elisabetta Soldini.

427. Benitez, Vincent P. "Narrating Saint Francis's Spiritual Journey: Referential Pitch Structures and Symbolic Images in Olivier Messiaen's *Saint François d'Assise*." In *Poznan Studies on Opera*. Volume 4, *Theories of Opera*, ed. Maciej Jablonski, 363–411. Poznan, Poland: Publishing House of the Poznan Society for the Advancement of the Arts and Sciences, 2004. 460 p. ISBN 837063401X. ML 1700.1.T46 2004.

Drawn from the sixth chapter of the author's dissertation (see item 429), this study investigates the dramatic design of *Saint François d'Assise* from a tonal/color perspective in order to interpret the development of grace in Saint Francis's soul, the opera's dramatic nexus. It focuses on Saint Francis's spiritual journey and the musical techniques that inform the various stages along his path.

428. Benitez, Vincent P. "Simultaneous Contrast and Additive Designs in Olivier Messiaen's Opera, *Saint François d'Assise*." *Music Theory Online* 8/2 (August 2002). ISSN: 1067–3040.

Explores Messiaen's claim regarding the role of simultaneous contrast in his approach to composition. Not only includes discussions of the use of simultaneous contrast in the work of Robert Delaunay (1885–1941), the composer's favorite painter, but also makes a case for their musical counterparts in *Saint François d'Assise*.

429. Benitez, Vincent P. "Pitch Organization and Dramatic Design in *Saint François d'Assise* of Olivier Messiaen." Ph.D. dissertation, Indiana University, 2001. vi, 456 p.

Considers how Messiaen uses different techniques of pitch organization to enhance the dramatic design of his opera, *Saint François d'Assise*. To set a foundation for its investigation, the study examines the opera's religious subjects, musical themes, formal designs, and harmonic vocabulary.

430. Braun, William R. "One Saint in Three Acts." *Opera News* 67/3 (September 2002): 46–51. ISSN: 0030–3607.

In anticipation of the American premiere of *Saint François d'Assise* in San Francisco in 2002, Braun describes the opera's background, dramatic design, performing forces, use of leitmotifs and birdsongs, and relations of sound and color for readers of *Opera News*.

431. Couvignou, Lionel. "*Saint François d'Assise*." In *Portrait(s) d'Olivier Messiaen* (item 241), 161–69.

An examination of the genesis and musical style of *Saint François d'Assise*. Recounts the commissioning of the opera by Rolf Liebermann in the presence of then President Georges Pompidou, describes Messiaen's conception of the opera's drama and the texts that inspired it, discusses his employment of musical themes to delineate the opera's characters, considers the use and significance of birdsong in the work, and notes Messiaen's block-like approach to form based on contrasts of timbre, use of instrumental and choral forces, and harmonic writing.

432. Fischer, Michel. "Olivier Messiaen: 'Saint François d'Assise (scènes franciscaines)': Un itinéraire musical du cheminement de la grace." *Analyse musicale* 49 (December 2003): 47–65. ISSN: 0295–3722.

Attempts to comprehend the drama of *Saint François d'Assise* by considering Saint Francis's path to grace. Examines scenes three through five and seven through eight in which the friar's encounter with the Leper, the dochmiac rhythm symbolizing the imposition of grace, the Angel's fourfold appearances, and the friar's request both to suffer and love as Christ did on the Cross, are considered significant elements of the opera's dramaturgy. Contains a selected bibliography and discography.

433. Gárdonyi, Zsolt. "Phänomene harmoniegeschichtlicher Kontinuität in Olivier Messiaens Oper *Saint François d'Assise.*" *Melos* 47/3 (1985): 58–66.

Focuses on the structural characteristics of the octatonic collection (i.e., the second mode of limited transposition) as used in the Angel's music of scenes four and five of *Saint François d'Assise*. Notes the major triads derived from an equal partitioning of the collection that often accompany the Angel. Also considers Messiaen's use of the octatonic collection historically by comparing it with that of Liszt, Debussy, Ravel, Scriabin, Bartók, and Stravinsky.

434. Grenier, Robert. "Recollections on Singing Messiaen's *Saint François d'Assise.*" *The Opera Quarterly* 18/1 (Winter 2002): 58–65. ISSN: 0736–0053.

Written by a singer who co-sang the role of Frère Bernard during the first production of *Saint François d'Assise* in Paris in 1983. Contains his memories of the experience and of his working relationship with Messiaen and his wife, Yvonne Loriod-Messiaen, including: (1) performers dealing with the large size of the musical scores; (2) intimidation of the singers by the huge orchestra; (3) the Messiaens' gracious hospitality, modest mode of living, use of intense colors (especially red) all over their apartment, and seriousness with which both regarded the rehearsals; (4) discovery that Messiaen felt it was his duty to France to compose an opera; (5) the mixed public reaction to the premiere; and (6) the powerful impressions of joy and suffering produced by the two scenes containing Saint Francis's sermon to the birds and receiving of the stigmata. Reflecting years later, the author considers the opera as being not principally about the voice but as posing profound questions concerning the saint's spiritual quest (to greater self-discipline) and that those ideas should remain predominant.

435. Griffiths, Paul. "*Saint François d'Assise.*" In *The Messiaen Companion* (item 240), 488–509.

In this essay, Griffiths gives an overview of *Saint François d'Assise*, noting its genesis, dramatic plot, musical themes, and performance history. He concludes by ruminating on Messiaen as a creative figure in the late twentieth century as seen through his opera. Griffiths considers *Saint François* as an iconic work that reflects Messiaen's tendency to mix reality with its representation in his music. He also views *Saint François* as an example of Messiaen's approach to composition, in which he combined a singular focus with multiple compositional techniques: nothing was seemingly excluded in the musical depiction of the opera's dramatic events.

436. Griffiths, Paul. *"Saint François d'Assise."* *Grove Music Online*, ed. Laura Macy. [www.grovemusic.com]. Accessed 22 July 2006.

Online version of the *New Grove*'s dictionary article. See item 437.

437. Griffiths, Paul. *"Saint François d'Assise."* In *The New Grove Dictionary of Opera*, ed. Stanley Sadie, 4:126–27. 4 vols. London: Macmillan, 1992. ISBN: 0935859926. ML 102.O6 N5 1992.

Summarizes the opera's performing forces and dramatic design. Regards *Saint François d'Assise* as a spiritual drama that focuses on the development of grace in Saint Francis's soul. There is no dramatic continuity either within or among the opera's eight scenes; instead, the work suggests a cycle of stained-glass windows through its static content. Includes descriptions of the dramatic events in each scene. Evaluates the place of *Saint François* in Messiaen's œuvre.

438. Guiberteau, Francine. "Le *Saint François d'Assise* d'Olivier Messiaen: Événement et avènement." *Analyse musicale* 1 (November 1985): 61–83. ISSN: 0295–3722.

Examines the opera's musical themes from melodic and harmonic perspectives. Remains somewhat close to Messiaen's analytical views by focusing on the tritone's role in shaping melodies, pointing out palindromic pitch structures, and identifying chords—at times incorrectly—through the use of his analytical labels.

439. Hill, Camille Crunelle. "Saint Thomas Aquinas and the Theme of Truth in Messiaen's *Saint François d'Assise*." In *Messiaen's Language of Mystical Love* (item 236), 143–67.

Draws on the writings of Saint Thomas Aquinas, Saint Francis, Franciscan writers like Père Louis-Antoine, and Messiaen in order to examine the composer's exploration of the concept of truth in *Saint François d'Assise*. According to the author, Messiaen develops the idea by means of a musical "Theme of Truth" sung by the character of the Angel to words paraphrased from the *Summa Theologiae* of Aquinas. Based upon the modes of limited transposition, the pitches of this theme evoke visual colors in Messiaen's synesthesia. Aquinas's text on truth and Messiaen's modes combine "sacred truth with visual and tonal color to create a music of 'éblouissement'" (dazzlement). The only drawback to this otherwise well-written article are its incorrect modal analyses. Extension of the author's doctoral dissertation (see item 440).

440. Hill, Camille Crunelle. "The Synthesis of Messiaen's Musical Language in His Opera *Saint François d'Assise*." Ph.D. dissertation, University of Kentucky and the University of Louisville, 1996. xi, 379 p.

A study of the elements of Messiaen's musical language and how they are integrated into the grand mosaic that forms *Saint François d'Assise*. Hill's treatment of pitch materials involves identifying the modes of limited transposition and their shaping of melodic themes, chords not derived from the modes, and serial techniques in musical passages. Argues for a mosaic form in the opera composed of pitch and timbral elements that accumulate to create larger musical-dramatic designs.

441. Hirsbrunner, Theo. "Die Farben der Himmlischen Stadt: Zu Oliver Messiaens Oper 'Saint François d'Assise'." In *Mahagonny: Die Stadt als Sujet und Herausforderung des (Musik-) Theaters*, ed. Jürgen Kühnel, Ulrich Müller, Oswald Panagl, Peter Csobádi, Gernot Gruber, and Franz Viktor Spechtler, 357–64. Anif/Salzburg: Mueller-Speiser, 2000.

Discusses the importance of sound-color relationships in Messiaen's music. Notes the pivotal role played by stained-glass windows in Messiaen's sound-color aesthetic, as seen by his appreciation of the windows at Sainte-Chapelle and Notre-Dame. Analyzes *Saint François d'Assise* using Messiaen's aesthetic ideas regarding perfect beauty and quasi-celestial harmony.

442. Keym, Stefan. *Farbe und Zeit: Untersuchungen zur musiktheatralen Struktur und Semantik von Olivier Messiaens* Saint François d'Assise. Studien und Materialien zur Musikwissenschaft, vol. 26. Hildesheim: Georg Olms Verlag, 2002. xi, 557 p. ISBN: 3487116618. MT 100.M47 K49 2002.

In an exhaustive study of the musical-theatrical structure and semantics of *Saint François d'Assise*, Keym attempts to achieve a synthesis between formal-compositional and theological-semantic analytical approaches by investigating how color and time interact. He looks at the development of Messiaen's musical language in terms of color and time, as well as each item individually. Keym concludes with an examination of *Saint François* as religious musical theater. The book contains four appendices, namely: (1) a technical glossary explaining Messiaen's harmonic language and device of symmetrical permutations; (2) photocopied pages from one of Messiaen's sketchbooks for the opera; (3) an overview of the opera's drama; and (4) a table listing the opera's textual sources.

443. Ozilou, Marc. "Olivier Messiaen: 'Saint François d'Assise': La musique comme vérité du livret." *Analyse musicale* 49 (December 2003): 66–73. ISSN: 0295–3722.

An analysis of the libretto of *Saint François d'Assise*. Maintains that the libretto is more than just a dramatic narrative but a work in which the listener must be actively engaged. Through a libretto that reveals the vantage point from which one listens, *Saint François*, like a contemporary work of art of any period, rejuvenates one's capacity to form aesthetic opinions.

444. Palmer, David. "Messiaen's *Saint François d'Assise.*" *The Diapason* (May 1984): 6. ISSN: 0012–2378.

Essentially the same essay on *Saint François d'Assise* as that published in *The American Organist* (see item 445). Describes: the opera's background; dramatic design; performing forces; costumes, sets, and lighting; and musical elements, particularly birdsong. Provides a critique of the performances of *Saint François* in Paris on 1, 3, and 6 December 1983. Concludes by placing the opera within the context of Messiaen's œuvre, declaring it to be "a grand summation of [his] musical language, intensified and fused for the first time with his own parallel visual elements."

445. Palmer, David. "*Saint François d'Assise*: An Opera by Messiaen." *The American Organist* 18 (March 1984): 46–48. ISSN: 0164–3150.

A summary of *Saint François d'Assise* from musical and dramatic vantage points. Notes that the musical language of the opera is reminiscent of the style Messiaen developed since the 1960s, as typified by *La Transfiguration de Nôtre-Seigneur Jésus-Christ, Méditations sur le mystère de la Sainte Trinité*, and *Des canyons aux étoiles*. Of interest is the discussion of harmony and color, rhythmic techniques, and birdsong. Finally, because the author attended performances of the opera in Paris on 1, 3, and 6 December 1983, he is able to provide readers with some comments about the quality of the production, which was superior in his opinion.

446. Petersen, Nils Holger. "Messiaen's *Saint François d'Assise* and Franciscan Spirituality." In *Messiaen's Language of Mystical Love* (item 236), 169–93.

Provides an historical backdrop to *Saint François d'Assise* by exploring the medieval spiritual traditions connected with the Franciscan movement of the early thirteenth century and their relationship to the opera. The emphasis on Saint Francis's spiritual growth and the use of historical costumes and decor accord well with twelfth- and thirteenth-century musical-dramatic and pictorial traditions. The opera not only alludes to the medieval liturgy through vocal gestures that hint at the differences between recitation and melodic singing, but also evokes Gothic spirituality and mendicant piety through the distinction between the development of Saint Francis's feelings and biblical and liturgical praises.

ORCHESTRAL WORKS

Les Offrandes oubliées

447. Klassen, Janina. "Theologischer Regenbogen: *Les offrandes oubliées* von Olivier Messiaen." *Jahrbuch des Staatlichen Instituts für Musikforschung Preußischer Kulturbesitz* (1998): 268–76. ISSN: 0572–6239.

Examines the religious symbolism, formal structure, and pitch content (i.e., modes of limited transposition) of *Les Offrandes oubliées*.

Turangalîla-Symphonie

448. Barber, Charles Frederick. "Messiaen and His *Turangalîla-Symphonie*. D.M.A. final project, Stanford University, 1991. iv, 127 p.

Considers the compositional and performance history of the *Turangalîla-Symphonie* and its position not only in Messiaen's œuvre but also in that of other twentieth-century composers attempting similar goals. Includes a discussion of the factors that influenced the *Turangalîla-Symphonie*, a movement-by-movement analysis, and an appendix (no. 6) suggesting conducting strategies in order to resolve the work's rehearsal and performance problems.

449. Bradbury, William C. "Messiaen and Gamelan: An Analysis of Gamelan in the 'Turangalîla-symphonie'." D.M.A. Thesis, vol. 2, Cornell University, 1991. 102 p.

Investigates the influence of Balinese gamelan music on the *Turangalîla-Symphonie*. Uses the work of Colin McPhee to summarize gamelan gong and *kebyar* styles. Analyses the symphony, noting how Messiaen based some of his percussion parts on Balinese musical practices and included compositional elements stemming from gamelan timbres, melodic devices, and colotomic structures.

450. Burkat, Leonard. "Current Chronicle." *The Musical Quarterly* 36/2 (April 1950): 259–68. ISSN: 0027–4631.

The first known English-language article on the *Turangalîla-Symphonie* from an author who attended the work's world premiere in Boston. Burkat describes the symphony's musical components in a movement-by-movement commentary, highlighting many of the work's rhythmic aspects.

451. Davidson, Audrey Ekdahl. *Olivier Messiaen and the Tristan Myth* (item 227), 63–106.

Includes an analysis of the *Turangalîla-Symphonie* in chapter three. Based upon the author's dissertation (item 228).

452. Davidson, Audrey Jean Ekdahl. "Olivier Messiaen's Tristan Trilogy: Time and Transcendance" (item 228), 181–280.

A dissertation on Messiaen's Tristan trilogy that includes an analysis of the *Turangalîla-Symphonie* in chapters five and six.

453. Fancher, Joseph E. "Pitch Organization in the *Turangalîla-Symphonie* of Olivier Messiaen." Ph.D. dissertation, University of Oregon, 2003. xv, 313 p.

Examines pitch organization in the *Turangalîla-Symphonie* from the perspectives of pitch-class set theory and neo-Schenkerian analysis. Argues that Messiaen employs an (016) trichord as a generative pitch cell for the entire symphony, which not only informs the construction of larger pitch collections on the surface but also relates temporally distant sections of music to each other. Focuses on modal pitch collections to the neglect of nonmodal ones in the work.

454. Herchenröder, Martin. "Komponieren nach Messiaen." *Musik und Kirche* 4 (July-August 1993): 188–96. ISSN: 0024–4471.

Despite Messiaen's overrated historical importance (according to the author) in the development of serialism, Herchenröder believes that he has still influenced many composers, especially those interested in mathematical approaches. The author analyzes the Introduction to the *Turangalîla-Symphonie* in order to show how Messiaen's diverse musical techniques can motivate a wide variety of compositional approaches.

455. Hook, Julian. "Rhythm in the Music of Messiaen: An Algebraic Study and an Application in the *Turangalîla Symphony*." *Music Theory Spectrum* 20/1 (Spring 1998): 97–120. ISSN: 0195–6167.

Systematic study of rhythm in the music of Messiaen using algebraic terminology and notation. Classifies fifty rhythms from the *Turangalîla Symphony* as either arising from generative, periodic, progressive, or recursive procedures. Considers interactions between pitch and rhythm and different rhythms upon each other. The author's employment of the term "rhythmic characters" to describe the many rhythmic processes at work in the symphony is incorrect. Messiaen's conception of rhythmic characters, which has been articulated unequivocally by the composer in his numerous interviews, lectures, and treatises, and echoed by many sources in the secondary literature, is much more narrow in scope. It centers around the tripartite polyrhythmic structuring of a musical passage where one rhythm augments at each repetition, another diminishes at each repetition, and the third rhythm stays the same. In his attempt to connect his work aesthetically to Messiaen's compositional approach, the author either appears ignorant of the Messiaen literature or does not deem it necessary to distinguish his interpretation of the term rhythmic characters from that found in most other sources.

456. Samuel, Claude. "Olivier Messiaen n'est plus obscur pour le grand publique." *L'Intransigeant*, 13 October 1961.

Not examined.

457. Schweizer, Klaus. *Olivier Messiaen: Turangalîla-Symphonie*. Meisterwerke der Musik, vol. 32. Munich: Wilhelm Fink Verlag, 1982. 79 p. ISBN: 3770520734. MT 130.M37 S4 1982.

An examination of the *Turangalîla-Symphonie* through formal, pitch, and rhythmic analysis. The study is divided into three parts: part one is an introduction that focuses on the genesis and first performances of the work; part two, the majority of the study, is a movement-by-movement analysis of the symphony; and part three contains answers to questions concerning compositional aesthetics, a publisher's note (translated into German) from the Durand edition of the *Turangalîla-Symphonie*, Messiaen's liner notes (translated into German) from two RCA recordings of the symphony, and reviews of the work's premiere in Boston from the *Boston Herald* and first performance in Europe (Aix-en-Provence) from *Epoque* (both translated into German).

458. Youngblood, Joseph. "Some Rhythmic Features in Messiaen's *Turangalîla Symphony*." *Percussionist* 15 (Spring-Summer 1978): 117–20. ISSN: 0553–6499.

A short article that examines the use of rhythm in selected percussion passages from the fourth ("Chant d'amour II") and sixth ("Jardin du sommeil d'amour") movements of the *Turangalîla-Symphonie*. The essay considers the construction of these passages and how their parts are integrated in their respective rhythmic textures. It likens Messiaen's rhythmic effects in the fourth movement to those produced by the *talea* of a fourteenth-century isorhythmic motet.

Réveil des oiseaux

459. Oh, Seung-Ah. "Olivier Messiaen's Composition Techniques in *Réveil des Oiseaux*." Ph.D. dissertation, Brandeis University, 2005. viii, 88 p.

Studies how form, pitch, and timbre are treated in *Réveil des oiseaux* from an organic perspective. Analyzes four different birdsongs (nightingale, blackbird, song thrush, and golden oriole) to determine how a limited collection of pitch materials is permutated. Looks at Messiaen's approach to "resonant harmony" with or without a fundamental in order to grasp how he colors birdsongs. The author's use of the term "permutation" to describe how Messiaen constructs birdcalls is misleading, for permutation implies a rigorous reordering of materials; "recombination" might have been a better term to use. Finally, the study suffers from numerous typographical errors.

Oiseaux exotiques

460. Bessière, Marie. "Oiseaux exotiques, d'Olivier Messiaen: De la nature à l'œuvre musicale." *Analyse musicale* 7 (April 1987): 62–67. ISSN: 0295-3722.

    Analyzes the ways in which Messiaen codified his musical language as exemplified in *Oiseaux exotiques*. Examines the use of birdsong in the piece, and to a lesser extent Greek meters and Hindu rhythms, in order to show how Messiaen enriched and adapted the orchestral, harmonic, thematic, and rhythmic elements of his musical style. Includes analytical charts.

461. Blarr, Oskar Gottlieb. *Oiseaux exotiques.* In *Musik-Konzepte 28: Olivier Messiaen* (item 243), 108–22.

    Stylistic and structural analysis of *Oiseaux exotiques*. Looks at the work in relation to its orchestration, formal relationships, layering of rhythmic and timbral elements, and pitch structure.

462. Hill, Peter and Nigel Simeone. *Olivier Messiaen:* Oiseaux exotiques. Landmarks in Music Since 1950. Aldershot, Hants, England, and Burlington, VT: Ashgate, 2007. ISBN: 9780754656306 (hardback); 9780754656302 (paperback).

    Not examined. Due to appear in July 2007. According to information provided by Ashgate, Hill and Simeone regard *Oiseaux exotiques* as the first successful synthesis of Messiaen's music and his passion for ornithology. They provide background information about the piece, examine Messiaen's work in relation to the 1950s avant garde, and consider his involvement with the concerts of the Domaine musical, for which *Oiseaux exotiques* was written.

Sept Haïkaï: Esquisses japonaises

463. Ohia, Chinyerem Maduakolam Nduka. "Messiaen's Rhythmic Techniques and Their Structural Application in *Sept Haïkaï*." Ph.D. dissertation, University of Pittsburgh, 1989. x, 230 p.

    Investigates Messiaen's use of rhythm as a form-generating device in his music. After examining the origins of Messiaen's rhythmic techniques, the study discusses how they are applied structurally in *Sept Haïkaï* in order to show how they both generate and unify the work. Pitch as a structural force is also considered, but primarily in terms of how it complements rhythm. Rhythm is the structural force behind the first, second, fourth, and seventh movements of *Sept Haïkaï*, whereas birdsong materials and sound-color structures form the basis of the third and sixth, and fifth movements, respectively. Concludes that what unifies *Sept Haïkaï* is the juxtaposition of materials, which are all superimposed in layers.

Couleurs de la Cité céleste

464. Kemmelmeyer, Karl-Jürgen. "Olivier Messiaen, 'Couleurs de la cité céleste'—Farben der himmlischen Stadt, 1963: Versuch einer didaktischen Aufbereitung für die S II." In *Musik und Bildung* 20/11 (item 251), 806–13.

    Analyzes the use of symmetrical permutations (interversions 13–15), Greek meters, Hindu rhythms, birdsong, biblical quotations, sound-color relationships, plainchant, and form in *Couleurs de la Cité céleste*. Also addresses the history and theological basis of the work, especially with respect to time. As the subtitle indicates, intended for use in German secondary schools.

465. Montgomery, Mary Ann. "Musical and Poetical Structures in Olivier Messiaen's *Couleurs de la Cité Céleste* and Ted Hughes's *Crow*." Ph.D. diss., Ohio University, 1989. viii, 301 p.

    Tests the validity of Walter Pater's statement (found in an 1873 essay on Giorgione in *The Renaissance*) that "all the arts aspire to the condition of music," by analyzing Messiaen's *Couleurs de la Cité céleste* and then comparing its structures and processes with those found in four poems ("Crow's First Lesson," "Crow Tyrannosaurus," "Crow Improvises," and "Littleblood") from Ted Hughes's *Crow*. Attempts to find meaning in the structural grammars of the two works. To understand the compositional aesthetics and techniques of *Couleurs*, examines Messiaen's *Technique de mon langage musical* and Claude Samuel's *Conversations with Olivier Messiaen.* Concludes that the four poems of Ted Hughes's *Crow* achieve the "conditions" of *Couleurs,* thus proving Pater's thesis.

466. Quilling, Howard Lee. "An Analysis of Olivier Messiaen's *Couleurs de la Cité céleste.*" Ph.D. dissertation, University of California at Santa Barbara, 1984. 40 p.

    A short study of Messiaen's *Couleurs de la Cité céleste.* After considering his compositional techniques from historical, mystical, and religious perspectives, the author attempts to demonstrate how Messiaen's preoccupations with birdsong, color, religion, and rhythm came together in the *Couleurs de la Cité céleste.* Detailed charts are supplied showing the structure of the work, its orchestration, and the location of musical components.

Et exspecto resurrectionem mortuorum

467. Cheong, Wai-Ling. "Composing with Pre-composed Chords in the Finale of *Et exspecto resurrectionem mortuorum.*" *Revue de Musicologie* 90/1 (2004): 115–32. ISSN: 0035–1601.

    Investigates Messiaen's use of the chords of transposed inversions on the same bass note, the first chords of contracted resonance, and turning chords in the Finale of *Et exspecto resurrectionem mortuorum.* Argues that these chord types were pre-composed and that Messiaen had employed them systematically in his works from 1960 onward. Notes that while these chords may be fixed in their pitch-class content and intervallic spacing, they are used with some flexibility in the Finale, primarily through the use of added notes that complete triads embedded in these chords, and through the alteration of a chord's intervallic spacing to accommodate registral spans established by the doubling of melodic notes. Finally, points out how Messiaen emphasizes conventional triads embedded in these chords through registral disposition, doublings, and orchestration, leading the author to speculate that these chords may be heard as colored triads.

468. Renshaw, Jeffrey. "Olivier Messiaen's *Et Exspecto*: An Interpretative Analysis." *The Instrumentalist* (November 1991): 28–34. ISSN: 0020–4331.

    Looks at *Et exspecto resurrectionem mortuorum,* noting each movement's use of melody, harmony, rhythm, and timbre. Follows these observations with conducting suggestions. The article is poorly written, with inaccurate statements about Messiaen's life and music interspersed within its sections. Not recommended.

Des canyons aux étoiles

469. Carl, Beate. *Olivier Messiaens Orchesterwerk "Des canyons aux étoiles": Studien zu Struktur und Konnex*, 2 vols. Kassel: Bärenreiter, 1994. ISBN: 3761811721. MT 130.M37 C37 1994.

    Considers *Des canyons aux étoiles* within the context of not only Messiaen's late musical style but also his entire orchestral œuvre. Looks at the piece's overall musical design, spiritual and programmatic aspects, pitch organization, and musical style in each movement. Does not address specific elements of Messiaen's later harmonic vocabulary, such as the chords of transposed inversions on the same bass note, in the study.

    Reviews: Theo Hirsbrunner, *Musiktheorie* 14/2 (1999): 179.

470. Steinitz, Richard. *"Des canyons aux étoiles."* In *The Messiaen Companion* (item 240), 460–87.

    A refreshing look at *Des canyons aux étoiles* from the vantage points of symbolism and structure, architecture, timbre, harmony, and compositional aesthetics. The author begins by exploring symbolic elements in the work, especially the *langage communicable* (a representation of the alphabet by specific pitches and durations) in the second and fourth movements, and how the music grows by accretion. He then looks at what makes the piece's large-scale architecture work, moving on to an examination of timbre and harmony, noting in the latter case the vast harmonic continuum that Messiaen uses in the work and how phrases often resolve to major triads. Finally, the author argues that through his approach to music, Messiaen is close in spirit to the nature-worshipping German Romantics of the early nineteenth century, who advocated a new synthesis of art and religion.

Un Sourire

471. Irvine, Catherine Anne. "The Interrelations of Formal Structure, Harmony, Register, and Instrumentation in Messiaen's *Un Sourire*." M.M. thesis, The University of Western Ontario, 1999. x, 184 p.

    Examines how Messiaen approaches form, harmony, register, and instrumentation in *Un Sourire*. Analyses harmony from the standpoints of the modes of limited transposition and pitch-class set theory. While the modal analysis is deemed to be inconclusive, asserts that pitch-class set analysis, in conjunction with a study of registral arrays, produced better results. While using pitch-class set theory as an analytical tool, does not identify nor explore the structural aspects of the nonmodal chords found in the music, making several statements that have more to do with American post-tonal theory than with Messiaen's perspectives on harmony. Nevertheless, one of the better master's theses on Messiaen.

Éclairs sur l'Au-Delà

472. Dingle, Christopher Philip. *Messiaen's Final Works: Developments in Style and Technique.* Aldershot Hants, England, and Burlington, VT: Ashgate, forthcoming. ISBN: 0754606333.

    Forthcoming. Not examined.

473. Dingle, Christopher Philip. "Understated Charm: Style and Technique in the Last Works of Olivier Messiaen." 2 vols. Ph.D. dissertation, University of Sheffield, 2000. vii, 389 p. (vol. 1); iii, 244 p. (vol. 2).

    Argues that Messiaen's late music underwent a definite stylistic change motivated by the composition of his opera *Saint François d'Assise.* To support the thesis, the dissertation examines the musical characteristics of seven works composed after *Saint François,* with special attention paid to harmony. The study focuses on the eleven-movement work *Éclairs sur l'Au-Delà,* analyzing each movement before considering the work as a whole.

474. Griffiths, Paul. "*Éclairs sur l'au-delà.*" In *The Messiaen Companion* (item 240), 510–25.

    Griffiths begins the article by situating *Éclairs sur l'Au-Delà* within Messiaen's later music. Unlike the grand summations that characterize the composer's output from *La Transfiguration de Nôtre-Seigneur Jésus-Christ* to *Livre du Saint Sacrement,* Griffiths considers *Éclairs sur l'Au-Delà* as a continuation of Messiaen's creative activities, suggesting a consistency of thought as a composer. Griffiths then looks at the sequence of miniatures from which *Éclairs sur l'Au-Delà* emerged (*Petites esquisses d'oiseaux, Un Vitrail et des oiseaux, La Ville d'En-Haut, Un Sourire,* and the *Pièce pour piano et quatuor à cordes*) before moving on to overviews of each movement.

475. Tölle, Julian Christophe. *Olivier Messiaen:* Éclairs sur l'Au-Delà: *Die christlich-eschatologische Dimension des Opus ultimum.* Europäische Hochschulschriften, Reihe 36, Musikwissenschaft, Band 191. Frankfurt am Main: Peter Lang, 1999. 341 p. ISBN: 3631348460. ML 410. M595 T65 1999.

Examines the eschatological elements of *Éclairs sur l'Au-Delà*. After establishing an interpretative framework, analyzes the work's eleven movements. Relates the musical language of each movement to Messiaen's *Traité de rythme, de couleur, et d'ornithologie* and information gleaned from Yvonne Loriod-Messiaen. Notes the significance of birdsong and number symbolism in the work. Interprets the titles and quotations placed at the beginning of each movement as referring to Messiaen's life and work. In the appendix, includes a chronology of Messiaen's later compositions from 1984–92, an incomplete chronology of the genesis and writing of *Éclairs sur l'Au-Delà*, musical illustrations of Messiaen's later harmonic vocabulary, a listing of the birdsongs used in the piece, an index of names, and a bibliography.

Reviews: Stefan Keym, *Die Musikforschung* 55/3 (July/September 2002): 330–31.

CHAMBER WORKS

Quatuor pour la fin du Temps

476. Bernstein, David Stephen. "Messiaen's *Quatuor pour la fin du temps*: An Analysis Based Upon Messiaen's Theory of Rhythm and His Use of Modes of Limited Transposition." D.M. dissertation, Indiana University, 1974. 132 p.

Notes many of the compositional techniques explained in the *Technique de mon langage musical*, especially those pertaining to rhythm and the modes of limited transposition, and observes how they are applied in the *Quatuor pour la fin du Temps*. Begins by describing the most important procedures associated with Messiaen's use of rhythm and the modes of limited transposition. Moves on to analyses of the pitch, rhythmic, and formal contents of each movement of the *Quatuor*. Closes the study by summarizing the most significant pitch and rhythmic techniques found in the *Quatuor*, as well as considering Messiaen's contribution to contemporary music as seen through this ground-breaking work.

477. Chen, Jo-Yu. "A Curricular Prototype to Enhance Compositional Skills through Improvisation Based on Messiaen's *Quatuor pour la fin du temps*." D.Ed. dissertation, Columbia University, 2005. 162 p.

Using selected excerpts from Messiaen's *Quatuor pour la fin du Temps*, develops a graduate-level curricular prototype in order to show classical pianists how to improve their compositional skills and theoretical understanding through extemporization. Chose Messiaen for the subject of the dissertation because he is said to be underrepresented in performance and theoretical study. Views Messiaen as possessing diverse compositional techniques that could be used as examples in the prototype. Moreover, his writings supply composers and performers with direct information. Designed the prototype for a wide variety of music-educational contexts. Believes that by relating the "threads of conscious thought and planning to those of intuition and spontaneity, a solid rationale can be built for improvisation as a precursor to composition" (pp. 8–9). After outlining the study's methodology in chapter three, tests its theories in chapter four through a series of improvisational activities, using rhythm and pitch elements from the *Quatuor* as organizational components.

478. Christensen, Erik. *The Musical Timespace: A Theory of Music Listening*. 2 vols. Aalborg, Denmark: Aalborg University Press, 1996. 174 p. (vol. 1), 67 p. (vol. 2). ISBN: 8773075256. MT6.C465 1996 (IUCAT).

Includes analyses of the rhythmic and pitch elements of the first ten measures of the "Abîme des oiseaux" from the *Quatuor pour la fin du Temps* (pp. 95–96, 101–2). Cites the passage as an example of additive rhythm, "where temporal patterns are created by the free addition of short durations." Looks at the use of pitch from the standpoint of contour, mode, and melodic soundspace.

479. Gonin, Philippe. "Le *Quatuor pour la fin du Temps* d'Olivier Messiaen: Temps et écriture musicale." *Analyse musicale* 44 (Sept 2002): 42–54. ISSN: 0295–3722.

Explores how Messiaen's Christian faith influenced his attempt to understand musical time through the *Quatuor pour la fin du Temps*. Looks at the piece's rhythmic, pitch, and formal aspects and how these elements contribute to this goal. Contains a schematic plan of the quartet's movements, along with a bibliography and a discography.

480. Lauerwald, Hannelore. "Er musizierte mit Olivier Messiaen als Kriegsgefangener: Der französische Cellist Étienne Pasquier im Gespräch mit Hannelore Lauerwald." *Das Orchester* 47/1 (1999): 21–23.

An important source describing the genesis and world premiere of the *Quatuor pour la fin du Temps*. Lauerwald interviewed cellist Étienne Pasquier of the Pasquier Trio shortly before his death in 1997 about his recollections regarding the composition and first performance of Messiaen's *Quatuor*. Like Messiaen, Pasquier was a prisoner at Stalag VIII A in Görlitz, Silesia. He was the cellist for the world premiere of the *Quatuor*. Although Pasquier was aware of Messiaen's reputation as a musician before World War II, he had never met Messiaen until their service together in the military near Verdun where he, as a corporal, was Messiaen's superior. After their capture following a battle with the Germans, they, along with other soldiers, were held in a large field in Toul, near Nancy, before their transferal to Stalag VIII A. It was there that they met the clarinettist Henri Akoka for whom Messiaen wrote a piece for solo clarinet, which eventually became the "Abîme des oiseaux," the third movement of the *Quatuor*. Akoka performed the piece in the field with Pasquier serving as a "music stand" (in other words, he held the music while Akoka played).

When Pasquier arrived at Stalag VIII A, he was assigned to the camp's cooking detail. He mentions how he would always give Messiaen an extra serving of food when the guards were not looking, and how the Germans allowed Messiaen to compose music in the corner of Hut 27B that was used as a church. Pasquier recounts how he went on a supervised trip to Görlitz in order to buy a cello after collecting money from his fellow prisoners to pay for the instrument. Soon after that, Messiaen wrote a trio for violin, clarinet, and cello that he, Akoka, and violinist Jean Le Boulaire played. Pasquier asserts that the trio became the "Intermède" of the *Quatuor*, the work's fourth movement. He also notes the many times he, Akoka, Le Boulaire, and Messiaen (after he was provided with a piano) rehearsed the *Quatuor* after it was completed from 6 p.m. to 10 p.m. in the camp's theater.

Finally, Pasquier describes the premiere of the *Quatuor* that took place on Wednesday, 15 January 1941. He estimated the size of the audience to be 400 based on the number of seats in the theater (at odds with Messiaen's estimate of several thousand), described how he and his fellow performers were attired, characterized the premiere as a complete success, and stated emphatically that he played on a cello with four strings, not three as maintained by Messiaen. The interview concludes with Pasquier describing how he, Messiaen, Akoka, and Le Boulaire were released from the camp with the aid of forged documents (stating that they were all "musician-soldiers") and a sympathetic German officer. Pasquier also mentions the premiere of the *Quatuor* at the Théâtre des Mathurins in Paris after their release with Messiaen at the piano, Pasquier on cello, Pasquier's brother Pierre on violin, and André Vacellier on clarinet. Pasquier closes by stating that it was Messiaen's fame as a composer that ultimately freed him, Akoka, and Le Boulaire.

481. Lauerwald, Hannelore. "Quartett auf das Ende der Zeiten: Olivier Messiaen als Kriegsgefangener in Görlitz." *Das Orchester* 43/5 (1995): 17–19.

Describes Messiaen's life as a prisoner of war in Stalag VIII A in Görlitz, Silesia, from the time of his capture by the Germans in the summer of 1940 to his repatriation back to France in 1941, where he assumed the post of Professor of Harmony at the Paris Conservatoire. Notes that while in captivity, Messiaen found solace by studying various musical scores that he was allowed to keep. Details camp life at Stalag VIII A. As a hospital orderly in the French army, Messiaen was assigned to the camp's medical detail, something that he has not mentioned in interviews. Talks about how Messiaen responded to getting together with Pasquier, Akoka, and Le Boulaire by composing a trio. Rehearsed in the camp's washrooms, the piece became the "Intermède" of the *Quatuor pour la fin du Temps*. Discusses the cultural life at the camp and Messiaen's role in it, mentioning his lecture on color and numerical symbolism in the Book of Revelation as witnessed by a priest, the Abbé Jean Brossard. Describes the world premiere of the *Quatuor* on 15 January 1941, noting how cold it was on that day and how the theater was filled to capacity with about 400 people. Closes by talking about Messiaen's repatriation back to France, life in Paris in the early 1940s, and his membership in an association of former French prisoners of war founded in 1965.

482. Matheson, Iain G. "The End of Time: A Biblical Theme in Messiaen's *Quatuor*." In *The Messiaen Companion* (item 240), 234–48.

A shorter version of an essay originally published in *Text as Pretext: Essays in Honour of Robert Davidson*, ed. Robert P. Carroll (see item 630).

483. Morris, David. "A Semiotic Investigation of Messiaen's 'Abîme des oiseaux'." *Music Analysis* 8/1–2 (1989): 125–58. ISSN: 0262–5245.

A semiotic analysis of "Abîme des oiseaux," the third movement of the *Quatuor pour la fin du Temps*, highlighting the work's hierarchical structure. The analysis is modeled after Jean-Jacques Nattiez's study of Edgard Varèse's *Density 21.5*. (Jean-Jacques Nattiez, "Densité 21.5 de Varèse: Essai d'analyse sémiologique," in *Monographies de sémiologie et d'analyses musicales*, No. 2 [Montréal: University of Montréal, Groupe de Recherches en Sémiologie musicale, 1975]; trans. and rev. as "Varèse's *Density 21.5*: A Study in Semiological Analysis," *Music Analysis* 1/3 [October 1982]: 243–340.) It attempts to find "possible poietic evidence to support its initial, 'neutral' findings." Because Messiaen talked extensively about his compositional techniques in the *Technique de mon langage musical*, the author believes it possible to "corroborate a neutrally conducted semiotic investigation with the composer's own views."

484. Pasquier, Étienne. "Hommage à Olivier Messiaen." In *Olivier Messiaen, homme de foi: Regard sur son œuvre d'orgue* (item 238), 91–92.

Another important source about the genesis and first performance of the *Quatuor pour la fin du Temps* from the cellist who was involved in the work's world premiere. Duplicates information found in Hannelore Lauerwald's interview of Pasquier (see item 480). Étienne Pasquier was guardian of a postern at the Citadel of Vauban just outside of Verdun where he first met Messiaen. As a corporal, Pasquier was Messiaen's superior and assigned him to guard duty. After the forces in which they served were defeated by the Germans in 1940, he and Messiaen were taken prisoner together and sent to Stalag VIII A in Görlitz, Silesia. While awaiting transfer to the Stalag, Messiaen and Pasquier, along with other prisoners, were held for several days in a large field in Toul, near Nancy. There they were with all of their companions, one of whom was a clarinetist named Henri Akoka, who had been allowed to keep his instrument. Messiaen wrote a piece for solo clarinet for Akoka that the clarinetist played while there. According to Pasquier, this piece became the "Abîme des oiseaux," the third movement of the *Quatuor pour la fin du Temps*. While at Stalag VIII A, Messiaen was recognized by the Germans for being the accomplished musician that he was. He subsequently received permission to perform the chamber music work on which he had been working, the *Quatuor*, at the Stalag. Rehearsals ensued with Messiaen at the piano, Pasquier playing the cello, Akoka the clarinet, and Jean Le Boulaire the violin, with the world premiere occurring on 15 January 1941.

485. Pople, Anthony. *Messiaen:* Quatuor pour la fin du Temps. Cambridge Music Handbooks, ed. Julian Rushton. Cambridge: Cambridge University Press, 1998. ISBN: 0521584973 (hard); 0521585384 (paperback). ML 410.M595 P58 1998.

Examines Messiaen's musical style through an analysis of the *Quatuor pour la fin du Temps*. Includes an introduction that describes not only Messiaen's musical influences but also the quartet's genesis, theological underpinning, and first performance; separate chapters devoted to a discussion of each movement; and a concluding chapter that considers the *Quatuor*'s position within the context of the composer's musical output. A concise source that explains Messiaen's compositional techniques in the quartet, comparing the quartet's passages at times either with those from the composer's other works or hypothetical models.

Reviews: Christopher Mark, "Messiaen: 'Quatuor pour la fin du temps'," *Music & Letters* 82 (February 2001): 143–45; and Diane Luchese, *Music Theory Online* 5/2 (March 1999).

486. Rischin, Rebecca. *For the End of Time: The Story of the Messiaen Quartet*. Ithaca, NY: Cornell University Press, 2003. ISBN: 0801441366. ML 410.M595 R57 2003.

Recounts the circumstances surrounding the composition and premiere of Messiaen's *Quatuor pour la fin du Temps*. Based on interviews and correspondence with Yvonne Loriod-Messiaen; Étienne Pasquier and Jean Le Boulaire, cellist and violinist, respectively, of the original quartet; relatives of Henri Akoka, the quartet's clarinetist; and witnesses to the work's premiere. Challenges Messiaen's recollections of which movement was composed first (the "Intermède" according to Messiaen or the "Abîme des oiseaux" according to Pasquier), whether or not Messiaen composed the work in the latrines or barracks, how many strings the cello had (three according to Messiaen or four according to Pasquier), and the number of prisoners in the audience at the work's premiere (5,000 according to Messiaen or 400, the capacity of the camp's theater, according to Hannelore Lauerwald's research in Polish archives). Suffers from an inadequate command of the sources related to its historical narrative, resulting in errors too numerous to cite here. The reader is encouraged to consult reviews by Leslie Sprout and Nigel Simeone (listed below) for more information.

Reviews: Leslie Sprout, *MLA Notes* 61/2 (December 2004): 423–25; M. Neil, *Choice* 41/10 (June 2004): 1891; Nigel Simeone, *The Musical Times* 145/1886 (Spring 2004): 91–94; Alex Ross, "Revelations: The Story behind Messiaen's 'Quartet for the End of Time'," *The New Yorker* (22 March 2004): 96–97; Alan Hirsch, *The Booklist* 100/6 (15 November 2003): 561–62; and [Anonymous], *Publisher's Weekly*, 13 October 2003, 69.

487. Rischin, Rebecca. "Music for Eternity: A New History of Messiaen's *Quartet for the End of Time*." D.M.A. treatise, The Florida State University, 1997. xvii, 370 p.

The basis for Rischin's book, *For the End of Time: The Story of the Messiaen Quartet* (see item 486). Examines the events surrounding the composition and premiere of Messiaen's *Quatuor pour la fin du Temps*. Spent a great deal of time conducting research in France, Germany, and Poland, especially collecting information from the surviving members of the Messiaen circle and their relatives, in order to refute the clichés and misconceptions surrounding the music's genesis and premiere. Chapters one through four provide background information about the *Quatuor*, whereas chapter five focuses on the work's first performance in the prison camp. Chapters six through seven discuss the liberation of the *Quatuor*'s four musicians, its Paris premiere, and Messiaen's post-war musical career. Chapter eight includes interviews of Étienne Pasquier, Jean Le Boulaire, relatives of Henri Akoka, and Yvonne Loriod-Messiaen.

488. Ross, Mark Alan. "The Perception of Multitonal Levels in Olivier Messiaen's 'Quatuor pour la fin du temps.'" Ph.D. dissertation, University of Cincinnati, 1977. iii, 247 p.

Views the harmonic structure of Messiaen's music in terms of multitonal levels, based on an investigation of compositional techniques discussed in the *Technique de mon langage musical*. Analyzes the *Quatuor pour la fin du Temps* and selected movements from *Poèmes pour Mi* and *Chants de Terre et de Ciel* to illustrate the presence of multitonal levels, which result, according to the author, from the expansion and elaboration of the modes of limited transposition. Chapter one includes a discussion of Charles Blanc-Gatti's ideas about sound-color relationships as articulated in the painter's *Sons et couleurs* (see item 650). Finally, the author's name is incorrectly listed in various sources as "Mark Alan Rose."

489. Straus, Joseph N. *Introduction to Post-Tonal Theory*, 3d ed. Upper Saddle River, NJ: Pearson Prentice Hall, 2005. xi, 273 p. ISBN: 0131898906. MT 40.S96 2005.

An analysis of a passage from Messiaen's "Abîme des oiseaux." See item 696.

ORGAN WORKS

Le Banquet céleste

490. Smith, Rollin. "*Le Banquet céleste.*" In *Music: The AGO-RCCO Magazine* 12/12 (item 244), 35.

A comparison of the original edition of *Le Banquet céleste* published in 1934 with the second edition published in 1960. Details the revisions Messiaen made to the original edition's registration indications, tempo and metronome markings, time signature, and interpretational suggestions.

Apparition de l'Église éternelle

491. Busch, Hermann J. "Olivier Messiaen: Apparition de l'Église éternelle: Beobachtungen und Anmerkungen zur Interpretation." *Orgel International: Zeitschrift für Orgelbau und Orgelmusik* 2/5 (1998): 48–49. ISSN: 1433–6464.

A performer's examination of a frequently played organ work of Messiaen. Notes the structural elements of the piece, such as: the pulsing bass characterized by Greek metric patterns; the second, third, and seventh modes of limited transposition; the immense crescendo and decrescendo; and open fifths. For the author, the work does not require a virtuoso. Considers Messiaen's registrations for the piece as conceived on the Cavaillé-Coll organ at La Trinité and how to adapt them to a German organ, as well as aspects of pacing. The use of the crescendo/decrescendo technique is characteristic of the French symphonic organ.

L'Ascension: Quatre Méditations symphoniques pour orgue

492. Holloway, Clyde. "The Organ Works of Olivier Messiaen and Their Importance in His Total *Oeuvre*" (item 212).

Holloway's consideration of *L'Ascension* is worth looking at for those desiring information about the organ version (see pp. 252–56). Although he considers the orchestral version first, his remarks about the first, second, and fourth movements apply to the organ version. Holloway discusses the challenges Messiaen faced when he transcribed *L'Ascension* for organ. He examines "Transports de joie d'une âme devant la gloire du Christ qui est la sienne," a new third movement that replaced the orchestral version's "Alléluia sur la trompette, Alléluia sur la cymbale," which Messiaen deemed as too problematic for transcription.

493. Siffler, Paul J. "An Analysis of Messiaen's Tempi and Phrasing in His Recorded Performance of *L'Ascension*." *Music: The American Organist* 43/11 (November 1960): 22. ISSN: 0164–3150.

An analysis of Messiaen's recorded performance of *L'Ascension* on the Cavaillé-Coll organ at La Trinité on the Ducretet-Thomson label. Discusses Messiaen's tempi via different metronome markings and notes their relative strictness or freedom within a movement. Considers the use of rubato as it relates to musical gestures, the observance of crescendo and diminuendo markings, and the employment of attacks and releases.

La Nativité du Seigneur

494. Foltz, Carolyn R. "Analysis of Compositional Techniques Used by Olivier Messiaen in *La Nativité du Seigneur.*" M.A. thesis, Kent State University, 1965. v, 47 p.

    A survey of the compositional devices used by Messiaen in *La Nativité du Seigneur*. After summarizing the contents of the *Technique de mon langage musical*, discusses how Messiaen uses rhythm, melody, form, and harmony in each of the work's movements. Summarizes the compositional devices used in each movement through the use of tables.

495. Hassman, Carroll. "Messiaen: An Introduction to His Compositional Techniques and An Analysis of *La Nativité.*" *The Diapason*, pt. 1 (December 1971): 22–23; pt. 2 (January 1972): 26–27. ISSN: 0012–2378.

    Surveys Messiaen's compositional techniques before proceeding to an analytical discussion of selected pieces in *La Nativité du Seigneur*. The survey of compositional techniques in part one draws heavily from the *Technique de mon langage musical*. The analytical discussion in part two takes a look at Messiaen's use of pitch (particularly the modes of limited transposition), rhythm, form, and various developmental procedures in "La Vierge et l'Enfant," "Les Enfants de Dieu," and "Dieu parmi nous."

496. Hochreither, Karl. "Olivier Messiaen: *La Nativité du Seigneur*: Eine Einführung unter besonderer Berücksichtigung der in diesem Werk angewandten kompositorischen Methoden." In *Festschrift für Michael Schnieider zum 65. Geburtstag*, 64–78. Berlin: Merseburger, 1974. 100 p. ISBN: 3875370821. ML 55.S365 1974.

    An introduction to the compositional techniques of Messiaen as seen through *La Nativité du Seigneur*. Examines the composer's use of the modes of limited transposition, nonretrogradable rhythms, augmentation and diminution, rhythmic polyphony, Hindu rhythms, melodic intervals, melodic contours derived from musical works or plainchant, birdsong, and form.

497. Romig, David W. and J. Melvin Butler. "Messiaen's *La Nativité du Seigneur* as a Setting for a Christmas Communion Service." In *Music: The AGO-RCCO Magazine* 12/12 (item 244), 32–34.

    Recalls a Christmas communion service at the Downtown United Presbyterian Church in Rochester, New York, on 1 January 1978 that was built around the music of Messiaen's *La Nativité du*

Seigneur. The service was developed by J. Melvin Butler, director of music and organist, and the Reverend David W. Romig, one of the ministers of the church. Romig composed a prose-poem for each of the work's nine meditations, replacing traditional liturgical texts in the service. Since the authors believe that the service was a memorable worship experience, they encourage other churches either to use the service intact or modify it for their specific theological or denominational needs.

498. Thissen, Paul. "Zahlensymbolik im Orgelwerk Messiaens" (item 356), 93–97.

    Includes an analysis of the numerological structure and religious symbolism found in "Jésus accepte la souffrance."

499. Thissen, Paul. "Zahlensymbolik im Orgelwerk von Olivier Messiaen" (item 357), 115–31.

    A longer and more developed version of the author's 1989 article found in item 356. Includes an analysis of "Jésus accepte la souffrance."

500. Zimmerman, Heinz Werner. "The Technique of Messiaen's 'La Nativité du Seigneur'." Translated from the German by Audrey Davidson. *Universitas: A Journal of Religion and the University* 4 (1966): 123–34. ISSN: 0566–1943.

    Examines *La Nativité du Seigneur* in relation to Messiaen's compositional techniques of the 1930s and 40s. After giving an overview of Messiaen's life and work, looks at *La Nativité* from the standpoint of its theological symbolism as discussed in Messiaen's preface. The rest of the article focuses on how aspects of the composer's musical language are reflected in the piece. The translator does not provide the original source for the article.

Les Corps glorieux

501. Michaely, Aloyse. "Messiaens Trinitästraktate" (item 290), 90–98.

    Considers how the musical materials of "Le Mystère de la Saint Trinité" are used to depict the Persons of the Trinity.

502. Thissen, Paul. "Zahlensymbolik im Orgelwerk von Olivier Messiaen" (item 357), 115–31.

    A longer and more developed version of the author's 1989 article found in item 356. Includes an analysis of the number symbolism found in "Le Mystère de la Saint Trinité."

Messe de la Pentecôte

503. Bingham, Seth. "Messiaen's Pentecostal Organ Mass." *Organ Institute Quarterly* 3 (Winter 1953): 9–18. ISSN: 0474–4748.

Descriptive overview of the *Messe de la Pentecôte* noting each movement's use of organ registration, form, themes, and pitch and rhythmic techniques. Bingham concludes with a discussion of Messiaen's compositional style based on his examination of the *Messe de la Pentecôte*. He evaluates how effective the work's musical elements are in communicating Messiaen's religious message.

504. Gut, Serge. *Le Groupe de Jeune France: Yves Baudrier, Daniel[-]Lesur, André Jolivet, Olivier Messiaen*. Paris: Honoré Champion, 1977. 158 p. ISBN: 2852030306. ML 390.G98.

Includes brief analyses of each movement of the *Messe de la Pentecôte* (see pp. 102–8).

505. Hohlfeld-Ufer, Ingrid. *Die musikalische Sprache Olivier Messiaen: Dargestellt an dem Orgelzyklus* Die Pfingstmesse. With an appendix by Almut Rößler (*Zur Interpretation der Orgelwerke Messiaens*). Duisburg: Gilles & Francke, 1978. 127 p. ISBN: 3921104416. ML 410.M595 H6.

A study of the elements of Messiaen's musical language as seen through an analysis of the *Messe de la Pentecôte*. Considers the composer's religious beliefs, ideas about time and eternity, thoughts about the meaning of liberty, and synthesis of both the sacred and secular in his music. Analyzes each movement of the *Messe de la Pentecôte* from the perspective of pitch and rhythm, noting, for instance, Messiaen's use of irrational rhythms, chord successions, Hindu rhythms treated as rhythmic characters, modes, permutations of a five-note series, a melody derived from plainchant alternating with melodies based on Hindu rhythms, special chords such as the chord on the dominant and chord of contracted resonance, and birdsong. The book includes an appendix by Almut Rößler that includes two essays on the interpretation of Messiaen's organ works.

506. Lora, Donna Bishop. "Characteristics of Olivier Messiaen's Compositional Style with Illustrations from the *Messe de la Pentecôte*." M.M. thesis, Bowling Green State University, 1973. iii, 56 p.

Attempts to elucidate the primary characteristics of Messiaen's compositional style through an analysis of the last two movements of the *Messe de la Pentecôte*, "Communion (Les oiseaux et les sources)" and "Sortie (Le vent de l'Esprit)." Before analyzing the two pieces in question, considers influences on Messiaen's compositional style as well as summarizes his compositional techniques as expressed in the *Technique de mon langage musical.*

507. Thissen, Paul. "Zahlensymbolik im Orgelwerk Messiaens" (item 356), 93–97.

Includes an analysis of the numerological structure and religious symbolism found in the "Offertoire."

508. Thissen, Paul. "Zahlensymbolik im Orgelwerk von Olivier Messiaen" (item 357), 115–31.

A longer and more developed version of the author's 1989 article found in item 356. Includes an analysis of the "Offertoire."

509. Weber, Paul Mathew. "Messiaen the Theologian." *The American Organist* 40/3 (March 2006): 70–72. ISSN: 0164–3150.

In an effort to fully appreciate Messiaen's music, attempts to reconcile the tools of musical analysis with the composer's theology by looking at the third movement of the *Messe de la Pentecôte,* "Consécration (Le don de Sagesse)."

Livre d'orgue

510. Cohalan, Aileen, R.S.C.J. "Messiaen: Reflections on *Livre d'Orgue.*" *The American Organist* 2/7 (July 1968): 26–27, 37–39; 11 (November 1968): 28–30, 56; 12 (December 1968): 28–31. ISSN: 0164–3150.

Three-part series that examines the *Livre d'orgue.* Asserts that to understand any work of art more fully, one must evaluate both the work and the person who produced it. Part one considers various elements, influences, and qualities—the expression of the sensuous, Debussy, rhythm, the modes of limited transposition, serialism, and the use of birdsong—that characterize Messiaen's music. Parts two and three analyze the individual movements of the *Livre d'orgue,* explaining Messiaen's use of rows and permutational techniques.

511. Forte, Allen. "Olivier Messiaen as Serialist." *Music Analysis* 21/1 (March 2002): 3–34. ISSN: 0262–5245.

This article is part of a larger study of serialism from 1921 to 1951. It views Messiaen as composing serial music from 1949 to 1951, inexplicably turning to a different, presumably avian, compositional aesthetic in the supposedly non-serial *Catalogue d'oiseaux,* after the composition of the *Livre d'orgue.* The article regards Messiaen's serial music as remarkable for its innovative techniques, and encourages its inclusion in the dodecaphonic canon. To advance its argument, the article focuses on "Reprises par interversion," the first piece from the *Livre d'orgue*, systematically examining it for its use of rhythmic characters, ordering procedures among its twelve-tone rows, and contour and symmetry. While the article offers many insights into the structure of "Reprises par interversion," its connection to Messiaen is tangential at best. In its attempt to portray a secular, dodecaphonic Messiaen who is interested primarily in teaching his students how to outdo the composers of the second Viennese School, the article ignores Messiaen's ideas on time and eternity, which are important components of his approach to serial writing. As a result, the article presents an incomplete picture of both Messiaen as serialist and "Reprises par interversion."

512. Heiß, Hellmut. "Struktur und Symbolik in 'Reprises par interversion' und 'Les mains de l'abîme' aus Olivier Messiaens 'Livre d'orgue'." *Zeitschrift für Musiktheorie* 1/2 (1970): 32–38. ISSN: 0342-3395.

Author states that he gained valuable insights into the structure and symbolism of "Reprises par interversion" and "Les Mains de l'abîme" through personal conversations with Messiaen. Examines the construction of the rows in both pieces, showing how continuity is preserved through the sharing of set classes (pitch-class sets related by transposition or inversion). In "Reprises par interversion," looks at the organization of other musical parameters besides that of rhythm. In "Les Mains de l'abîme," discusses aspects of form, the use of permutation in relation to "Reprises par interversion," and tonal centers.

513. Heiß, Hellmut. "Struktur und Symbolik in 'Les yeux dans les roues' aus Olivier Messiaens 'Livre d'orgue'." *Zeitschrift für Musiktheorie* 3/2 (1972): 22–27. ISSN: 0342-3395.

A continuation of the author's earlier article on the *Livre d'orgue* (see item 512). Investigates the rows used in the three strata of "Les Yeux dans les roues." Considers their structure and how they cohere both individually and in relation to other parts. Discusses why some tones are eliminated in the manual parts (usually to avoid duplication with a note in the pedal part). Examines how the music reflects the vision of Ezekiel from the Hebrew Bible (Ezekiel 1:18, 20).

514. Seidel, Elmar. "Messiaens *Livre d'orgue*." *Musik und Altar* 10/6/167 (May-June 1958): 167–74.

Regards Messiaen as one of the most important composers of postwar Europe, whose extension of ordering procedures to non-pitch parameters influenced the likes of Boulez, Nono, and Stockhausen. It is within this framework that the author places the *Livre d'orgue*, which he considers as expanding the possibilities of the post-war serial style in striking new ways. What follows in the rest of the article is a movement-by-movement summary of the *Livre d'orgue*, highlighting the major pitch and rhythmic techniques employed in each piece.

515. Trawick, Eleanor. "Serialism and Permutation Techniques in Olivier Messiaen's *Livre d'orgue.*" *Music Research Forum* (1991): 15–35. ISSN: 1042–1262.

Examines "Les Yeux dans les roues," the sixth piece from the *Livre d'orgue*, as a point of departure for an investigation of Messiaen's approach to serialism. Characterizes the composer's approach and its relationship to the European serialist tradition as neglected by scholars. Views Messiaen's serial techniques as innovative primarily because of the composer's *closed* (movement from the extremes to the center) and *open fan* (from the center to the extremes) permutational techniques and their effect on pitch relationships. The first part of the article focuses on a general examination of Messiaen's permutational techniques, formalizing them mathematically through "F" (closed fan), "R" (retrograde), and "RF" (open fan) operations on a twelve-element series and their combinations into chains. The second part of the article considers serial techniques in "Les Yeux dans les roues" from the standpoint of pitch. Regards the right- and left-hand parts as each containing a "meta-row" of six distinct twelve-tone rows, while the pedal line features a single row that undergoes five different order permutations.

516. Zacher, Gerd. "*Livre d'Orgue*—eine Zumutung." In *Musik-Konzepte 28: Olivier Messiaen* (item 243), 92–107.

Analysis of each movement of the *Livre d'orgue*. Regards the music's biblical citations as referring to the work's musical structure and its challenges to the listener rather than to poetical titles or a literary program. In a word, they serve as key elements for building a critical grasp of the music. Concludes that Messiaen's complex theology is represented successfully by a compact use of symbolism.

Méditations sur le mystère de la Sainte Trinité

517. Fanselau, Rainer. "Die musikalischen Ausdrucksformen des Dreifaltigkeitsmysteriums in Olivier Messiaens 'Méditations sur le Mystère de la Sainte Trinité'." In *Musik und Bildung* 20/11 (item 251), 796–805.

Examines a varied topography with respect to the *Méditations sur le mystère de la Sainte Trinité*: musical themes, religious symbolism, depictions of nature, representations of divine love, and organ registrations. Includes a chart (see Example 4) that lists the use of the *langage communicable*, birdsong, modes, special rhythmic devices, plainchant, and biblical passages within the work, along with the formal design of each movement. Considers Messiaen's representation of nature in terms of his utilization of birdsong. Views birdsongs as connoting "constructive freedom" in both a theological and musical-syntactical sense. Examines the birdsongs of the second movement according to how they appear in sketchbooks, sonograms, and the movement itself (see Example 7). Finally, argues that the coloristic effects produced by Messiaen's organ registrations devised at La Trinité are weakened when played on other types of organs (despite the composer's acceptance of those instruments).

518. Fishell, Janette. "Old Symbols—New Language: An Examination of Olivier Messiaen's *Méditations sur le Mystère de la Sainte Trinité.*" In *The Diapason* 79 (item 245), 12–15.

   A discussion of the *Méditations sur le mystère de la Sainte Trinité* that focuses on the ways Messiaen uses number symbolism, the *langage communicable*, chant, and birdsong to translate his trinitarian theology into music. Notes: how aspects of unity and contrast are achieved through various musical and theological relationships between movements; how the structure of the work is influenced by numerical considerations; how the *langage communicable* is used, especially with respect to motives; and how chant and birdsong are incorporated into the work.

519. Gillock, Jon, trans. "Messiaen ... Communicable Language." *Music: The AGO-RCCO Magazine* 8/4 (April 1974): 30–32, 42. ISSN: 0027–4208.

   In this article, Gillock gives an abbreviated English translation of Messiaen's explanation of the *langage communicable* from the preface to the *Méditations sur le mystère de la Sainte Trinité*. He also provides analytical notes to each Meditation based on Messiaen's commentaries, emphasizing the musical design and theological symbolism of each piece. Used as a part of his program notes that accompanied his performance of the New York City premiere of the *Méditations* on 15 January 1974.

520. Gilmer, Carl. "Messiaen's Musical Language in *Méditations sur le Mystère de la Sainte Trinité.*" D.M.A. research paper and lecture recital, Memphis State University, 1978. vi, 62 p.

Examines the compositional techniques utilized by Messiaen in the *Méditations sur le mystère de la Sainte Trinité*. Explains the construction of the *langage communicable* and how it is used to quote trinitarian texts from the *Summa Theologiae* of Saint Thomas Aquinas. Also looks at the composer's use of the modes of limited transposition, birdsongs, color and timbre, Hindu *decî-talâs*, nonretrogradable rhythms, Greek meters, and plainchant. Appears to be oblivious to Messiaen's later nonmodal harmonic language throughout the paper. Closes the study with a discussion of the work's religious connotations.

521. Grotjahn, Rebecca. "Meditationen, Geheimnisse, Zufälle: Messiaens Konzept der *langage communicable*." *Frankfurter Zeitschrift für Musikwissenschaft* 5 (2002): 94–110.

An examination of the *langage communicable* as used both musically and symbolically in the *Méditations sur le mystère de la Sainte Trinité*.

522. Michaely, Aloyse. "Messiaens Trinitästraktate" (item 290), 90–98.

Studies how the musical materials of the fifth movement of *Méditations sur le mystère de la Sainte Trinité* are used to depict the Persons of the Trinity.

523. Schlee, Thomas Daniel. "Olivier Messiaen: 'Méditations sur le mystère de la Sainte Trinité'." Ph.D. dissertation, University of Vienna, 1984. iii, 475 p.

Examines the compositional origins and musical techniques of *Méditations sur le mystère de la Sainte Trinité*. Analyzes the work in detail from thematic, harmonic, and rhythmic perspectives. Compares the music of Messiaen with that of Dukas and Langlais.

524. Thissen, Paul. "Zahlensymbolik im Orgelwerk von Olivier Messiaen" (item 357), 115–31.

A longer and more developed version of the author's 1989 article found in item 356. Includes an examination of the number symbolism found in the themes and structure of the *Méditations sur le mystère de la Sainte Trinité*.

Livre du Saint Sacrement

525. Bruach, Agustí. "Beziehungen zwischen Farbe, Programm und musikalischer Struktur im Orgelzyklus *Livre du Saint Sacrement* Olivier Messiaens." Edited by Peter Williams. *The Organ Yearbook: A Journal for the Players & Historians of Keyboard Instruments* 31 (2002): 145–54. ISSN: 0920–3192.

Stylistic analysis of the *Livre du Saint Sacrement*. Examines relationships between color, programmatic content, and musical structure in "Institution de l'Eucharistie" and "Les deux murailles d'eau."

526. Landale, Susan. "Olivier Messiaen: *Livre du Saint Sacrement*." In *L'Orgue: Revue trimestrielle* 224 (item 246), 24–42.

Discusses the background of the *Livre du Saint Sacrement* with particular reference to Messiaen's improvisations during the celebration of the Office at La Trinité, Dom Columba Marmion's "Christ dans ses mystères," and a historical trip to Jerusalem where Messiaen wanted to notate the birdsongs that Christ supposedly heard. Considers the eighteen movements of the work, remarking briefly on the musical techniques and symbolic elements found in each movement.

527. Mittelstadt, James A. "Olivier Messiaen's *Livre du Saint Sacrement*." M.M. thesis, Cleveland State University, 2000. viii, 331 p.

Investigates Messiaen's *Livre du Saint Sacrement* to determine whether or not Messiaen developed a distinctive late style. Contains an overview of the work from structural, theological, and musical perspectives, along with a more detailed look at individual movements. The study is marred by an insistence on the recurring use of mode 7 in the *Livre*, a ten-note collection that Messiaen rarely if ever used in his later music.

528. Rößler, Almut. "Gedanken zu Olivier Messiaens 'Livre du Saint Sacrement'." *Musica* 43/2 (March/April) 1989: 134–37. ISSN: 0027–4518.

Reflections on the *Livre du Saint Sacrement* from one of the world's leading interpreters of Messiaen's organ music. Considers the use of color, harmony, sound-painting, birdsong, and musical symbolism, especially the *langage communicable*, in the piece.

PIANO WORKS

Préludes

529. Derfler, Barbara Joan. "Claude Debussy's influence on Olivier Messiaen: An Analysis and Comparison of Two Preludes." M.M. thesis, University of Alberta, 1999. 82 p.

Compares Debussy's "La Cathédrale engloutie" and Messiaen's "Cloches d'angoisse et larmes d'adieu" in order to investigate Debussy's influence on Messiaen. To establish a framework for the study, turns to Harold Bloom's theory of "Anxiety as Influence" as adapted by Kevin Korsyn and Joseph N. Straus. Views Bloom's theory as one in which one composer strives to surpass a predecessor by misreading or revising his or her work. By examining the compositional techniques used by Debussy and Messiaen in their respective preludes from a formalist perspective, along with applying Straus's theory of influence, asserts that Debussy's influence on Messiaen can be shown.

530. Hirsbrunner, Theo. "Die 'Preludes' für Klavier von Olivier Messiaen." *Musica* 4 (July/August 1988): 361–65. ISSN: 0027–4518.

Overview of the eight preludes for piano by Messiaen. Identifies Messiaen's compositional devices; compares his musical techniques with those of other composers, particularly Debussy and Ravel; and considers the role of sound-color relationships in the work, although in a skeptical fashion. For Hirsbrunner, sounds are sounds and colors are colors.

Visions de l'Amen

531. Ngim, Alan Gerald. "Olivier Messiaen as a Pianist: A Study of Tempo and Rhythm Based on His Recordings of *Visions de l'Amen*." D.M.A. essay, University of Miami, 1997.

Studies Messiaen work as a pianist through an examination of his performance style of tempo (especially tempo rubato) and rhythm in his recordings of *Visions de l'Amen*. Asserts that there are numerous discrepancies between Messiaen's recordings and the printed score. Concludes that they are due in part to limitations in notating tempo rubato. Focuses on tempo and tempo change, markings that influence rhythm, and Messiaen's solos. Tries to comprehend the rhythmic vocabulary of *Visions de l'Amen* by cataloguing rhythmic techniques and tempos in order to determine their function and meaning in the music, comparing recordings made by Messiaen and Yvonne Loriod-Messiaen with those by other pianists, and studying and performing the work. Summarizes the study by offering a performance guide to the work.

Vingt Regards sur l'Enfant-Jésus

532. Amper, Leslie. "Messiaen's *Vingt regards sur l'Enfant-Jésus*." *Keyboard Classics* 8/5 (1988): 44–45. ISSN: 1044–3266.

A performer's guide to Messiaen's *Vingt Regards sur l'Enfant-Jésus*. Provides information about Messiaen's musical style. Consulted Yvonne Loriod-Messiaen in order to better comprehend the music.

Due to the exigencies of space, examines the first piece, "Regard du Père." Gives performance suggestions regarding tempo and the voicing of chords. Looks at how Messiaen treats the "Theme of God" in subsequent pieces (pp. 5–6, 10–11, 15, and 20).

533. Anderson, Shane Dewayne. "*Vingt regards sur l'Enfant-Jésus* by Olivier Messiaen: An Analysis of Its Content, Spiritual Significance and Performance Practice." D.M.A. treatise, University of Texas at Austin, 1999. x, 117 p.

Analyzes how harmony, melody, and rhythm convey extra-musical meaning in *Vingt Regards sur l'Enfant-Jésus*, providing a foundation for a performer's understanding of the music. Includes interpretative suggestions for each piece in the study.

534. Bowlby, Christopher S. "*Vingt regards sur l'Enfant-Jésus*: Messiaen's Means of Conveying Extra-Musical Subtext." D.M.A. dissertation, University of Washington, 2005. vi, 80 p.

Attempts to address how Messiaen's approach to musical structure conveys extra-musical meaning in *Vingt Regards sur l'Enfant-Jésus*. Examines how his compositional elements and processes are employed to contribute to the symbolism of each movement as well as the entire work. Relies exclusively on the *Technique de mon langage musical* with no mention of the *Traité de rythme*, especially in its discussion of *Vingt Regards*.

535. Bruhn, Siglind. "The Spiritual Layout in Messiaen's Contemplations of the Manger." In *Messiaen's Language of Mystical Love* (item 236), 247–67.

In an analysis of *Vingt Regards sur l'Enfant-Jésus*, argues for a structural design based on the piece's spiritual contents and the musical symbols that represent them. Uncovers a fourfold division within the piano cycle's twenty pieces, and associates spiritual events with their musical symbols throughout the essay.

536. Bruhn, Siglind. *Images and Ideas in Modern French Piano Music: The Extra-Musical Subtext in Piano Works by Ravel, Debussy, and Messiaen*. Aesthetics in Music, no. 6, ed. Edward Lippman. Stuyvesant, New York: Pendragon Press, 1997. xxxiii, 425 p. ISBN: 0945193955. ML 724.B78 1997.

As part of an examination of musical compositions inspired by poems or paintings in which the verbal or visual stimulus is translated into musical form, considers *Vingt Regards sur l'Enfant-Jésus* by Messiaen. Argues that *Vingt Regards*, along with other pieces by Debussy and Ravel, can be understood as "portraying and nuancing, commenting on and interpreting a non-musical stimulus," namely the religious subheadings of its individual movements. Part three ("Spiritual Concepts and Divine Attributes," pp. 229–375) is devoted to an examination of *Vingt Regards*. Looks at the relationships between subtext and music, concluding that they can be categorized on a scale ranging from pictorial to interior meanings. Includes overviews of Messiaen's musical language and *Vingt Regards* in Appendixes two and three, respectively.

Reviews: Theo Hirsbrunner, *Die Musikforschung* 54/3 (July-September 2001): 323; Thomas Daniel Schlee, *Österreichische Musikzeitschrift* 56/6 (June 2000): 87–88.

537. Bruhn, Siglind. *Musikalische Symbolik in Olivier Messiaens Weihnachtsvignetten: Hermeneutisch-analytische Untersuchungen zu den* Vingt regards sur l'Enfant-Jésus. Publikationen des Instituts für Musikanalytik Wien, Band 4. Frankfurt am Main: Peter Lang, 1997. 253 p. ISBN: 3631310978. ML 410.M595 B78 1997.

A hermeneutic interpretation of *Vingt Regards sur l'Enfant-Jésus*. Provides an introduction that surveys Messiaen's life and œuvre, theological and artistic influences, and musical language, concluding with an overview of the musical materials of *Vingt Regards*. Examines the religious symbols of *Vingt Regards* and how they are developed and expressed in the music.

538. Bruhn, Siglind. "Symbolic Representations of Divine Attributes in the Musical Language of Olivier Messiaen Exemplified in His Piano Cycle 'Vingt regards sur l'Enfant-Jésus'." *Symmetry: Culture and Science* 3/4 (1992): 431–57. ISSN: 0865–4824.

Studies Messiaen's musical representations of the divine in *Vingt Regards sur l'Enfant-Jésus*. Attempts to show correlations between the piece's musical parameters and structure, and the symbolic images contained in Messiaen's commentaries. Concludes that Messiaen's musical language can be interpreted as symbolic because it contains representations of theological ideas and images.

539. Burge, David. "Olivier Messiaen's *Vingt Regards sur L'Enfant-Jésus*." *Keyboard* 10/1 (January 1984): 66. ISSN: 0730–0158.

In his monthly workshop column, Burge examines Messiaen's *Vingt Regards sur L'Enfant-Jésus*. After providing background information on the piece, Burge discusses its stylistic aspects, such as its unique approach to musical time, lack of harmonic progression, and use of added values, virtuosic passages, and juxtaposition as a means to foster musical variety and formal continuity.

540. Carl, Beate. "Rhythmus, Metrum und die Verknüpfung von Tondauer und- höhe in Olivier Messiaens Klavierzyklus 'Vingt regards sur l'Enfant-Jésus'." *Die Musikforschung* 49/4 (October-December 1996): 383–402. ISSN: 0027–4801.

Emphasizes how the smallest durational value is used as the basis for many rhythmic elements of *Vingt Regards sur l'Enfant Jésus*. Looks at Messiaen's use of Indian rhythms, primary numbers, rhythmic canons, nonretrogradable rhythms, and rhythmic characters. Shows how duration and pitch are treated independently of each other, with duration considered as being more important than pitch.

541. Ennis, Paula. "A Study of Coherence and Unity in Messiaen's Cycle *Vingt Regards sur L'Enfant-Jésus*." D.M. document, Indiana University, 1979. viii, 99 p.

Examines how compositional techniques in the *Technique de mon langage musical* contribute to the musical unity and coherence of *Vingt Regards sur l'Enfant-Jésus*. After providing background information on Messiaen and considering the position of *Vingt Regards* in his œuvre, focuses on techniques associated with pitch, number symbolism, cyclic themes, birdsong, and rhythm that enhance the piano cycle's coherence. Analyzes movements six, ten, fifteen, and twenty and considers their interpretative challenges.

542. Hill, Matthew Richard. "Messiaen's *Regard du Silence* as an Expression of Catholic Faith." D.M.A. dissertation, University of Wisconsin—Madison, 1995. iv, 73 p.

Investigates how religious faith can impact musical perception when that faith is an integral part of the music, through an analysis of Messiaen's *Regard du Silence*. Chapter one ("Contemplating Silence") introduces the idea of faith as unknowing knowledge that becomes a means to unite with the divine. Argues that when music expresses this type of faith, it is associated with silence, and that is what *Regard du Silence* attempts to describe. Accordingly, considers how this piece is a contemplation of the mystical silence of faith. Chapter two ("Expressing Silence") develops interpretative strategies based on the ideas articulated in chapter one in order to understand the music from a structural perspective. Chapter three ("Silence as a Dark Night") focuses on the mysticism of the work, especially as a contemplation of silence. Relates *Regard du Silence* to Saint John of the Cross's view of faith as a "dark night."

543. Hopkins, Stephen O. "Rhythmic, Melodic, and Harmonic Integration in Olivier Messiaen's *Vingt regards sur l'Enfant-Jésus*, with Reference

to *Technique de mon langage musical.*" M.M. thesis, The Florida State University, 1985. iii, 177 p.

Analyzes *Vingt Regards sur l'Enfant-Jésus* in relation to the *Technique de mon langage musical* in order to reveal the piece's integration of rhythm, melody, and harmony. After providing background information on Messiaen and his works in chapter one, summarizes the contents of the *Technique* in chapter two. Examines how rhythmic, melodic, harmonic, and formal elements are employed in each movement of *Vingt Regards* in chapter three. Relies on the *Technique* to identify various compositional devices. Considers *Vingt Regards* from a large-scale perspective in order to ascertain how the music coheres.

544. Joos, Maxime. "Olivier Messiaen: *Vingt Regards sur l'Enfant-Jésus*: Analyse, perception et interprétation." *Analyse musicale* 44 (Sept 2002): 67–98. ISSN: 0295–3722.

Considers *Vingt Regards sur l'Enfant-Jésus* from three perspectives: (1) a stylistic examination of the piece, considering Messiaen's own ideas, with author commentary, and including charts outlining the main aspects of each movement (form, pitch space, rhythm, themes, and theological symbolism); (2) that of the listener—how the work is perceived; and (3) that of the performer—in this instance, through an interview with pianist Pierre-Laurent Aimard, a noted interpreter of Messiaen's works. Contains a bibliography and discography.

545. Lee, Hyeweon. "Olivier Messiaen's *Vingt regards sur l'Enfant-Jésus*: A Study of Sonority, Color, and Symbol." D.M.A. thesis, University of Cincinnati College-Conservatory of Music, 1992. vi, 136 p.

Thinks of *Vingt Regards sur l'Enfant-Jésus* as representing Messiaen's musical style and aesthetics in toto. With that as a backdrop, explores the metaphysical aspects of *Vingt Regards* and assesses Messiaen's "achievements in timbre." Examines the composer's musical aesthetics, use of symbolism in *Vingt Regards*, and timbral approach to harmony. Concludes with a discussion of sound-color relationships as found in the piece.

546. McKinnon, Heather Price. "Symbolism and Theology as Compositional Genesis in *Vingt regards sur l'Enfant-Jésus* by Olivier Messiaen." D.M.A. essay, University of Iowa, 1991. iv, 94 p.

Relates the symbolic elements described in the texts and titles of *Vingt Regards sur l'Enfant-Jésus* to the compositional techniques used in the music. Includes a biography, thoughts on time and sound-color relationships in Messiaen's music, and a movement-by-movement analysis of *Vingt Regards.*

547. Michaely, Aloyse. "Verbum Caro: Die Darstellung des Mysteriums der Inkarnation in Olivier Messiaens 'Vingt Regards sur l'Enfant-Jésus'." *Hamburger Jahrbuch für Musikwissenschaft* 6 (1983): 225–345. ISSN: 0342–8303.

In keeping with the author's later volume published in 1987 (see item 216), an exhaustive study of *Vingt Regards sur l'Enfant-Jésus* based on the thesis that the theology behind the work determines the entire compositional design, from its smallest details to its overall structure. Modal-tonal and chromatic-atonal pitch elements are linked with specific theological ideas.

548. Morris, Betty Ann Walker. "Symbolism and Meaning in *Vingt regards sur l'Enfant-Jésus* by Olivier Messiaen: A Lecture Recital, Together with Three Recitals of Selected Works." D.M.A. dissertation, North Texas State University, 1978. ix, 20 p.

A lecture recital (given on 10 April 1978) focusing on the symbolic content of Messiaen's *Vingt Regards sur l'Enfant-Jésus*. Argues that a complete understanding of the composer's music comes only in the context of its literary associations. Examines how number symbolism, cyclic themes, the literary idea of a spiral, birdsong, and Shakespeare, in conjunction with compositional devices such as *agrandissement asymétrique* (a technique where during several repetitions of a musical idea or passage, some notes are transposed up a half step, others are transposed down a half step, while others remain stationary) and repetitious passages in alternating thirds, contribute to a fuller understanding of the piece.

549. Mulder, Karen L. "Messiaen's Complicated Contemplations." *Christianity Today* 40/8 (15 July 1996): 52. ISSN: 0009–5753, 1551–1855.

Pianist Jacqueline Chew reflects on her association with and playing of Messiaen's *Vingt Regards sur l'Enfant-Jésus*.

550. Piirainen, Jr., John Ruben. "Olivier Messiaen's *Par Lui tout a été fait*: A Performer's Guide." M.M. thesis, Bowling Green State University, 1997. viii, 54 p.

Analyzes *Par Lui tout a été fait* in order to establish interpretative criteria for performers. Drawing heavily from Messiaen's *Technique de mon langage musical*, considers the use of rhythm, melody, form, and harmony in light of the piece's symbolism, which is the key, in the author's opinion, to unlocking its interpretative secrets. Also examines the technical considerations the piece poses for pianists, along with its philosophical implications.

551. Seifert, Charles Ernest. "Messiaen's *Vingt regards sur l'Enfant-Jésus*: A Historical and Pedagogical Study." Ed.D. thesis, University of Illinois at Urbana-Champaign, 1989. vii, 316 p.

One of the better performance guides to *Vingt Regards sur l'Enfant-Jésus*. Attempts to help interpreters gain a better understanding of the work through an examination of its interdisciplinary elements, namely, music, theology, philosophy, and visual art. Investigates how the French cultural milieu during the German occupation of Paris from 1940 to 1944 influenced the composition of *Vingt Regards*. Considers how Messiaen's family shaped his compositional aesthetics. Examines how musical techniques described in the *Technique de mon langage musical* were utilized in *Vingt Regards*. Looks at the religious influences of *Vingt Regards*, compiles a dictionary of symbols associated with the piece, and describes its musical style.

552. Whitmore, Brooks Blaine. "Rhythmic Techniques in Olivier Messiaen's *Vingt Regards sur l'Enfant-Jésus*." D.M.A. treatise, University of Texas at Austin, 2000. xiii, 145 p.

Surveys the rhythmic techniques used in *Vingt Regards sur l'Enfant-Jésus*. Following a "life-and-works" chapter, examines the elements of Messiaen's rhythmic language and the roles theology, nature, plainchant, ancient Greek and Hindu rhythms, and composers such as Debussy, Stravinsky, and Bartók played in their formulation. After analyzing the rhythmic techniques used in *Vingt Regards*, looks at how rhythm is utilized in Messiaen's later piano works in order to show how his approach to rhythm developed.

Quatre Études de rythme

553. Barash, Amari Pepper. "Cadential Gestures in Post-Tonal Music: The Constitution of Cadences in Messiaen's *Île de feu I* and Boulez'[s] *Première Sonate*, First Movement." D.M.A. dissertation, The City University of New York, 2002. xiv, 123 p.

In a study that attempts to define what constitutes a cadence in post-tonal music, looks at Messiaen's "Île de feu I,", the first piece from the *Quatre Études de rythme*, in chapter two (pp. 18–48). Provides an overview of the music's large-scale structure before examining cadences and their indicators, along with non-cadential moments, in the piece. To sum, the study attempts to define what a post-tonal cadence is, as well as offer theoretical ideas regarding musical boundaries and grouping in lieu of clear harmonic norms. It also seeks to supply more information about cadences to performers in order to enhance their interpretative insights. Includes the score of "Île de feu I" in Appendix A (pp. 110–13).

554. Covington, Kate. "Visual Perception vs. Aural Perception: A Look at *Mode de valeurs et d'intensités*." *Indiana Theory Review* 3/2 (1980): 4–11. ISSN: 0271-8022.

Contrasts the visual and aural aspects of "Mode de valeurs et d'intensités" in order to show how they mutually inform one's understanding of the piece, with the aural aspects taking precedence. The goal is to hear the work with shape and direction and not as a series of random notes. After providing a conventional explanation of the piece's structure that elucidates Messiaen's methodology, the author interprets the music as comprised of six planes of sound or strata, with each plane composed of notes united by similarities in register, dynamics, articulation, and duration. Employs graphs to illustrate various details about the piece's multi-layered structure.

555. Guertin, Marcelle. "Sémiologie et Interprétation: Quelques Aspects d'*Île de feu* 2 d'Olivier Messiaen." Montréal, P.Q., Canada: Faculté de musique, Université de Montréal, [1974?]. 184 p. ML 410.M595 G8 1974.

A stylistic examination of "Île de feu 2" focusing on how its main theme is transformed. Views the superior resonance (notes added above a sonority in order to transform its timbre) used above the main theme in mm. 1–7, and the lower-pitched material that accompanies the main theme in its first transformation in mm. 28–34, as counter-themes that participate in the main theme's structural development. Emphasizes the connection between analysis and performance, stressing that analysis allows a performer to understand a work objectively in all of its details so that he or she may bring forth a better interpretation. Closes with a short chapter on the relationship between *sémiologie* (i.e., semiotics) and interpretation.

556. Hirsbrunner, Theo. "Olivier Messiaen's 'Neumes Rhythmiques' [sic]." In *Musik und Bildung* 20/11 (item 251), 814–18.

An examination of Messiaen's "Neumes rythmiques." Considers the piece's genesis as well as place in *Quatre Études de rythme*. Questions Messiaen's characterization of "Mode de valeurs et d'intensités" as a mere exercise, musically worth nothing, by noting the use of similar compositional procedures in "La Chouette Hulotte" from the *Catalogue d'oiseaux* and "Les Stigmates" from *Saint François d'Assise*. Accordingly, concludes that technical procedures are a significant part of Messiaen's theologically oriented music. Looks at the rhythmic elements of Messiaen's musical language, believing that these and other elements coalesce to form a personal musical style of which "Neumes rythmiques" is a good example. Accordingly, "Mode de valeurs et d'intensités" is not the only path to a music of compositional complexity. The rest of the article is devoted to an analysis of the work. The rhythmic construction at the beginning (Example 1) suggests the tripartite structuring of rhythmic characters. Considers the role of color in the work by looking at the way Messiaen uses superior and inferior resonance to enhance melodic lines (Example 2). Also examines the play of color created by the contrast of extreme registers on the piano (Example 3), which are organized by nonretrogradable rhythms. Discusses aspects of Messiaen's approach to harmony by noting how two "atonal" chords (Example 4) are based upon the interval of a tritone and minor second (an "016" trichord from pitch-class perspectives). Relates the structuring of these sonorities to chords at the beginning of Boulez's Second Sonata.

557. Lee, John Madison. "Harmonic Structures in the 'Quatre Études rythmiques' of Olivier Messiaen." Ph.D. dissertation, Florida State University, 1972. v, 71 p.

This short study (58 pages of text) investigates the intervallic content, spacing, doubling, and spelling of the chords found in Messiaen's *Quatre Études de rythme* in order to understand the harmonic language of the *Études*. The study first uses a computer-based approach to distinguish sonorities by interval-class content, noting each sonority type's number of occurrences in all four pieces. It then interprets the computer data, classifying Messiaen's chords according to the frequency with which they are pedaled, producing two categories of sonorities: *simple structures* (chords consisting of one to seven tones that are usually not pedaled) and *aggregate structures* (chords consisting of seven or more tones that are normally pedaled). Finally, it considers the spacing, doubling, and spelling of Messiaen's chords for further insights into his harmonic language.

558. Schweizer, Klaus. "Olivier Messiaens Klavieretude 'Mode de valeurs et d'intensités'." *Archiv für Musikwissenschaft* 30/2 (1973): 128–46. ISSN: 0003-9292.

Valuable study of "Mode de valeurs et d'intensités." Considers its position within the context of both post-war European serialism and Messiaen's œuvre. Examines the work's modal design and how it is realized in the music. Also includes a discussion of *Cantéyodjayâ* and Boulez's opinions about Messiaen's compositional techniques (drawn from *Stocktakings from an Apprenticeship*; see items 652 and 653) and "Mode de valeurs."

Catalogue d'oiseaux

559. Cheong, Wai-Ling. "Symmetrical Permutation, the Twelve Tones, and Messiaen's *Catalogue d'oiseaux.*" *Perspectives of New Music* 45/1 (Winter 2007): 110–37. ISSN: 0031–6016.

Not examined.

560. Freeman, Robin. "Courtesy Towards the Things of Nature: Interpretations of Messiaen's 'Catalogue d'oiseaux'." *Tempo* 192 (April 1995): 9–14. ISSN: 0040–2982.

An examination of the *Catalogue d'oiseaux* as seen through reviews of two recordings by Anatole (*sic*) Ugorski (Deutsche Grammophon 439 214–2; see item B.209) and Peter Hill (Unicorn Kanchana DKPCD 9062, 9075, 9090; see item B.210). Considers the piano cycle's aesthetic and compositional style before examining the work in relation to the two recordings in question. Quoting Messiaen in an interview with Brigitte Massin (see item 171), establishes an artistic connection between Messiaen's birds and the tapestries of Jean Lurçat. Regards Lurçat's tapestries as a possible model for the *Catalogue*, since Messiaen might have viewed Lurçat's work at the Trocadero in 1958.

561. Hirsbrunner, Theo. "Magic and Enchantment in Olivier Messiaen's *Catalogue d'oiseaux.*" In *Messiaen's Language of Mystical Love* (see item 236), 195–212.

A descriptive and somewhat rambling essay that breaks little ground. States that Messiaen was inspired to compose because of his Roman Catholic faith, love of nature, and fascination with the "Tristan and Isolde" myth. Music was the vehicle by which he praised God, especially the divine revealed in nature and human love. Describes the contents of the *Catalogue d'oiseaux*. Though there are no human beings in the work, and God is never mentioned, Messiaen suggests that God is indeed present in these French birds and their environmental settings. In short, he "reaches beyond, into universality."

562. Kim, Paul Sung-Il. "Olivier Messiaen's *Catalogue d'Oiseaux* for Solo Piano: A Phenomenological Analysis and Performance Guide." Ph.D. dissertation, New York University, 1989. xi, 458 p.

Kim analyzes the *Catalogue d'oiseaux* based on the methods of Jan LaRue and Thomas Clifton. He argues that this "bifurcation of the analytical method" is productive because the style-analytical approach of LaRue, which is concerned with objectively examining a piece's musical components, reinforces Clifton's more subjective and philosophical phenomenological approach. After offering a biographical sketch of Messiaen, general introduction to his piano music, survey of his work with birdsong, and overview of the *Catalogue*, Kim proceeds to the heart of the study in which he analyzes six pieces from the *Catalogue* in depth using his bifurcated method, concluding each analysis with a "Performance Guide" where interpretative issues are explored.

563. Philips, John. "The Modal Language of Olivier Messiaen: Practices of *Technique de mon langage musical* as Reflected in *Catalogue d'Oiseaux*." D.M.A. dissertation, Peabody Conservatory, 1977. iv, 440 p.

Studies aspects of modality found in the solo piano music of Messiaen with a special emphasis on the *Catalogue d'oiseaux*. Considers the compositional techniques in the *Technique de mon langage musical*, in order to lay a foundation for the detailed discussion of Messiaen's music that is to follow. Looks at the modes of limited transposition, modal elements in piano works that postdate the *Technique*, which tend toward a total chromatic idiom, and sound-color relationships. Applies these findings to a study of *Catalogue d'oiseaux*.

564. Sun, Shu-Wen. "Birdsong and Pitch-Class Sets in Messiaen's 'L'Alouette Calandrelle.'" D.M.A. dissertation, University of Oregon, 1995. xiv, 152 p.

Attempts to understand 'L'Alouette Calandrelle' by comprehending its structural details, in order to perform the piece more artistically. Uses Messiaen's ideas from the *Technique de mon langage musical* as a backdrop from which to generate three large-scale analytical parameters of time, sonority, and pitch that are used to further a better understanding of the music. Pitch-class set theory not only is employed to analyze pitch and interval-class content but, more importantly, reveals details of continuity, similarity, and variety on different structural levels that would be difficult to uncover otherwise.

Petites esquisses d'oiseaux

565. Buchler, Michael H. "Relative Saturation of Subsets and Interval Cycles as a Means for Determining Set-Class Similarity." 2 vols. Ph.D. dissertation, University of Rochester, 1997. xxiii, 204 p. (vol. 1); 130 p. (vol. 2).

In a dissertation that investigates the intervallic and cyclic contents of pitch-class sets and the number and types of subsets with which they are saturated, analyzes "Le Merle noir," the second piece from Messiaen's *Petites esquisses d'oiseaux* (1985), in chapter four. Since chords derived from symmetrical collections are common elements of Messiaen's harmonic language, employs the "cyclic saturation similarity measure" (CSATSIM) defined in chapter two to compare pitch-class sets in "Le Merle noir." To facilitate the comparison of these sets, uses the "cyclic saturation vector" (CSATV) weighting value of 1.2. Concludes that CSATSIM was "quite useful in interpreting the progression of set types in the A [mm. 1–4, 10–13, 20–23, and 31–36] and C [mm. 7–9, 17–19, 26–30, and 38–40] sections of [the] work [where bird calls were not represented]," but less useful in the B sections (mm. 5–6, 14–16, 24–25, 37) where bird calls were represented.

VOCAL AND CHORAL WORKS

Trois Mélodies

566. Henstein, Robert John. "An Analysis of Three Song Cycles for Soprano and Piano by Olivier Messiaen."

    See item 336.

Poèmes pour Mi

567. Bradshaw, Susan. "Susan Bradshaw writes about the orchestral transcription of Messiaen's 'Poèmes pour Mi.'" *The Listener* 85/2189 (11 March 1971): 313.

    An examination of the orchestral transcription of "Poèmes pour Mi" in relation to the original version for voice and piano. Looks at the original version first, considering its text, musical language, and form. Discusses the orchestral version next, commenting on how successful Messiaen was in his transcription, especially how the piano part is rethought in terms of an orchestral palette, which at times brings out musical details previously unnoticed.

568. Henstein, Robert John. "An Analysis of Three Song Cycles for Soprano and Piano by Olivier Messiaen."

    See item 336.

569. Lyman, Rebecca. "Olivier Messiaen's *Poèmes pour Mi* for Voice and Piano: An Analysis of His Musical Language and Its Relationship to the Text." D.M. document, Indiana University, 1995. iv, 93 p.

A performer's analysis of *Poèmes pour Mi*. Relies on the *Technique de mon langage musical* to describe the work's musical language and compositional techniques. Focuses on how the modes of limited transposition are used in the piece, especially in relationship to the text. Also looks at the roles of added value and psalmody in the music. After an introductory chapter that includes an overview of Messiaen's compositional style as reflected mainly by the *Technique*, analyzes the nine songs from *Poèmes pour Mi* individually in each of the following nine chapters. Discusses aspects of coherence and the form of the piece in the conclusion.

570. Reeves, Janice E. Rogers. "Theological Symbolism in Olivier Messiaen's *Poèmes pour Mi*: An Interpretive and Set[-]Theoretic Analysis." D.M.A. dissertation, University of Missouri—Kansas City, 1997. xii, 140 p.

One of the better performer's discussions of a work by Messiaen. The study is divided into two parts: part one (pp. 12–43) is an analysis of the poetry, while part two (pp. 45–119) is a pitch-class set analysis of the music. In part one, the author delves into the religious and romantic connotations of each poem. She bases her interpretation of Messiaen's use of theological symbolism in *Poèmes pour Mi* on biblical passages and writings suggested by the composer's poetry. In some of her analyses, the author stresses the linguistic development of French words and Messiaen's symbolic employment of verbs and nouns. In part two, the analysis of the music is presented in relation to the modes of limited transposition. The modes are examined from set-theoretic perspectives. They are analyzed as pitch-class sets and compared intervallically with similar sets, discussed in connection with their methods of incorporation in *Poèmes pour Mi*, and considered in relation to their consistency of usage. The author concludes that through its regular use of the modes, along with other pitch-class sets, *Poèmes pour Mi* resembles a medieval morality play in which the modes participate as hypothetical characters.

Chants de Terre et de Ciel

571. Henstein, Robert John. "An Analysis of Three Song Cycles for Soprano and Piano by Olivier Messiaen."

See item 336.

572. Keith, Lizanne. "An Analysis of Olivier Messiaen's 'Chants de Terre et de Ciel' from the Perspective of *The Technique of My Musical Language*." M.M. thesis, University of Tulsa, 1997. v, 147 p.

As a rationale for the study's investigation, cites Messiaen's statement at the end of the *Technique de mon langage musical* that the song cycle *Chants de Terre et de Ciel* was highly representative of his musical style and should be studied closely for that very reason. Analyses the six songs of *Chants de Terre et de Ciel* according to the melodic, harmonic, rhythmic, and formal techniques laid out in Messiaen's treatise.

Trois petites Liturgies de la Présence Divine

573. Gut, Serge. *Le Groupe de Jeune France: Yves Baudrier, Daniel[-]Lesur, André Jolivet, Olivier Messiaen* (item 504), 109–20.

    Includes a stylistic analysis of the complete *Trois petites Liturgies de la Présence Divine*.

574. Simeone, Nigel. "Messiaen and the Concerts de la Pléiade: 'A Kind of Clandestine Revenge Against the Occupation.'" *Music and Letters* (November 2000): 551–69. ISSN: 0027–4224.

    Examines the genesis, rehearsal, performance, and reception of *Trois petites Liturgies de la Présence Divine*. See item 309.

Harawi: Chant d'Amour et de Mort

575. Anderson, Christine Lynn. "A Singer's Examination of Olivier Messiaen's *Harawi: Chant d'Amour et de Mort*." D.M.A. thesis, University of Cincinnati, 1982. iii, 87 p.

    An examination of *Harawi* that attempts to make the work more accessible to singers. After providing introductory material about Messiaen's life, religious views, musical language, as well as information on the music of the Incas and the Quechua language, the study considers the symbolic content, musical structure, and interpretative demands of each individual movement.

576. Davidson, Audrey Ekdahl. "Messiaen's Use of Peruvian Sources in His *Harawi* Song Cycle." *Michigan Academician* 12/1 (Summer 1979): 47–59. ISSN: 0026–2005.

    Investigates Messiaen's appropriation of Peruvian materials from Raoul and Marguérite d'Harcourt's *La musique des Incas et ses survivances* in *Harawi*, along with their musical transformation by means of his compositional techniques (Raoul and Marguérite d'Harcourt, *La musique des Incas et ses survivances*, 2 vols. [Paris: Geuthner, 1925]). Explores the symbolism of the song cycle, especially its emphasis on love and death, claiming that the composer's use of Peruvian sources was pivotal in giving these elements depth and substance. The article is based on the author's dissertation "Olivier Messiaen's Tristan Trilogy: Time and Transcendance" (see item 228). Aspects of the article were incorporated into her book *Olivier Messiaen and the Tristan Myth* (see item 227).

577. Davidson, Audrey Ekdahl. *Olivier Messiaen and the Tristan Myth* (item 227), 23–62.

Includes an analysis of *Harawi* in chapter two. Based upon the author's dissertation (see item 228).

578. Davidson, Audrey Jean Ekdahl. "Olivier Messiaen's Tristan Trilogy: Time and Transcendance" (item 228), 60–180.

A dissertation devoted to Messiaen's Tristan trilogy that includes an analysis of *Harawi* in chapters two through four.

579. Gut, Serge. *Le Groupe de Jeune France: Yves Baudrier, Daniel[-]Lesur, André Jolivet, Olivier Messiaen* (item 504), 94–102.

Includes a stylistic analysis of the first, fifth, and tenth songs from *Harawi*.

Cinq Rechants

580. Davidson, Audrey Ekdahl. *Olivier Messiaen and the Tristan Myth* (item 227), 107–32.

Includes an analysis of *Cinq Rechants* in chapter four. Based upon the author's dissertation (see item 228).

581. Davidson, Audrey Ekdahl. "Olivier Messiaen's *Cinq Rechants*: The Conclusion of His Tristan Trilogy." *The Centennial Review* 25/1 (Winter 1981): 48–58. ISSN: 0008–0901X.

An examination of Messiaen's *Cinq Rechants*, the third and final part of the composer's Tristan trilogy. Interprets the work as completing the theme of love and death as experienced in the Tristan story. Although noting some aspects of form and texture, is preoccupied with the work's poetic images and symbolic elements. The article is based on the author's dissertation "Olivier Messiaen's Tristan Trilogy: Time and Transcendance" (see item 228). Aspects of the article were incorporated into her book *Olivier Messiaen and the Tristan Myth* (see item 227).

582. Davidson, Audrey Jean Ekdahl. "Olivier Messiaen's Tristan Trilogy: Time and Transcendance" (item 228), 281–368.

A dissertation devoted to Messiaen's Tristan trilogy that includes an analysis of *Cinq Rechants* in chapter seven.

583. Edgerton, Robert A. "An Analysis for Performance of Messiaen's *Cinq Rechants*." D.M. document, Indiana University, 1973. iv, 251 p.

A performer's guide to *Cinq Rechants*. Places the work within the context of Messiaen's œuvre. Analyses the work's text, form, texture, and structure before considering interpretative issues and rehearsal techniques associated with its performance.

584. Gottwald, Clytus. "Fragment über Messiaen." In *Musik-Konzepte 28: Olivier Messiaen* (item 243), 78–91.

A two-part essay. The first part addresses characteristics of Messiaen's musical style, particularly the *style oiseau*. Views the *style oiseau* as an aspect of musical realism that reveals the religious qualities of Messiaen's music as specific phenomena, rather than as elements subordinate to religion. The second part of the essay deals with the first movement of *Cinq Rechants*.

585. Prost, Christine. "Questions de rythme et d'interprétation: *Le Printemps* de Claude Le Jeune [et] *Cinq Rechants* d'Olivier Messiaen." *Analyse musicale* 9 (October 1987): 33–42. ISSN: 0295–3722.

Examines the use of rhythm, along with its concomitant problems of interpretation, in "Pedre le sens" from *Le Printemps* by Claude Le Jeune and the first, second, and third movements of *Cinq Rechants* by Messiaen in order to shed more light on their compositional aesthetics. Although it purports to compare works by Le Jeune and Messiaen, the article is more of a study of *Cinq Rechants* than anything else. Notes the melodic nature of *Cinq Rechants* and how it exhibits traces of plainchant, the songs of the troubadours (albas—dawn songs), Peruvian folksongs (*Yaraví*—songs of love and death), and isorhythmic motets. But these heterogeneous elements, according to the author, are unified by the modal color of the scales employed and an approach to rhythm derived from the free multiplication of a small base value. Considers various melodic-rhythmic figures used by Messiaen in the first movement as neumes. Also looks at that piece's mode of pitches, durations, and intensities, and counterpoints based on Hindu rhythmic patterns. Concludes the study by comparing the rhythmic approaches of Le Jeune and Messiaen, emphasizing how they are related more by their conceptions of rhythm rather than by their treatments of it.

586. Schlee, Thomas Daniel. "Die *Cinq Rechants* von Olivier Messiaen." In *Zum Verhältnis von zeitgenössischer Musik und zeitgenössischer*

Dichtung, ed. Otto Kolleritsch, 121–35. Studien zur Wertungsforschung, Band 20. Vienna: Universal Edition für Institut für Wertungsforschung, 1988. 208 p. ISBN: 3702401903. ML 55.S92 Bd. 20.

This article consists of a general examination of *Cinq Rechants* followed by analyses of each movement. Regards *Cinq Rechants* as one of the classic works of contemporary choral literature and as occupying a key place in Messiaen's œuvre. It features not only novel choral writing but also innovative relationships between text and music. Examines the invented language used in *Cinq Rechants*, especially how the text is related to rhythm and color. Describes the influence of Claude Le Jeuene's *Printemps* on the structuring of rhythm and form in *Cinq Rechants*. In the second part of the article, considers aspects of form, text, and compositional technique in each movement.

587. Wiest, Lori Jean. "Olivier Messiaen's *Cinq Rechants*: The Importance of Rhythm as a Structural Element." D.M.A. document, University of Arizona, 1990. 40 p.

Regards *Cinq Rechants* as the culmination of and a framework within which to study Messiaen's rhythmic discoveries. Through an exploration of Greek meters, Hindu rhythmic patterns, and plainchant, along with techniques associated with canon, ostinato, and polymeter, Messiaen developed rhythmic techniques that involved adding short values to given rhythmic patterns and unconventional approaches to augmentation and diminution. Through an analysis of its form, meter adaptation, music-text relationships, and texture, *Cinq Rechants* can shed more light on Messiaen's approach to rhythm.

La Transfiguration de Nôtre-Seigneur Jésus-Christ

588. Bradshaw, Susan. "Messiaen's 'Transfiguration'." *The Listener* 84/2155 (16 July 1970): 93.

Examines Messiaen's *La Transfiguration de Nôtre-Seigneur Jésus-Christ* from a stylistic point of view. Considers *La Transfiguration* as a "supreme example of sustained musical thought functioning simultaneously at many levels—demanding, in return, an equally sustained, flexible and imaginative concentration from the listener." Briefly discusses the music's texts, scoring, structure, influences, and technical procedures.

589. Dingle, Christopher Philip. "La statue reste sur son piédestal: Messiaen's *La Transfiguration* and Vatican II." *Tempo* (April 2000): 8–11. ISSN: 0040–2982.

Explores the impact the Vatican II reforms of the Roman Catholic Church had on Messiaen's compositional style. Posits that although Messiaen must have found these reforms difficult to deal with because of his conservative religious beliefs, he reacted to them by composing *La Transfiguration de Nôtre-Seigneur Jésus-Christ*, a musical statement that alludes, according to the author, to pre-Vatican II thought and practice. *La Transfiguration* initiates, moreover, a process of "monumental consolidation" in which it serves as the first in a line of religious works in which both progressive and traditional elements are frequently juxtaposed.

590. Dingle, Christopher Philip. "Olivier Messiaen: *La Transfiguration de Nôtre-Seigneur, Jésus-Christ*: A Provisional Study." 2 vols. Master of Philosophy thesis, University of Sheffield, 1994. vi, 131 p. (vol. 1); 133 p. (vol. 2).

Considers the musical and theological aspects of *La Transfiguration de Nôtre-Seigneur Jésus-Christ* in order to obtain a better grasp of Messiaen's compositional intentions for the work. Regards *La Transfiguration* as Messiaen's preeminent religious work due to the control theological concerns have over musical ones, and a change of musical style, labeled as "Consolidatory Monumentalism." To set the stage for an analysis of the composition's fourteen movements, the thesis examines Messiaen's work before composing *La Transfiguration*, the theological and musical structure of the piece, and the effect Vatican II reforms had on Messiaen. Theological issues related to "light," "mystery," and "transcendence" dominate the study's discussion.

591. Mellers, Wilfrid. *"La Transfiguration de Nôtre-Seigneur Jésus-Christ."* In *The Messiaen Companion* (item 240), 448–59.

Outlines the musical structure and content of *La Transfiguration de Nôtre-Seigneur Jésus-Christ*. Views the work as a blend of Christian Passion music with Gospel narration and a celebratory oratorio. Notes the work's "mosaic of Latin texts" intended by Messiaen to evoke the mystery of Christ's Transfiguration, along with its large-scale structure, before proceeding to a movement-by-movement analysis. The article has some interesting things to say about the piece, but unfortunately fails to support its contentions.

592. Michel, Alain. "La Transfiguration et la Beauté: d'Olivier Messiaen à Urs von Balthasar." In *La Recherche Artistique présente hommage à Olivier Messiaen* (item 247), 86–89.

Perceptive study of the text of *La Transfiguration* and its religious symbolism. Included in the *La Recherche Artistique* program booklet at Messiaen's request. Originally published in the *Bulletin de l'Association Guillaume Budé* (December 1974).

593. Schweizer, Klaus. "Materialdenken und Stilbildung bei Olivier Messiaen: Anmerkungen zu Satz VI des Oratoriums 'La Transfiguration de Notre Seigneur Jésus-Christ'." *Schweizer Jahrbuch für Musikwissenschaft/ Annales suisses de musicology* 8–9 (1988–89): 95–114.

Views the movement as a complex whole in which individual strata, such as avian polyphony, harmonic counterpoint, and texted vocal lines, blend. The extraneous materials, such as bird calls, Gregorian chant, Indian rhythmic patterns, and musical citations are not only transformed but also absorbed completely into Messiaen's musical language, acquiring new meaning as a result.

594. Simeone, Nigel. "Towards 'un succès absolument formidable': The Birth of Messiaen's *La Transfiguration*." *The Musical Times* 145/ 1887 (Summer 2004): 5–24. ISSN: 0027–4666.

Traces the genesis of Messiaen's *La Transfiguration* through the correspondence between Messiaen and Maria Madalena de Azeredo Peridigão (1924–89), Director of the Music Department of the Gulbenkian Foundation in Lisbon, Portugal. A fascinating read containing materials previously unpublished (besides the correspondence and extracts from Messiaen's diaries) that reveals the path which led to the final version of one of Messiaen's most important compositions. Parts of the article are derived from Peter Hill and Nigel Simeone, *Messiaen* (see item 210).

ELECTRONIC WORKS

Timbres-Durées (unpublished)

595. Goléa, Antoine. "Tendances de la musique concrète." *La Revue musicale: Vers une musique expérimentale*, no. 236 (1957): 36–44. ISSN: 0768–1593.

In this examination of *musique concrète* in which its short history is interpreted as consisting of four trends (toward direct expression, abstraction, pure music, and the most important works which combine these trends), analyzes Messiaen's composition for tape, *Timbres-Durées* (see pp. 36–37, 39, 41–43). Notes how it is based on four rhythmic characters that are developed by means of twenty-four sequences. Considers the piece as exemplifying the trend towards abstraction in *musique concrète*. Includes a reproduction of Messiaen's graphic score for the piece.

7

Accounts of Messiaen and His Work in Sources Devoted to Other Topics

This chapter includes accounts of Messiaen and his work in sources devoted to other topics, such as articles and essays in collections, books and textbooks, dissertations and other unpublished documents, and dictionary and encyclopedia articles. The section on books and textbooks is geared to students.

ARTICLES AND ESSAYS IN COLLECTIONS

596. Asplund, Christian. "A Body Without Organs: Three Approaches—Cage, Bach, and Messiaen." *Perspectives of New Music* 35/2 (Summer 1997): 171–87. ISSN: 0031–6016.

   Asks the question, "What is the purpose of music?" For Cage, Bach, and Messiaen, it is to effect a spiritual communion between more than one entity. While Cage attempted to quiet the mind of a listener in order to make it more receptive to divine influence, and Bach strove to move the listener toward humility and penance through an emotional catharsis, Messiaen sought to provide the listener with a sensual glance of what lies beyond time and space. Most of the article focuses on Messiaen's sense of what the purpose of music is, surveying his ideas on the glorified body, dazzlement, sound-color relationships, the perception of divine mysteries, sacred music, stained-glass windows and light, and joy and glory.

597. Barber, Charles. "Olivier Messiaen." In *Music of the Twentieth-Century Avant-Garde: A Biocritical Sourcebook*, ed. Larry Sitsky, 299–304. With a foreword by Jonathan D. Kramer. Westport, CT:

Greenwood Press, 2002. xx, 660 p. ISBN: 0313296898. ML 390. M9574 2002.

In keeping with the goals of the book, a non-technical entry on Messiaen of approximately 3,000 words in which his musical contributions are interpreted from historical and social vantage points. Geared to the music lover as well as the music student and the music professional. Includes a selected works list and a bibliography to encourage further investigation.

598. Barraqué, Jean. "Rythme et développement." *Polyphonie* IX (1954): 47–73.

In an article focusing on contemporary rhythmic techniques, Barraqué considers the contributions of Messiaen by examining *Vingt Regards sur l'Enfant-Jésus, Cinq Rechants, Messe de la Pentecôte*, the *Turangalîla-Symphonie*, and *Mode de valeurs et d'intensités* (pp. 58–63). Referring to Messiaen as "the pure rhythmicist" (le rythmicien pur), Barraqué surveys the composer's rhythmic techniques, noting his manipulation of rhythmic cells through the multiplication of a small base value, and use of variation procedures such as retrograde movement, nonretrogradable rhythms, added value, and exact and inexact augmentation and diminution. Barraqué also touches upon: Hindu *deçi-tâlas*; Greek metric patterns; interversions, which for Barraqué arise from a serial dialectic; rhythmic characters; and the quasi-serialism evinced by *Mode de valeurs et d'intensités*. In his discussions of Machaut's *Messe de Notre-Dame* and Stravinsky's *Danse Sacrale*, Barraqué demonstrates his debt to Messiaen by analyzing these works in terms of rhythmic cells.

599. Barraud, Henry. "French Religious Music: Precursors and Innovators." *Musical America* 72 (February 1952): 26, 108, 146.

A survey of French religious music in the twentieth century that includes a discussion of Messiaen. Barraud questions the religious value of Messiaen's music, despite the composer's claim to be an exclusively religious musician. In offering his opinion, Barraud recalls his thoughts of six years ago when he was skeptical of Messiaen's supposed contention of being a mystical composer. For Barraud, great mystics attempt to give concrete form to their spiritual experiences, losing themselves in the contemplation of immanent truth. They are not preoccupied with material results, as Messiaen appears to be when he talks about his music. With respect to Barraud's current thoughts, little has changed. While acknowledging changes made by Messiaen in response to the public criticism of his work in the 1940s (e.g., not writing as many "interminable" commentaries, and retreating from mysticism by referring to himself as a theological composer), Barraud believes there was a decline in the religious quality of Messiaen's music since the composition of *La Nativité du Seigneur*. Because of the introduction of musical elements in later works such as the *Trois petites Liturgies de la Présence Divine, Vingt Regards sur l'Enfant-Jésus*, and the *Turangalîla-Symphonie* that evoke an atmosphere of sensuality, which seems to contradict the composer's intentions of promoting the truths of his faith, Barraud refuses to refer to Messiaen as an important religious musician.

600. Benitez, Vincent P. "Narrating Saint Francis's Spiritual Journey: Referential Pitch Structures and Symbolic Images in Olivier Messiaen's *Saint François d'Assise*." In *Poznan Studies on Opera*. Volume 4, *Theories of Opera*, ed. Maciej Jablonski, 363–411. Poznan, Poland: Publishing House of the Poznan Society for the Advancement of the Arts and Sciences, 2004. 460 p. ISBN: 837063401X. ML 1700.1.T46 2004.

An analysis of Saint Francis's spiritual journey in terms of a tonal-color narrative. See item 427.

601. Bingham, Seth. "Organ Personalities, Part II." *The American Organist* 46/10 (October 1963): 12–18. ISSN: 0164–3150.

A brief discussion of Messiaen (pp. 16–17) in a survey of mid-twentieth-century organists and organ builders. States that Messiaen's musical idiom arises not from liturgical chant, as in the case of Jean Langlais, but from traditional Hindu music, bird calls, harmonic sequences derived from the modes of limited transposition ("new scales with altered steps and half-steps"), added values, and certain "theological" formulas. Does not delve into questions concerning pitch structure, registration, or symbolism in Messiaen's works, since they have been dealt with, according to the author, in his article on the *Messe de la Pentecôte* (see item 503). Encourages the reader to examine Messiaen's *Technique de mon langage musical* for a better understanding of his compositional aesthetics and techniques.

602. Bingham, Seth. "Glimpses Over the French Horizon." *The American Organist* 42/1 (January 1959): 16–19, 27. ISSN: 0164–3150.

A discussion of Messiaen (pp. 18–19, 27) within a commentary on the French musical scene in the late 1950s. Describes Messiaen's organ playing at an eleven o'clock mass at La Trinité on 29 June 1958. Discusses the controversy ignited by the premiere of the composer's *Trois petites Liturgies de la Présence Divine* in the "Le Cas Messiaen" affair, described by Claude Rostand in his brochure entitled "Olivier Messiaen." Looks at *Trois petites Liturgies* in more detail in order to characterize Messiaen's musical language more fully for the reader. Reflects on Messiaen's views regarding his music and Catholic faith.

603. Boivin, Jean. "Olivier Messiaen et le Québec: Une présence et une influence déterminante sur la création musicale de l'après-guerre." *Canadian University Music Review/Revue de musique des universités canadiennes* 17/1 (1996): 72–97. ISSN: 0710–0353.

Describes the influence of Messiaen as both composer and teacher on the thought and avant-garde music of prominent Québécois composers between 1945 and 1960. Many of these musicians attended Messiaen's famous analysis class at the Paris Conservatoire. Some eventually became prominent teachers in Canada, contributing to the dissemination of Messiaen's compositional ideas on pitch and rhythm. Among the composers discussed in this article are Françoise Aubut, Jocelyne Binet, Sylvio Lacharité, Serge Garant, Clermont Pépin, Roger Matton, and Gilles Tremblay. Contains a list of Messiaen's best-known Canadian students.

604. Boulez, Pierre. *Points de repère*. Textes réunis et présentés par Jacques Nattiez. Deuxième édition revue et corrigée (1985). Paris: Christian Bourgois éditeur, 1981, 1985. 587 p. ISBN: 2267002760. ML 60.B796 P6 1985.

Several essays on Messiaen (pp. 338–52, 566–71) in a collection of writings by Boulez. They include: "Vision et revolution" ("Vision and Revolution"), "Le temps de l'utopie" ("The Utopian Years"), "Une classe et ses chimères" ("A Class and Its Fantasies"), "Rétrospective" ("Retrospective"), and "La toute puissance de l'exemple" ("The Power of Example"). The texts are drawn from television and radio broadcasts devoted to Messiaen, the publication *L'artiste musicien de Paris*, and tributes on the occasions of Messiaen's fiftieth (Domaine musical concert, 15 April 1959) and seventieth birthdays (concert featuring a performance of *Des canyons aux étoiles*, Paris Opéra, 10 December 1978). The essays cover Boulez's thoughts on Messiaen's work as a teacher and composer, echoing, in the latter case, his previous writings on Messiaen's rhythmic techniques.

605. Boulez, Pierre. *Orientations: Collected Writings by Pierre Boulez*. Edited by Jean-Jacques Nattiez. Translated from the French by Martin Cooper. Cambridge: Harvard University Press, 1986. ISBN: 0674643755. ML 60.B796 P613 1986.

English translation of *Points de repère*. Based on the second, revised French edition of 1985. The arrangement of the essays on Messiaen is different from that found in *Points de repère*; Cooper believed it better to group the two collections of essays found in the original into one for the translation.

606. Boulez, Pierre. "Pierre Boulez hielt Laudatio zum 70. Geburtstag von Olivier Messiaen." *Österreichische Musikzeitschrift* 34/2 (February 1979): 93–96. ISSN: 0029–9316.

A German translation of "La toute puissance de l'exemple" ("The Power of Example") by Boulez, a speech given during a performance of *Des canyons aux étoiles* at the Paris Opéra on 10 December 1978 celebrating Messiaen's seventieth birthday, as well as a review of other concerts in Paris honoring the composer in late November-early December 1978, by Thomas Daniel Schlee.

607. Brooks, Gerard. "French and Belgian Organ Music after 1800." In *The Cambridge Companion to the Organ*, ed. Nicholas Thistlethwaite and Geoffrey Webber, 263–78. Cambridge: Cambridge University Press, 1998. xiv, 340 p. ISBN: 0521573092 (hardback); 0521575842 (paperback). ML 550.C35 1998.

Brief discussion of Messiaen (pp. 277–78) in the context of French organ music after 1800. Messiaen's organ music, like Alain's, is characterized as falling outside of the French symphonic organ tradition of Widor and Dupré. It is viewed as atmospheric and full of religious imagery. The use of harmony in the organ works is regarded as coloristic rather than functional, and the approach to form as atypical, where themes are generated from developments rather than being subjected to them. Finally, mention is made of the importance of the modes of limited transposition and the use of birdsong in the later organ works.

608. Brown, Royal S. "French Music Since Debussy and Ravel." *High Fidelity and Musical America* (September 1973): 50–65. ISSN: 0018–1463.

A survey of twentieth-century French music from *Les Six* to Iannis Xenakis that mentions the music of Messiaen. Considers Messiaen as one of the twentieth century's most original and influential composers. Because of his religious mysticism, Messiaen developed new notions of musical time that had a significant impact on later composers.

609. Clements, Andrew. "Western Europe, 1945–70." In *Modern Times: From World War I to the Present*, ed. Robert P. Morgan, 257–88. Englewood Cliffs, NJ: Prentice Hall Inc., 1994. x, 464 p. ISBN: 0135901340 (hardback); 0135901596 (paperback). ML 197.M72.

Includes a discussion of Messiaen's significance as both a teacher and composer in the development of musical culture in Western

Europe after World War II (see pp. 257–63). Views his analysis class at the Paris Conservatoire as particularly crucial in the development of radical movements, especially total serialism, because of its broad-minded eclecticism, which pointed the way to the future for younger European composers. Also looks at Boulez, Stockhausen, and Goeyvaerts and their interactions with Messiaen. Notes the importance of Messiaen's *Mode de valeurs et d'intensités* for the development of total serialism, especially the effect it had on Stockhausen and Goeyvaerts.

610. Davidson, Audrey. "The Tristan Myth and Olivier Messiaen." *Substance and Manner: Studies in Music and the Other Arts*, 45–61. With a preface by Herbert M. Schueller. Saint Paul, MN: Hiawatha Press, 1977. xii, 103 p. ISBN: 0930276019 (hardback); 0930276000 (paperback). ML 60.D24.

Examines the Tristan trilogy—*Harawi*, *Turangalîla-Symphonie*, and *Cinq Rechants*—in relation to Messiaen's compositional world. Traverses a broad range of cultural subjects in order to connect the trilogy to its intellectual, literary, and symbolic aspects. The essay is one of seven by the author that traces not only the continuity of musical ideas and styles throughout history but also that of the other arts, giving the book an interdisciplinary tone. Derived from chapter one of the author's dissertation on the Tristan trilogy (see item 228).

611. Demarquez, Suzanne. "Youth and Spirit Take Over in French Music." *Musical Courier* (1 October 1948): 7.

Survey of French music after Debussy, Ravel, Fauré, Dukas, and Roussel that includes a discussion of Messiaen. Although acknowledging the varied nature of Messiaen's musical language, notes the pivotal role religion plays in his approach to composition. Flowing from this compositional aesthetic are the *Quatuor pour la fin du Temps*, *Visions de l'Amen*, *Vingt Regards sur l'Enfant-Jésus*, and the *Trois petites Liturgies de la Présence Divine*. Concludes by mentioning Messiaen's influence as a teacher at the Paris Conservatoire. Interestingly, Yvonne Loriod is described at the end of the article as a gifted young composer whose work cannot be evaluated due to the small number of compositions performed.

612. Fallon, Robert. "Composing Subjectivity: Maritain's Poetic Knowledge in Stravinsky and Messiaen." In *Jacques Maritain and the Many Ways of Knowing*, ed. Douglas A. Ollivant with an introduction by George Anastapio, 284–302. Washington, D.C.: American Maritain Association, 2002. xii, 330 p.

Within a study of Maritain's poetic knowledge where subjectivity is central to its expression, Fallon looks at Messiaen's *La Nativité du Seigneur* in order to show that "the relationship between poetic knowledge and subjectivity is closer than even Maritain asserted." Like Stravinsky, Messiaen was influenced by Maritain in his compositional aesthetics. Unlike the Russian composer, Messiaen's subjectivity was "firmly planted and his notion of truth clear." In its Thomistic theme of truth, *La Nativité du Seigneur* is strongly indicative of Maritain's influence and points to Messiaen's view of himself as a French Catholic organist composing works that are sincere and genuine.

613. Fano, Michel. "L'Expérience pedagogique." In *Éclats/Boulez*, ed. Claude Samuel with the collaboration of Jacqueline Muller, 6–7. Paris: Éditions du Centre Pompidou, 1986. 143 p. ISBN: 2858503427. ML 410.B773 S193.

In this collection honoring Pierre Boulez on his sixtieth birthday and IRCAM (*L'Institut de Recherche et Coordination Acoustique/Musique*) on its tenth anniversary, Michel Fano describes his time as a student in Messiaen's analysis class in 1950 in order to point out Messiaen's admiration for Boulez's music. He recounts the time when Messiaen had Boulez come to his analysis class to analyze his *Deuxième Sonate* for piano (1948). Fano states that it took Boulez several meetings to discuss the work. Moreover, Fano notes how Boulez, in contrast to the deliberate and slow discourse of Messiaen, dissected the piece rapidly while simultaneously speaking and playing at the piano. Every observation and thought, Fano states, was at a high intellectual level.

614. Goehr, Alexander. "The Messiaen Class." In *Finding the Key: Selected Writings of Alexander Goehr*, ed. Derrick Puffett, 42–57. London: Faber and Faber, 1998. xiii, 321 p. ISBN: 0571193102. ML 410.G563 A3 1998 (IUCAT).

A valuable source about Messiaen as a teacher at the Paris Conservatoire in the 1950s. See item 417.

615. Goléa, Antoine. "French Music since 1945." Translated by Lucile H. Brockway. *The Musical Quarterly* 51/1 (January 1965): 22–37. ISSN: 0027–4631.

A survey of French music since 1945. Regards the music of France as playing a pivotal role in the development of modern music since 1910. Considers Debussy, Messiaen, and Boulez as contributing the most to this revolution in musical language. Views Messiaen as building upon the work of Debussy in the areas of modal scales and rhythm. This prompted Messiaen to regard pitch and rhythm, along with other parameters like timbre, as independent of each other, which points the way to Boulez. Discusses the influence of Messiaen's teaching at the Paris Conservatoire on a younger generation of composers. Also looks at *Mode de valeurs et d'intensités* and its impact on the postwar musical scene in Europe. After considering Boulez's musical style, concludes the essay with an examination of the music of several different composers, including Gilbert Amy, Jean-Louis Martinet, and Serge Nigg, all former pupils of Messiaen.

616. Goléa, Antoine. "Tendances de la musique concrète." *La Revue musicale: Vers une musique expérimentale* (item 595).

Includes a discussion of *Timbres-Durées*.

617. Griffiths, Paul. "Master and Pupil." *The New Yorker* 68/30 (September 14 1992): 85–89. ISSN: 0028–0792X.

Discusses the music and compositional techniques of Messiaen and Boulez along with recent performances of their works. Considers the mutual influences the two composers had upon one another.

618. Hamel, Peter Michael. "Universalismus in der zeitgenössischen Musik am Beispiel der Wirkungsgeschichte von John Cage und Olivier Messiaen." *Musica* 48/1 (January/February 1994): 4–9. ISSN: 0027–4518.

Examines the notion of universality in the music of Cage and Messiaen. Looks at how both composers incorporated material found in nature into their works. Discusses several works by each composer in the process. For the author, both composers represent a non-European, critical universality.

619. Hamilton, David. "A Synoptic View of the New Music." *High Fidelity* Magazine (September 1968): 44–61. ISSN: 0018–1455.

In a survey of music after 1945, includes discussions of the influence of Messiaen's work as a teacher at the Paris Conservatoire (p. 46) and composer (p. 51) on the generation of European musicians coming of age at that time.

620. Hirsbrunner, Theo. "Die Rückkehr zur Magie in der Musik: Zur Konjunktion Varèse—Jolivet—Messiaen." *Dissonanz* 79 (February 2003): 4–9. ISSN: 1422–7371.

Investigates the influence of Varèse on Jolivet and Messiaen. Although Varèse's works were not well received in Paris during the 1930s, Jolivet and Messiaen both expressed an interest in his music, with Jolivet even becoming a student of Varèse. Discusses Jolivet's *Mana* in relation to Messiaen's comments on the work. Finally, looks at the founding of La Jeune France.

621. Hirsbrunner, Theo. "Deutsches und französisches Musikdenken am Beispiel von Schönberg und Messiaen." *Archiv für Musikwissenschaft* 55/1 (1998): 72–86. ISSN: 0003–9292.

Compares and contrasts German and French musical thought by examining the musical aesthetics of Schoenberg and Messiaen. Concludes that rhythm and timbre are more important for Messiaen than Schoenberg, who preferred to emphasize harmony and the development of motives and themes in his serial techniques.

622. Hirsbrunner, Theo. "Messiaen und Boulez." In *Das musikalische Kunstwerk: Geschichte, Ästhetik, Theorie*, ed. H. Danuser, H. de la Motte-Habe, S. Leopold, and N. Miller, 753-66. Festschrift Carl Dahlhaus zum 60. Geburtstag. Laaber: Laaber-Verlag, 1988. xii, 826 p. ISBN: 3890071449. ML 55.D185 1988.

A condensed version of Hirsbrunner's "Messiaen und Boulez" essay in *Olivier Messiaen: Leben und Werk* (see item 211). Evaluates the compositional techniques of Messiaen and Boulez, as well as their relationships to musical tradition. Maintains that while Boulez adopted some of Messiaen's techniques in a more objective form, he criticized Messiaen from time to time, hence inverting their earlier relationship as teacher and student.

623. Hochreither, Karl. "Olivier Messiaen: *La Nativité du Seigneur*: Eine Einführung unter besonderer Berücksichtigung der in diesem Werk angewandten kompositorischen Methoden." In *Festschrift für Michael Schnieder zum 65. Geburtstag*, 64–78. 100 p. Berlin: Merseburger, 1974. ISBN: 3875370821. ML 55.S365 1974.

An examination of *La Nativité du Seigneur*. See item 496.

624. Hughes, Allen. "French Musical Scene: Pierre Boulez Is a Key Figure." *Musical America* 77 (February 1957): 34, 120.

An essay on the French musical scene from the 1920s to mid-1950s in which Messiaen is discussed. Views Messiaen and André Jolivet as two composers who transcended the "warmed-over sentiments and styles" associated with most French music of the 1930s. Their compositional approaches were driven by their attitudes toward religion. This led both of them to explore musical techniques from non-Western cultures as well as incorporate modern inventions such as the Ondes Martenot into their works. Also considers Messiaen's significance as a teacher at the Paris Conservatoire in the 1940s and 50s.

625. Jolas, Betsy. "Milhaud, Messiaen: Maître et maître." In *Le Conservatoire de Paris: deux cents ans de pédagogie, 1795–1995*, ed.

Anne Bongrain and Alain Poirier, with the collaboration of Marie-Hélène Coudroy-Saghaï, 371–77. Paris: Buchet-Chastel, 1999. 444 p. ISBN: 2283017742. MT 3.P2 C35 (IUCAT).

In this article, Jolas expresses her appreciation of the work of Milhaud and Messiaen as teachers at the Paris Conservatoire, with whom she both studied. See item 419.

626. Koozin, Timothy. "Spiritual-Temporal Imagery in Music of Olivier Messiaen and Toru Takemitsu." *Contemporary Music Review* 7 (1993): 185–202. ISSN: 0749–4467.

Koozin considers the philosophical and technical parallels between Messiaen's and Toru Takemitsu's (1930–96) handling of musical time. He notes that the works of both composers are metaphorical in nature, and that these metaphors generate similarly functioning musical structures despite their origins in different cultural and spiritual traditions. Works analyzed in this study include Messiaen's *Quatuor pour la fin du Temps*, and Takemitsu's *Les yeux clos II* (1988) and *Quatrain II* (1977), a piece influenced by Messiaen's *Quatuor* both in musical expression and instrumentation.

627. Loranquin, Albert. "Messiaen et Claudel." *Le Bulletin des lettres* 48/ 497 (15 June 1990): 209–13. ISSN: 0007–4489.

An examination of the aesthetics and theologies of Messiaen and the poet Paul Claudel (1868–1955). Considers their similarities and differences.

628. van Maas, Sander. "The Reception of Aquinas in the Music of Olivier Messiaen." In *Aquinas as Authority*, ed. Paul van Geest, Harm Goris, and Carlo Leget, 317–31. A Collection of Studies Presented at the Second Conference of the *Thomas Instituut te Utrecht*, December 14–16, 2000. Leuven: Peeters, 2002. xviii, 338 p. ISBN: 9042910747. B 765.T54 T375 2000.

A multipart paper that examines the relationship between Saint Thomas Aquinas and Messiaen. Examines the general position of music in Aquinas's theology before focusing on parallels between Aquinas and Messiaen as related to theologies of light, form, and concordance. Considers the religious symbolism of the *Méditations sur le mystère de la Sainte Trinité*. Reflects on the questions and problems raised by Messiaen's theological outlook.

629. Marie, Jean-Étienne. "Inverse Function: Differentiation and Integration in Messiaen and Boulez, Parts One and Two." *Sonus: A Journal of Investigations into Global Musical Possibilities* 2/1 (Fall 1981): 26–33; 5/1 (Fall 1984): 36–60. ISSN: 0739–229X.

This two-part article examines musical process in Messiaen and Boulez by considering their different compositional approaches as analogous to differentiation and integration, respectively, in mathematical process. Part one (Fall 1981) studies differentiation in Messiaen's "L'échange" from *Vingt Regards sur l'Enfant-Jésus*, while part two (Fall 1984) considers integration in Boulez's "Trope," entitled "Parenthesis," from the Third Piano Sonata. The articles are excerpted from the author's *Trois Discours sur le Musical* (La Calade, Aix-en-Provence: Édisud, 1983).

630. Matheson, Iain G. "The End of Time: A Biblical Theme in Messiaen's *Quatuor*." In *Text as Pretext: Essays in Honour of Robert Davidson*, ed. Robert P. Carroll, 200–214. Sheffield, England: JSOT Press, 1992. 307 p. ISBN: 1850752958. BS 1192.5.A1 T49 1992 (IUCAT).

Asks if music can engage the Bible at a theological level beyond that of a verbal or narrative one. Suspects that such musical engagement may be impossible, and uses Messiaen's *Quatuor pour la fin du Temps* as a means to examine that suspicion. While acknowledging Messiaen's pictorial representation of Revelation 10:1–7, the *Quatuor*'s scriptural basis, in the titles of each movement, focuses instead on the composer's view of the biblical text as a starting point for a musical work that considers time from theological perspectives. Examines the *Quatuor* from the standpoint of rhythm, noting the composer's use of isorhythm and nonretrogradable rhythms. Concludes that the *Quatuor* is biblical in a more general way, not because of its textual association with the Book of Revelation, but because it shares the same concerns as the Bible, that is, time, space, eternity, transcendence, and meaning. However, while the Bible attempts to depict the "Word in words," thus revealing it to be a secondary text, the *Quatuor*'s music, or, for that matter, any music relating to transcendent truths, can only depict itself, thus revealing it to be its own primary text and reality.

631. Rorem, Ned. *Pure Contraption: A Composer's Essays*. New York: Holt, Rinehart and Winston, 1974. vii, 149 p. ISBN: 0030110211. ML 60.R784 P9.

Rorem's essay on Messiaen ("A Note on Messiaen," pp. 94–96) captures the contradictions that typify Messiaen's art. His music is quintessentially French because it features an economy of means when its dazzling colors are stripped away. His works are mostly long and not developed organically as in the classical sonata; rather, they consist of collections of ideas that are often sustained through literal repetition. His works, moreover, may be structured around

Hindu talas and accompanied by Christian epigraphs. Rorem describes Messiaen's art as being propelled by a public joy that is, in the final analysis, a private matter between him and his God. Finally, Rorem believes that Messiaen's commentaries on his works are of no benefit either to his listeners or to him as a means to understand or explain his music. But he is clearly the most important French composer of his generation, for his music is distinguished by both original sounds and order in an age of "eye-music."

632. Rorem, Ned. *Setting the Tone: Essays and a Diary.* New York: Coward, McCann & Geoghegan, 1983. Reprint, New York: Limelight Editions, 1984. 383 p. ISBN: 0879100249 (paperback). ML 410.R693 A33 1984.

In birthday tributes to both Messiaen and Elliott Carter on the occasion of their seventieth birthdays in 1978 (see "Messiaen and Carter on Their Birthdays, pp. 146–48"), Rorem repeats observations published in an earlier essay (see item 631) about the contradictions that typify Messiaen's art, in order to compare and contrast Messiaen with Carter. In Rorem's opinion, these two great masters are diametric opposites: for example, where Messiaen embraces literal repetition Carter shuns it. The greatest contrast between the two composers, however, is that Messiaen bloomed well before Carter: Messiaen's musical identity was already present in 1928, whereas Carter's did not manifest itself until 1946 with the advent of his Piano Sonata. Rorem concludes that both composers were concerned with the ear in an age of "eye-music," and that their respective musics reside in an originality tempered by order, not chaos. Originally published in *Tempo* 127 (December 1978): 22–24.

633. Rößler, Almut. "Messiaen und die deutsche Orgel." In *Festschrift für Michael Schnieder zum 65. Geburtstag*, 62–63. Berlin: Merseburger, 1974. 100 p. ISBN: 3875370821. ML 55.S365 1974.

Short essay highlighting Messiaen's approach to the registration of his organ music on a non-French instrument. During the First and Second Düsseldorf Messiaen Festivals in 1968 and 1972, respectively, Rößler accompanied Messiaen on both of his visits to Düsseldorf's Johanneskirche and was able to observe him register his organ music on the church's 1954 Beckerath organ. She noticed that Messiaen was flexible in his approach to organ registration, modifying his conceptions of a piece to match the organ and acoustical setting. For an abridged English translation of this essay, see item 396.

634. Schauerte-Maubouet, Helga. "Duruflé et ses amis: Maurice Duruflés Rezeption durch Jehan Alain, Jean Langlais und Olivier Messiaen

während der 1930er Jahre." *Organ: Journal für die Orgel* 6/1 (2003): 56–62. ISSN: 1435–7941.

Looks at Duruflé during the 1930s and 40s through Jehan Alain, Jean Langlais, and Messiaen. Compares Messiaen with Alain, mentions "Le Cas Messiaen," and discusses Messiaen's relationship with Langlais.

635. Schubert, Giselher. "Zum Verhältnis von musikalischer Poetik und Musiktheorie in 20. Jahrhundert: Hinweise auf französische und deutsche Komponisten." *Musiktheorie* 3 (1988): 225–35. ISSN: 0177–4182.

Considers the degree to which French (Messiaen, Dukas, Milhaud, Boulez) and German (Schoenberg, Eisler, Hindemith) composers developed certain theoretical convictions in the wake of their creative activities. Examines Messiaen's early theoretical ideas as reflected in the *Technique de mon langage musical* (pp. 225–27). Outlines and critiques the treatise's contents.

636. Simeone, Nigel. "An Exotic Tristan in Boston: The First Performance of Messiaen's *Turangalîla-Symphonie.*" In *King Arthur in Music.* Volume 52, Arthurian Studies, ed. Richard Barber, 105–25. Cambridge: D.S. Brewer, 2002. viii, 190 p. ISBN: 0859917673. ML 3849.K55 2002.

Considers Messiaen's commentaries on the *Turangalîla-Symphonie*, particularly the inspiration he drew from the Tristan myth, and the critical reception of the first performances of the work in Boston and New York, as well as early performances in Great Britain and France. Examines the connection between the mental health of Messiaen's first wife Claire Delbos and the composer's increasing attraction to the Tristan myth beginning in the early 1940s. The survey of generally indifferent responses to the *Turangalîla-Symphonie* in the American press encapsulates many criticisms of Messiaen's music that appear throughout the literature.

637. Simeone, Nigel. "*La Spiral* and *La Jeune France*: Group Identities." *The Musical Times* 143/1880 (Autumn 2002): 10–36. ISSN: 0027–4666.

Documents the musical activities of *La Spiral* and *La Jeune France*, two groups whose memberships overlapped. Messiaen, along with André Jolivet and Daniel-Lesur, was a member of both groups. According to Simeone, the common thread linking *La Spiral* and *La Jeune France* was the Schola Cantorum, where most members served as faculty members. Discusses Messiaen's musical activities in relation to both groups, especially performances of various works, including the premiere of *La Nativité du Seigneur*.

638. Simeone, Nigel. "Music at the 1937 Paris Exposition: The Science of Enchantment." *The Musical Times* 143/1878 (Spring 2002): 9–17. ISSN: 0027–4666.

Looks at the music performed during the 1937 Paris Exposition ("Exposition Internationale des Arts et des Techniques appliqués à la Vie Moderne"), particularly the series of "Fêtes de la lumiére," which consisted of displays of illuminated fountains and fireworks along the banks of the Seine River, accompanied by newly commissioned musical works by the city of Paris. Includes an examination of Messiaen's contribution, *Fête des belles eaux*, for six Ondes Martenot.

639. Simeone, Nigel. "Music Publishing in Paris under the German Occupation." *Brio* 38/1 (Spring/Summer 2001): 2–17. ISSN: 0007–0173.

Summarizes the publishing output of serious music by fifteen important Parisian firms during the German Occupation of Paris from June 1940 until August 1944. Within that framework, considers the activities of Messiaen's publishers Durand and Alphonse Leduc. In May 1942, Durand published the *Quatuor pour la fin du Temps*. It is rightly considered as the high point of Durand's publishing record during the Occupation (see pp. 4–6). From 1942–44, Alphonse Leduc published three of Messiaen's works (see p. 11), the organ cycle *Les Corps glorieux*, the *Rondeau* for solo piano, and both volumes of the *Technique de mon langage musical*.

640. Smalley, Roger. "Debussy and Messiaen." *The Musical Times* 109/1500 (February 1968): 128–31. ISSN: 0027–4666.

Part of a series of articles that attempts to understand Debussy through his influence on other composers. Begins by looking at the impact of Debussy's *Pelléas et Mélisande* on Messiaen, moving on to the older musician's influence on Messiaen's approaches to melody and harmony as articulated in the *Technique de mon langage musical*. Notes similarities between Debussy's use of scales and Messiaen's use of the modes of limited transposition. Observes further similarities in their use of formal processes and how extra-musical elements shape their music.

641. Sprout, Leslie A. "Messiaen, Jolivet, and the Soldier-Composers of Wartime France." *The Musical Quarterly* 87/2 (Summer 2004): 259–304. ISSN: 0027–4631.

Examines Messiaen's *Quartet for the End of Time* in relation to the music written by French soldier/composers in order to challenge long-held assumptions associated with the piece, especially the idea that the experience of Messiaen's wartime captivity cannot be found in the work. Investigates the French public's perception of the music of its soldier/composers and Messiaen's *Quartet*, noting that their compositions, unlike the *Quartet*, received generally positive reviews by wartime critics. Also takes issue with Denise Tual's claims, which are echoed by Nigel Simeone in a 2000 article on Messiaen (see item 309), that there was a ban on contemporary French music during the German occupation, and that the programming of this music at the Concerts de la Pléiade was indicative of an artistic resistance movement. Includes two appendices, one containing translated excerpts from reviews of the Paris premiere of the *Quartet* on 24 June 1941 by Marcel Delannoy, Arthur Honegger, and Serge Moreux, and a translation of an account of the *Quartet*'s world premiere by a fellow prisoner named Marcel Haedrich (see item 843). Highly recommended.

642. Stuckenschmidt, Hans Heinz. "Contemporary Techniques in Music." *The Musical Quarterly* 49/1 (January 1963): 1–16. ISSN: 0027–4631.

In a survey of contemporary styles and techniques from approximately 1900 to 1960, Stuckenschmidt examines the work of Messiaen (pp. 7–9, 10, 11, 13–14). He regards Messiaen's musical techniques as a welcome contrast to the serial techniques of Schoenberg, Berg, and Webern. He hails Messiaen as the first composer to combine series of chords with series of rhythms in his *Quatuor pour la fin du Temps*, and views his modes of limited transposition as viable alternatives to twelve-tone rows. In a discussion about the application of serial techniques to *musique concrete*, Stuckenschmidt describes procedures found in Messiaen's *Timbres-Durées*.

643. Tenzer, Michael. "Western Music in the Context of World Music." In *Modern Times: From World War I to the Present*, ed. Robert P. Morgan, 388–410. Englewood Cliffs, NJ: Prentice Hall Inc., 1994. x, 464 p. ISBN: 0135901340 (hardback); 0135901596 (paperback). ML 197.M72.

Tenzer examines Western music's increasing assimilation of non-Western musical elements in the second half of the twentieth century. He views the world's musical cultures as relativistic, interacting, and constantly changing. It is within this cross-cultural framework that he examines "Gagaku," the fourth movement of Messiaen's *Sept Haïkaï*. Tenzer notes the diverse influences that compose Messiaen's later music of the 1960s to 90s, which suggest aspects of Asian music, such as multi-layered textures that are in static relationships with one another, and a nonlinear approach to musical time in which the music seems to start and stop in an arbitrary manner. He proceeds to an examination of how "Gagaku" evokes the ancient Japanese music of the same name, focusing on how certain instrumental combinations suggest the sounds of the *hichiriki* (a reed instrument that carries the primary melody), the *ryuteki* (a flute-like instrument that sounds a secondary melody), and *sho* (a bamboo mouth organ). He also looks at how "Gagaku" differs from its counterpart, as in its less restrained approach to pitch materials and rhythm, and in its lack of evoking the aesthetic demeanor characteristic of this Japanese music.

644. Toop, Richard. "Messiaen/Goeyvaerts, Fano/Stockhausen, Boulez." *Perspectives of New Music* (Fall-Winter 1974): 141–69. ISSN: 0031–6016.

Considers the development of European integral serialism by examining not only Messiaen's *Mode de valeurs et d'intensités* (1949), Stockhausen's *Kreuzspiel* (1951), and Boulez's *Structures* I (1951–52) but also Sonatas for Two Pianos by Karel Goeyvaerts (1950–51) and Michel Fano (1951), respectively, which link, in the author's estimation, Messiaen's piece to those by Stockhausen and Boulez. Provides background information on, as well as a thoughtful analysis of, *Mode de valeurs*. Notes stylistic similarities that *Mode de valeurs* shares with the late Ars Antiqua motet ("the simultaneous presentation of three speeds in the three voices") and the piece's various permutational techniques, although note order is based ultimately on taste and expediency. For the author, the main achievement of *Mode de valeurs* is the combination of pointillism with a rhythmic dynamism.

645. Whittall, Arnold. "Stravinsky and Music Drama." *Music and Letters* 50/1 (January 1969): 63–67. ISSN: 0027–4224.

In a short article that probes Stravinsky's relationship to Wagnerian music drama, Whittall compares Stravinsky with Messiaen. Stravinsky was hostile to Wagner for a variety of reasons, one of them being his rejection of the idea that a work of art could be put on the same level as sacred ritual. For Stravinsky, human beings can judge a work of art because it is the result of human activity; they do not have the right to judge the sacred, for to do so would be blasphemous. Since he no longer composed church music per se (i.e., organ music) and used nature instead as a symbol of praise, Messiaen was more disposed to accept Wagner. His music is always descriptive, utilizing sensual images more directly than Wagner, although his use of form exhibits stricter controls.

BOOKS AND TEXTBOOKS

646. Abraham, Gerald. *The Concise Oxford History of Music*. London: Oxford University Press, 1985. 968 p. ISBN: 0193113198 (hard); 019284010X (paperback). ML 160.A27 1985.

   Discussions of Messiaen's music in relation to the music of Indonesia (p. 572), the Ondes Martenot and quarter-tone music (p. 831), and European music after 1945 (pp. 847–48, 849, 855).

647. Antokoletz, Elliott. *Twentieth-Century Music*. Upper Saddle River, NJ: Prentice Hall, 1998. xiv, 546 p. ISBN: 0139341269. ML 197.A63 1992.

   Considers how the Ondes Martenot is used in the sixth movement, "Jardin du sommeil d'amour," of the *Turangalîla-Symphonie* (p. 347). Also examines *Mode de valeurs et d'intensités* in a discussion of total serialization in Europe (pp. 370–72).

648. Austin, William W. *Music in the Twentieth Century: From Debussy through Stravinsky*. New York: W. W. Norton & Company, Inc., 1966. xx, 708 p. ML 197.A9.

   Discussion of Messiaen (pp. 390–95) in which he is viewed as the most important composer between Debussy and Boulez. However, takes him to task for his musical and emotional excesses, particularly with respect to his use of harmony, form, and programmatic elements. Examines the components of Messiaen's musical language, attending to melody, harmony, rhythm, and birdsong, while tracing the development of the composer's style.

649. Berry, Wallace. *Structural Functions in Music*. Englewood Cliffs, NJ: Prentice-Hall, Inc., 1976. xii, 447 p. ISBN: 0138539030. MT 6.B465 S8.

   Includes discussions of Messiaen's *Reprises par interversion* (p. 311), *Mode de valeurs et d'intensités* (p. 409), and *Ile de feu II* (pp. 409–13) within the larger context of rhythm and meter in chapter three.

650. Blanc-Gatti, Charles. *Sons et couleurs*, 2d ed. With a preface by Ivanhoé Rambosson. Paris: Victor Attinger, 1947. ML 3840.B62 1900Z.

   Contains a brief mention of Messiaen (p. 69). By 1931, Messiaen had met the Swiss painter Charles Blanc-Gatti (1890–1965), who experienced *synopsia*, a type of colored-hearing synesthesia which enabled him to actually see colors and shapes when he listened to music. With the painter's assistance, Messiaen established an early correlation between certain sounds and colors. In *Sons et couleurs*, Blanc-Gatti notes that when he painted the sounds that he had heard while listening to Messiaen's *La Nativité du Seigneur*, the composer recognized and confirmed them as the colors that he had envisioned in his organ work.

651. Bonds, Mark Evan. *A History of Music in Western Culture*, 2d ed. Upper Saddle River, NJ: Pearson Prentice Hall, 2006. xviii, 701 p. ISBN: 0131931040. ML 160.B75 2006.

   Discusses the "Liturgie de cristal" from the *Quatuor pour la fin du Temps* in a section on chamber music, from a chapter devoted to tonal traditions in twentieth-century music (chapter 22, "The Tonal Tradition," pp. 608–11). After providing information about the quartet's background and context, focuses on the unsynchronized harmonic and rhythmic ostinatos of "Liturgie de cristal." Concludes with some observations about how the piece reflects twentieth-century conceptions of tonality. Later in the book, considers Messiaen's role in the development of integral serialism by looking at *Mode de valeurs et d'intensités* (pp. 621–22).

652. Boulez, Pierre. *Relevés d'apprenti*. Textes réunis et présentés par Paule Thévenin. Paris: Éditions du Seuil, 1966. 385 p. ML 60.B796 R4.

   This source contains remarks by Boulez on the importance of Messiaen's rhythmic techniques. In "Proposals" ("Propositions," pp. 65–74), Boulez acknowledges Messiaen's innovations in the field of rhythm (the separation of rhythm from pitch, added values, rhythmic canons, rhythmic pedals, the symmetrical or asymmetrical augmentation of rhythmic cells, and the distinction between retrogradable and nonretrogradable rhythms), stating that they are established principles that should be enriched. In "Stravinsky Remains" ("Stravinsky demeure," pp. 75–145) where he analyzes the *Rite of Spring* in terms of the development of rhythmic cells, Boulez demonstrates a debt to Messiaen's analysis of the same work as published in the second volume of the *Traité de rythme* (see item 90). Later in the book, Boulez reiterates the importance of Messiaen's contributions to rhythm (pp. 174–75), as well as discusses how the notion of chromaticism is extended to other musical elements in Messiaen's *Mode de valeurs et d'intensités* (p. 284).

653. Boulez, Pierre. *Stocktakings from an Apprenticeship*. Collected and presented by Paule Thévenin. Translated from the French by Stephen Walsh, with an introduction by Robert Piencikowski. Oxford: Clarendon Press, 1991. xxix, 316 p. ISBN: 0193112108. ML 60.B796 R413 1991.

The most recent English translation of *Relevés d'apprenti*. Superior to the Weinstock translation (item 654). Not only helps the reader with Boulez's literary allusions but also identifies the sources of the musical examples that he uses from his works.

654. Boulez, Pierre. *Notes of an Apprenticeship*. Texts collected and presented by Paule Thévenin. Translated from the French by Herbert Weinstock. New York: Alfred A. Knopf, 1968. 398 p. ML 60.B796 R43.

First English translation of *Relevés d'apprenti*. Virtually unknown in the United Kingdom. Problematic in quality.

655. Brindle, Reginald Smith. *The New Music: The Avant-garde since 1945*, 2d ed. London: Oxford University Press, 1987. 222 p. ISBN: 0193154714 (hard), 0193154684 (paperback). ML 197.B77 1987.

Comments on Messiaen's music and style within the context of avant-garde music since 1945. Describes the structural principles of *Mode de valeurs et d'intensités* and how they were carried further by Boulez in *Structures Ia* (pp. 23–33). Also looks at Messiaen's fascination for proportion and number as expressed in the *Technique de mon langage musical* (pp. 47–48), and how Eastern music influenced him (pp. 134–35, 159).

656. Bruhn, Siglind. *Images and Ideas in Modern French Piano Music: The Extra-Musical Subtext in Piano Works by Ravel, Debussy, and Messiaen*. Aesthetics in Music, no. 6, ed. Edward Lippman. Stuyvesant, New York: Pendragon Press, 1997. xxxiii, 425 p. ISBN: 0945193955. ML 724.B78 1997.

A discussion of *Vingt Regards sur l'Enfant-Jésus*. See item 536.

657. Burkholder, J. Peter, Donald Jay Grout, and Claude V. Palisca. *A History of Western Music*, 7th ed. New York: W. W. Norton & Company, 2006. xxviii, 965 p. ISBN: 0393979911. ML 160.G872 2006.

Discusses Messiaen's life, works, and compositional style (pp. 909–12). Also considers the impact of *Mode de valeurs et d'intensités* on Boulez and his writing of *Structures* (pp. 918–19). Regards Messiaen as "the most important French composer born in the twentieth century." Uses the "Liturgie de cristal" from the *Quatuor pour la fin du Temps* to illustrate Messiaen's compositional techniques as described in the *Technique de mon langage musical*.

658. Christensen, Erik. *The Musical Timespace: A Theory of Music Listening* (see item 478).

Includes analyses of the rhythmic and pitch elements of the first ten measures of the "Abîme des oiseaux" from the *Quatuor pour la fin du Temps* (pp. 95–96, 101–2).

659. Cogan, Robert, and Pozzi Escot. *Sonic Design: The Nature of Sound and Music*. Englewood Cliffs, NJ: Prentice-Hall, Inc., 1976. xvi, 496 p. ISBN: 0138227268. MT 6.C63 S6.

Contains discussions of Messiaen's modes of limited transposition (pp. 182–83) within a larger study of symmetrical pitch collections, and *Ile de feu II* (pp. 289–92) within a larger examination of rhythmic serialism. Also includes a brief mention of nonretrogradable rhythms (p. 293).

660. Cook, Nicholas. *Analysing Musical Multimedia*. Oxford and New York: Oxford University Press, 2000. xiv, 290 p. ISBN: 0198167377 (paperback). ML 3849.C66 2000 (IUCAT).

In a study of the general principles of musical multimedia, Cook examines the colored-hearing synesthesia of Messiaen in relation to the idea that while synesthesia "provides some hints as to what multimedia is …, it supplies an illuminating model of what multimedia is *not*" (chapter 1: "Synaesthesia and Similarity," pp. 29–33). Cook notes the multidimensional aspects of Messiaen's music as seen through the coloristic descriptions he included in his compositions, and the suggestions he made in his interviews that the only true appreciation of his work arises when both hearing and vision are combined. Accordingly, Cook considers color as an essential element of Messiaen's music. However, since Messiaen experienced only *imaginary* colors in his synesthesia, Cook concludes that his music cannot serve as a model for multimedia because it does not consist of the "perceived interaction of real sounds and *real* colours." In short, synesthesia "may be an enabling condition for multimedia, but it is not a sufficient one."

661. Cross, Jonathan. *The Stravinsky Legacy*. Cambridge: Cambridge University Press, 1998. xii, 282 p. ISBN: 0521563658. ML 410.S932 C87 1998.

Considers Stravinsky's impact on Messiaen as a composer. In chapter two ("Block forms," pp. 46–55), posits that "Stravinsky's *early* works up to the *Symphonies of Wind Instruments* … influenced Messiaen most directly" with respect to formal procedures (p. 47). Includes discussions of *Cantéyodjayâ*, *Couleurs de la Cité céleste*, and *Et exspecto resurrectionem mortuorum*. Considers it likely that the *Symphonies of Wind Instruments* served as a model for *Cantéyodjayâ*.

Regards *Couleurs de la Cité céleste* and *Et exspecto resurrectionem mortuorum* as Messiaen's own "symphonies of wind instruments."

In chapter 3 ("Structural rhythms," pp. 112–19), investigates the influence of Stravinsky's rhythmic techniques, as exemplified especially in the *Rite of Spring*, on the composition of *Chronochromie* and the *Turangalîla-Symphonie*. Finally, examines *Et exspecto resurrectionem mortuorum* in relation to chapter four's theme of "Ritual theatres" (pp. 149–51).

662. Cytowic, Richard E. *Synesthesia: A Union of the Senses*. With a Foreword by Ayub K. Ommaya. Springer Series in Neuropsychology, ed. Harry A. Whitaker. New York: Springer-Verlag, 1989. xiv, 354 p. ISBN: 0387968075. QP 435.C97 1989.

Consideration of Messiaen's synesthetic perceptions (pp. 263–69) from a neurologist specializing in synesthesia. Although he was unable to examine Messiaen personally and therefore develop a medical perspective on the composer's synesthesia, Cytowic concludes that Messiaen exemplifies the connections between synesthesia, art, and number that he argues for in his book. Most of Cytowic's discussion of Messiaen's synesthesia is drawn from the composer's *Technique de mon langage musical*, 1967 conversations with Claude Samuel, and liner notes from a 1977 recording of *Des canyons aux étoiles* on the Erato label.

663. Grant, Morag Josephine. *Serial Music, Serial Aesthetics*: *Compositional Theory in Post-War Europe*. Cambridge: Cambridge University Press, 2001. 272 p. ISBN: 0521804582 (hardback). ML 3877.G73 2001.

Discussion of Messiaen's *Mode de valeurs et d'intensités* in light of the serial aesthetic of post-war Europe (pp. 61–63). Also mentions Stockhausen's criticism of the arithmetic series from *Mode de valeurs et d'intensités* (durational units multiplied by 1 through 12) as inadequate for the calculation of rhythm in serial works (pp. 136–37).

664. Griffiths, Paul. *Modern Music: A Concise History*, rev. ed. London: Thames and Hudson, 1994. 216 p. ISBN: 0500202788. ML 197.G74 1994.

Surveys elements that comprise Messiaen's musical style and how they are reflected in his music (pp. 120–28). Discusses the composer's adoption of Eastern elements, his use of modality, especially as a means to express human and divine love, birdsong, and sound-color relationships. Also includes remarks on the importance of *Mode de valeurs et d'intensités* for the post-war musical scene in Europe (pp. 132–33).

665. Griffiths, Paul. *Modern Music: The Avant-garde since 1945.* New York: George Braziller, 1981. 331 p. ISBN: 0807610186 (paperback). ML 197.G76 1981b.

Notes Messiaen's importance as a composer and teacher at the Paris Conservatoire since 1945. Begins by examining his influence as a teacher for French composers (especially Boulez) of the late 1940s who were rethinking their approaches to music (pp. 19–25). Looks at *Mode de valeurs et d'intensités* and its influence on younger European composers, as well as the permutational techniques used in *Ile de feu II* (pp. 47–51). Finally, considers Messiaen's use of plainsong in *Couleurs de la Cité céleste* (pp. 190–91) and his integration of Eastern elements into his musical style (p. 196).

666. Gut, Serge. *Le Groupe de Jeune France: Yves Baudrier, Daniel[-]Lesur, André Jolivet, Olivier Messiaen.* Paris: Honoré Champion, 1977. 158 p. ISBN: 2852030306. ML 390.G98.

Within an examination of La Jeune France, discusses Messiaen and his music (see pp. 75–120). Surveys his life; provides an overview of his works; looks at his compositional techniques; and considers his aesthetics with respect to his ideas on faith, sound-color relationships, rhythm, ornithology, and the magical. Analyzes the first, fifth, and tenth songs of *Harawi*; the *Messe de la Pentecôte*; and the *Trois petites Liturgies de la Présence Divine.* Closes the chapter with some general considerations of Messiaen's œuvre. Includes a list of works through 1974 (pp. 135–37).

667. Hinson, Maurice. *Guide to the Pianist's Repertoire.* 3d ed. Bloomington: Indiana University Press, 2000. xli, 933 p. ISBN: 0253336465 (hard); 0253213487 (paperback). ML 128.P3 H5 2000.

Includes an entry on Messiaen's piano music (pp. 535–38). Begins with an overview of his musical style. Each piano work (including his transcription of *Les Offrandes oubliées*) is listed chronologically. In each annotation identifies the publisher, describes the musical style, and ascertains levels of difficulty. Concludes with a short bibliography.

668. Hirsbrunner, Theo. *Die Musik in Frankreich im 20. Jahrhundert.* Laaber: Laaber-Verlag, 1995. 287 p. ISBN: 389007197X. ML 270.5.H57 1995.

In a book devoted to French music of the twentieth century, Hirsbrunner examines Messiaen's musical contributions. In chapter three ("1929–45," pp. 147–70) he considers Messiaen's early life and formative influences, the *Préludes* for piano, his relationship with Jolivet in the 1930s, and *Harawi*. In chapter four ("1945–65," pp. 171–220)

Hirsbrunner addresses Messiaen's connection to serialism by discussing the quasi-serial manipulation of different musical parameters in *Cantéyodjayâ*, *Mode de valeurs et d'intensités*, and *La Chouette Hulotte*, where fixed sound-durations are employed freely in musical passages. He compares Messiaen's modal approach with compositional techniques used by Boulez, especially in *Structures Ia*. Later in the chapter, Hirsbrunner explores the Messiaen/Boulez relationship in more detail (p. 193–203).

669. Hirsbrunner, Theo. "Ein neuer Begriff von der Zeit: Olivier Messiaens geistiges Vermächtnis." In *Von Richard Wagner bis Pierre Boulez: Essays* (item 337).

A discussion of musical time in the works of Messiaen.

670. Hodeir, André. *La musique depuis Debussy.* Paris: Presses Universitaires de France, 1961. 222 p. ML 390.H65 (IUCAT).

In chapter six, "Olivier Messiaen" (pp. 81–105), Hodeir surveys Messiaen's life, works, and musical style through the late 1950s. He examines the composer's approach to rhythm by considering elements that reflect its ametrical nature, such as rhythms derived from Hindu *deçi-tâlas* and primary numbers, unconventional approaches to augmentation and diminution, added values, nonretrogradable rhythms, rhythmic pedalpoints and canons, and rhythmic characters. Hodeir also examines Messiaen's approach to pitch by looking at the modes of limited transposition. Since he believes that form is the most basic component of music, Hodeir is critical of Messiaen's approach to form, which he believes is his ultimate failure as a composer. Despite his rhythms and modes, Hodeir characterizes Messiaen's music as resting upon "poverty-stricken, outmoded structures" that in the end evoke a "sense of monotony and inertia."

671. Hodeir, André. *Since Debussy: A View of Contemporary Music.* Translated by Noel Burch. Da Capo Press Music Reprint Series. New York: Da Capo Press, 1975. 256 p. ISBN: 0306706628. ML 197.H63 1975 (IUCAT).

English translation of item 670.

672. Honegger, Arthur. *Je suis compositeur.* Paris: Éditions du Conquistador, 1951. 188 p. ML 410.H79 A3.

In his 1951 autobiography, Honegger mentions Messiaen several times (pp. 58–59, 69–70, 111–12, 168–72). Messiaen's name especially comes up when Honegger discusses questions of compositional craft. While advocating that composers should strive for a more rational method of notation, free of difficulties that would interfere with the reading of their music, he characterizes Messiaen's manner of notation as complicated. Moreover, Messiaen has never been able to explain to him the reasons behind his procedures. Honegger also states that the extra-musical aspects Messiaen associates with his work are reflected in his writing. In discussing the present and future of music, Honegger expresses his admiration for Messiaen, who is certainly ahead of his generation. Although he mentions several works of Messiaen from the 1940s that he likes, and talks about the *Technique de mon langage musical* and aspects of Messiaen's musical language, he remains skeptical of Messiaen's rhythmic techniques, which are only important on paper and not perceived by listeners.

673. Honegger, Arthur. *Incantation aux fossiles.* Lausanne: Éditions d'Ouchy, 1948. 220 p. ML 60.H78.

In this collection of critical essays there is a discussion of Messiaen's work from the 1940s (pp. 95–100). Honegger considers Messiaen's *Quatuor pour la fin du Temps*, compositional aesthetics, and musical language. He also conveys his admiration for Messiaen's *Visions de l'Amen*.

674. Jameux, Dominique. *Pierre Boulez.* Paris: Fayard Fondation SACEM, 1984. 492 p. ISBN: 2213010773. ML 410.B773 J3 1984.

In this biography of Boulez, includes discussions of his relationship with Messiaen as a student (pp. 24–29), the influence of Messiaen's *Mode de valeurs et d'intensités* on the writing of *Structures 1a* (pp. 69–71), Messiaen's support of and participation in the concerts of the Domaine musical (pp. 86, 90), and the hints of Messiaen's compositional influence in his Piano Sonatas (pp. 295, 314, 373–76) and *Pli selon pli* (p. 382).

675. Jameux, Dominique. *Pierre Boulez.* Translated by Susan Bradshaw. Cambridge, MA: Harvard University Press, 1991. xiii, 422 p. ISBN: 0674667409. ML 410.B773 J313 1990.

English translation of item 674.

676. Jaquet-Langlais, Marie-Louise. *Jean Langlais (1907–1991): Ombre et Lumière.* Paris: Éditions Combre, 1995.

Given Messiaen's close relationship with Langlais ever since the two met as students in Dupré's organ class at the Paris Conservatoire in 1927, there are extensive references to Messiaen in this volume. Included in this book is Messiaen's analysis of Langlais's *Messe Solennelle* (1949) reproduced in his own handwriting on p. 163 (see item 82).

677. Jolivet, Hilda. *Avec André Jolivet.* With a preface by Maurice Schumann. Paris: Flammarion, 1978. 302 p. ISBN: 2080640615. ML 410.J69 J6.

A biography of André Jolivet by his widow Hilda that includes references to Messiaen. Quotes part of Messiaen's preface to *Mana* (pp. 126–29) and notes his admiration for Jolivet's *Danse Incantatoire* (p. 137).

678. Kramer, Jonathan D. *The Time of Music: New Meanings, New Temporalities, New Listening Strategies.* New York: Schirmer Books, 1988. xviii, 493 p. ISBN: 0028725905. ML 3850.K72 1988.

Presents an overview of moment form in the music of Messiaen in order to show how the composer gradually embraced moment time (pp. 213–17). Believes that Messiaen's music links early Stravinsky with the Stockhausen circle.

679. Lester, Joel. *Analytical Approaches to Twentieth-Century Music.* New York: W. W. Norton & Company, Inc., 1989. x, 303 p. ISBN: 0393957624. MT 6.L365 A5 1989.

Uses movements from Messiaen's *Quatuor pour la fin du Temps* to illustrate diverse facets of post-tonal theory (chaps. 2–16 passim). Includes a discussion of Messiaen's serial techniques involving non-twelve-tone series and rhythm (pp. 263–66).

680. Longchampt, Jacques. *Le Bon Plaisir: Journal de musique contemporaine.* Paris: Éditions Plume, 1994.

An essay on Messiaen (pp. 32–49) amongst others devoted to Dimitri Shostakovich, Daniel-Lesur, Pierre Schaeffer, and Jehan Alain. Considers his life and music via a compilation of reviews from *Le Monde.*

681. Machlis, Joseph. *Introduction to Contemporary Music*, 2d ed. New York: W. W. Norton & Company, Inc., 1979. xxv, 694 p. ISBN: 0393090264. ML 197.M11 1979.

Discussion of Messiaen in relation to the European musical scene after World War II ("Part Five: The Second Revolution: Four Representative European Composers," pp. 467–73). After considering Messiaen's musical style, Machlis looks at the *Quatuor pour la fin du Temps*, drawing from Messiaen's remarks about the piece in the writing of his commentary.

682. Morgan, Robert P. *Twentieth-Century Music: A History of Musical Style in Modern Europe and America.* New York: W. W. Norton & Company, 1991. xvii, 554 p. ISBN: 039395272X. ML 197.M675 1990.

Examines Messiaen's musical style in the context of the serial revolution in France (pp. 335–40). Notes Messiaen's systematic approach to composition, as demonstrated in his separation of musical parameters and rigorous discussion of each in the *Technique de mon langage musical*. Also discusses Messiaen's borrowing of preexistent musical materials and his transformation of them, and abstract precompositional designs.

683. Murray, Michael. *French Masters of the Organ: Saint-Saens, Franck, Widor, Vierne, Dupré, Langlais, Messiaen*. New Haven: Yale University Press, 1998. 245 p. ISBN: 0300072910. ML 396.M87 1998.

In his essay on Messiaen (pp. 180–205), Murray examines the roles rhythm and time, harmony and color, and registration and timbre play in Messiaen's organ music. He begins by looking at Messiaen's early musical influences, such as the poetical intuitions of his mother Cécile Sauvage, the mountainous landscapes of the Dauphiné region in France, the plays of Shakespeare, and musical dramas by Gluck, Mozart, Berlioz, and Debussy. After mentioning the composer's student years at the Paris Conservatoire, Murray proceeds to the focus of his essay, a consideration of Messiaen's musical style and its relationship to his organ music, from *Le Banquet céleste* to *Livre du Saint Sacrement*. Murray concludes his essay (and the book) by viewing Messiaen as the culmination of the French romantic organ tradition that began "with the young Cavaillé-Coll's journey to Paris" (p. 203).

Reviews: Benjamin Van Wye, *MLA Notes* 55/4 (June 1999): 925.

684. Murray, Michael. *Marcel Dupré: The Work of a Master Organist*. With a foreword by Jacques Barzun. Boston: Northeastern University Press, 1985. xxv, 259 p. ISBN: 0930350650 (hard); 0930350669 (paperback). ML 416.D83 M9 1985.

In his book on Marcel Dupré, Murray includes references to Messiaen, one of Dupré's most brilliant students. He cites passages from Messiaen's homage to Dupré written in *Le Courrier Musical de France* (see item 74) shortly after Dupré's death in 1971 (pp. 4, 222), the influence of Dupré's *Symphonie-Passion* for organ on Messiaen's musical idiom (p. 81), and Dupré's demonstrated regard for Messiaen and his music (p. 195).

685. Myers, Rollo H. *Modern French Music: From Fauré to Boulez*. New York: Praeger, 1971. Reprint, New York: Da Capo Press, 1984. 210 p. ISBN: 0306761580. ML 270.5.M9 1984.

In chapter nine entitled "Messiaen, Boulez and After" (pp. 152–78), Myers places the music of Messiaen and Boulez within the context of post-war music in France, noting their roles as trendsetters during this time. Myers surveys Messiaen's life and works through *La Transfiguration de Nôtre-Seigneur Jésus-Christ* (1965–69). While acknowledging Messiaen's influence on a generation of musicians as both a pedagogue and composer, as well as noting the uniqueness of Messiaen's attempts to express his Roman Catholic faith in an age of unbelief, Myers takes issue with what he sees as the incongruity between Messiaen's complex musical language and banal musical ideas. For Myers, Messiaen's descriptions about his musical goals not only border on excessive emotion but also hinder an objective evaluation of his music.

686. Peyser, Joan. *To Boulez and Beyond: Music in Europe Since the Rite of Spring*. With a foreword by Charles Wuorinen. New York: Billboard Books, 1999. xvii, 382 p. ISBN: 0823078752. ML 240.5.P49 1999.

Includes information on Messiaen's relationship to Boulez (pp. 157–60, 180–82). Describes his first contact with Boulez when Boulez entered his harmony class at the Paris Conservatoire in the fall of 1944, his relationship with Boulez in the later 1940s, and the impact of *Mode de valeurs et d'intensités* on Boulez's compositional aesthetics. Suffers from a lack of documentation.

687. Pozzi, Raffaele. "'Le rythme chez Mozart': Alcune osservazioni analitiche di Olivier Messiaen sull'accentuazione ritmica in Mozart." In *Bericht über den Internationalen Mozart-Kongreß Salzburg 1991*, ed. Rudolph Angermüller, Dietrich Berke, Ulrike Hofmann, and Wolfgang Rehm, 613–24. Kassel: Bärenreiter, 1992. ISSN: 0077–1805.

An examination of Messiaen's views on melodic accentuation in the music of Mozart. Compares Messiaen's readings of passages from Mozart's works with those by Grosvenor Cooper and Leonard B. Meyer in *The Rhythmic Structure of Music* (Chicago and London: The University of Chicago Press, 1960), Fred Lerdahl and Ray Jackendoff in *A Generative Theory of Tonal Music* (Cambridge, MA: MIT Press, 1983), and Jonathan D. Kramer in *The Time of Music* (see item 678).

688. Riley, Charles A., II. *Color Codes: Modern Theories of Color in Philosophy, Painting and Architecture, Literature, Music, and Philosophy.* Hanover, NH: University Press of New England, 1995. xi, 351 p. ISBN: 0874516714. NX 650.C676 R56 1995.

In a chapter entitled "Color in Music" (see pp. 287–89), Riley considers Messiaen as the master colorist of the late twentieth century. Messiaen surpassed the colorism of his contemporaries through his use of chromaticism, orchestration, and sound-color relationships.

Influenced by Wagner and French composers such as Berlioz, Debussy, and Ravel, Messiaen's colorism, while striving ideally for chromatic fullness, manifested itself in highly diverse ways. By assigning cosmic powers to his use of sound-color relationships, Messiaen achieved a heroic colorism that surpassed Wagner's.

689. Rostand, Claude. *La Musique française contemporaine*. 4th ed. Paris: Presses Universitaires de France, 1971. 126 p. ML 270.5.R7 1971.

Discussion of Messiaen in chapter four, "Le Groupe de La Jeune France" (pp. 52–72). Mentions "Le Cas Messiaen," and then critiques his compositional aesthetics and musical language (pp. 56–66). Looks at music through *Oiseaux exotiques*.

690. Rostand, Claude. *La Musique française contemporaine*. Translated as *French Music Today* by Henry Marx. New York: Merlin Press, 1955. 147 p. ML 270.5.R713.

English translation of item 689.

691. Routley, Erik. *Twentieth[-]Century Church Music*. Carol Stream, Il: Agape, 1984. 244 p. ISBN: 0916642232. ML 3131.R68 1984.

A consideration of Messiaen's organ music within the context of twentieth-century church music (pp. 82, 130–33, 143, 145). Routley praises Messiaen for initiating a rebirth of organ music in the twentieth century through his skillful exploitation of the organ's rhythmic qualities in his works. Messiaen regarded the organ's method of expressing musical sounds through duration and timbre as liberating, not limiting. He discovered and subsequently demonstrated in his works how the organ could fulfill itself as a musical instrument. Routley discusses Messiaen's organ music through the *Messe de la Pentecôte*. He interprets *Apparition de l'Église éternelle* as a study in simple duration and uses "Les Bergers" from *La Nativité du Seigneur* to illustrate various facets of Messiaen's musical style. The book was originally published in 1964 by Herbert Jenkins, Limited in London.

692. Roy, Jean. *Présences contemporaines Musique française*. Paris: Nouvelles Éditions Debresse, 1962. 488 p. ML 390.R89.

General "life and works" overview of Messiaen through 1960 (pp. 361–84). Also contains a selected bibliography, biographical chronology, listing of works by genre, and a selected discography.

693. Salzman, Eric. *Twentieth-Century Music: An Introduction*, 4th ed. Upper Saddle River, NJ: Prentice-Hall, Inc., 2002. xiv, 337 p. ISBN: 0130959413. ML 197.S17 2002.

Brief discussion of Messiaen's musical style (pp. 159–60). Considers him not only as the father of the European avant-garde but also as a highly original figure. States that Messiaen's music consists of a mixture of disparate elements and is comparable to the music of Varèse in terms of sonority and spatial form.

694. Simeone, Nigel. *Paris: A Musical Gazetteer.* New Haven: Yale University Press, 2000. ix, 299 p. ISBN: 0300080530 (cloth), 0300080549 (paperback). ML 21.F7 S56 2000.

Provides valuable information on Messiaen, such as: his residences (65 rue Rambuteau, 77 rue des Plantes, 13 villa du Danube, 230 rue Marcadet, pp. 97–99); institutions where he worked (La Trinité, pp. 170–71, Conservatoire de Musique, pp. 214–17, École Normale de Musique, p. 218, Schola Cantorum, pp. 222–23); and publishers (Durand, pp. 228–29, Leduc, p. 231).

695. Sims, Bryan R. *Music of the Twentieth-Century: Style and Structure.* New York: Schirmer Books, 1986. xiv, 450 p. ISBN: 0028725808. MT 6.S534 M9 1986.

Survey of Messiaen's life, works, and musical style (pp. 403–9). While acknowledging that the sources of his music are eclectic, maintains that their use is determined by his Catholic faith and ideas about human love and nature. Considers Messiaen's approaches to rhythm, harmony, and melody. As a work that exemplifies his musical style, looks at *Couleurs de la Cité céleste.* Also includes separate discussions of the modes of limited transposition in the context of symmetric sets (pp. 37–38), *Mode de valeurs et d'intensités* in relation to postwar European serialism (pp. 86, 345), and Messiaen's rhythmic language in relation to twentieth-century approaches to rhythm and meter (pp. 107–8).

696. Straus, Joseph N. *Introduction to Post-Tonal Theory,* 3d ed. Upper Saddle River, NJ: Pearson Prentice Hall, 2005. xi, 273 p. ISBN: 0131898906. MT 40.S96 2005.

Uses a passage from Messiaen's "Abîme des oiseaux," the third movement of the *Quatuor pour la fin du Temps,* to explain the octatonic collection and the transposition of its constituent subsets by minor thirds and tritones (pp. 145–47).

697. Strinz, Werner. *Variations sur l'inquiétude rythmique: Untersuchungen zur morphologischen und satztechnischen Funktion des Rhythmus bei Olivier Messiaen, Pierre Boulez und Jean Barraqué,* 2 vols. Europäische Hochschulschriften, Reihe 36, Musikwissenschaft, Band 223. Frankfurt am Main: Peter Lang, 2003. ISBN: 3631396260. MT 90.S77 (IUCAT).

Devotes two chapters to an examination of rhythm in the music of Messiaen. In chapter two (pp. 19–66), looks at Messiaen's ideas about ametrical music (where a small base value is freely multiplied), arsis and thesis, melodic accentuation (derived from Vincent d'Indy), and the expansion of nonharmonic tones and their incorporation into his music. Surveys Messiaen's rhythmic styles, considering the *Quatuor pour la fin du Temps* as the key to understanding his conception of rhythm. Investigates Messiaen's use of rhythmic cells, durational rows, chromatic durations, and rhythm in relation to the complete work. In chapter six (pp. 173–96), focuses on Messiaen's works from 1949–51, analyzing "Mode de valeurs et d'intensités," the first movement ("Entrée [Les langues de feu]") from the *Messe de la Pentecôte*, and the second ("Pièce en trio [I]"), fifth ("Pièce en trio [II]"), and seventh movements ("Soixante-Quatre durées") from the *Livre d'Orgue*.

Reviews: Theo Hirsbrunner, *Österreichische Musikzeitschrift* 59/5 (May 2004): 81–82.

698. Stuckenschmidt, Hans Heinz. *Twentieth[-]Century Music*. Translated from the German by Richard Deveson. New York: McGraw-Hill Book Company, 1976. 256 p. ML 197.S7752 T9 1969b.

Includes three discussions of Messiaen (pp. 147–49, 167–68, and 204–7). The first examines the importance of religion in Messiaen's music, the second focuses on his rhythmic language in relation to classical Indian music, and the third studies the influence of mathematics on his compositional techniques, which is evinced by rhythmic pedals in the "Liturgie de cristal" of the *Quatuor pour la fin du Temps*, the modes of limited transposition, and the quasi-serial techniques of *Mode de valeurs et d'intensités* and *Timbres-Durées*.

699. Taruskin, Richard. *The Oxford History of Western Music*. 6 vols. Oxford: Oxford University Press, 2005. ISBN: 0195169794. ML 160.T18 2005 v. 1–6.

Two discussions of Messiaen in volumes 4 and 5 that cover early- and late-twentieth century music, respectively. The first one (volume 4, pp. 229–42) examines his musical style as seen through *La Nativité du Seigneur*, *Les Corps glorieux*, *Quatuor pour la fin du Temps*, *Technique de mon langage musical*, and the *Turangalîla-Symphonie*. States incorrectly that Messiaen used the first and second modes of limited transposition (whole-tone and octatonic scales, respectively) more frequently than any other modes in his music ("the ones most frequently used by far, even by him [Messiaen]"). On the contrary, that honor goes to modes two and three. Since Messiaen believed that Debussy and Dukas used the whole-tone scale so successfully in their works, mode one is seldom used in his music. When it is, it is often placed in a polymodal texture. The second discussion (volume 5, pp. 22–30, 35–37) centers on *Mode de valeurs et d'intensités* and its influence on Boulez's writing of *Structures Ia*. There is no further consideration of Messiaen in volume 5, particularly with respect to his music of the 1960s to 1990s.

700. Toesca, Maurice. *Cinq ans de patience*. Paris: Éditions Émile-Paul, 1975. 377 p. PQ 2639.O53 Z513.

In a journal kept from 1939 to 1944 describing Parisian life during World War II, Toesca recounts his interactions with Messiaen. They include receiving a note from the composer about *La Nativité du Seigneur* (p. 197), discussing a proposed radio program featuring the recitation of Toesca's *Les douze regards* with musical accompaniment supplied by Messiaen (pp. 298, 348–49), and attending performances of the *Quatuor pour la fin du Temps* (pp. 279–81), *Visions de l'Amen* (pp. 298–302), and *Vingt Regards sur l'Enfant-Jésus* (pp. 348–49). Toesca found Messiaen's music troubling, primarily because of its mixture of both extreme dissonance and sweet consonance. He was also critical of Messiaen's practice of supplying verbal commentaries about his works before their performance.

701. Vincent, John Nathaniel. *The Diatonic Modes in Modern Music*. Hollywood, CA: Curlew Music Publishers, Inc., 1974. x, 394 p. ML 3812.V7 1974 (IUCAT).

Short discussion of Messiaen (pp. 373–74) within the context of twentieth-century modal practice, in which the concept of tonality has been broadened. Uses two excerpts from "L'Ange aux parfums" of *Les Corps glorieux* to illustrate that "a complex sound-texture, even highly chromatic and/or dissonant, may be invested with tonality through combining it with a diatonic melodic line (Major, Minor, modal, exotic or 'constructed')."

702. Vogt, Hans, in collaboration with Maja Bard, Mathias Bielitz, Hans Peter Haller, Hans-Peter Raiß, and Angelus Seipt. *Neue Musik seit 1945*, 3d ed., rev. and enl. Stuttgart: Philipp Reclam jun., 1982. 538 p. ISBN: 3150102030. ML 197.V64 1982.

Views Messiaen in relation to music after World War II. Notes the innovative approach to rhythm in the *Quatuor pour la fin du Temps* and the Dionysian character of Messiaen's music as reflected in the *Turangalîla-Symphonie* (p. 19), as well as the extension of the serial principle to non-pitch parameters in *Mode de valeurs et d'intensités* (pp. 24–25). In the section of the book devoted to the extended examination of selected pieces (Teil III), there is a rhythmic analysis of the *Messe de la Pentecôte* by Hans-Peter Raiß (pp. 249–53).

703. Watkins, Glenn. *Soundings: Music in the Twentieth Century.* New York: Schirmer Books, 1988. xviii, 728 p. ISBN: 0028732901. ML 197.W44 1988.

Discussions of Messiaen's musical style and works interspersed throughout the volume (pp. 216, 224, 481–86, 498, 506–9, 622–23, 672–74). Covers a wide variety of topics in relation to Messiaen's musical style, such as rhythmic characters, the modes of limited transposition, nonretrogradable rhythms, isorhythm, the serialization of non-pitch parameters, added resonance, synesthesia, and Messiaen's influence on Boulez.

704. Whittall, Arnold. *Musical Composition in the Twentieth Century.* New York: Oxford University Press, 1999. vi, 419 p. ISBN: 0198166842 (hardback); 0198166834 (paperback). ML 197.W55 1999.

Three essays on Messiaen that survey his music and compositional style, set within a larger stylistic discussion of Michael Tippett, Messiaen, and Elliott Carter. For the author, all three composers approached style and structure in a fundamentally modernist vein. The first essay (*Messiaen I*, pp. 243–46) examines Messiaen's early musical style and works through the *Turangalîla-Symphonie.* It makes some questionable statements regarding how the modes of limited transposition make extended tonality possible, by the strategic placement of relatively more consonant (added-sixth chords) and dissonant structures (chords containing a minor second) within a passage of music. The second essay (*Messiaen II*, pp. 252–57) discusses Messiaen's compositional style from 1949–69, covering *Mode de valeurs et d'intensités* through *Méditations sur le mystère de la Sainte Trinité.* The third essay (*Messiaen III*, pp. 262–63) looks at Messiaen's music since the mid-1970s, viewing it as a series of epilogues, at times grand and at other times modest in scope.

705. Wittlich, Gary E., ed. *Aspects of Twentieth-Century Music.* Englewood Cliffs, NJ: Prentice-Hall, Inc., 1975. xi, 483 p. ISBN: 0130493465. ML 197.A8.

Three of the book's authors (DeLone, Winold, and Kliewer) use passages from Messiaen's music, along with the preface to the *Quatuor pour la fin du Temps*, as part of their investigations of twentieth-century approaches to timbre and texture, rhythm, and melody, respectively. The examples include: (1) "L'Ange aux parfums" from *Les Corps glorieux* to illustrate contrapuntal aspects of fuller textures (pp. 173–74); (2) "Danse de la fureur, pour les sept trompettes," the sixth movement of the *Quatuor pour la fin du Temps*, and part of the preface to the *Quatuor* translated into English, to explain some of Messiaen's rhythmic techniques (pp. 261–63); and (3) *Couleurs de la Cité céleste* to show a melody of timbres (pp. 285–86).

706. Xenakis, Iannis. *Arts/Sciences, alliages: Iannis Xenakis, Olivier Messiaen, Michel Ragon, Olivier Revault d'Allonnes, Michel Serres, Bernard Teyssèdre.* Paris: Casterman, 1979. 151 p. ISBN: 220323170X. ML3800.X38.

The text of this book is a transcription made from the tape recordings of Iannis Xenakis's thesis defense for his *doctorat d'Etat* at the University of Paris, Sorbonne on 18 May 1976. After a statement from Xenakis, each member of the jury took turns questioning him, with other members periodically joining the conversation. Instead of opening with a statement like his colleagues, Messiaen asked Xenakis four questions, one right after the other.

707. *Arts/sciences, alloys: The Thesis Defense of Iannix Xenakis before Olivier Messiaen, Michel Ragon, Olivier Revault d'Allonnes, Michel Serres, and Bernard Teyssédre.* Translated by Sharon Kanach. Aesthetics in Music No. 2. New York: Pendragon Press, 1985. x, 133 p. ISBN: 0918728223. ML 3800.X3813 1985.

English translation of item 706.

DISSERTATIONS AND OTHER UNPUBLISHED DOCUMENTS

708. Barash, Amari Pepper. "Cadential Gestures in Post-Tonal Music: The Constitution of Cadences in Messiaen's *Île de feu I* and Boulez'[s] *Première Sonate*, First Movement" (item 553).

An analysis of the cadential factors at work in "Île de feu I," the first piece from the *Quatre Études de rythme*, in chapter two.

709. Buchler, Michael H. "Relative Saturation of Subsets and Interval Cycles as a Means for Determining Set-Class Similarity" (item 565).

An analysis of "Le Merle noir," the second piece from the *Petites esquisses d'oiseaux* (1985), in chapter four.

710. Conrad, Bridget F. "The Sources of Jolivet's Musical Language and His Relationships with Varèse and Messiaen," 2 vols. Ph.D. dissertation, City University of New York, 1994. xxxi, 537 p. (vol. 1); ix, 141 p. (vol. 2).

An examination of Jolivet's musical language in relation to that of Varèse and Messiaen. Considers Jolivet's relationship to Messiaen in the latter part of the dissertation. In chapter nine (pp. 394–437), describes Jolivet's association with Messiaen and the other musicians of *La Spirale* and *Jeune France* during the 1930s. Jolivet and Messiaen exchanged ideas at this time, each to their mutual benefit. In particular, Jolivet introduced the music of Varèse to Messiaen and the other members of *La Jeune France*. In chapter ten (pp. 438–65), looks at similarities between the musical-aesthetic outlooks of the two composers. The next chapter (pp. 466–519) includes an examination of various aspects of Messiaen's musical language in relation to Jolivet's, in order to highlight how their compositional innovations were related but different. In the conclusion (pp. 526–37), reflects on how Jolivet is part of the same musical tradition shared by Messiaen and Varèse. An added bonus: includes excerpts from interviews of Messiaen conducted in Paris in May-June 1987 where Messiaen discusses Jolivet and his music. Highly recommended.

711. Covington, Katherine Russell. "A Study of Textural Stratification in Twentieth-Century Compositions." Ph.D. dissertation, Indiana University, 1982. xiii, 147 p.

Considers the role of texture in the analysis of twentieth-century music. Develops a definition of textural stratification. Discusses how textural strata are characterized by various musical elements, such as time, timbre, register, dynamics, different types of melodic and harmonic activity, rhythm, meter, and density. Concludes the study by exploring how textural strata are related. Messiaen's *Mode de valeurs et d'intensités* and *Sept Haïkaï* are among the pieces analyzed in this study.

712. Derfler, Barbara Joan. "Claude Debussy's influence on Olivier Messiaen: An Analysis and Comparison of Two Preludes." M.M. thesis, University of Alberta, 1999. 82 p.

An examination of "Cloches d'angoisse et larmes d'adieu" from the *Préludes* for piano. See item 529.

713. Hickman, Melinda Lee. "Meaning in Piano Music with a Religious Theme: A Philosophical and Historical Approach." D.M.A. thesis, University of Cincinnati College-Conservatory of Music, 2001. vi, 195 p.

Within a study on the communication of musical meaning, analyzes Messiaen's *Vingt Regards sur l'Enfant-Jésus* (Chapter VI: "The Twentieth Century," pp. 137–77). Focuses on the expressive devices used in *Vingt Regards* to convey meaning. Prefaces the analysis with an overview of twentieth-century aesthetics and biographical information pertaining to Messiaen's faith.

714. Hopkins, Stephen. "A Comparative Analysis of Selected Works of Alexander Scriabin and Olivier Messiaen for Solo Piano." Ph.D. dissertation, The Florida State University, 1993. ix, 552 p.

Using pitch-class set theory, investigates the piano music of Scriabin and Messiaen for their similarities in pitch organization. Views Messiaen's use of the modes of limited transposition as comparable to the scale collections employed by Scriabin. Considers principles of symmetry and periodicity as fundamental to each composer's handling of pitch. Works examined are Scriabin's last five piano sonatas and Five Preludes, op. 74, and Messiaen's *Vingt Regards sur l'Enfant-Jésus* and *Petites esquisses d'oiseaux*.

715. Koh, Hwee Been. "East and West: The Aesthetics and Musical Time of Toru Takemitsu." Ph.D. dissertation, Boston University, 1998. xiii, 294 p.

In this study of Toru Takemitsu's compositional practice and its relationship to his philosophical aesthetics, the author includes a discussion of how the richness of harmonic color and sense of timelessness in Messiaen's music influenced the Japanese composer (see pp. 68–71). Examines how Takemitsu responded to Messiaen's musical style through his handling of pitch structure and formal designs in his music.

716. Ming, Christina Tio Ee. "The Avant Garde and Its 'Others': Orientalism in Contemporary Art Music." Ph.D. dissertation, University of Southampton, 2000.

Explores cross-cultural interactions in contemporary art music. Seeks to develop a critical framework for interpreting the influence of and allusions to East Asian elements in such music, one that would emphasize the transformation of ethnocentric narratives into more inclusive ones, rather than their subversion. Examines the music of four contemporary composers: Olivier Messiaen, Karlheinz Stockhausen, Peter Sculthorpe, and Toru Takemitsu. Looks at Messiaen's "Gagaku," the fourth movement of *Sept Haïkaï*, in chapter one.

717. Montgomery, Mary Ann. "Musical and Poetical Structures in Olivier Messiaen's *Couleurs de la Cité Céleste* and Ted Hughes's *Crow*."

An examination of *Couleurs de la Cité céleste*. See item 465.

718. Shadinger, Richard Cole. "The Sacred Element in Piano Literature: A Historical Background and an Annotated Listing." D.M.A. dissertation, The Southern Baptist Theological Seminary, 1974. ix, 205 p.

Discussion of Messiaen and *Vingt Regards sur l'Enfant-Jésus* (pp. 40–41) in the context of a study that investigates the sacred element in music for the piano. Also includes *Vingt Regards* as a part of its "Annotated Listing of Sacred Piano Literature" (pp. 124–25).

719. Sprout, Leslie A. "Music for a 'New Era': Composers and National Identity in France, 1936–46." Ph.D. dissertation, University of California, Berkeley, 2000. xiii, 427 p.

Includes discussions of Messiaen within a study that examines the French government's 1938 program to revitalize contemporary French music. Mentions a performance of Messiaen's *Les Offrandes oubliées* conducted by Charles Munch at a "Composers in the Camps" concert on 11 January 1942 (pp. 176–77). Speculates as to why Messiaen did not receive any financial support as a composer from the Vichy regime, despite his academic credentials, post as a professor of harmony at the Paris Conservatoire, position as titular organist at La Trinité, and expressions of devout Catholicism. Yet, notes how Honegger consistently supported Messiaen during this time through his positive reviews of the premieres of the *Quatuor pour la fin du Temps* and *Visions de l'Amen* (pp. 181–82). Discusses the reception of Messiaen's *Quatuor* by most Parisian critics, who, although acknowledging the sincerity of Messiaen's religious beliefs, were bewildered by the *Quatuor*'s mysticism and musical language (pp. 184–85). Finally, describes Messiaen's influence on Boulez as a teacher, the unruly behavior of Messiaen's students protesting at performances of Stravinsky's neoclassical works in the music concerts of the Orchestre national in 1945, and Messiaen's growing reputation as a composer in the later 1940s (pp. 369–74).

720. Trevitt, John. "The Role of the Diminished Seventh and Related Phenomena in the Development of Harmonic Dissension from Beethoven to Messiaen, with Special Reference to Claude Debussy." Ph.D. dissertation, The University of East Anglia, 1975.

Examines the relationship of the diminished seventh chord to certain modes of limited transposition. Traces the history of chromaticism based on the diminished seventh chord in the music from the late eighteenth through twentieth centuries. Maintains that a new musical language involving the modes of limited transposition emerged in the music of Debussy from 1880–1900. Discusses the development of this modal language in the works of Debussy, as well as Ravel and Stravinsky, from 1901–14. Investigates the decline of modality after 1914 and its revival in the music of Messiaen (see chapter 6, pp. 134–49).

DICTIONARY AND ENCYCLOPEDIA ARTICLES

721. Griffiths, Paul. "Messiaen, Olivier." *Grove Music Online*, ed. Laura Macy. [www. grovemusic.com]. Accessed 22 July 2006.

Online version of the *New Grove*'s dictionary article. See item 722.

722. Griffiths, Paul. "Messiaen, Olivier." In *The New Grove Dictionary of Music and Musicians*, ed. Stanley Sadie and J. Tyrrell, 2d ed., 16:491–504. 29 vols. London: Macmillan, 2001. ISBN: 1561592390. ML 100.N48 2001.

Overview of Messiaen's life, compositional aesthetics, musical language, and works. Divided into five sections: (1) Life; (2) Theology; (3) Musical Elements; (4) Works to 1950; and (5) Works after 1950. The discussion of Messiaen's harmonic elements focuses on the modes of limited transposition to the exclusion of his later non-modal chords (e.g., chords of transposed inversions on the same bass note). Includes a list of works and an extensive bibliography.

723. Griffiths, Paul. "Messiaen, Olivier." In *The New Grove Twentieth-Century French Masters*, 221–48. New York: W. W. Norton, 1986. 291 p. ISBN: 0393022846 (hard); 0393303500 (paperback). ML 390.N498 1986.

An earlier version of Griffiths's 2001 article for *The New Grove Dictionary of Music and Musicians* (see item 722). Does not include a discussion of Messiaen's theology, nor does it consider any works after *Saint François d'Assise* (1975–83).

724. Griffiths, Paul. "*Saint François d'Assise*." *Grove Music Online*, ed. Laura Macy. [www.grovemusic.com]. Accessed 22 July 2006.

Online version of the *New Grove*'s dictionary article. See item 437.

725. Griffiths, Paul. "*Saint François d'Assise*." In *The New Grove Dictionary of Opera* (item 437), 4:126–27.

See item 437.

726. Griffiths, Paul. "Messiaen, Olivier." In *The Thames and Hudson Encyclopedia of 20th-Century Music*, 118–19. London: Thames and Hudson Inc., 1986. 207 p. ML 197.G75 1986 (IUCAT).

Biographical and stylistic survey of Messiaen and his music. Includes a list of works through 1975.

727. Hindley, Geoffrey, ed. "Serialism," "Messiaen, Olivier." In *Larousse Encyclopedia of Music*, 372–73, 404–5. With an introduction by

Anthony Hopkins. Seacaucus, NJ: Chartwell Books Inc., 1976. ISBN: 0890090599. ML 160.L34 1971B.

This English language edition is based on *La Musique: les hommes; les instruments; les œuvres*, ed. M. Norbert Dufourcq (Paris: Augé, Gillon, Hollier-Larousse, Morceau et Cie, Librairie Larousse, 1965). It includes two essays, one on Messiaen's role in the development of total serialism ("Serialism," pp. 372–73) as seen through *Mode de valeurs et d'intensités*, and the other on his life and works ("Messiaen," pp. 404–5).

728. Sherlaw Johnson, Robert. "Olivier Messiaen and Pierre Boulez." In *Heritage of Music*. Volume 4, *Music in the Twentieth Century*, ed. Michael Raeburn and Alan Kendall, 267–77. New York: Oxford University Press, 1990. ISBN: 019520493X (set). ML 160.H527 1989.

In the part of the article devoted to Messiaen (pp. 267–72), Johnson not only summarizes the composer's life and works, but also discusses aspects of his musical style, such as color and mode, serial processes, and birdsong (particularly in relation to the *Catalogue d'oiseaux*), closing with some remarks on his influence. Because the *Heritage of Music* is touted as an illustrated history of music, the article includes numerous pictures.

729. Keym, Stefan. "Messiaen, Olivier." In *Die Musik in Geshichte und Gegenwart*, ed. Ludwig Finscher, Zweite, neubearbeitete Ausgabe, Personenteil 12:63–81. 26 Bände in zwei Teilen. Kassel: Bärenreiter-Verlag, 2004. ISBN: 3761811225.

This excellent survey of Messiaen's life and works includes discussions of his musical language, chronological development as a composer, compositional genres, and work as a teacher and theorist. Contains comprehensive discussions of his harmonic and rhythmic elements. Besides a list of works, provides a thorough bibliography that includes sources related to the topic of spirituality in Messiaen's music. Highly recommended.

730. Messiaen, Olivier and J. Roy. "Messiaen, Olivier." In *Dictionnaire de la musique: Les Hommes et leurs œuvres*, ed. Marc Honegger, 2:713.

See item 73.

731. Pople, Anthony. "Messiaen, Olivier." In *Contemporary Composers*, ed. Brian Morton and Pamela Collins, 649–52. With a preface by Brian Ferneyhough. Chicago and London: St. James Press, 1992. xvi, 1019 p. ISBN: 1558620850. ML 105.C75 1992.

Includes a brief biography, a list of works with place and date of first performance as well as selected discographical information, a selected bibliography, and a discussion of Messiaen's musical style and its place within contemporary music.

732. Randel, Don Michael, ed. "Messiaen, Olivier." In *The Harvard Biographical Dictionary of Music*, 582–83. Cambridge, MA: The Belknap Press of Harvard University Press, 1996. x, 1013 p. ISBN: 0674372999. ML 105.H38 1996.

Short biography of Messiaen followed by a discussion of his musical style. Not only addresses the significance of the Roman Catholic faith, the Tristan legend, and birdsong in order to understand Messiaen's music, but also discusses various musical techniques related to rhythm, pitch, and timbre. Contains a list of selected works and a bibliography.

733. Slonimsky, Nicolas, Laura Kuhn, and Dennis McIntire. "Messiaen, Olivier." In *Baker's Biographical Dictionary of Musicians*, ed. Nicolas Slonimsky and Laura Kuhn, Centennial ed., 4:2420–21. 6 vols. New York: Schirmer Books, 2001. ISBN: 0028655257. ML 105.B16 2001.

Basic biography and style analysis of Messiaen and his music. Includes a list of selected works, writings, and bibliography. Contains some inaccuracies with respect to dating (e.g., Messiaen spent one year in a German prison camp in Görlitz, not two as the entry maintains) and omits keyboard works after 1969 and the *Traité de rythme, de couleur, et d'ornithologie (1949–1992)* in its list of works and writings.

734. Slonimsky, Nicolas. "Messiaen, Olivier." In *Baker's Biographical Dictionary of Twentieth-Century Classical Musicians*, ed. Laura Kuhn and Dennis McIntire. New York: Schirmer Books, 1997. xii, 1595 p. ISBN: 0028712714. ML 105.S612 1997.

Compact life and works survey of Messiaen. Contains biographical data and a description of Messiaen's musical style. Concludes with a list of works and a selected bibliography.

735. Slonimsky, Nicolas; updated by Laura Diane Kuhn. *Music Since 1900*, 6th ed. New York: Schirmer Reference/Gale Group, 2001. xvii, 1174 p. ISBN: 0028647874. ML 197.S634 2001.

In a descriptive chronology listing significant musical events of the twentieth century from 1 January 1900 through 14 December 2000, this final edition of *Music Since 1900* features numerous entries on Messiaen. Besides the dates of his birth and death, it lists dates of premieres and important concerts of his works. It also interprets Messiaen's use of birdsongs in *Chronochromie* as a modern example of Neo-Romanticism (pp. 1080–81).

736. Sadie, Stanley, ed. "Messiaen, Olivier." In *The Norton/Grove Concise Encyclopedia of Music*, 484–85. New York: W. W. Norton & Company, 1988. 850 p. ISBN: 0393026205. ML 100.N88 1988.

Short summary of Messiaen's life and works. Includes a list of selected compositions but no bibliography.

737. Tremblay, Gilles. "Messiaen, Olivier." In *Dictionary of Contemporary Music*, ed. John Vinton, 474–78. New York: E.P. Dutton & Co., Inc., 1974. xiv, 834 p. ISBN: 0525091254. ML 100.V55.

One of the best dictionary articles on Messiaen by an author who studied with the composer at the Paris Conservatoire in the 1950s. The article covers Messiaen's life and work, mentioning elements of his compositional aesthetics that are not brought up in similar accounts, such as the role of distant harmonics in altering timbres, or the role of quantitative and qualitative time in the formation of the composer's rhythmic techniques. Includes a list of principal compositions and writings, along with a selected bibliography.

8

Selected Listings of Reviews of Books, Essay Collections, Monographs, Treatises, World Premieres, and Significant Performances

SELECTED REVIEWS OF BOOKS, ESSAY COLLECTIONS, MONOGRAPHS, AND TREATISES

BOIVIN, Jean. *La classe de Messiaen* [item 203].

> 738. Bardez, Jean-Michel. "*La classe de Messiaen* de Jean Boivin." *Circuit* 9/1 (1998): 27–40.

> 739. Dingle, Christopher. *Tempo* 202 (October 1997): 25–26.

BRUHN, Siglind. *Images and Ideas in Modern French Piano Music* [item 537].

> 740. Hirsbrunner, Theo. *Die Musikforschung* 54/3 (July-September 2001): 323.

> 741. Schlee, Thomas Daniel. *Österreichische Musikzeitschrift* 56/6 (June 2000): 87–88.

BRUHN, Siglind, ed. *Messiaen's Language of Mystical Love* [item 236].

> 742. Benitez, Vincent P. *MLA Notes* 56/2 (December 1999): 424–26.

CARL, Beate. *Olivier Messiaens Orchesterwerk "Des canyons aux étoiles"* [item 469].

> 743. Hirsbrunner, Theo. *Musiktheorie* 14/2 (1999): 179.

DAVIDSON, Audrey Ekdahl. *Olivier Messiaen and the Tristan Myth* [item 227].

744. Sullivan, Tim. *Journal of Musicological Research* 22/1–2 (January–June 2003): 174–77.

745. Mardirosian, Haig. *The American Organist* 36/10 (October 2002): 85–86.

746. Behrens, J. *Choice* 39/11–12 (July/August 2002): 1970.

GRIFFITHS, Paul. *Olivier Messiaen and the Music of Time* [item 208].

747. Whittall, Arnold. *The Music Review* 46/3 (August 1985): 226–28.

HILL, Peter, ed. *The Messiaen Companion* [item 240].

748. Burbank, Richard D. *MLA Notes* 53/1 (September 1996): 76–77.

749. Palmer, David. *The Diapason* 87/2 (February 1996): 8–9.

750. Anderson, Julian. "Writ Small." *The Musical Times* 136/1830 (August 1995): 434–35.

HILL, Peter and Nigel Simeone. *Messiaen* [item 210].

751. Braun, William R. *Opera News* 71/1 (July 2006): 64.

752. Neil, M. *Choice* 43/8 (April 2006): 1413.

753. Thomson, Andrew. "All for Jesus." *The Musical Times* 147/1894 (Spring 2006): 73–80.

754. Schiff, David. "Music for the End of Time." *The Nation* 282/6 (13 February 2006): 25–29.

755. Rindom, Ditlev. "Illuminating the Beyond: The Life and Work of Olivier Messiaen." *The Cambridge Quarterly* 35/2 (2006): 188–91.

756. Schueneman, Bruce R. *Library Journal* 130/16 (1 October 2005): 78.

HIRSBRUNNER, Theo. *Olivier Messiaen: Leben und Werk* [item 211].

757. Rößler, Almut. *Musica* 43/2 (March/April 1989): 165–66.

758. Rößler, Almut. *Musik und Kirche* 58/6 (1988): 303–4.

HSU (Forte), Madeleine. *Olivier Messiaen, the Musical Mediator* [item 230].

759. Timbrell, Charles. *The American Music Teacher* 47/3 (December 1997-January 1998): 69, 71.

JOHNSON, Robert Sherlaw. *Messiaen* [item 213].

760. Griffiths, Paul. "Deux Regards." *The Musical Times* 116/1592 (October 1975): 881–83.

761. Drew, David. *Times Literary Supplement.* 12 September 1975, 1030.

762. Newlin, Dika. *Library Journal* 100/13 (July 1975): 1328.

MESSIAEN, Olivier. *Olivier Messiaen: Music and Color: Conversations with Claude Samuel.* **Translated by E. Thomas Glasow** [item 176].

763. Benitez, Vincent P. *Indiana Theory Review* 17/2 (Fall 1996): 93–102.

764. Dingle, Christopher. *Tempo* 192 (April 1995): 29–30, 32.

MESSIAEN, Olivier. *Technique de mon langage musical* [item 88].

765. Dingle, Christopher. "Messiaen and Ravel [Includes a review of the 2000 edition of the *Technique de mon langage musical*]." *Tempo* 59/231 (January 2005): 61–62.

766. Anhalt, Istvan. Review of the *Technique of My Musical Language*, trans. John Satterfield. *The Canadian Music Journal* 2 (Autumn 1957): 67, 69, 71.

767. Galkin, Elliott W. *The Technique of My Musical Language*, trans. John Satterfield. *Notes* 14/4 (September 1957): 575–76.

768. Jacobi, Frederick. "Messiaen's Language: Birds and Butterflies" [Review of the 1944 edition of the *Technique de mon langage musical*]. *Modern Music* 23/3 (Summer 1946): 231–32.

MESSIAEN, Olivier. *Traité de rythme, de couleur, et d'ornithologie (1949–1992)* [item 90].

769. Dingle, Christopher. Reviews of vol. 1, *Tempo* 192 (April 1995): 29–30, 32; vols. 2 and 3, *Tempo* 202 (October 1997): 25–26; vol. 4,

Tempo 205 (July 1998): 26–27; vols. 5–7, *Tempo* 58/227 (January 2004): 41–46.

770. Boivin, Jean. "*Le Traité de rythme, de couleur, et d'ornithologie d'Olivier Messiaen* (tomes I, II, III et IV)." *Circuit* 9/1 (1998): 17–26.

MESSIAEN, Olivier and Yvonne Loriod-Messiaen. *Ravel: Analyses des Œuvres pour Piano de Maurice Ravel* [item 92].

771. Dingle, Christopher. "Messiaen and Ravel." *Tempo* 59/231 (January 2005): 61–62.

MICHAELY, Aloyse. *Die Musik Olivier Messiaens: Untersuchungen zum Gesamtschaffen* [item 216].

772. Rößler, Almut. *Musica* 43/2 (March/April 1989): 166–67.

MURRAY, Michael. *French Masters of the Organ: Saint-Saens, Franck, Widor, Vierne, Dupré, Langlais, Messiaen* [item 683].

773. Van Wye, Benjamin. *MLA Notes* 55/4 (June 1999): 925.

NICHOLS, Roger. *Messiaen* [item 218].

774. Lawrence, Arthur. [Review of the First Edition.] *The Diapason* 70 (December 1978): 4.

775. Griffiths, Paul. "Deux Regards [Review of the First Edition]." *The Musical Times* 116/1592 (October 1975): 881–83.

POPLE, Anthony. *Messiaen:* **Quatuor pour la fin du Temps** [item 485].

776. Mark, Christopher. "Messiaen: 'Quatuor pour la fin du temps'." *Music & Letters* 82 (February 2001): 143–45.

777. Luchese, Diane. *Music Theory Online* 5/2 (March 1999).

RISCHIN, Rebecca. *For the End of Time: The Story of the Messiaen Quartet* [item 486].

778. Sprout, Leslie. *MLA Notes* 61/2 (December 2004): 423–25.

779. Neil, M. *Choice* 41/10 (June 2004): 1891.

780. Simeone, Nigel. "Après la guerre: *For the End of Time: The Story of the Messiaen Quartet*." *The Musical Times* 145/1886 (Spring 2004): 91–94.

781. Ross, Alex. "Revelations: The Story behind Messiaen's 'Quartet for the End of Time'." *The New Yorker* (22 March 2004): 96–97.

782. Hirsch, Alan. *The Booklist* 100/6 (15 November 2003): 561–62.

783. [Anonymous]. *Publisher's Weekly*, 13 October 2003, 69.

RÖßLER, Almut. ***Contributions to the Spiritual World of Olivier Messiaen: With Original Texts by the Composer*** [item 180].

784. Palmer, David. *The Diapason* 77/11 (November 1986): 6.

SAMUEL, Claude. ***Entretiens avec Olivier Messiaen*** [item 181].

785. Gardiner, Bennitt. "Dialogues with Messiaen [Review of *Entretiens avec Olivier Messiaen*, by Claude Samuel]." *Musical Events* (October 1967): 6–9.

SAMUEL, Claude. ***Conversations with Olivier Messiaen.* Translated by Felix Aprahamian** [item 182].

786. Lawrence, Arthur. *The Diapason* 70 (December 1978): 4.

SIMEONE, Nigel. ***Olivier Messiaen: A Bibliographical Catalogue of Messiaen's Works*** [item 6].

787. Hirsbrunner, Theo. *Dissonanz* 66 (November 2000): 55.

788. Morris, David. *MLA Notes* 57/1 (September 2000): 116.

STRINZ, Werner. ***Variations sur l'inquiétude rythmique*** [item 697].

789. Hirsbrunner, Theo. *Österreichische Musikzeitschrift* 59/5 (May 2004): 81–82.

TÖLLE, Julian Christophe. ***Olivier Messiaen:* Éclairs sur l'Au-Delà: *Die christlich-eschatologische Dimension des Opus ultimum*** [item 475].

790. Keym, Stefan. *Die Musikforschung* 55/3 (July/September 2002): 330–31.

SELECTED REVIEWS OF WORLD PREMIERES AND SIGNIFICANT PERFORMANCES OF MESSIAEN'S WORKS

Opera

Saint François d'Assise

World Premiere, Paris, 1983

791. Petit, Pierre. "*Saint François d'Assise* d'Olivier Messiaen: L'Art naif de la mosaïque." *Le Figaro*, 29 November 1983.

792. Rockwell, John. "Paris Opéra: The Debut of Messiaen['s] [*Saint*] *François*." *The New York Times*, 30 November 1983.

793. Samuel, Claude. "Un opéra messianique." *Le Matin*, 30 November 1983.

794. Stadlen, Peter. "Messiaen's St. Francis of Assisi." *Daily Telegraph*, 30 November 1983.

795. Griffiths, Paul. "Holy Mystery, Pastel Panto." *The Times*, 1 December 1983.

796. Schweizer, Klaus. "Eine unmögliche grossartige Opera." *Basler Zeitung*, 1 December 1983.

797. Cairns, David. "A Fresco for St. Francis." *Sunday Times*, 4 December 1983.

798. Doucelin, Jacques. "Cinq heures d'opéra: un pari difficile: *Saint François d'Assise.*" *L'Aurore*, 12 December 1983.

799. Toop, Richard. "Messiaen's 'Saint François'." *Contact* 28 (1984): 49–50.

800. Head, Raymond. "First Performances: 'Saint François d'Assise (Scènes Franciscaines)'." *Tempo* 148 (March 1984): 19–21.

801. Pasler, Jann. "St. Francis at the Opéra." *The Musical Times* 125/1693 (March 1984): 149–51.

Salzburg Festival 1992

802. B., R. "Messiaen's *Saint François d'Assise* at Salzburg." *Musical Opinion* 115 (October 1992): 408.

803. DiGaetani, John. "Salzburg Festival 1992: Taking Risks." *Opera Monthly* (November 1992): 26–29.

San Francisco 2002

804. Kosman, Joshua. "A Heavenly Premiere: S.F. Opera Pulls Off Complex Messiaen Masterpiece 'Saint Francois d'Assise'." *San Francisco Chronicle*, 30 September 2002, section D, 1.

805. Page, Tim. "'St. Francois,' Worthy of a Pilgrimage." *The Washington Post*, 30 September 2002, section C, 01.

806. Ruhe, Pierre. "Runnicles' 'Francis' a Triumph: U.S. Stage Premiere in San Francisco." *The Atlanta Journal-Constitution*, 30 September 2002, section E, 1.

807. Swed, Mark. "A Glorious Journey: The French Opera 'Saint François d'Assise' Has Its First American Staging in a Dazzling and Immense Production by the San Francisco Opera." *Los Angeles Times*, 30 September 2002, section F, 1.

808. Waleson, Heidi. "Misreading Messiaen's Ecstatic Vision." *Wall Steet Journal* (Eastern edition), 3 October 2002, section D, 6.

809. Winn, Steven. "A Strange and Transfixing Opera: Impact of Messiaen's 'Saint Francois d'Assise' Depends on the Staging." *San Francisco Chronicle*, 13 October 2002, 14.

810. Ross, Alex. "Sacred Monster." *The New Yorker* 78/32 (28 October 2002): 112–13.

811. Harvey, Dennis. *"Saint François d'Assise." Variety* 389/1 (18–24 November 2002): 36.

812. Crowley, Paul, S.J. "Music of the Invisible: Messiaen's *Saint François d'Assise." Commonweal* 129/22 (20 December 2002): 17–18.

813. Rich, Allan. "San Francisco." *Opera News* 67/7 (January 2003): 79–80.

Paris, 2004

814. Mudge, Stephen. *Opera News* (January 2005): 61–62.

Orchestral Works

Les Offrandes oubliées: Méditation symphonique pour Orchestre

815. Schmitt, Florent. *Le Temps*, 24 February 1931.

816. Baruzi, Joseph. "Concerts Straram (19 février)." *Le Ménestrel*, 27 February 1931, 95.

817. Febvre-Longeray, A., "Concerts Straram (19 et 26 février)." *Le Courrier musical*, 15 March 1931, 186.

818. Tournemire, Charles. "Société des Concerts du Conservatoire." *Le Courrier musical*, 15 December 1931, 594.

Le Tombeau resplendissant

819. Altomont, Claude. "Orchestre Symphonique de Paris, Dimanche 12 février." *Le Ménestrel*, 17 February 1933, 69.

820. D., F. "Les Concerts symphoniques à Paris." *Le Courrier musical*, 1 March 1933, 113.

Hymne au Saint-Sacrement

821. Le Flem, Paul. *Comœdia*, 27 March 1933.

822. B[elvianes], M[arcel]. "Concerts divers: Concerts Straram." *Le Ménestrel*, 31 March 1933, 134.

823. Brillant, Maurice. "Musique sacrée, musique profane." *L'Aube*, 31 March 1933.

824. Schmitt, Florent. "Les Concerts Straram: *Hymne au Saint-Sacrement* de M. Messiaen." *Le Temps*, 8 April 1933.

825. Imbert, Maurice. "Les Concerts Symphoniques à Paris." *Le Courrier musical*, 15 April 1933, 196.

Turangalîla-Symphonie

826. Gavoty ("Clarendon"), Bernard. "Les *Trois Tâla* d'Olivier Messiaen." *Le Figaro*, 18 February 1948.

827. Elie, Rudolph. "Symphony Concert [...] Turangalîla Symphony of Olivier Messiaen." *Boston Herald*, 3 December 1949.

828. Smith, Warren Storey. "Symphony Concert." *Boston Post*, 3 December 1949.

829. Downes, Olin. "Bernstein Leads Messiaen's Work." *The New York Times*, 11 December 1949.

830. Kolodin, Irving. "The Music Makers: Messiaen, Thebom, Flagstad and Puccini Make News." *The New York Sun*, 12 December 1949.

Réveil des oiseaux

831. Périsson, Jacques. "Le *Réveil des Oiseaux* d'Olivier Messiaen [first Paris performance]." *Le Conservatoire* 29, January 1954, 17–18.

Oiseaux exotiques

832. Demarquez, Suzanne. "Premiéres auditions: Domaine musical (Petit Théâtre Marigny [10.3])." *Guide du concert* 107, 23 March 1956, 867.

Chronochromie

833. Rostand, Claude. "Bataille pour «Chronochromie»?: Cinq rappels, à Besançon, pour cette «Couleur du temps» que de très jeunes gens ont pourtant sifflée" [Besançon Festival, 13 September 1961]. *Le Figaro littéraire*, 23 September 1961, 4.

Des canyons aux étoiles

834. Griffiths, Paul. "MUSIC REVIEW; Pursuing an Aim to Startle [Alice Tully Hall, New York City, 14 March 1999]." *The New York Times*, 17 March 1999.

835. Ross, Alex. "Splendor in the Canyons: Messiaen Ascends [Alice Tully Hall, New York City, 14 March 1999]." *The New Yorker* (5 April 1999): 88–89, 91.

Éclairs sur l'Au-Delà

836. Griffiths, Paul. "First Performances: Messiaen: *'Eclairs sur l'au-delà ... '.*" *Tempo* 183 December (1992): 40–41.

Concert à quatre

837. Stevens, David. "In Paris, a First – Maybe Last – Concert." *International Herald Tribune*, 28 September 1994.

Chamber and Instrumental Works

Thème et variations

838. Altomont, Claude. "Cercle musical de Paris (22 novembre)." *Le Ménestrel*, 2 December 1932, 490.

839. B[elvianes], M[arcel]. "Société Nationale (14 janvier)." *Le Ménestrel*, 20 January 1933, 25.

Quatuor pour la fin du Temps

840. M.,V. "*Première au Camp.*" *Lumignon: Bi-mensuelle du Stalag VIIIA*, no. 1; 1 April 1941, 3–4.

A review of the world premiere of the *Quatuor pour la fin du Temps* by an author known only by his initials "V. M." Important historically for its recognition that a masterpiece had just been performed and for its account of the audience's reaction to the work. (I want to express my gratitude to Nigel Simeone for providing me with a scan of this document from his private collection ["Nigel Simeone, private collection"]. For an English translation of the review, see Hill and Simeone, *Messiaen* [item 210], 101–2.) The newspaper also contains an article on the *Quatuor* by Messiaen (see item 53).

841. Honegger, Arthur. "Le Quatour Bouillon; Olivier Messiaen." *Comœdia*, 12 July 1941.

842. Delannoy, Marcel. "Depuis le mysticisme jusqu'au sport." *Les Nouveaux Temps*, 13 July 1941.

843. H[aedrich], M[arcel]. "Une grande premiere au Stalag VIII C [*sic*]: Olivier Messiaen présente son 'Quatuor pour la fin des [*sic*] Temps'." *Le Figaro*, 28 January 1942, 2.

An eye-witness account of the premiere of the *Quatuor pour la fin du Temps*. Haedrich recalls the event by describing the performance of each movement and the audience's reactions. The atmosphere of the event, moreover, is compared to that of a contentious Parisian premiere.

844. Bruyr, José. "Les Concerts de la semaine." *Aujourd'hui*, 9 December 1942.

845. Jourdanet, Charles. "Il y a soixante ans en Allemagne: Messiaen créait *Quatuor pour la fin du temps* au stalag." *Nice-Matin*, 15 January 2001.

An eye-witness account of the premiere of the *Quatuor pour la fin du Temps*. Jourdanet estimates the audience's size at the concert to be about 150, notes how Messiaen provided commentaries to each of the *Quatuor*'s eight movements before they were played, and describes the audience's reaction to the work as mixed. He also mentions how Messiaen was given special treatment when he was composing the *Quatuor*, although he had to struggle with a lot of noise while writing the work's third movement, the "Abîme des oiseaux."

Organ Works

Complete Organ Works

846. Hughes, David Joseph. "Transports de joie: Paul Jacob's Musical Odyssey." *The American Organist* 36/12 (December 2002): 38.

  Describes six concerts throughout the United States in 2002 in which Jacobs played the complete organ works of Messiaen at each venue.

Le Banquet céleste

847. "Piccolo." "Some Recent French Organ Music." *The Musical Times* (June 1936): 528 and 537–39.

L'Ascension: Quatre Méditations symphoniques pour orgue

848. P., M. *Le Ménestrel*, 3 February 1935.

849. Raugel, Félix. "Récital d'orgue d'Olivier Messiaen." *Le Monde musical*, 28 February 1935.

850. "Piccolo." "Some Recent French Organ Music." *The Musical Times* (June 1936): 528 and 537–39.

La Nativité du Seigneur

851. Barraud, Henry. "*La Nativité du Seigneur* d'Olivier Messiaen: Société Nationale." *L'Art musical*, 6 March 1936.

852. André, George. "Musique: Olivier Messiaen." *Les Nouvelles littéraires*, 14 March 1936.

853. D[andelot], G[eorges]. "*La Nativité du Seigneur* d'Olivier Messiaen." *Le Monde musical*, 31 March 1936.

854. Martelli, Henri. "Olivier Messiaen: *La Nativité du Seigneur*." *La Revue musicale* 165, April 1936, 291–92.

855. "Piccolo." "Some Recent French Organ Music." *The Musical Times* (June 1936): 528 and 537–39.

Les Corps glorieux

856. de Gibon, Jean. "Corps glorieux d'Olivier Messiaen." *Écho du Pays de Redon*, 8 December 1951.

Review of a radio broadcast of *Les Corps glorieux* played by Messiaen. Norbert Dufourque, a faculty member at the Paris Conservatoire, served as the program's commentator.

Méditations sur le mystère de la Sainte Trinité

World Premiere, Washington, D.C., 20 March 1972

857. Wyton, Alec. "Méditations sur le mystère de la Sainte Trinité." *Music: The AGO-RCCO Magazine* 6/5 (May 1972): 23, 56.

New York City, 15 January 1974 (Jon Gillock)

858. Raver, Leonard. "Olivier Messiaen's *Méditations sur le mystère de la Sainte Trinité*: A Review of the Music and Its First New York Performance." *Music: The AGO-RCCO Magazine* 8/4 (April 1974): 27, 30.

Piano Works

Préludes

859. Baruzi, Joseph. "Société Nationale de Musique (1er mars)." *Le Ménestrel*, 7 March 1930, 110–11.

860. Demarquez, Suzanne. "Société Nationale, 1er mars." *Le Courrier musical*, 15 March 1930, 194.

861. Dandelot, Georges. *Le Monde musical*, 31 March 1930.

Fantaisie burlesque

862. B[elvianes], M[arcel]. "S.M.I. (8 février)." *Le Ménestrel*, 17 February 1933, 70.

863. Dandelot, Georges. "S.M.I." *Le Monde musical*, 28 February 1933.

864. Petit, Henri. "S.M.I." *Le Courrier musical*, 1 March 1933, 116.

Pièce pour le Tombeau de Paul Dukas

865. Vinteuil, Roger. "Société Nationale de la Musique (25 avril)." *Le Ménestrel*, 1 May 1936, 145.

Visions de l'Amen

866. Honegger, Arthur. "Olivier Messiaen à la Pléiade." *Comœdia*, 15 May 1943.

867. Delannoy, Marcel. "Du plastique au mystique." *Les Nouveaux Temps*, 16 May 1943.

868. Clarendon [Gavoty, Bernard]. "Musique de chambre." *Le Figaro*, 13 May 1952.

Vingt Regards sur l'Enfant-Jésus

869. Bruyr, José. "Un jeune grand musicien: Olivier Messiaen." *Paris mondial*, 3 April 1945.

870. Gavoty ("Clarendon"), Bernard. "Les Concerts: Regard sur Olivier Messiaen." *Le Figaro*, 3 April 1945.

871. Roland-Manuel. "Olivier Messiaen et ses *Vingt Regards sur l'Enfant-Jésus*." *Combat*, 3 April 1945.

872. Auric, Georges. "*Vingt Regards sur l'Enfant-Jésus*." *Les Lettres français*, 7 April 1945.

873. Dufresse, Henri. "*Vingt Regards sur l'Enfant-Jésus* – Yvonne Loriod." *Images musicales*, 25 March 1949.

874. Goléa, Antoine. "Les *Vingt Regards sur l'Enfant-Jésus*." *Images musicales*, 25 March 1949.

Catalogue d'oiseaux

875. Demarquez, Suzanne. "Premiéres auditions [...] Domaine musical (Gaveau 30.3)." *Guide du concert* 151, 12 April 1957, 893.

876. Demarquez, Suzanne. "Le *Catalogue d'oiseaux* d'Olivier Messiaen." *Guide du concert*, 233, 1 May 1959, 42.

Vocal and Choral Works

Trois Mélodies

877. Belvianes, Marcel. "Société Nationale de Musique (14 février)." *Le Ménestrel*, 20 February 1931, 84.

878. Plé, Simone. "Les Concerts: Société Nationale (14 février)." *Le Courrier musical*, 1 March 1931, 154.

879. Dandelot, Georges. *Le Monde musical*, 31 January 1935, 26.

La Mort du Nombre

880. Baruzi, Joseph. "S.M.I. (25 mars)." *Le Ménestrel,* 3 April 1931, 155.

881. Plé, Simone. "Les Concerts: Société Nationale (28 mars), S.M.I. (25 mars). *Le Courrier musical*, 15 April 1931, 261–62.

L'Ensorceleuse

882. Bertrand, Paul. "Concours de Rome." *Le Ménestrel* 10 July 1931, 303–4.

Poèmes pour Mi

883. Demarquez, Suzanne. "Société Nationale." *L'Art musical*, 19 March 1937.

884. Arrieu, Claude. "Sociéte Nationale." *Le Monde musical*, 31 March 1937.

885. Vinteuil, Roger. "La Spirale (28 avril)." *Le Ménestrel*, 7 May 1937, 147–48.

886. Capdevielle, Pierre. "La Spirale: Claire Delbos et Olivier Messiaen." *Le Monde musical*, 31 May 1937, 140.

887. Hirsch, Michel-Léon. "La Jeune France (4 juin) [first performance of the orchestral version of "Action de grâces']." *Le Ménestrel* 11 June 1937, 180–81.

888. Auclert, Pierre. "Marcelle Bunlet et O. Messiaen aux Heures Alpines." *Le Petit Dauphinois*, 20 January 1938.

889. F., R. "Société Nationale de Musique." *Le Ménestrel*, 28 January 1938, 21.

890. Demarquez, Suzanne. "Jeune France 1938 – Daniel-Lesur: *Pastorale* – André Jolivet: *Poémes pour l'enfant* – Yves Baudrier: *Eleonora* – Olivier Messiaen: *Poémes pour Mi*." *La Revue musicale* 184 (June 1938): 382–83.

Chants de Terre et de Ciel

891. Hirsch, Michel-Léon. "Le Triton (23 janvier)." *Le Ménestrel*, 3 February 1939, 28.

Trois petites Liturgies de la Présence Divine

892. Bernard[-Delapierre], Guy. "Une date dans l'histoire de la musique: Les *Liturgies* d'Olivier Messiaen." *Le Pays*, 25 April 1945, 1–2.

893. Roland-Manuel. "Georges Auric, Olivier Messiaen." *Les Lettres françaises*, 28 April 1945.

894. Vallas, Léon. "Olivier Messiaen." *Le Progrès*, 25 January 1949.

La Transfiguration de Nôtre-Seigneur Jésus-Christ

895. Rostand, Claude. "*La Transfiguration de Notre-Seigneur* d'Olivier Messiaen au Festival Gulbenkian de Lisbonne." *Le Figaro littéraire*, 16 June 1969.

896. Crichton, Ronald. "Gulbenkian Festival." *The Musical Times* 110/1518 (August 1969): 860.

897. Dennis, Brian. "Messiaen's 'La Transfiguration'." *Tempo* 94 (Autumn 1970): 29–30.

898. Gill, Dominic. "The Proms' [British premiere, London; 17 July 1970]." *The Musical Times* 111/1531 (September 1970): 908.

9

Other Source Materials: Messiaen Web Sites, Competitions, Conferences, and Festivals

This chapter surveys source materials on Messiaen found primarily on the internet. They include resources on his life and work, competitions, conferences, and festivals. Some overlap between sources is inevitable. The following entries are arranged in alphabetical order.

MESSIAEN WEB SITES

899. Aimard, Pierre-Laurent. "Pierre-Laurent Aimard." [http://warner classics.com/artistbiography.php?artist=2575]. Accessed 4 August 2007.

Web site with biographical and other information on the distinguished French pianist and interpreter of Messiaen's music.

900. Answers.com. "Olivier Messiaen." [http://www.answers.com/topic/olivier-messiaen?cat=entertainment]. Accessed 4 August 2007.

Contains several entries on Messiaen from different encyclopedias.

901. Austbø, Håkon. "Håkon Austbø." [http://www.austbo.info/]. Accessed 4 August 2007.

Personal Web site of Håkon Austbø, a Norwegian concert pianist living in the Netherlands, noted for his interpretations of Messiaen's music.

902. Ball, Malcolm. "The Olivier Messiaen Page." [http://www.olivier messiaen.org/messhome.htm]. Accessed 4 August 2007.

Bibliographic entries for selected articles, books, and book chapters, as well as a biography containing personal reminiscences, and several short articles and reviews. Also includes links to reviews, a list of Messiaen's works and recordings, a photo gallery, news about concerts and conferences, and links to other Web sites that provide information on Messiaen.

903. Bate, Jennifer. "Jennifer Bate: Concert Organist." [http://www.classical-artists.com/jbate/default.htm]. Accessed 4 August 2007.

Personal Web site of British concert organist Jennifer Bate, a noted interpreter of Messiaen's music.

904. BBC Radio. "Olivier Messiaen: Renaissance Man." [http://www.bbc.co.uk/radio3/sundayfeature/pip/i87gt/]. Accessed 4 August 2007.

Short description of a radio program devoted to interviews by Tom Service with four persons whose lives were influenced by Messiaen: Pierre Boulez; Olivier Latry; Pierre-Laurent Aimard; and Père Jean-Rodolphe Kars. This 30-minute interview was conducted on 15 August 2004.

905. British Broadcasting Corporation (BBC). "COMPOSERS: Olivier Messiaen." [http://www.bbc.co.uk/music/artist/gx3n/]. Accessed 4 August 2007.

A "one-minute" bio, links to several audio examples and an analysis, and links to other Messiaen-related Web sites.

906. Chamber Music Society of Lincoln Center. "For Olivier Messiaen, and the End of Time." [http://intermissionimpossible.org/?cat=3]. Accessed 4 August 2007.

Recollection of a 1984 performance of the *Quartet for the End of Time* in Alice Tully Hall. Includes links to other Messiaen Web sites.

907. Crowley, Paul. *Commonweal*. "Music of the invisible: Messiaen's 'Saint Francis'." [http://www.encyclopedia.com/doc/1G1-95953596.html]. Accessed 4 August 2007.

Article on Messiaen's opera, *Saint François d'Assise*. Describes the opera's plot and themes, and reviews the U.S. premiere of the work in San Francisco in 2002.

908. DMOZ Open Directory Project. "Messiaen, Olivier." [http://dmoz.org/Arts/Music/Composition/Composers/M/Messiaen,_Olivier/]. Accessed 4 August 2007.

Page listing links to other Web sites with: (1) a directory of MP3s; (2) a biography from the *Concise Oxford Dictionary of Music*; (3) selection of quality MIDI files; (4) biographical data; (5)

recommended CDs; (6) books and sheet music; (7) bibliography; and (8) links to biographical essays. Also contains a discography, list of works, some previously unpublished material, and photos. Links to automatic Messiaen searches by over ten Internet search engines.

909. Durand-Salabert-Eschig Éditions Musicales. [http://www.durand-salabert-eschig.com/english/index.html]. Accessed 4 August 2007.

Web site of Durand, one of Messiaen's publishers.

910. Éditions Alphonse Leduc. [http://alphonseleduc.com/english/index.htm]. Accessed 4 August 2007.

Web site of the major publisher of Messiaen's works.

911. Gillock, Jon. "Jon Gillock, Organist." [http://www.jongillock.com/]. Accessed 4 August 2007.

Personal Web site of American concert organist Jon Gillock, a noted interpreter of Messiaen's music. Important because of his long association with Messiaen.

912. Glandaz, Olivier. "Olivier Glandaz, Organ Technician: The Love of Beautiful Sound." [http://www.glandaz.com/]. Accessed 4 August 2007.

Web site of Parisian organ builder associated with Messiaen and the Cavaillé-Coll organ at La Trinité for fourteen years. Includes personal reminiscences along with photos of Messiaen and the Trinité organ.

913. Global Music Network. "Messiaen, Olivier." [http://www.gmn.com/composers/composer.asp?id=88]. Accessed 4 August 2007.

Biographical essay and list of selected works. Links to audio files of several compositions.

914. Gottlieb, Jay. "Jay Gottlieb." [http://jaygottlieb.free.fr/uk/bio.htm]. Accessed 4 August 2007.

Personal Web site of an American concert pianist who worked closely with Messiaen and Yvonne Loriod-Messiaen.

915. Griffiths, Paul. "Paul Griffiths: Words and Music." [http://www.disgwylfa.com/index.php?f=data_home&a=0]. Accessed 4 August 2007.

Web site of noted Messiaen author Paul Griffiths. Contains information on his librettos, presentations, and music books.

916. Hakim, Naji. "Naji Hakim: Composer - Organist - Improviser." [http://www.najihakim.com/]. Accessed 4 August 2007.

Personal Web site of Lebanese-born French organist/improviser/composer who succeeded Messiaen at La Trinité in Paris.

917. HighBeam Encyclopedia. "Olivier Messiaen." [http://www.encyclo
     pedia.com/doc/1E1-Messiaen.html]. Accessed 4 August 2007.

     Short biographical article and links to other Messiaen-related Web
     articles.

918. Hill, Peter. "Professor Peter Hill." [http://www.shef.ac.uk/music/
     staff/ph/phhomepage.html]. Accessed 4 August 2007.

     Web site at the University of Sheffield with information on faculty
     member and concert pianist Peter Hill, distinguished interpreter of
     Messiaen's music.

919. IMDb (Internet Movie Database). "Olivier Messiaen." [http://us.imdb.
     com/name/nm0582093/]. Accessed 4 August 2007.

     Includes a production of Messiaen's opera, *Saint François d'Assise*, on
     French television, with links listing performers and basic information.

920. IRCAM – Centre Georges Pompidou. "Olivier Messiaen." [http://
     mac-texier.ircam.fr/textes/c00000066/]. Accessed 4 August 2007.

     Biographical essay in French on Messiaen, and a catalogue of works
     with extensive information on many of his pieces.

921. Kelley, Robert T. "Tradition, the Avant Garde, and Individuality in
     the Music of Olivier Messiaen: Musical Influences in Méditations
     sur l[e] [m]ystère de la Sainte-Trinité." [http://www.robertkelleyphd.
     com/index.htm?homepage.htm&1]. Accessed 4 August 2007.

     A Web site that includes a stylistic examination of Messiaen's music
     as seen through the *Méditations sur le mystère de la Sainte Trinité*.
     (Click on the "Music Theory" link to find the article.)

922. Latry, Olivier. "European Concert Organists: Olivier Latry." [http://
     www.concertorganists.com/htdocs/artistdocs/latry.html]. Accessed 4
     August 2007.

     Web site with biographical and other information on the French
     organist noted for his interpretations of Messiaen's music.

923. Muraro, Roger. "Roger Muraro." [http://rogermuraro.artistes.universal
     music.fr/]. Accessed 4 August 2007.

     Personal Web site of French concert pianist Roger Muraro, a specia-
     list in Messiaen's music.

924. Music & Vision: The World's First Daily Internet Music Magazine.
     "Olivier Messiaen." [http://search.freefind.com/find.html?id=6500658&
     pageid=r&mode=ALL&query=Messiaen]. Accessed 4 August 2007.

Includes links to online articles and reviews of compact discs and performances related to the music of Messiaen.

925. Musica et Memoria. "Olivier Messiaen (1908–92)." [http://www.musi mem.com/messiaen.htm]. Accessed 4 August 2007.

Excellent biographical and stylistic information on Messiaen in French by Joachim Havard de la Montagne. Includes photos.

926. musicteachers.co.uk. "Composers and Their Music No. 1: Olivier Messiaen." [http://www.musicteachers.co.uk/resources/]. Accessed 4 August 2007.

Extensive guide on Messiaen's music in a .pdf version freely available for download, that considers his background and training, compositional style, musical language, and influences. To access, click on: "Olivier Messiaen: An Introduction."

927. Nagano, Kent. "Kent Nagano." [http://www.kentnagano.com/]. Accessed 4 August 2007.

The official Web site of Kent Nagano, distinguished conductor of Messiaen's works.

928. Naxos Digital Services. "Messiaen, Olivier (1908–92)." [http://www. naxos.com/composerinfo/689.htm]. Accessed 4 August 2007.

Page on the Naxos corporate Web site with basic information about Messiaen's compositions for orchestra, organ, piano, and chamber ensembles, with a selected discography and hyperlinks so that one can listen to pieces if logged in as a subscriber.

929. *The New York Times.* "Olivier Messiaen." [http://topics.nytimes.com/ top/reference/timestopics/people/m/olivier_messiaen/index.html?8qa]. Accessed 4 August 2007.

List of article titles, with author's names and one-sentence descriptions. Title is a hyperlink to either a free preview or page where access to the full article may be purchased. Most articles appear to be announcements of or reviews of performances featuring works by Messiaen. Also covered are compact disc recordings.

930. San Francisco Symphony. "Meet the Composers: Olivier Messiaen." [http://www.sfsymphony.org/templates/composer.asp?nodeid=206]. Accessed 4 August 2007.

Page on the symphony's Web site with a "life and works" essay (with information taken from *The Grove Concise Dictionary of Music*) and a list of selected works in various categories.

931. Shenton, Andrew. "oliviermessiaen.net"/Boston University's Messiaen Project (BUMP). [http://oliviermessiaen.net/index.shtml]. Accessed 4 August 2007.

Site begun by Andrew Shenton, a music faculty member at Boston University, in September 2006, as part of "BUMP," Boston University's Messiaen Project, which centers on the life and work of Messiaen. Currently in its infancy. Will serve as host for online, peer-reviewed articles. Also includes or will include: biographical information; a list of works accessible by title, genre, or date; descriptions of Messiaen's musical language and influences upon his music; current scholarship concerning Messiaen; reviews; interviews; discography; videography; and links to audio, visual, and streaming media.

932. Soylent Communications. "Olivier Messiaen," on beta version of NNDB. [http://www.nndb.com/people/875/000044743/]. Accessed 4 August 2007.

Page with a "life and works" essay, and a few links to pages on other composers.

933. Weir, Gillian. "Olivier Messiaen: The Organ Works." [http://gillian weir.com/cds/messiaen.shtml]. Accessed 4 August 2007.

British concert organist Gillian Weir's personal Web site, where reviews of her performances of Messiaen's organ works are listed.

934. *Wikipedia*. "Olivier Messiaen." [http://en.wikipedia.org/wiki/Olivier_ Messiaen]. Accessed 4 August 2007.

Annotated article on Messiaen's life and music. Includes musical examples and many links within the text to terms, compositions, and people. Contains a complete list of works, list of references, and links to other Messiaen sites.

935. W. W. Norton. "Olivier Messiaen." [http://www2.wwnorton.com/ classical/composers/messiaen.htm]. Accessed on 4 August 2007.

One-page biography, plus a short list of selected works, and links to two audio clips.

COMPETITIONS

936. Concours Internationaux de la Ville de Paris (CIVP). "Concours Olivier Messiaen." [http://www.civp.com/messiaen/amessiaen.html]. Accessed 4 August 2007.

Official Web site of the "Olivier Messiaen Competition," which is devoted to the performance of contemporary piano music. Includes the rules of future and recent past competitions, information on the jury of 2003, sponsors, schedule of events, and lists of recent past award winners. Date of the next competition is listed.

937. Orchestre symphonique de Montréal. "The Olivier Messiaen International Prize." [http://www.composition.osm.ca/en/index_epreuves_messiaen.cfm?screen=1280]. Accessed 4 August 2007.

Official Web site of the Montréal Symphony Orchestra's "Olivier Messiaen International Prize" in composition. Description of the contest, prizes, rules, juries, partners, press, registration, and contact information. Also includes downloadable audio extracts of interviews with Yvonne Loriod-Messiaen and Gilbert Amy, downloadable video extracts of Kent Nagano and Gilles Tremblay, and a biography of Messiaen.

CONFERENCES

938. Birmingham Conservatoire. "Messiaen 2008 International Centenary Conference." [http://www.conservatoire.uce.ac.uk/messiaen/]. Accessed 4 August 2007.

Conference to be held at the Birmingham Conservatoire on 21–24 June 2008 to celebrate the centenary of the birth of Messiaen. Will feature scholarly paper presentations and performances.

939. Boston University. "Olivier Messiaen – BUMP Inaugural Conference." [http://oliviermessiaen.net/news/conferences/bump.html]. Accessed 4 August 2007.

Conference hosted by Boston University's Messiaen Project on 21–22 September 2006. Featured speakers included Peter Hill, Andrew Shenton, and Nigel Simeone. Several scholarly papers presented, roundtable discussion, and two recitals.

940. Boston University. "Messiaen the Theologian." [http://oliviermessiaen. net/news/conferences/bump2007.html]. Accessed 4 August 2007.

Conference to be hosted by Boston University's Messiaen Project on 12–13 October 2007 that will center on the theological aspects of Messiaen's work. Keynote speaker will be Stephen Schloesser. In addition to paper presentations, the conference will include a performance of Messiaen's *Fantaisie* for violin and piano (1933), along with a screening of Paul Festa's film, "Apparition of the Eternal Church."

941. Forum on Music and Christian Scholarship. [http://www.fmcs.us/]. Accessed 4 August 2007.

Annual conference held at various locations in the spring. Has often featured one or more scholarly paper presentations dealing with religious aspects of Messiaen's music. The 2007 Annual Meeting was held at Yale University, Institute of Sacred Music, on 9–10 March 2007 and included a special session on Messiaen.

942. University of Sheffield. "Messiaen 2002 International Conference." [http://www.shef.ac.uk/music/staff/cd/Messiaen/Messiaen1.html]. Accessed on 4 August 2007.

Conference hosted by the University of Sheffield on 20–23 June 2002 to commemorate the tenth anniversary of Messiaen's death. Keynote addresses, scholarly paper presentations, and concerts dealing with Messiaen's music.

FESTIVALS

943. Église de la Trinité. *Olivier Messiaen, homme de foi: Regard sur son œuvre d'orgue.* Paris: Trinité Média Communication, 1995. 104 p.

See item 238.

944. English Bach Festival. [http://www.ebf.org.uk/index.php]. Accessed 4 August 2007.

Official Web site of the English Bach Festival, with photos and information on the festival's history and recent past productions. Because the English Bach Festival has promoted contemporary music in Great Britain since the 1960s, Messiaen's music was celebrated every so often with Messiaen and Yvonne Loriod-Messiaen present and/or involved as performers. For reviews of two such occasions, see Dominic Gill, "Messiaen in London," *The Musical Times* 109/1056 (August 1968): 748; and Paul Griffiths, "Visions and Meditations: A Messiaen Festival," *The Musical Times* 114/1564, (June 1973): 592–94.

945. Gillock, Jon. *Celebration Messiaen: The Complete Works for Organ.* Special Program Book in Honor of the Ninetieth Anniversary of the Birth of Olivier Messiaen. Edited by Madame Francine Matiffa. New York: The Riverside Church in the City of New York, 1999. 56 p.

See item 239.

946. "Messiaen 2002 International Festival on the 10th Anniversary of his Death." [http://www.messiaen.de/start.htm]. Accessed 4 August 2007.

Festival at the Kreuzeskirche, Essen on 1 April – 30 May 2002 featuring performances and discussions of Messiaen's music.

947. Messiaen au Pays de la Meije. "Du Spirituel dans la musique" (Spirituality in Music). [http://www.festival-messiaen.com/ang/programme.html]. Accessed 4 August 2007.

Tenth Annual "Messiaen au Pays de la Meije" Festival, held from 19–29 July 2007 in the towns of La Grave and Villar d'Arène in the French Alps, near Messiaen's country home. Each yearly festival normally consists of a ten-day series of concerts, talks, and other events, celebrating themes predominant in Messiaen's life and music in a beautiful mountain setting that he loved. The theme for 2007 is "Spirituality in Music."

948. Southbank Centre. "Messiaen Festival Throughout 2008." [http://www.southbankcentre.co.uk/all-events/just-announced/music]. Accessed 4 August 2007.

In celebration of the centenary of his birth, major interpreters of Messiaen's music will perform his works at this London performing arts venue and across the city throughout the 2008 season, as well as those works that inspired him and compositions by his pupils and younger colleagues. The festival will begin and end with performances by the Ensemble Intercontemporain (EIC) from Paris, with Pierre-Laurent Aimard as soloist.

Appendix 1
List of Musical Works by Olivier Messiaen

This list is compiled from the following sources: (1) Olivier Messiaen, *Technique de mon langage musical* (item 88), 107–9; (2) Robert Sherlaw Johnson, *Messiaen* (item 213), 197–205; (3) Harry Halbreich, *Olivier Messiaen* (item 209); (4) Paul Griffiths, *Olivier Messiaen and the Music of Time* (item 208), 257–68; (5) Christopher Dingle, "List of Works and Discography," in *The Messiaen Companion*, ed. Peter Hill (item 240), 536–65; (6) Nigel Simeone, *Olivier Messiaen: A Bibliographical Catalogue of Messiaen's Works* (item 6); (7) Paul Griffiths, "Olivier Messiaen," in *New Grove Dictionary of Music and Musicians* (item 722), 16:502–3; (8) Raffaele Pozzi, *Il suono dell'estasi: Olivier Messiaen dal* Banquet céleste *alla* Turangalîla-symphonie (item 232), 195–211; and (9) the commercial catalogue of Messiaen's works published by Alphonse Leduc & Cie (1995).

Messiaen's works are arranged into the following categories:

- Opera
- Orchestral
- Chamber and Instrumental
- Organ
- Piano
- Vocal and Choral
- Electronic

Each entry includes the following information (where appropriate):

- Title and subtitle (in the original French)
- Individual movements or section titles
- Date and place of composition and orchestration
- Date and place of premiere, as well as performers, soloists, performing ensemble and conductor
- Publisher
- Soloists or dramatic characters
- Scoring, which includes strings of letters denoting voice parts in a chorus, and/or numbers denoting woodwind, brass, and/or string players in an instrumental ensemble or orchestra

Except for a few instances, discrepancies between sources are corrected without comment. Finally, unless otherwise indicated, all texts are by Messiaen.

I. OPERA

A.1. *Saint François d'Assise: Scènes franciscaines*

Act I:

Scene 1:	Scene 2:	Scene 3:
La Croix	Les Laudes	Le Baiser au Lépreux

Act II:

Scene 4:	Scene 5:	Scene 6:
L'Ange voyageur	L'Ange musicien	Le Prêche aux oiseaux

Act III:

Scene 7:	Scene 8:
Les Stigmates	La Mort et la nouvelle Vie

Date of composition and orchestration: composed 1975–79, orchestrated 1979–83, according to Messiaen (orchestrated 1977–82, according to Hill and Simeone; see Claude Samuel and Olivier Messiaen, *Olivier Messiaen: Music and Color: Conversations with Claude Samuel*, item 176, p. 216; Hill and Simeone, *Messiaen*, item 210, pp. 323–37.)

Premiere: 28 November 1983, Paris Opéra; Christiane Eda-Pierre (L'Ange), José van Dam (Saint François), Kenneth Riegel (Le Lépreux), Philippe Duminy – Michel Philippe (Frère Léon), Georges Gautier (Frère Massée), Michel Sénéchal (Frère Élie), Jean-Philippe Courtis – Robert Grenier (Frère Bernard); Sandro Sequi, producer; Giuseppe Crisolini-Malatesta, designer; Jean Laforge, chorusmaster; Chorus and Orchestra of the Paris Opéra, Seiji Ozawa, conductor

Publisher: Alphonse Leduc (Paris, 1983, 1988–92): full score, libretto

Characters: L'Ange (soprano), Saint François (baritone), Le Lépreux (tenor), Frère Léon (baritone), Frère Massée (tenor), Frère Élie (tenor), Frère Bernard (bass), Frère Sylvestre (bass), Frère Rufin (bass)

Scoring:

Chorus: s.s.m-s.a.a.t.t.bar.b.b. – 15 voices per part

Orchestra: 7.4.7.4 – 6.4.3.3 – xylophone, xylorimba, marimba, glockenspiel, vibraphone, 3 Ondes Martenot, 5 percussion – 16.16.14.12.10 (with 5 strings)

II. ORCHESTRAL WORKS

A.2. *Fugue en ré mineur* (unpublished)

Date and place of composition: 1928, Paris

A.3. *Le Banquet eucharistique* (unpublished)

(In an interview with Brigitte Massin [*Olivier Messiaen: une poétique du merveilleux,* item 171, 44–45], Messiaen stated that *Le Banquet eucharistique* and the organ work *Le Banquet céleste* were related. As a nineteen-year-old student of Dukas at the Paris Conservatoire, Messiaen composed *Le Banquet eucharistique* first, and then reworked one part of it for organ to become *Le Banquet céleste*.)

Date and place of composition: 1928, Fuligny, Aube

Date and place of premiere: 1928 or 1929, Paris Conservatoire; student orchestra, Henri Rabaud, conductor

A.4. *Simple Chant d'une âme* (unpublished)

Date and place of composition: 1930, Paris

A.5. *Les Offrandes oubliées: Méditation symphonique pour Orchestre*

Date and place of composition: 1930, Fuligny, Aube

Premiere: 19 February 1931, Théâtre des Champs-Élysées, Paris; Orchestre Straram, Walter Straram, conductor

Publisher: Durand (Paris, 1931): study score, piano reduction

Scoring: 3.3.3.3 – 4.3.3.1; timpani, percussion; strings

A.6. *Le Tombeau resplendissant*

Date and place of composition: 1931, Fuligny, Aube

Premiere: 12 February 1933, Paris; Orchestre Symphonique de Paris, Pierre Monteux, conductor

Publisher: Durand (Paris, 1997): study score

Scoring: 3.3.3.3 – 4.3.3.1; timpani, 4 percussion; strings

A.7. *Hymne au Saint-Sacrement*

Date and place of composition: 1932, Paris

Premiere: 23 March 1933, Théâtre des Champs-Élysées, Paris; Orchestre Straram, Walter Straram, conductor

Publisher: Broude Brothers (New York, 1947/1974): study score (the original version of this work was published by Durand, Paris [rental only], and was subsequently lost in 1944. In 1947, Messiaen reconstructed the work [as *Hymne*] from memory for a performance conducted by Leopold Stokowski in New York. The reconstructed version was published by Broude Brothers in 1947 [rental only], and then in a newly engraved study score [no. 16 of "Contemporary Composers: Study Score Series"] in 1974. For evidence of the original version, see Simeone, *Olivier Messiaen: A Bibliographical Catalogue of Messiaen's Works* [item 6], 30.)

Scoring: 3.3.3.3 – 4.3.3.0; timpani, percussion; strings

A.8. *L'Ascension: Quatre Méditations symphoniques pour orchestre*

(Messiaen transcribed movements 1, 2, and 4 for organ in 1933–34; see item A.38.)

1. Majesté du Christ demandant sa gloire à son Père
2. Alléluias sereins d'une âme qui désire le ciel
3. Alléluia sur la trompette, Alléluia sur la cymbale
4. Prière du Christ montant vers son Père

Date and place of composition: May 1932, Paris – July 1932, Neussargues, Cantal; orchestrated May-July 1933, Monaco

Premiere: 9 February 1935, Paris; Concerts Siohan, Robert Siohan, conductor

Publisher: Alphonse Leduc (Paris, 1948): study score

Scoring: 3.3.3.3 – 4.3.3.1 – timpani, percussion – 16.16.14.12.10

A.9. *Turangalîla-Symphonie*

1. Introduction
2. Chant d'amour I
3. Turangalîla I
4. Chant d'amour II
5. Joie du sang des étoiles
6. Jardin du sommeil d'amour
7. Turangalîla II
8. Développement de l'amour
9. Turangalîla III
10. Final

Date of composition: 17 July 1946 – 29 November 1948

Premiere: 2 December 1949, Symphony Hall, Boston; Yvonne Loriod, piano; Ginette Martenot, Ondes Martenot; Boston Symphony Orchestra, Leonard Bernstein, conductor

Publisher: Durand (Paris, 1953): study score, solo parts for piano and Ondes Martenot; Durand (Paris, 1992): revised version, 1990

Scoring: 3.3.3.3 – 4.5.3.1 – piano solo, Ondes Martenot solo, glockenspiel, celesta, vibraphone, 5 percussion – 16.16.14.12.10

A.10. *Réveil des oiseaux*

Date of composition: Completed in 1953

Premiere: 11 October 1953, Donaueschingen; Yvonne Loriod, piano; Südwestfunk Orchestra, Hans Rosbaud, conductor

Publisher: Durand (Paris, 1955): study score, solo part for piano

Scoring: 4.3.4.3 – 2.2.0.0 – piano solo, celesta, xylophone, glockenspiel, 2 percussion – 8.8.8.8.6

A.11. *Oiseaux exotiques*

Date of composition: 5 October 1955 – 23 January 1956

Premiere: 10 March 1956, Petit Théâtre Marigny, Paris; Yvonne Loriod, piano; Domaine Musical, Rudolf Albert Vega, conductor

Publisher: Universal (Vienna, 1959/1995): study score, solo part for piano

Scoring: 2.1.3.1 – 2.1.0.0 – piano solo, glockenspiel, xylophone, 5 percussion

A.12. *Chronochromie*

  1. Introduction
  2. Strophe I
  3. Antistrophe I
  4. Strophe II
  5. Antistrophe II
  6. Épôde
  7. Coda

Date of composition: 1959–60

Premiere: 16 October 1960, Donaueschingen; Südwestfunk Orchestra, Hans Rosbaud, Conductor

Publisher: Alphonse Leduc (Paris, 1963): study score

Scoring: 4.3.4.3 – 4.4.3.1 – glockenspiel, xylophone, marimba, 3 percussion – 16.16.14.12.10

A.13. *Sept Haïkaï: Esquisses japonaises*

  1. Introduction
  2. Le parc de Nara et les lanternes de pierre
  3. Yamanaka-cadenza
  4. Gagaku
  5. Miyajima et le torii dans le mer
  6. Les oiseaux de Karuizawa
  7. Coda

Date of composition: 1962

Premiere: 30 October 1963, Odéon, Paris; Yvonne Loriod-Messiaen, piano; Orchestre du Domaine musical, Pierre Boulez, conductor

Publisher: Alphonse Leduc (Paris, 1966): study score, solo part for piano

Scoring: 2.3.4.2 – 0.1.1.0 – piano solo, xylophone, marimba, 4 percussion – 8.0.0.0.0

A.14. *Couleurs de la Cité céleste*

Date of composition: 1963

Premiere: 17 October 1964, Donaueschingen; Yvonne Loriod-Messiaen, piano; Orchestre du Domaine Musical, Pierre Boulez, conductor

Publisher: Alphonse Leduc (Paris, 1966): study score, solo part for piano

Scoring: 0.0.3.0 – 2.4.4.0 – piano solo, xylophone, xylorimba, marimba, 3 percussion

A.15. *Et exspecto resurrectionem mortuorum*

1. Des profondeurs de l'abîme, je crie vers toi, Seigneur: Seigneur, écoute ma voix!
2. Le Christ, ressuscité des morts, ne meurt plus; la mort n'a plus sur lui d'empire
3. L'heure vient où les morts entendront la voix du Fils de Dieu ...
4. Ils ressusciteront, glorieux, avec un nom nouveau—dans le concert joyeux des étoiles et les acclamations des fils du ciel
5. Et j'entendis la voix d'une foule immense ...

Date and place of composition: 1964, Petichet, Isère

Premiere: 7 May 1965, Sainte Chapelle, Paris; Domaine Musical, Serge Baudo, conductor

Publisher: Alphonse Leduc (Paris, 1966): study score

Scoring: 5.4.5.4 – 6.4.4.2 – 3 percussion

A.16. *Des canyons aux étoiles*

Première partie

1. Le désert
2. Les Orioles
3. Ce qui est écrit sur les étoiles ...
4. Le Cossyphe d'Heuglin
5. Cedar Breaks et le Don de Crainte

Deuxième partie

6. Appel interstellaire
7. Bryce Canyon et les rochers rouge-orange

Troisième partie

8. Les ressucités et le chant de l'étoile Aldébaran
9. Le Moqueur polyglotte
10. La Grive des bois
11. Omao, Leiothrix, Elepaio, Shama
12. Zion Park et la Cité céleste

Date of composition: 1971–74

Premiere: 20 November 1974, Alice Tully Hall, New York; Yvonne Loriod-Messiaen, piano; Musica Aeterna, Frederic Waldman, conductor

Publisher: Alphonse Leduc (Paris, 1978): full score, solo part for piano

Scoring: 4.3.4.3 – 3.3.3.0 – piano solo, glockenspiel, xylorimba, 5 percussion – 6.0.3.3.1

A.17. *Un Vitrail et des oiseaux*

Date of composition: 1986

Premiere: 26 November 1988, Théâtre des Champs-Élysées, Paris; Yvonne Loriod-Messiaen, piano; Orchestre de l'Ensemble Inter-contemporain, Pierre Boulez, conductor

Publisher: Alphonse Leduc (Paris, 1992): full score

Scoring: 4.4.5.3 – 0.1.0.0 – piano solo, xylophone, xylorimba, marimba, 5 percussion

A.18. *La Ville d'En-Haut*

Date of composition: 1987

Premiere: 17 November 1989, Salle Pleyel, Paris; Yvonne Loriod-Messiaen, piano; BBC Symphony Orchestra, Pierre Boulez, conductor

Publisher: Alphonse Leduc (Paris, 1994): full score, solo part for piano

Scoring: 5.4.5.3 – 6.4.3.1 – piano solo, glockenspiel, xylophone, xylorimba, marimba, 4 percussion

A.19. *Un Sourire*

Date of composition: 1989

Premiere: 5 December 1991, Théâtre du Châtelet, Paris; Orchestre Philharmonique de Radio-France, Marek Janowski, conductor

Publisher: Alphonse Leduc (Paris, 1994): full score

Scoring: 4.4.3.3 – 4.1.0.0 – xylophone, xylorimba, 2 percussion – 16.16.14.12.0

A.20. *Éclairs sur l'Au-Delà*

1. Apparition du Christ glorieux
2. La Constellation du Sagittaire
3. L'Oiseau-Lyre at la Ville-Fianceé
4. Les Élus marqués du sceau
5. Demeurer dans l'Amour …
6. Les Sept Anges aux sept trompettes
7. Et Dieu essuiera toute larme de leurs yeux …
8. Les Étoiles et la Gloire
9. Plusieurs Oiseaux des arbres de Vie

10. Le Chemin de l'Invisible
11. Le Christ, lumière du Paradis

Date of composition: 1988–92

Premiere: 5 November 1992, New York; New York Philharmonic, Zubin Mehta, conductor

Publisher: Alphonse Leduc (Paris, 1998): full score

Scoring: 10.4.10.4 – 6.5.3.3 – crotales, glockenspiel, xylophone, xylorimba, marimba, 10 percussion – 16.16.14.12.10

A.21. *Concert à quatre*

(Commissioned by Myung-Whun Chung and Heinz Holliger, the *Concert à quatre* was completed after Messiaen's death [27 April 1992] by his widow Yvonne Loriod-Messiaen, with assistance from George Benjamin and Heinz Holliger. According to Griffiths [liner notes to *Concert à quatre*; Deutsche Grammophon 445 947–2; p. 6—see item B.58], Loriod-Messiaen orchestrated the second part of the first movement and all of the last movement. She inserted a cadenza of bell sounds and birdsongs into the finale, with the birdsongs played in separate tempos by the four soloists.)

1. Entrée
2. Vocalise (The second movement is a transcription of the earlier *Vocalise-étude* for soprano and piano; see item A.67.)
3. Cadenza
4. Rondeau

Date of composition: 1990–92

Premiere: 26 September 1994, Opéra-Bastille, Paris; Catherine Cantin, flute; Heinz Holliger, oboe; Yvonne Loriod-Messiaen, piano; Mstislav Rostropovich, cello; Orchestre de l'Opéra Bastille, Myung-Whun Chung, conductor

Publisher: Alphonse Leduc (Paris, 1998): full score

Scoring: flute solo, oboe solo, piano solo, cello solo – 7.5.7.5 – 4.5.3.1–xylophone, xylorimba, marimba, glockenspiel, celesta, 7 percussion – 16.16.14.12.10

III. CHAMBER AND INSTRUMENTAL

A.22. *Fugue sur un sujet de Georges Hüe* (unpublished)

(Messiaen wrote this fugue as part of his first [but unsuccessful] attempt to win the Prix de Rome in 1930. It has a time signature of 2/2 and a tempo marking of "Assez vif." See Simeone, *A Bibliographical Catalogue of Messiaen's Works* [item 6], 189. For a reproduction of the first page of the manuscript, see Alain Périer, *Messiaen* [item 219], 23.)

Date of composition: 1930 or 1931

Scoring: Four unspecified parts, written in open score using soprano, alto, tenor, and bass clefs

A.23. *Thème et variations*

(Messiaen wrote this work for his first wife, the violinist-composer Claire Delbos. In dedicating the work to Delbos, Messiaen did not follow the usual custom of listing her name on the dedicatory page of the publication. Instead, he had the word "pour" followed by an E placed on the fourth space of a treble clef staff. In French solmization, E is assigned the syllable "Mi," which was Messiaen's nickname for Delbos. For information on Delbos and her life with Messiaen, see Simeone, *A Bibliographical Catalogue of Messiaen's Works* [item 6], 34–35.)

Date and place of composition: 1932, Paris

Premiere: 22 November 1932, Salle Debussy, Cercle Musical de Paris, Paris; Claire Delbos, violin; Olivier Messiaen, piano

Publisher: Alphonse Leduc (Paris, 1934): score and violin part

Scoring: violin and piano

A.24. *Fantaisie*

Date and place of composition: 1933, Paris

Publisher: Durand (Paris, 2006)

Scoring: violin and piano

A.25. *Quatuor pour la fin du Temps*

1. Liturgie de cristal
2. Vocalise, pour l'Ange qui annonce la fin du Temps
3. Abîme des oiseaux
4. Intermède
5. Louange à l'Éternité de Jésus
6. Danse de la fureur, pour les sept trompettes
7. Fouillis d'arcs-en-ciel, pour l'Ange qui annonce la fin du Temps
8. Louange à l'Immortalité de Jésus

Date and place of composition: 1940–41, Stalag VIII A, Görlitz, Silesia (Gorlice, Poland). (Most of the *Quatuor pour la fin du Temps* was composed while Messiaen was a prisoner at Stalag VIII A. Movements III, V, and VIII, however, have different origins: Movement III was written—according to Étienne Pasquier—in a large open field, near Nancy, where Messiaen was waiting to be transferred to Stalag VIII A; Movement V is based on a section from the *Fête des belles eaux* [1937], a work for six Ondes Martenot; and Movement VIII is a reworking of the second section of the *Diptyque* for organ. See Étienne Pasquier, "Hommage à Olivier Messiaen," in *Olivier Messiaen, homme de foi: Regard sur son œuvre d'orgue*, 91–92 [item 238]; Rebecca Rischin, *For the End of Time: The Story of the Messiaen Quartet* [item 486], 12, 16–17; and Simeone, *A Bibliographical Catalogue of Messiaen's Works* [item 6], 71–73.)

Premiere: 15 January 1941, Stalag VIII A, Görlitz, Silesia; Jean Le Boulaire, violin; Henri Akoka, clarinet; Étienne Pasquier, cello; Olivier Messiaen, piano

Publisher: Durand (Paris, 1942): score; parts for violin, clarinet, and cello; and study score

Scoring: violin, clarinet, cello, and piano

A.26. *Le Merle noir*

(This work was written for the competitive examination in flute at the Paris Conservatoire.)

Date and place of composition: 1951 [March 1952, according to Hill and Simeone (item 210, pp. 199–200).], Paris

Premiere: 1951 [1952], Conservatoire, Concours, Paris

Publisher: Alphonse Leduc (Paris, 1952): score, part for flute

Scoring: flute and piano

A.27. *Chant donneé*

(Messiaen composed *Chant donneé* as a tribute to his teacher Jean Gallon [1878–1959], a professor of harmony at the Paris Conservatoire, whose post he occupied from 1941–47.)

Date of composition: Before February 1953

Publisher: (Published in) *64 Leçons d'Harmonie offertes en hommage à Jean Gallon [...] par ses élèves*; Durand (Paris, 1953)—piece can be found on pp. 87–88.

Scoring: Four unspecified parts, written in open score using soprano, alto, tenor, and bass clefs

A.28. *Chant dans le style Mozart* (unpublished)

(The *Chant dans le style Mozart* was written for the competitive examination in clarinet at the Paris Conservatoire.)

Date and place of composition: 1986, Paris

Scoring: clarinet and piano

A.29. *Pièce pour piano et quatuor à cordes*

(This work was composed for the 90th birthday of Alfred Schlee and the 90th anniversary of Universal Edition.)

Date of composition: 1991

Premiere: 18 November 1991, Vienna; Harald Ossberger, piano; Arditti String Quartet

Publisher: Universal (Vienna, 1992)

Scoring: piano and string quartet: full score, part for piano (The full score also serves as parts for the string quartet ["Partitur=Stimme"]; the piano part is the same as the full score except that page turns have been rearranged for the convenience of the performer.)

IV. ORGAN

A.30. *Esquisse modale* (unpublished)

Date and place of composition: 1927, Paris

A.31. *Le Banquet céleste*

Date and place of composition: 1928, Fuligny, Aube (Some sources list 1926 as the date of composition for *Le Banquet céleste* based on information given in the 1960 edition. But in an interview with Brigitte Massin [*Olivier Messiaen: une poétique du merveilleux*, item 171, 44–45], Messiaen claimed that he was 19 years old when he composed *Le Banquet céleste*, which means that it was probably composed in 1928 [Messiaen was born on 10 December 1908]. See n. 2 above.)

Premiere: 28 May 1935, La Trinité, Paris; Marcel Dupré, organ

Publisher: First edition: Alphonse Leduc (Paris, 1934)

Revised edition: Alphonse Leduc (Paris, 1960—for the principal differences between the 1934 and 1960 editions, see Simeone, *A Bibliographical Catalogue of Messiaen's Works* [item 6], 3–4.)

A.32. *L'Hôte aimable des âmes* (unpublished)

Date and place of composition: 1928, Fuligny, Aube

A.33. *Variations écossaises* (unpublished)

Date and place of composition: 1928, Paris

A.34. *Offrande au Saint-Sacrement*

Date of composition: ca. 1928

Publisher: Alphonse Leduc (Paris, 2001)

A.35. *Prélude*

Date of composition: late 1929, Paris

Publisher: Alphonse Leduc (Paris, 2002)

A.36. *Diptyque: Essai sur la vie terrestre et l'éternité bienheureuse*

(Although various sources provide titles for the two sections of this work ["La vie terrestre, avec ses agitations inutiles," and "Le Paradis"], they are not found in the first edition [as well as all reprints] of the *Diptyque*. Instead, the sections are distinguished only by tempo and metronome markings—*Modéré* [quarter note=50] and *Très lent* [eighth note=58].)

Date and place of composition: 1930, Paris

Premiere: Before 28 December 1930, La Trinité, Paris; Olivier Messiaen, organ

Publisher: Durand (Paris, 1930)

A.37. *Apparition de l'Église éternelle*

Date and place of composition: 1932, Paris

Premiere: ca. 1932, La Trinité, Paris; Olivier Messiaen, organ

Publisher: First edition: Henry Lemoine (Paris, 1934)

Second edition: Henry Lemoine (Paris, 1985—in 1985, Lemoine issued a new edition of this work [using the 1934 plates] with revised dynamic markings and registration indications provided by Messiaen. In 1993, Lemoine issued a newly engraved version of the 1985 edition, incorporating minor alterations as well as facsimiles of the autograph title page and part of the manuscript.)

Third edition: Henry Lemoine (Paris, 1993)

A.38. *L'Ascension: Quatre Méditations symphoniques pour orgue*

1. Majesté du Christ demandant sa gloire à son Père

2. Alléluias sereins d'une âme qui désire le ciel
3. Transports de joie d'une âme devant la gloire du Christ qui est
   la sienne (Messiaen transcribed movements 1, 2, and 4 of the
   orchestral version of *L'Ascension* for organ. Because he considered the orchestral version's third movement ["Alléluia sur la
   trompette, Alléluia sur la cymbale"] as less amenable to organ
   transcription, Messiaen composed a new third movement—the
   first of his large organ toccatas—for the organ work.)
4. Prière du Christ montant vers son Père

Date and place of composition: 1933, Neussargues, Cantal (movements 1 and 4); 1934, Paris (movements 2 and 3)

Premiere: 28 May 1935, La Trinité, Paris; Olivier Messiaen, organ

Publisher: Alphonse Leduc (Paris, 1934)

A.39. *La Nativité du Seigneur: Neuf Meditations pour orgue*

1. La Vierge et l'Enfant
2. Les Bergers
3. Desseins éternels
4. Le Verbe
5. Les Enfants de Dieu
6. Les Anges
7. Jésus accepte la souffrance
8. Les Mages
9. Dieu parmi nous

Date and place of composition: 1935, Grenoble

Premiere: Individual movements: 1935, La Trinité, Paris; Olivier
Messiaen, organ. Complete performance: 27 February 1936, concert
of Les Amis de l'Orgue, La Trinité, Paris; Daniel-Lesur (movements
1–3), Jean Langlais (movements 4–6), and Jean-Jacques Grunenwald (movements 7–9), organists

Publisher: Alphonse Leduc (Paris, 1936)

A.40. *Les Corps glorieux: Sept Visions brèves de la Vie des Ressuscités pour
orgue*

1. Subtilité des Corps glorieux
2. Les Eaux de la Grâce
3. L'Ange aux parfums
4. Combat de la mort et de la vie
5. Force et Agilité des Corps glorieux
6. Joie et Clarté des Corps glorieux
7. Le Mystère de la Saint Trinité

Date and place of composition: 1939; completed on 25 August 1939 at Petichet, Isère,

Premiere: 15 November 1943, La Trinité, Paris; Olivier Messiaen, organ

Publisher: Alphonse Leduc (Paris, 1942)

A.41. *Messe de la Pentecôte*

1. Entrée (Les langues de feu)
2. Offertoire (Les choses visibles et invisbles)
3. Consécration (Le don de Sagesse)
4. Communion (Les oiseaux et les sources)
5. Sortie (Le vent de l'Esprit)

Date and place of composition: 1949, Tanglewood—1950, Paris

Premiere: 1951, during the liturgical office of Pentecost, La Trinité, Paris; Olivier Messiaen, organ

Publisher: Alphonse Leduc (Paris, 1951)

A.42. *Livre d'orgue*

1. Reprises par interversion
2. Pièce en trio: Pour le Dimanche de la Sainte-Trinité
3. Les Mains de l'abîme: Pour les Temps de Pénitence
4. Chants d'oiseaux: Pour le Temps Pascal
5. Pièce en trio: Pour le Dimanche de la Sainte-Trinité
6. Les Yeux dans les roues: Pour le Dimanche de la Pentecôte
7. Soixante-Quatre durées

Date and places of composition: 1951[-52]: Movements 1, 2, and 6, Paris; Movement 3, Montagnes du Dauphiné, vallée de la Romanche; Movement 4, pré Perrin de Fuligny, forêt de St-Germain-en-Laye, branderaie de Gardépée, Charente (April 1952—Hill and Simeone state that the fourth movement could not have been completed before April 1952 [see item 210, p. 201], thus the *Livre d'orgue* was actually completed in that year rather than 1951 according to Messiaen); Movement 5, devant les glaciers du Râteau, de la Meije et du Tabuchet; Movement 7, Champs de Petichet

Premiere: 23 April 1952, Villa Berg, Stuttgart; Olivier Messiaen, organ

Publisher: Alphonse Leduc (Paris, 1953)

A.43. *Verset pour la fête de la Dédicace*

(This piece was written for the competitive examination in organ at the Paris Conservatoire that took place on 13 June 1961. First prizes were awarded to Raffi Ourgandjian [unanimous], Christian Manen [unanimous], Yves Devernay, and Francine Guiberteau [see Simeone, *A Bibliographical Catalogue of Messiaen's Works* (item 6), 135; and Timothy J. Tikker, "The Organs of Olivier Messiaen" (item 400), 13, n. 41].)

Date and place of composition: December 1960, Paris

Premiere: 13 June 1961, Concours, Paris Conservatoire

Publisher: Alphonse Leduc (Paris, 1961)

A.44. *Monodie*

(According to liner notes by Yvonne Loriod-Messiaen in *Olivier Messiaen: Inédits* [Éditions Jade 7432167411–2, p. 4—see B.147], this piece was written at the request of Jean Bonfils—Messiaen's assistant at La Trinité—for his organ method book. The piece was published as a part of that book in 1963 by the Schola Cantorum, and then in 1998 by Alphonse Leduc, who acknowledged the Schola Cantorum's permission to reproduce the work on its title page. Simeone [*A Bibliographical Catalogue of Messiaen's Works* (item 6), 139] posits, based upon a private communication from Christopher Dingle, that Messiaen might have composed *Monodie* for a sight-reading examination at the Schola Cantorum.)

Date of composition: 1963

Premiere: 19 May 1998, Westminster Cathedral, London; Gillian Weir, organ

Publisher: Alphonse Leduc (Paris, 1998)

A.45. *Méditations sur le mystère de la Sainte Trinité*

1. Le Père inengendré (although untitled in the score, the meditations are titled in later sources, such as Catherine Massip, ed., *Portrait(s) d'Olivier Messiaen* [item 241], 171; and Messiaen's notes on the work in *Olivier Messiaen, homme de foi: Regard sur son œuvre d'orgue* [item 238], 49–58. See also Simeone, *A Bibliographical Catalogue of Messiaen's Works* [item 6], 150–53.)
2. La Sainteté de Jésus-Christ
3. "La relation réelle en Dieu est réellement identique à l'essence"
4. "Je suis, je suis!"
5. Dieu est immense, éternel, immuable – Le Souffle de l'Esprit – Dieu est Amour
6. Le Fils, Verbe et Lumière
7. "Le Père et le Fils aiment, par le Saint-Esprit, eux-mêmes et nous"

    8. Dieu est simple

    9. "Je suis Celui qui Suis"

Date of composition: 1969

Premiere: 20 March 1972, Basilica of the Immaculate Conception, Washington D.C.; Olivier Messiaen, organ

Publisher: Alphonse Leduc (Paris, 1973)

A.46. *Livre du Saint Sacrement*

    1. Adoro te

    2. La Source de Vie

    3. Le Dieu caché

    4. Acte de Foi

    5. Puer natus est nobis

    6. La manne et le Pain de Vie

    7. Les ressuscités et la Lumière de Vie

    8. Institution de l'Eucharistie

    9. Les ténèbres

    10. La Résurrection du Christ

    11. L'apparition du Christ ressuscité à Marie-Madeleine

    12. La Transsubstantiation

    13. Les deux murailles d'eau

    14. Prière avant la communion

    15. La joie de la grâce

    16. Prière après la communion

    17. La Présence multipliée

    18. Offrande et Alléluia final

Date of composition: 1984

Premiere: 1 July 1986, Metropolitan Methodist Church, Detroit; Almut Rößler, organ

Publisher: Alphonse Leduc (Paris, 1989)

V. PIANO

A.47. *La Dame de Shalott* (unpublished)

Date and place of composition: 1917, Grenoble

A.48. *La Tristesse d'un grand ciel blanc* (unpublished)

Date and place of composition: 1925, Paris

A.49. *Préludes*

    1. La colombe

2. Chant d'extase dans un paysage triste
3. Le nombre léger
4. Instants défunts
5. Les sons impalpables du rêve (in *A Bibliographical Catalogue of Messiaen's Works* [item 6, p. 7], Simeone notes that the "opening of no. V and a nine-bar fragment of no. VI are published in [Nicolas] Obouhow's experimental notation on pp. 21 and 23 of *Collection Nicolas Obouhow: Pièces pour piano transcrites en nouvelle notation simplifiée Nicolas Obouhow* [plate number D. & F. 13,261, 1947].")
6. Cloches d'angoisse et larmes d'adieu
7. Plainte calme
8. Un reflet dans le vent

Date and place of composition: 1928–29, Fuligny. Aube

Premiere: 1 March 1930, Salle Erard, Société Nationale, Paris; Henriette Roget, piano (although Henriette Roget gave the first public performance of the *Préludes* on 1 March 1930, Messiaen played them on 28 January 1930 at a private performance of the Concerts Durand in Paris; see Simeone, *A Bibliographical Catalogue of Messiaen's Works* [item 6], 7.)

Publisher: Durand (Paris, 1930)

A.50. *Fantaisie burlesque*

Date and place of composition: 1932, Paris

Premiere: 8 February 1933, École Normale de Musique, Société Musicale Indépendante, Paris; Robert Casadesus, piano

Publisher: Durand (Paris, 1932)

A51. *Morceau de Lecture à vue*

(*Morceau de Lecture à vue* was one of three test pieces written by Messiaen for the École Normale de Musique when he was a faculty member there in the 1930s. It appeared in a musical supplement of *Le Monde musical* for 31 October 1934. See Hill and Simeone, *Messiaen* [item 210], 50, for a facsimile reproduction of the piece.)

Date and place of composition: 1934, Paris

Publisher: Durand (Paris, forthcoming)

A.52. *Pièce pour le Tombeau de Paul Dukas*

Date and place of composition: Summer 1935, Grenoble (Paul Dukas died on 18 May 1935)

Premiere: 25 April 1936, École Normale de Musique, Société Nationale, Paris; Joaquín Nin, piano

Publisher: First published in *Le Tombeau de Paul Dukas: Supplément Musical de la Revue musicale* (Paris, May-June 1936—Messiaen's piece can be found on pp. 23–24. Tony Aubin, Elsa Barraine, Manuel De Falla, Julien Krein, Gabriel Pierné, Joaquín Rodrigo, Guy Ropartz, and Florent Schmitt also submitted pieces for *Le Tombeau de Paul Dukas*.). After Messiaen's death, the piece was published separately by Durand in an edition prepared by Yvonne Loriod-Messiaen (Durand—Paris, 1996).

A.53. *Rondeau*

(This piece was written in 1943 for the competitive examination in piano at the Paris Conservatoire. First prizes were awarded to Yvonne Loriod and Jean-Michel Damase [see Simeone, *A Bibliographical Catalogue of Messiaen's Works* (item 6), 79].)

Date and place of composition: 1943, Paris

Premiere: 1943, Concours, Paris Conservatoire

Publisher: Alphonse Leduc (Paris, 1943)

A.54. *Visions de l'Amen*

1. Amen de la Création
2. Amen des étoiles, de la planète à l'anneau
3. Amen de l'Agonie de Jésus
4. Amen du Désir
5. Amen des Anges, des Saints, du chant des oiseaux
6. Amen du Jugement
7. Amen de la Consommation

Date and place of composition: 1943, Paris

Premiere: 10 May 1943, Galerie Charpentier (76 rue du Faubourg Saint-Honoré), Concerts de la Pléiade, Paris; Yvonne Loriod, Olivier Messiaen, pianos I and II

Publisher: Durand (Paris, 1950)

Scoring: Two pianos

A.55. *Vingt Regards sur l'Enfant-Jésus*

1. Regard du Père
2. Regard de l'étoile
3. L'échange
4. Regard de la Vierge

    5. Regard du Fils sur le Fils
    6. Par Lui tout a été fait
    7. Regard de la Croix
    8. Regard des hauteurs
    9. Regard du Temps
   10. Regard de l'Esprit de joie
   11. Première communion de la Vierge
   12. La parole toute puissante
   13. Noël
   14. Regard des Anges
   15. Le baiser de l'Enfant-Jésus
   16. Regard des prophètes, des bergers et des Mages
   17. Regard du silence
   18. Regard de l'Onction terrible
   19. Je dors, mais mon coeur veille
   20. Regard de l'Église d'amour

Date and place of composition: 23 March – 8 September 1944, Paris

Premiere: 26 March 1945, Salle Gaveau, Paris; Yvonne Loriod, piano

Publisher: Durand (Paris, 1947)

A.56. *Cantéyodjayâ*

Date and place of composition: 15 July – 15 August 1948 [1949], Tanglewood, Massachusetts. (According to Hill and Simeone [*Messiaen* (item 210), 180], Messiaen's 1948 date for *Cantéyodjayâ* is wrong because his first visit to Tanglewood actually took place in July-August 1949. They state that "Messiaen was so convinced by his error that he went to the trouble of redating several of his Tanglewood photographs." Griffiths ["Olivier Messiaen," *New Grove Dictionary of Music and Musicians*—item 722] and other sources list the date as 1949.)

Premiere: 23 February 1954, Concerts du Domaine musical, Paris; Yvonne Loriod, piano

Publisher: Universal (Vienna, 1953)

A.57. *Quatre Études de rythme*

(The first editions of these works indicate that Messiaen may not have initially conceived of them as a set. It was only after their separate publication that he gave the four works their collective title of *Quatre Études de rythme*, stipulating that they should be played in the order given below. See Simeone, *A Bibliographical Catalogue of Messiaen's Works* [item 6], 105.)

1. Île de feu I
2. Mode de valeurs et d'intensités
3. Neumes rythmiques
4. Île de feu II

Dates and places of composition: *Ile de feu I* – 1950, Paris; *Mode de valeurs et d'intensités* – 1949, Darmstadt/Paris; *Neumes rythmiques* – Tanglewood, 1949; *Ile de feu II* – 1950, Paris

Premiere: 1950, Tunis; Olivier Messiaen, piano

Publisher: Durand (Paris, 1950)

A.58. *Catalogue d'oiseaux*

Premier livre:

1. Le Chocard des Alpes
2. Le Loriot
3. Le Merle bleu

Deuxième livre:

4. Le Traquet Stapazin

Troisième livre:

5. La Chouette Hulotte
6. L'Alouette Lulu

Quatrième livre:

7. La Rousserolle Effarvatte

Cinquième livre:

8. L'Alouette Calandrelle
9. La Bouscarle

Sixième livre:

10. Le Merle de roche

Septième livre:

11. La Buse variable
12. Le Traquet rieur
13. Le Courlis cendré

Date of composition: October 1956 – 1 September 1958

Premiere: 15 April 1959, Salle Gaveau, Concerts du Domaine musical, Paris; Yvonne Loriod, piano

Publisher: Alphonse Leduc (Paris, 1964)

A.59. *Prélude* (1964).

Date and place of composition: 1964

Publisher: Durand (Paris, 2000)

A.60. *La Fauvette des jardins*

Date and place of composition: 1970, Petichet, Isère

Premiere: 7 November 1972, Espace Pierre Cardin, Paris; Yvonne Loriod-Messiaen, piano

Publisher: Alphonse Leduc (Paris, 1972)

A.61. *Petites esquisses d'oiseaux*

1. Le Rouge-gorge
2. Le Merle noir
3. Le Rouge-gorge
4. La Grive musicienne
5. Le Rouge-gorge
6. L'Alouette des champs

Date and place of composition: 1985

Premiere: 26 January 1987, Théâtre de la Ville, Paris; Yvonne Loriod-Messiaen, piano

Publisher: Alphonse Leduc (Paris, 1988)

VI. VOCAL AND CHORAL

A.62. *Deux Ballades de Villon* (unpublished—the texts of these unpublished songs are by the French poet François Villon [1431–1463]. Debussy's *Trois Ballades de Villon* [1910] for voice and piano may have inspired the twelve-year old Messiaen to compose these songs.)

1. Épître à ses amis
2. Ballade des pendus

Date and place of composition: 1921, Paris

Scoring: Voice and piano

A.63. *Trois Mélodies*

1. Pourquoi?
2. Le Sourire (The text of *Le Sourire* is by the French poetess Cécile Sauvage, Messiaen's mother.)
3. La Fiancée perdue

Date and place of composition: 1930, Paris

Premiere: 14 February 1931, Société Nationale, Paris; Louise Matha, soprano; Olivier Messiaen, piano. (According to Simeone [*A Bibliographical Catalogue of Messiaen's Works* (item 6), 11], 1930 is often incorrectly listed in various sources as the date of the first performance.)

Publisher: Durand (Paris, 1930/1946)

Scoring: Soprano and piano

A.64. *La Mort du Nombre*

Date and place of composition: 1930, Paris

Premiere: 25 March 1931, École Normale de Musique, Société Musicale Indépendante, Paris; Mme Guiberteau, soprano (replacing Georgette Mathieu); Jean Planel, tenor; M. Blareau, violin; Olivier Messiaen, piano

Publisher: Durand (Paris, 1931/1976)

Scoring: Soprano, tenor, violin, and piano

A.65. *L'Ensorceleuse* (unpublished)

(As part of his second unsuccessful attempt to win the Prix de Rome, Messiaen composed the cantata *L'Ensorceleuse* to a text by Paul Arosa [1890–1940] for the competition's final round in 1931. For more information on Messiaen's participation in the competition process of the Prix de Rome, see Hill and Simeone, *Messiaen* [item 210], 28–29, 32–34; and Simeone, *A Bibliographical Catalogue of Messiaen's Works* [item 6], 189–91.)

Date and place of composition: June 1931, Paris

Premiere: 4 July 1931, Académie des Beaux-Arts, Paris; Georgette Mathieu, soprano; Louis Arnot, tenor; Guénot, bass; Olivier Messiaen, piano

Scoring: Soprano, tenor, bass, and piano (or orchestra)

A.66. *Messe* (unpublished)

1. Kyrie
2. Gloria
3. Credo
4. Sanctus
5. Agnus

Date and place of composition: 1933, Neussargues, Cantal

Scoring: 8 sopranos and 4 violins

A.67. *Vocalise-étude*

Date and place of composition: 1935, Paris

Premiere: 1935, Conservatoire, Concours, Paris

Publisher: Alphonse Leduc (Paris, 1935/1937—in 1935, Alphonse Leduc published the *Vocalise-étude* as no. 151 of the series entitled *Répertoire Moderne de Vocalises-Études publiées sous la Direction de A. L. Hettich, Professeur au Conservatoire National de Paris.* Two years later, Leduc published the work in an anthology of the same name [*Répertoire Moderne de Vocalises-Études publiées sous la Direction de A. L. Hettich, Professeur au Conservatoire National de Paris, nouvelle édition, 3e recueil pour voix élevées*]. See Simeone, *A Bibliographical Catalogue of Messiaen's Works* [item 6], 49.)

Scoring: Soprano and piano

A.68. *Poèmes pour Mi: Chant et Piano*

(*Poèmes pour Mi* was dedicated to Messiaen's first wife, Claire Delbos, whose familiar name was "Mi.")

Premier livre:

  1. Action de grâces
  2. Paysage
  3. La maison
  4. Épouvante

Deuxième livre:

  5. L'Épouse
  6. Ta voix
  7. Les deux guerriers
  8. Le collier
  9. Prière exaucée

Date and place of composition: 1936, Petichet, Isère

Premiere: 28 April 1937, Salle des Concerts de la Schola Cantorum, La Spirale, Paris; Marcelle Bunlet, soprano; Olivier Messiaen, piano

Publisher: Durand (Paris, 1937)

Scoring: Soprano and piano

A.69. *Poèmes pour Mi: Grand Soprano dramatique et Orchestre* (orchestral version)

Premier livre:

  1. Action de grâces

    2. Paysage
    3. La maison
    4. Épouvante

Deuxième livre:

    5. L'Épouse
    6. Ta voix
    7. Les deux guerriers
    8. Le collier
    9. Prière exaucée

Orchestration: 1937, Paris

Premiere: *"Action de grâces only"*: 4 June 1937, second concert by La Jeune France, Salle Gaveau, Paris; Marcelle Bunlet, soprano; Orchestre de la Société des Concerts du Conservatoire, Roger Désormière, conductor

Complete performance: 1946, Belgian Radio Concert, Brussels; Marcelle Bunlet, soprano; Belgian National Radio Orchestra, Franz André, conductor. (According to Simeone [*A Bibliographical Catalogue of Messiaen's Works* (item 6), 57–58], there are discrepancies between various sources regarding the premiere of the orchestral version of *Poèmes pour Mi*. For example, while some sources—including Messiaen's liner notes to the Everest recording of *Poèmes pour Mi* [Lise Arseguest, soprano; Olivier Messiaen, piano; Everest 3269; sound recording]—give the date and location as listed above, Messiaen's liner notes to an Argo recording of *Poèmes pour Mi* [Felicity Palmer, soprano; BBC Symphony Orchestra, Pierre Boulez, conductor; Argo ZRG 703, 1973; sound recording] give the first performance as having occurred in 1946, at the Théâtre des Champs-Élysées in Paris, with Marcelle Bunlet as soloist accompanied by the National Orchestra of the O.R.T.F. under the direction of Roger Désormière. The Brussels concert is said, moreover, to have followed later that year, with Bunlet and the I.N.R. Orchestra conducted by André Cluytens as performers.)

Publisher: Durand (Paris, 1939): study score

Scoring: soprano – 3.3.2.3 – 4.3.3.1 – 3 percussion – strings (including 6 solo first violins, 6 solo second violins, 6 solo violas, 4 solo cellos)

A.70. *O sacrum convivium!: Motet au Saint-Sacrement pour chœur à quatre voix mixtes ou quatre solistes (avec accompagnement d'orgue ad libitum)*

(The work's Latin text is attributed to Saint Thomas Aquinas [1225–1274].)

Date and place of composition: 1937, Paris

Premiere: Possibly in 1937, at La Trinité, Paris (Simeone, *A Biblio-graphical Catalogue of Messiaen's Works* [item 6], 61.)

Publisher: Durand (Paris, 1937)

Scoring: s.a.t.b. chorus; or four soloists and organ

A.71. *Chants de Terre et de Ciel*

1. Bail avec Mi (pour ma Femme—"Bail avec Mi" is dedicated to Messiaen's first wife, Claire Delbos, whereas "Danse du bébé-Pilule" and "Arc-en-ciel d'innocence" are dedicated to Messiaen's son, Pascal, who was born on 14 July 1937.)
2. Antienne du silence (pour le jour des Anges gardiens)
3. Danse du bébé-Pilule (pour mon petit Pascal)
4. Arc-en-ciel d'innocence (pour mon petit Pascal)
5. Minuit pile et face (pour la Mort)
6. Résurrection (pour le jour de Pâques)

Date and place of composition: 1938, Petichet, Isère

Premiere: 23 January 1939, Triton, Paris; Marcelle Bunlet, soprano; Olivier Messiaen, piano. (At the work's premiere, the program and reviewer Michel-Léon Hirsch ["Le Triton (23 janvier)," *Le Ménes-trel*, 3 February 1939, 28] both refer to this song-cycle as "Prismes" [see Simeone, *A Bibliographical Catalogue of Messiaen's Works* (item 6), 63, 221]. The different title may be the reason why there is a discrepancy between the January date listed above and that found in Griffiths's *Olivier Messiaen and the Music of Time* [(item 208) 262], which gives the work's first performance as taking place on 6 March 1939 in Paris, with Marcelle Bunlet as soloist and Olivier Messiaen at the piano.)

Publisher: Durand (Paris, 1939)

Scoring: Soprano and piano

A.72. *Chœurs pour une Jeanne d'Arc* (unpublished)

1. Te Deum
2. Impropères

Date and place of composition: 1941, Neussargues, Cantal

Scoring: Large and small s.a.t.b. choirs

A.73. *Trois petites Liturgies de la Présence Divine*

    1. Antienne de la conversation intérieure (Dieu présent en nous ...)
    2. Séquence du Verbe, Cantique Divin (Dieu présent en lui-même ...)
    3. Psalmodie de l'Ubiquité par amour (Dieu présent en toutes choses ...)

Date and place of composition: 15 November 1943 – 15 March 1944, Paris

Premiere: 21 April 1945, Salle de l'Ancien Conservatoire, Concerts de la Pléiades, Paris; Chorale Yvonne Gouverné; Yvonne Loriod, piano; Ginette Martenot, Ondes Martenot; Orchestre de la Société des Concerts du Conservatoire, Roger Désormière, conductor

Publisher: Durand (Paris, 1952): study score, chorus part, revised solo parts for piano and Ondes Martenot in preparation

Scoring:

    Chorus: s.m-s.a. – 36 female voices

    Orchestra: piano solo, Ondes Martenot solo, celesta, vibraphone, 3 percussion – 8.8.6.6.4 (strings)

A.74. *Harawi: Chant d'Amour et de Mort*

    1. La ville qui dormait, toi
    2. Bonjour toi, colombe verte
    3. Montagnes
    4. Doundou tchil
    5. L'amour de Piroutcha
    6. Répétition planétaire
    7. Adieu
    8. Syllabes
    9. L'escalier redit, gestes du soleil
    10. Amour oiseaux d'étoile
    11. Katchikatchi les étoiles
    12. Dans le noir

Date and place of composition: 15 June – 15 September 1945, Petichet, Isère

Premiere: 24 June 1946, Salle des Fêtes, Mâcon; Marcelle Bunlet, soprano; Olivier Messiaen, piano

Publisher: Alphonse Leduc (Paris, 1949)

Scoring: dramatic soprano and piano

A.75. *Chant des Déportés*

Date of composition: 1945

Premiere: 2 November 1945, Concert de Musique Française à la Mémoire des Déportés morts en Allemagne, Palais de Chaillot, Paris; Pierre Boulez, piano; Orchestre National de la Radiodiffusion Française, Manuel Rosenthal conductor

Publisher: Alphonse Leduc (Paris, 1998)

Scoring:

Chorus: s.t. (in large numbers)

Orchestra: 3.2.3.3. – 4.3.3.1. – suspended and chinese cymbals, tamtam, bass drum, piano, glockenspiel – strings (in large numbers)

A.76. *Cinq Rechants*

Date and place of composition: December 1948 (February 1949 according to Hill and Simeone, *Messiaen* [item 210], 179), Paris

Premiere: 1949, Salle Erard, Paris; Chorale Marcel Couraud, Marcel Couraud, conductor

Publisher: Éditions Salabert (Paris, 1949)

Scoring: s.a.t.b. chorus – 3 voices per part

A.77. *La Transfiguration de Nôtre-Seigneur Jésus-Christ*

(The Latin text, arranged by Messiaen, is drawn from various sources: the Bible, namely, Genesis, Psalms, Wisdom of Solomon [considered deuterocanonical by Roman Catholics and apocryphal by Protestants], the Gospels according to Saints Matthew and Luke, the Epistle of Saint Paul to the Philippians, and the Epistle to the Hebrews; the *Summa Theologiae* of Saint Thomas Aquinas; the Office for the Feast of the Transfiguration; and the Roman Catholic Missal.)

Premier Septénaire:

1. Récit Évangélique
2. Configuratum corpori claritatis suae
3. Christus Jesus, splendor Patris
4. Récit Évangélique
5. Quam dilecta tabernacula tua
6. Candor est lucis aeternae
7. Choral de la Sainte Montagne

Deuxième Septénaire:

8. Récit Évangélique

9. Perfecte conscius illius perfectae generationis
10. Adoptionem filiorum perfectam
11. Récit Évangélique
12. Terribilis est locus iste
13. Tota Trinitas apparuit
14. Choral de la Lumière de Gloire

Date of composition and orchestration: 28 June 1965 – 20 February 1969

Premiere: 7 June 1969, Coliseu, Lisbon; Chœur Gulbenkian; Yvonne Loriod-Messiaen, piano; Mstislav Rostropovich, cello; Michel Debost, flute; Henry Druart, clarinet; Alain Jacquet, xylorimba; Jacques Delécluse, vibraphone; François Dupin, marimba; l'Orchestre de Paris, Serge Baudo, conductor

Publisher: Alphonse Leduc (Paris, 1972): full score

Scoring:

Chorus: s.s.m-s.a.a.t.t.bar.b.b. – 10 voices per part

Orchestra: 7 soloists: piano, cello, flute, clarinet, xylorimba, vibraphone, and marimba; 5.4.5.4. – 6.4.4.3. – 6 percussion – 16.16.14.12.10

VII. ELECTRONIC

A.78. *Fête des belles eaux*

(Messiaen reworked part of the *Fête des belles eaux* for cello and piano for the fifth movement ["Louange à l'Éternité de Jésus"] of the *Quatuor pour la fin du Temps* [see item A.25]. For more information on the genesis, first performance, and structure of the *Fête des belles eaux*, see Simeone, *A Bibliographical Catalogue of Messiaen's Works* [item 6], 192–94.)

1. Premières fusées
2. L'eau
3. Les fusées
4. L'eau
5. Les fusées
6. L'eau (à son maximum de hauteur)
7. Superposition de l'eau et des fusées

Date and place of composition: 1937, Paris

Premiere: 25 July 1937; along the banks of the Seine river; Fêtes du son, de l'eau, et de la lumière; Exposition Internationale des Arts et des Techniques appliqués à la vie moderne; Paris

Publisher: Alphonse Leduc (Paris, 2003): full score

Scoring: Six Ondes Martenot

A.79. *Deux Monodies en quarts de ton* (unpublished)

Date and place of composition: 1938, Paris

Scoring: Ondes Martenot

A.80. *Musique de scène pour un Œdipe* (unpublished)

(Scholars have been unable to identify the production of Oedipus for which this music was composed.)

Date and place of composition: 1942, Paris

Scoring: Ondes Martenot

A.81. *Timbres-Durées* (unpublished)

(After hearing the piece's realization by Pierre Henry, Messiaen withdrew the composition, claiming that it was "very bad." However, Antoine Goléa provided a different view of the work in a special issue of *La Revue musicale* devoted to musique concrète [see item 595, p. 41]. There Goléa not only cites a less negative assessment of the work by Messiaen but also describes it as being based on four rhythmic characters developed through twenty-four durational sequences. See Simeone, *A Bibliographical Catalogue of Messiaen's Works* [item 6], 196.)

Date of composition: 1952 (realized by Pierre Henry)

Scoring: Tape

A.82. *Feuillets inédits: Quatre piéces pour onde Martenot et piano*

Date of composition: Unknown (in her liner notes to *Olivier Messiaen: Inédits* [p. 4—see B.257], Yvonne Loriod-Messiaen states that Messiaen did not date these pieces. But he did leave pedagogical indications that the first piece was for "learning to read music" ["Solfège"] and the remaining pieces for "sight-reading" ["Déchiffrages"]. These indications are not present, however, in the published score.)

Publisher: Durand (Paris, 2001): full score

Scoring: Ondes Martenot and piano (in the same liner notes to *Olivier Messiaen: Inédits*, Loriod-Messiaen leaves the reader with the impression that the scoring of these pieces was not specified by Messiaen, and that she decided to arrange them for Ondes Martenot and piano ["Qui aurait pu résister à l'idée de les arranger pour Onde Martenot et piano, certaines mélodies semblant écrites pour le jeu au Ruban de l'Onde?"].)

Appendix 2
Selected Discography of Musical Works by Olivier Messiaen

With the exception of a "Collections" category, this selected discography of Messiaen's music lists commercially issued compact disc recordings by genre and individual pieces. Selections were limited to different recordings by Messiaen, Yvonne Loriod-Messiaen, and the more notable champions of Messiaen's music. Items are listed in reverse chronological and, if necessary, in alphabetical order according to the conductor or principal performer(s). Individual recordings are given multiple entries under each separate work. Some older recordings are listed along with their reissued counterparts in the *Messiaen Edition*.

I. COLLECTIONS

Collected Works

B.1. *Messiaen Edition*. Various performers, including Olivier Messiaen and Yvonne Loriod, and ensembles. Liner notes. Warner Classics 2564 62162–2, 2005. 18 CDs.

Organ

B.2. *Messiaen: Complete Organ Works*. Gillian Weir. Liner notes. Priory Records PRCD 921–25/6, 2004. 6 CDs.

B.3. *Messiaen: Complete Organ Works.* Olivier Latry. Liner notes. Deutsche Grammophon 471 480–82, 2002. 6 CDs.

B.4. *Messiaen: The Organ Works.* Jennifer Bate. Liner notes. Regis RRC 6001, 1980–87/2001. 6 CDs.

B.5. *Olivier Messiaen: Complete Organ Works.* Rudolf Innig. Liner notes. MD&G Records 3170009, 3170346, 3170621, 3170053, 3170622, 31706232, 1996–98. 7 CDs.

B.6. *Messiaen par lui-même: Organ Works.* Olivier Messiaen. Liner notes. EMI Classics CDZ 7 67401 2, 1957/1992. 4 CDs.

B.7. *The Complete Organ Music.* Hans-Ola Ericsson. Liner notes. Bis CD-409, CD-410, CD-441, CD-442, CD-464, CD-491/492; 1988–89. 6 CDs.

Piano

B.8. *Messiaen: Complete Works for Piano, Volumes 1–4.* Paul Kim. Liner notes. Centaur Records 2567/9, 2627/8, 2668, 2727; 2002–5. 7 CDs.

B.9. *Messiaen: Integrale de l'oeuvre pour piano seul.* Roger Muraro. Liner notes. Accord 461 907–2, 2001. 7 CDs.

B.10. *Messiaen: The Piano Works.* Peter Hill (with Benjamin Frith [*Visions de l'Amen*]). Liner notes. Unicorn-Kanchana Records RRC 7001, 1984–92. 7 CDs.

II. OPERA

Saint Francois d'Assise: Scènes franciscaines

B.11. Arnold Schoenberg Chor and Hallé Orchestra, Kent Nagano, conductor. José van Dam, Dawn Upshaw, and Chris Merritt. Liner notes. Deutsche Grammophon 445 176–2, 1999. 4 CDs.

B.12. ORF-Chor, Arnold Schönberg Chor, and Radio Symphonie Orchester Wien, Lothar Zagrosek, conductor. Dietrich Fischer-Dieskau, Rachel Yakar, and Kenneth Riegel. Liner notes. Orfeo C 485 9821, 1998. 2 CDs.

B.13. Chorus and Orchestra of l'Opéra de Paris, Seiji Ozawa, conductor. José van Dam, Christiane Eda-Pierre, and Kenneth Riegel. Liner notes. Cybelia CY 833836, 1983. (Reissued in 1998 on MSI CDMS 1193.) 4 CDs.

III. ORCHESTRAL WORKS

Les Offrandes oubliées: Méditation symphonique

B.14. *Messiaen Edition*. Orchestre Philharmonique de l'O.R.T.F., Marius Constant, conductor. Liner notes. Warner Classics 2564 62162–2, 2005. 18 CDs.

B.15. Orchestre de l'Opéra Bastille, Myung-Whun Chung, conductor. Liner notes. Deutsche Grammophon 445 947–2, 1995.

B.16. Orchestre de Paris, Serge Baudo, conductor. Liner notes. Summit Records DCD 122, 1991.

B.17. Orchestre Philharmonique de l'O.R.T.F., Marius Constant, conductor. Liner notes. Erato 4509-91707-2, 1971.

Le Tombeau resplendissant

B.18. Orchestre de l'Opéra Bastille, Myung-Whun Chung, conductor. Liner notes. Deutsche Grammophon 445 947–2, 1995.

Hymne au Saint-Sacrement

B.19. *Messiaen Edition*. Orchestre Philharmonique de l'O.R.T.F., Marius Constant, conductor. Liner notes. Warner Classics 2564 62162–2, 2005. 18 CDs.

B.20. Orchestre Philharmonique de l'O.R.T.F., Marius Constant, conductor. Liner notes. Erato 4509-91707-2, 1971.

L'Ascension: Quatre Méditations symphoniques pour orchestre

B.21. Bayerischer Rundfunk Orchester, Karl Anton Rickenbacher, conductor. Liner notes. Koch Schwann Musica Mundi 311 015 H1, 1988.

B.22. Orchestre Philharmonique de L'O.R.T.F, Marius Constant, conductor. Liner notes. Erato MO 4509-91706-2, 1966/71.

Turangalîla-Symphonie

B.23. *Messiaen Edition*. Berlin Philharmonic, Kent Nagano, conductor. Pierre-Laurent Aimard, piano, and Dominique Kim, Ondes Martenot. Liner notes. Warner Classics 2564 62162–2, 2005. 18 CDs.

B.24. Toronto Symphony Orchestra, Seiji Ozawa, conductor. Yvonne Loriod, Jeanne Loriod. Liner notes. RCA Red Seal 82876-59418-2, 2004.

B.25. Berlin Philharmonic, Kent Nagano, conductor. Pierre-Laurent Aimard, piano, and Dominique Kim, Ondes Martenot. Teldec 8573-82043-2, 2001.

B.26. Orchestre de l'Opéra Bastille, Myung-Whun Chung, conductor. Yvonne Loriod, Jeanne Loriod. Liner notes. Deutsche Grammophon 431 781–82, 1991.

Réveil des oiseaux

B.27. *Messiaen Edition*. Orchestre National de France, Kent Nagano, conductor. Yvonne Loriod, piano. Liner notes. Warner Classics 2564 62162–2, 2005. 18 CDs.

B.28. SWR Sinfonieorchester Baden-Baden und Freiburg, Europa-ChorAkademie, Hans Rosbaud, conductor. Yvonne Loriod, piano. Hänssler Classic 93.078, 2002. 2 CDs.

B.29. The Cleveland Orchestra, Pierre Boulez, conductor. Françoise Pollet, Pierre-Laurent Aimard, and Joela Jones. Deutsche Grammophon 453 478–2, 1997.

B.30. Orchestre National de France, Kent Nagano, conductor. Yvonne Loriod, Jeanne Loriod. Liner notes. Erato 0630-12702-2, 1996.

Oiseaux exotiques

B.31. Ensemble intercontemporain, Pierre Boulez, conductor. Yvonne Loriod. Liner notes. Montaigne MO 781111, 1994.

B.32. London Sinfonietta, Esa-Pekka Salonen, conductor. Paul Crossley, piano. Liner notes. CBS Masterworks: M2K 44762, 1988. 2 CDs.

Chronochromie

B.33. The Cleveland Orchestra, Pierre Boulez, conductor. Deutsche Grammophon 445 827–2, 1995.

B.34. Bayerischer Rundfunk Orchester, Karl Anton Rickenbacher, conductor. Liner notes. Koch Schwann Musica Mundi 311 015 H1, 1988.

Sept Haïkaï: Esquisses japonaises

B.35. *Messiaen Edition.* Ensemble Ars Nova, Marius Constant, conductor. Yvonne Loriod, piano. Liner notes. Warner Classics 2564 62162–2, 2005. 18 CDs.

B.36. The Cleveland Orchestra, Pierre Boulez, conductor. Françoise Pollet, Pierre-Laurent Aimard, and Joela Jones. Deutsche Grammophon 453 478–2, 1997.

B.37. Ensemble intercontemporain, Pierre Boulez, conductor. Yvonne Loriod. Liner notes. Montaigne MO 781111, 1994.

Couleurs de la Cité céleste

B.38. *Messiaen Edition.* Group instrumental à percussion de Strasbourg, Orchestre du Domaine Musical, Pierre Boulez, conductor. Yvonne Loriod, piano. Liner notes. Warner Classics 2564 62162–2, 2005. 18 CDs.

B.39. Group instrumental à percussion de Strasbourg, Orchestre du Domaine Musical, and New York Philharmonic, Pierre Boulez, conductor. Yvonne Loriod, piano. Liner notes. Sony SMK 68 332, 1995.

B.40. Ensemble intercontemporain, Pierre Boulez, conductor. Yvonne Loriod, piano. Liner notes. Montaigne MO 781111, 1994.

B.41. London Sinfonietta, Esa-Pekka Salonen, conductor. Paul Crossley, piano. Liner notes. CBS Masterworks: M2K 44762, 1988. 2 CDs.

B.42. Group instrumental à percussion de Strasbourg, Orchestre du Domaine Musical, Pierre Boulez, conductor. Yvonne Loriod, piano. Liner notes. Erato MO 4509-91706-2, 1966/71.

Et exspecto resurrectionem mortuorum

B.43. *Messiaen Edition.* Group instrumental à percussion de Strasbourg, Orchestre du Domaine Musical, Pierre Boulez, conductor. Yvonne Loriod, piano. Liner notes. Warner Classics 2564 62162–2, 2005. 18 CDs.

B.44. The Cleveland Orchestra, Pierre Boulez, conductor. Deutsche Grammophon 445 827–2, 1995.

B.45. Group instrumental à percussion de Strasbourg, Orchestre du Domaine Musical, and New York Philharmonic, Pierre Boulez, conductor. Yvonne Loriod, piano. Liner notes. Sony SMK 68 332, 1995.

B.46. Orchestre de Paris, Serge Baudo, conductor. Liner notes. Summit Records DCD 122, 1991.

B.47. Group instrumental à percussion de Strasbourg, Orchestre du Domaine Musical, Pierre Boulez, conductor. Yvonne Loriod, piano. Liner notes. Erato 4509-91706-2, 1966/71.

Des canyons aux étoiles

B.48. *Messiaen Edition.* Ensemble Ars Nova, Marious Constant, conductor. Yvonne Loriod, piano; Georges Barboteu, horn; Alain Jacquet, xylorimba; and François Dupin, glockenspiel. Liner notes. Warner Classics 2564 62162–2, 2005. 18 CDs.

B.49. Orchestre Philharmonque de Radio France, Myung-Whun Chun, conductor. Roger Muraro, piano. Liner notes. Deutsche Grammonphon 471 617–2, 2002. 2 CDs.

B.50. Asko Ensemble, Schönberg Ensemble, and Slagwerkgroep den Haag, Reinbert de Leeuw, conductor. Liner notes. Montaigne MO 782035, 1994. 2 CDs.

B.51. London Sinfonietta, Esa-Pekka Salonen, conductor. Paul Crossley, piano. Liner notes. CBS Masterworks: M2K 44762, 1988. 2 CDs.

Un Vitrail et des oiseaux

B.52. Ensemble intercontemporain, Pierre Boulez, conductor. Yvonne Loriod. Liner notes. Montaigne MO 781111, 1994.

La Ville d'En-Haut

B.53. The Cleveland Orchestra, Pierre Boulez, conductor. Deutsche Grammophon 445 827–2, 1995.

Un Sourire

B.54. Orchestre de l'Opéra Bastille, Myung-Whun Chung, conductor. Liner notes. Deutsche Grammophon 445 947–2, 1995.

Éclairs sur l'Au-Delà

B.55. Berliner Philharmoniker, Sir Simon Rattle, conductor. Liner notes. EMI Classics 7243 5 57788 2 6, 2004.

B.56. Orchestre de l'Opéra Bastille, Myung-Whun Chung, conductor. Liner notes. Deutsche Grammophon 439 929–2, 1994.

B.57. Orchestre National de la Radio Polonaise, Katowice. Antoni Wit, conductor. Liner notes. Jade/Harmonia Mundi JAD C 099, 1994.

Concert à quatre

B.58. Orchestre de l'Opéra Bastille, Myung-Whun Chung, conductor. Catherine Cantin, Heinz Holliger, Yvonne Loriod, and Mstislav Rostropovich. Liner notes. Deutsche Grammophon 445 947–2, 1995.

IV. CHAMBER AND INSTRUMENTAL

Thème et variations

B.59. Scott St. John, violin; Patricia Parr, piano. Naxos 8.554824, 2001.

Quatuor pour la fin du Temps

B.60. *Messiaen Edition.* Huguette Fernandez, violin; Guy Deplus, clarinet; Jacques Neilz, cello; Marie-Madeleine Petit, piano. Liner notes. Warner Classics 2564 62162–2, 2005. 18 CDs.

B.61. Scott St. John, violin; Joaquin Valdepeñas, clarinet; David Hetherington, cello; Patricia Parr, piano. Liner notes. NAXOS 8.554824, 2001.

B.62. Gil Shaham, violin; Paul Meyer, clarinet; Jian Wang, cello; Myung-Whun Chung, piano. Liner notes. Deutsche Grammophon 289 469 052–2, 2000.

B.63. Vera Beths, violin; George Pieterson, clarinet; Anner Bijlsma, cello; Reinbert de Leeuw, piano. Philips D 105572, 1989.

B.64. Ida Kavafian, violin; Peter Serkin, piano; Fred Sherry, cello; Richard Stoltzman, clarinet. Liner notes. RCA Victor 7835–2-RG, 1976.

B.65. Huguette Fernandez, violin; Guy Deplus, clarinet; Jacques Neilz, cello; Marie-Madeleine Petit, piano. Liner notes. Erato 4509-91708-2, 1963.

Le Merle noir

B.66. *Olivier Messiaen: Inédits.* Christian Lardé, flute; Yvonne Loriod-Messiaen, piano. Jade 7432167411–2, 1999.

Chant dans le style Mozart *(unpublished)*

B.67. *Olivier Messiaen: Inédits.* Guy Deplus, Yvonne Loriod-Messiaen. Jade 7432167411–2, 1999.

Pièce pour piano et quatuor à cordes

B.68. *Olivier Messiaen: Inédits.* Yvonne Loriod-Messiaen, Quatuor Rosamonde. Jade 7432167411–2, 1999.

V. ORGAN

Le Banquet céleste

B.69. *Messiaen Edition.* Marie-Claire Alain. Liner notes. Warner Classics 2564 62162–2, 2005. 18 CDs.

B.70. *Messiaen: Complete Organ Works.* Gillian Weir. Liner notes. Priory Records PRCD 921–925/6, 2004. 6 CDs.

B.71. *Messiaen: Complete Organ Works.* Olivier Latry. Liner notes. Deutsche Grammophon 471 480–2, 2002. 6 CDs.

B.72. *Messiaen: The Organ Works.* Jennifer Bate. Liner notes. Regis RRC 6001, 1980–87/2001. 6 CDs.

B.73. *Olivier Messiaen: Complete Organ Works.* Rudolf Innig. Liner notes. MD&G Records 3170346, 1996–98. 7 CDs.

B.74. *Messiaen par lui-même: Organ Works.* Olivier Messiaen. Liner notes. EMI Classics CDZ 7 67401 2, 1957/1992. 4 CDs.

B.75. *The Complete Organ Music.* Hans-Ola Ericsson. Liner notes. Bis CD-409. 1988–89.

B.76. Marie-Claire Alain. Liner notes. Erato 2292-45470-2, 1988.

B.77. Louis Thiry. Liner notes. Caliope CAL 9928, 1986.

Offrande au Saint-Sacrement

B.78. *Messiaen: Complete Organ Works.* Gillian Weir. Liner notes. Priory Records PRCD 921–925/6, 2004. 6 CDs.

B.79. *Messiaen: Complete Organ Works.* Olivier Latry. Liner notes. Deutsche Grammophon 471 480–2, 2002. 6 CDs.

B.80. *Olivier Messiaen: Inédits.* Naji Hakim. Liner notes. Jade 7432167411–2, 1999.

Prélude

B.81. *Messiaen: Complete Organ Works.* Gillian Weir. Liner notes. Priory Records PRCD 921–925/6, 2004. 6 CDs.

B.82. *Messiaen: Complete Organ Works.* Olivier Latry. Liner notes. Deutsche Grammophon 471 480–2, 2002. 6 CDs.

B.83. *Olivier Messiaen: Inédits.* Naji Hakim. Liner notes. Jade 7432167411–2, 1999.

Diptyque: Essai sur la vie terrestre et l'éternité bienheureuse

B.84. *Messiaen: Complete Organ Works.* Gillian Weir. Liner notes. Priory Records PRCD 921–925/6, 2004. 6 CDs.

B.85. *Messiaen: Complete Organ Works.* Olivier Latry. Liner notes. Deutsche Grammophon 471 480–2, 2002. 6 CDs.

B.86. *Messiaen: The Organ Works.* Jennifer Bate. Liner notes. Regis RRC 6001, 1980–87/2001. 6 CDs.

B.87. *Olivier Messiaen: Complete Organ Works.* Rudolf Innig. Liner notes. MD&G Records 3170346, 1996–98. 7 CDs.

B.88. Jon Gillock. Liner notes. Jade 7313835752–2, 1995.

B.89. *Messiaen par lui-même: Organ Works.* Olivier Messiaen. Liner notes. EMI Classics CDZ 7 67401 2, 1957/1992. 4 CDs.

B.90. *The Complete Organ Music.* Hans-Ola Ericsson. Liner notes. Bis CD-409. 1988–89.

Apparition de l'Église éternelle

B.91. *Messiaen Edition.* Marie-Claire Alain. Liner notes. Warner Classics 2564 62162–2, 2005. 18 CDs.

B.92. *Messiaen: Complete Organ Works.* Gillian Weir. Liner notes. Priory Records PRCD 921–925/6, 2004. 6 CDs.

B.93. *Messiaen: Complete Organ Works.* Olivier Latry. Liner notes. Deutsche Grammophon 471 480–2, 2002. 6 CDs.

B.94. *Messiaen: The Organ Works.* Jennifer Bate. Liner notes. Regis RRC 6001, 1980–87/2001. 6 CDs.

B.95. *Olivier Messiaen: Complete Organ Works*. Rudolf Innig. Liner notes. MD&G Records 3170346, 1996–98. 7 CDs.

B.96. *Messiaen par lui-même: Organ Works*. Olivier Messiaen. Liner notes. EMI Classics CDZ 7 67401 2, 1957/1992. 4 CDs.

B.97. *The Complete Organ Music*. Hans-Ola Ericsson. Liner notes. Bis CD-409. 1988–89.

B.98. Marie-Claire Alain. Liner notes. Erato 2292-45470-2, 1988.

B.99. Louis Thiry. Liner notes. Caliope CAL 9928, 1986.

L'Ascension: Quatre Méditations symphoniques pour orgue

B.100. *Messiaen Edition*. Marie-Claire Alain. Liner notes. Warner Classics 2564 62162–2, 2005. 18 CDs.

B.101. *Messiaen: Complete Organ Works*. Gillian Weir. Liner notes. Priory Records PRCD 921–925/6, 2004. 6 CDs.

B.102. *Messiaen: Complete Organ Works*. Olivier Latry. Liner notes. Deutsche Grammophon 471 480–2, 2002. 6 CDs.

B.103. *Messiaen: The Organ Works*. Jennifer Bate. Liner notes. Regis RRC 6001, 1980–87/2001. 6 CDs.

B.104. *Olivier Messiaen: Complete Organ Works*. Rudolf Innig. Liner notes. MD&G Records 3170346, 1996–98. 7 CDs.

B.105. *Messiaen par lui-même: Organ Works*. Olivier Messiaen. Liner notes. EMI Classics CDZ 7 67401 2, 1957/1992. 4 CDs.

B.106. *The Complete Organ Music*. Hans-Ola Ericsson. Liner notes. Bis CD-409. 1988–89.

B.107. Louis Thiry. Liner notes. Caliope CAL 9926, 1986.

La Nativité du Seigneur: Neuf Meditations pour orgue

B.108. *Messiaen Edition*. Marie-Claire Alain. Liner notes. Warner Classics 2564 62162–2, 2005. 18 CDs.

B.109. *Messiaen: Complete Organ Works*. Gillian Weir. Liner notes. Priory Records PRCD 921–925/6, 2004. 6 CDs.

B.110. *Messiaen: Complete Organ Works*. Olivier Latry. Liner notes. Deutsche Grammophon 471 480–2, 2002. 6 CDs.

B.111. *Messiaen: The Organ Works*. Jennifer Bate. Liner notes. Regis RRC 6001, 1980–87/2001. 6 CDs.

B.112. *Olivier Messiaen: Complete Organ Works.* Rudolf Innig. Liner notes. MD&G Records 3170009, 1996–98. 7 CDs.

B.113. *Messiaen par lui-même: Organ Works.* Olivier Messiaen. Liner notes. EMI Classics CDZ 7 67401 2, 1957/1992. 4 CDs.

B.114. *The Complete Organ Music.* Hans-Ola Ericsson. Liner notes. Bis CD-410. 1988–89.

B.115. Marie-Claire Alain. Liner notes. Erato 2292–45470–2, 1988.

B.116. Wolfgang Rübsam. Liner notes. Bayer Records BR 100 004, 1988.

B.117. Louis Thiry. Liner notes. Caliope CAL 9928, 1986.

Les Corps glorieux: Sept Visions brèves de la Vie des Ressuscités pour orgue

B.118. *Messiaen: Complete Organ Works.* Gillian Weir. Liner notes. Priory Records PRCD 921–925/6, 2004. 6 CDs.

B.119. *Messiaen: Complete Organ Works.* Olivier Latry. Liner notes. Deutsche Grammophon 471 480–2, 2002. 6 CDs.

B.120. *Messiaen: The Organ Works.* Jennifer Bate. Liner notes. Regis RRC 6001, 1980–87/2001. 6 CDs.

B.121. *Olivier Messiaen: Complete Organ Works.* Rudolf Innig. Liner notes. MD&G Records 3170621, 1996–98. 7 CDs.

B.122. Jon Gillock. Liner notes. Jade 7313835752–2, 1995.

B.123. *Messiaen par lui-même: Organ Works.* Olivier Messiaen. Liner notes. EMI Classics CDZ 7 67401 2, 1957/1992. 4 CDs.

B.124. *The Complete Organ Music.* Hans-Ola Ericsson. Liner notes. Bis CD-442. 1988–89.

B.125. Louis Thiry. Liner notes. Caliope CAL 9926, 1986.

Messe de la Pentecôte

B.126. *Messiaen: Complete Organ Works.* Gillian Weir. Liner notes. Priory Records PRCD 921–925/6, 2004. 6 CDs.

B.127. *Messiaen: Complete Organ Works.* Olivier Latry. Liner notes. Deutsche Grammophon 471 480–2, 2002. 6 CDs.

B.128. *Messiaen: The Organ Works.* Jennifer Bate. Liner notes. Regis RRC 6001, 1980–87/2001. 6 CDs.

B.129. *Olivier Messiaen: Complete Organ Works.* Rudolf Innig. Liner notes. MD&G Records 3170622, 1996–98. 7 CDs.

B.130. *Messiaen par lui-même: Organ Works.* Olivier Messiaen. Liner notes. EMI Classics CDZ 7 67401 2, 1957/1992. 4 CDs.

B.131. *The Complete Organ Music.* Hans-Ola Ericsson. Liner notes. Bis CD-441. 1988–89.

B.132. Louis Thiry. Liner notes. Caliope CAL 9927, 1987.

Livre d'orgue

B.133. *Messiaen: Complete Organ Works.* Gillian Weir. Liner notes. Priory Records PRCD 921–925/6, 2004. 6 CDs.

B.134. *Messiaen: Complete Organ Works.* Olivier Latry. Liner notes. Deutsche Grammophon 471 480–2, 2002. 6 CDs.

B.135. *Messiaen: The Organ Works.* Jennifer Bate. Liner notes. Regis RRC 6001, 1980–87/2001. 6 CDs.

B.136. *Olivier Messiaen: Complete Organ Works.* Rudolf Innig. Liner notes. MD&G Records 3170622, 1996–98. 7 CDs.

B.137. *Messiaen par lui-même: Organ Works.* Olivier Messiaen. Liner notes. EMI Classics CDZ 7 67401 2, 1957/1992. 4 CDs.

B.138. *The Complete Organ Music.* Hans-Ola Ericsson. Liner notes. Bis CD-441. 1988–89.

B.139. Louis Thiry. Liner notes. Caliope CAL 9927, 1987.

Verset pour la fête de la Dédicace

B.140. *Messiaen: Complete Organ Works.* Gillian Weir. Liner notes. Priory Records PRCD 921–925/6, 2004. 6 CDs.

B.141. *Messiaen: Complete Organ Works.* Olivier Latry. Liner notes. Deutsche Grammophon 471 480–2, 2002. 6 CDs.

B.142. *Messiaen: The Organ Works.* Jennifer Bate. Liner notes. Regis RRC 6001, 1980–87/2001. 6 CDs.

B.143. *Olivier Messiaen: Complete Organ Works.* Rudolf Innig. Liner notes. MD&G Records 3170621, 1996–98. 7 CDs.

B.144. *The Complete Organ Music.* Hans-Ola Ericsson. Liner notes. Bis CD-442. 1988–89.

Monodie

B.145. *Messiaen: Complete Organ Works.* Gillian Weir. Liner notes. Priory Records PRCD 921–925/6, 2004. 6 CDs.

B.146. *Messiaen: Complete Organ Works.* Olivier Latry. Liner notes. Deutsche Grammophon 471 480–2, 2002. 6 CDs.

B.147. *Olivier Messiaen: Inédits.* Naji Hakim. Jade 7432167411–2, 1999.

Méditations sur le mystère de la Sainte Trinité

B.148. *Messiaen Edition.* Olivier Messiaen. Liner notes. Warner Classics 2564 62162–2, 2005. 18 CDs.

B.149. *Messiaen: Complete Organ Works.* Gillian Weir. Liner notes. Priory Records PRCD 921–925/6, 2004. 6 CDs.

B.150. *Messiaen: Complete Organ Works.* Olivier Latry. Liner notes. Deutsche Grammophon 471 480–2, 2002. 6 CDs.

B.151. *Messiaen: The Organ Works.* Jennifer Bate. Liner notes. Regis RRC 6001, 1980–87/2001. 6 CDs.

B.152. *Olivier Messiaen: Complete Organ Works.* Rudolf Innig. Liner notes. MD&G Records 3170053, 1996–98. 7 CDs.

B.153. Christopher Bowers-Broadbent. Liner notes. ECM Records ECM 1494, 1995.

B.154. *The Complete Organ Music.* Hans-Ola Ericsson. Liner notes. Bis CD-464. 1988–89.

Livre du Saint Sacrement

B.155. *Messiaen: Complete Organ Works.* Gillian Weir. Liner notes. Priory Records PRCD 921–925/6, 2004. 6 CDs.

B.156. *Messiaen: Complete Organ Works.* Olivier Latry. Liner notes. Deutsche Grammophon 471 480–2, 2002. 6 CDs.

B.157. *Messiaen: The Organ Works.* Jennifer Bate. Liner notes. Regis RRC 6001, 1980–87/2001. 6 CDs.

B.158. *Olivier Messiaen: Complete Organ Works.* Rudolf Innig. Liner notes. MD&G Records 31706232, 1996–98. 7 CDs.

B.159.　*The Complete Organ Music.* Hans-Ola Ericsson. Liner notes. Bis CD-491/492. 1988–89.

B.160.　Almut Rößler. Liner notes. Motette DCD 11061, 1987. 2 CDs.

VI. PIANO

Préludes

B.161.　*Messiaen Edition.* Yvonne Loriod. Liner notes. Warner Classics 2564 62162–2, 2005. 18 CDs.

B.162.　*Messiaen: Complete Works for Piano, Volume 4.* Paul Kim. Liner notes. Centaur Records 2727, 2005.

B.163.　*Messiaen: Integrale de l'oeuvre pour piano seul.* Roger Muraro. Liner notes. Accord 461 907–2, 2001. 7 CDs.

B.164.　*Olivier Messiaen: Piano Music, Volume 3.* Håkon Austbø. Liner notes. Naxos 8.554090, 1999.

B.165.　*Messiaen: The Piano Works.* Peter Hill (with Benjamin Frith [*Visions de l'Amen*]). Liner notes. Unicorn-Kanchana Records RRC 7001, 1984–92. 7 CDs.

B.166.　Michel Béroff. Liner notes. EMI Classics 7243 5 69668 2 6, 1978/ 1987. 2 CDs.

Les Offrandes oubliées *(transcribed for piano by Messiaen)*

B.167.　*Messiaen: Complete Works for Piano, Volume 4.* Paul Kim. Liner notes. Centaur Records 2727, 2005.

B.168.　*Olivier Messiaen: Piano Music, Volume 4.* Håkon Austbø. Liner notes. Naxos 8.554655, 2002.

Fantaisie burlesque

B.169.　*Messiaen: Complete Works for Piano, Volume 4.* Paul Kim. Liner notes. Centaur Records 2727, 2005.

B.170.　*Olivier Messiaen: Piano Music, Volume 4.* Håkon Austbø. Liner notes. Naxos 8.554655, 2002.

B.171.　*Messiaen: Integrale de l'oeuvre pour piano seul.* Roger Muraro. Liner notes. Accord 461 907–2, 2001. 7 CDs.

B.172. *Messiaen: The Piano Works.* Peter Hill (with Benjamin Frith [*Visions de l'Amen*]). Liner notes. Unicorn-Kanchana Records RRC 7001, 1984–92. 7 CDs.

Pièce pour le Tombeau de Paul Dukas

B.173. *Messiaen: Complete Works for Piano, Volume 4.* Paul Kim. Liner notes. Centaur Records 2727, 2005.

B.174. *Olivier Messiaen: Piano Music, Volume 4.* Håkon Austbø. Liner notes. Naxos 8.554655, 2002.

B.175. *Messiaen: Integrale de l'oeuvre pour piano seul.* Roger Muraro. Liner notes. Accord 461 907–2, 2001. 7 CDs.

B.176. *Olivier Messiaen: Inédits.* Yvonne Loriod-Messiaen. Liner notes. Jade 7432167411–2, 1999.

B.177. *Messiaen: The Piano Works.* Peter Hill (with Benjamin Frith [*Visions de l'Amen*]). Liner notes. Unicorn-Kanchana Records RRC 7001, 1984–92. 7 CDs.

Rondeau

B.178. *Messiaen: Complete Works for Piano, Volume 4.* Paul Kim. Liner notes. Centaur Records 2727, 2005.

B.179. *Olivier Messiaen: Piano Music, Volume 4.* Håkon Austbø. Liner notes. Naxos 8.554655, 2002.

B.180. *Messiaen: Integrale de l'oeuvre pour piano seul.* Roger Muraro. Liner notes. Accord 461 907–2, 2001. 7 CDs.

B.181. *Messiaen: The Piano Works.* Peter Hill (with Benjamin Frith [*Visions de l'Amen*]). Liner notes. Unicorn-Kanchana Records RRC 7001, 1984–92. 7 CDs.

Visions de l'Amen

B.182. *Messiaen Edition.* Katia and Mariélle Labéque. Liner notes. Warner Classics 2564 62162–2, 2005. 18 CDs.

B.183. *Messiaen: Complete Works for Piano, Volume 3.* Paul Kim (with Matthew Kim). Liner notes. Centaur Records 2668, 2004.

B.184. Maarten Bon and Reinbert de Leeuw. Liner notes. Montaigne MO 782159, 1994/2002.

B.185. *Messiaen: The Piano Works*. Peter Hill (with Benjamin Frith [*Visions de l'Amen*]). Liner notes. Unicorn-Kanchana Records RRC 7001, 1984–92. 7 CDs.

B.186. Alexandre Rabinovitch and Martha Argerich. Liner notes. EMI CDC 7 54050 2, 1990.

B.187. Katia and Mariélle Labeque. Liner notes. Erato 4509-91707-2, 1970.

Vingt Regards sur l'Enfant-Jésus

B.188. *Messiaen Edition*. Yvonne Loriod. Liner notes. Warner Classics 2564 62162–2, 2005. 18 CDs.

B.189. *Messiaen: Complete Works for Piano, Volume 2*. Paul Kim. Liner notes. Centaur Records 2627/8, 2003. 2 CDs.

B.190. *Messiaen: Integrale de l'oeuvre pour piano seul*. Roger Muraro. Liner notes. Accord 461 907–2, 2001. 7 CDs.

B.191. Pierre-Laurent Aimard, piano. Teldec 3984-26868-2, 2000. 2 CDs.

B.192. Håkon Austbø. Naxos 8.550829/30, 1993. 2 CDs.

B.193. *Messiaen: The Piano Works*. Peter Hill (with Benjamin Frith [*Visions de l'Amen*]). Liner notes. Unicorn-Kanchana Records RRC 7001, 1984–92. 7 CDs.

B.194. Roger Muraro. Liner notes. Accord 465 334–2. 1991. 2 CDs.

B.195. Michel Béroff. Liner notes. EMI Classics 7243 5 69668 2 6, 1970/ 1987. 2 CDs.

B.196. Yvonne Loriod. Liner notes. Erato 4509-91705-2, 1975. 2 CDs.

Cantéyodjayâ

B.197. *Messiaen: Complete Works for Piano, Volume 3*. Paul Kim. Liner notes. Centaur Records 2668, 2004.

B.198. *Messiaen: Integrale de l'oeuvre pour piano seul*. Roger Muraro. Liner notes. Accord 461 907–2, 2001. 7 CDs.

B.199. *Messiaen: The Piano Works*. Peter Hill (with Benjamin Frith [*Visions de l'Amen*]). Liner notes. Unicorn-Kanchana Records RRC 7001, 1984–92. 7 CDs.

Quatre Études de rythme

B.200. *Messiaen Edition*. Yvonne Loriod. Liner notes. Warner Classics 2564 62162–2, 2005. 18 CDs.

B.201. *Messiaen: Complete Works for Piano, Volume 3.* Paul Kim. Liner notes. Centaur Records 2668, 2004.

B.202. *Messiaen: Integrale de l'oeuvre pour piano seul.* Roger Muraro. Liner notes. Accord 461 907–2, 2001. 7 CDs.

B.203. *Messiaen: The Piano Works.* Peter Hill (with Benjamin Frith [*Visions de l'Amen*]). Liner notes. Unicorn-Kanchana Records RRC 7001, 1984–92. 7 CDs.

Catalogue d'oiseaux

B.204. *Messiaen Edition.* Yvonne Loriod. Liner notes. Warner Classics 2564 62162–2, 2005. 18 CDs.

B.205. *Messiaen: Complete Works for Piano, Volume 1.* Paul Kim. Liner notes. Centaur Records 2567/9, 2002. 3 CDs.

B.206. *Messiaen: Integrale de l'oeuvre pour piano seul.* Roger Muraro. Liner notes. Accord 461 907–2, 2001. 7 CDs.

B.207. Håkon Austbø. Liner notes. Naxos 8.553532–34, 1997. 3 CDs.

B.208. Roger Muraro. Liner notes. Accord 465 768–2. 1997. 3 CDs.

B.209. Anatol Ugorski. Liner notes. Deutsche Grammophon 474 345–2, 1994. 3 CDs.

B.210. *Messiaen: The Piano Works.* Peter Hill (with Benjamin Frith [*Visions de l'Amen*]). Liner notes. Unicorn-Kanchana Records RRC 7001, 1984–92. 7 CDs.

Prélude

B.211. *Messiaen: Complete Works for Piano, Volume 4.* Paul Kim. Liner notes. Centaur Records 2727, 2005.

B.212. *Olivier Messiaen: Piano Music, Volume 4.* Håkon Austbø. Liner notes. Naxos 8.554655, 2002.

B.213. *Messiaen: Integrale de l'oeuvre pour piano seul.* Roger Muraro. Liner notes. Accord 461 907–2, 2001. 7 CDs.

B.214. *Olivier Messiaen: Inédits.* Yvonne Loriod-Messiaen. Liner notes. Jade 7432167411–2, 1999.

La Fauvette des jardins

B.215. *Messiaen Edition.* Yvonne Loriod. Liner notes. Warner Classics 2564 62162–2, 2005. 18 CDs.

B.216. *Olivier Messiaen: Piano Music, Volume 4.* Håkon Austbø. Liner notes. Naxos 8.554655, 2002.

B.217. *Messiaen: Complete Works for Piano, Volume 1.* Liner notes. Paul Kim. Centaur Records 2567/9, 2002. 3 CDs.

B.218. *Messiaen: Integrale de l'oeuvre pour piano seul.* Roger Muraro. Liner notes. Accord 461 907–2, 2001. 7 CDs.

B.219. Roger Muraro. Liner notes. Accord 461 646–2, 2001.

B.220. Anatol Ugorski. Liner notes. Deutsche Grammophon 474 345–2, 1994. 3 CDs.

B.221. *Messiaen: The Piano Works.* Peter Hill (with Benjamin Frith [*Visions de l'Amen*]). Liner notes. Unicorn-Kanchana Records RRC 7001, 1984–92. 7 CDs.

Petites esquisses d'oiseaux

B.222. *Messiaen Edition.* Yvonne Loriod. Liner notes. Warner Classics 2564 62162–2, 2005. 18 CDs.

B.223. *Messiaen: Complete Works for Piano, Volume 1.* Paul Kim. Liner notes. Centaur Records 2567/9, 2002. 3 CDs.

B.224. *Messiaen: Integrale de l'oeuvre pour piano seul.* Roger Muraro. Liner notes. Accord 461 907–2, 2001. 7 CDs.

B.225. Håkon Austbø. Naxos 8.553532–34, 1997. 3 CDs.

B.226. *Messiaen: The Piano Works.* Peter Hill (with Benjamin Frith [*Visions de l'Amen*]). Liner notes. Unicorn-Kanchana Records RRC 7001, 1984–92. 7 CDs.

VII. VOCAL

Trois Mélodies

B.227. *Mélodies.* Ingrid Kappelle, soprano; Håkon Austbø, piano. Brilliant Classics, 7448, 2004/2005.

La Mort du Nombre

B.228. *Olivier Messiaen: Inédits.* Hervé Lamy, Yvonne Loriod-Messiaen, Alain Louvier, Françoise Pollet, and Agnès Sulem-Bialobroda. Jade 7432167411–2, 1999.

Vocalise-étude

B.229. *Mélodies.* Ingrid Kappelle, soprano; Håkon Austbø, piano. Brilliant Classics, 7448, 2004/2005.

Poèmes pour Mi: Chant et Piano

B.230. *Messiaen Edition.* Maria Oràn, soprano, and Yvonne Loriod, piano. Liner notes. Warner Classics 2564 62162–2, 2005. 18 CDs.

B.231. *Mélodies.* Ingrid Kappelle, soprano; Håkon Austbø, piano. Brilliant Classics, 7448, 2004/2005.

Poèmes pour Mi: Grand Soprano dramatique et Orchestre *(orchestral version)*

B.232. The Cleveland Orchestra, Pierre Boulez, conductor. Françoise Pollet, Pierre-Laurent Aimard, and Joela Jones. Deutsche Grammophon 453 478–2, 1997.

O sacrum convivium!: Motet au Saint-Sacrement pour chœur à quatre voix mixtes ou quatre solistes (avec accompagnement d'orgue *ad libitum*)

B.233. London Sinfonietta Voices, Terry Edwards, conductor. Liner notes. Virgin Classics VC 7 91472–2, 1991.

Chants de Terre et de Ciel

B.234. *Messiaen Edition.* Maria Oràn, soprano, and Yvonne Loriod, piano. Liner notes. Warner Classics 2564 62162–2, 2005. 18 CDs.

B.235. *Mélodies.* Ingrid Kappelle, soprano; Håkon Austbø, piano. Brilliant Classics, 7448, 2004/2005.

Trois petites Liturgies de la Présence Divine

B.236. *Messiaen Edition.* Maîtrise et Orchestre de Chambre de la RTF, Marcel Couraud, conductor. Yvonne Loriod, piano, and Jeanne Loriod, Ondes Martenot. Liner notes. Warner Classics 2564 62162–2, 2005. 18 CDs.

B.237. Orchestre National de France, Kent Nagano, conductor. Yvonne Loriod, piano; Jeanne Loriod, Ondes Martenot. Liner notes. Erato 0630-12702-2, 1996.

B.238. Kühn Mixed Chorus/Bambini di Praga; Prague Symphony Orchestra, Bohumil Kulinsky, conductor. Yvonne Loriod, piano; Jeanne Loriod, Ondes Martenot. Liner notes. Supraphon 11 0404–2 231, 1991.

B.239. London Sinfonietta Chorus, London Sinfonietta, Terry Edwards, conductor. Rolf Hind, piano; Cynthia Millar, Ondes Martenot. Liner notes. Virgin Classics VC 7 91472–2, 1991.

Harawi: Chant d'Amour et de Mort

B.240. *Messiaen Edition.* Rachel Yakar, soprano, and Yvonne Loriod, piano. Liner notes. Warner Classics 2564 62162–2, 2005. 18 CDs.

B.241. *Mélodies.* Ingrid Kappelle, soprano; Håkon Austbø, piano. Brilliant Classics, 7448, 2004/2005.

B.242. Lucy Shelton, soprano, and John Constable, piano. Liner notes. Koch International Classics 3-7292-2 H1, 1999.

B.243. Veronica Lenz-Kuhn, soprano, and Wolfgang Kaiser, piano. Liner notes. Thorofon Classics CTH 2330, 1997.

B.244. Jane Manning, soprano, and David Miller, piano. Unicorn Records UKCD 2084, 1996.

B.245. Yumi Nara, soprano, and Jay Gottlieb, piano. ADDA 581139, 1991.

B.246. Rachel Yakar, soprano, and Yvonne Loriod, piano. Liner notes. Erato 2292-45505-2/9, 1988.

Chant des Déportés

B.247. *Olivier Messiaen: Inédits.* BBC Orchestra and Choir, Sir Andrew Davis, conductor. Jade 7432167411–2, 1999.

Cinq Rechants

B.248. *Messiaen Edition.* Solistes des chœurs de l'O.R.T.F., Marcel Couraud, conductor. Liner notes. Warner Classics 2564 62162–2, 2005. 18 CDs.

B.249. Kühn Chamber Soloists, Pavel Kühn, conductor. Liner notes. Supraphon 11 0404–2 231, 1991.

B.250. London Sinfonietta Voices, Terry Edwards, conductor. Liner notes. Virgin Classics VC 7 91472–2, 1991.

B.251. Solistes des chœurs de l'O.R.T.F., Marcel Couraud, conductor. Liner notes. Erato 4509-91708-2, 1968.

La Transfiguration de Nôtre-Seigneur Jésus-Christ

B.252. SWR Sinfonieorchester Baden-Baden und Freiburg, Europa Chor-Akademie, Hans Rosbaud, conductor. Yvonne Loriod, piano. Liner notes. Hänssler Classic 93.078, 2002. 2 CDs.

B.253. NDR-Chor, Rundfunkchor Berlin, Rundfunk-Sinfonieorchester Berlin, Karl Anton Rickenbacher, conductor. Yvonne Loriod, piano. Liner notes. Koch Classics CD 3-1216-2, 1999. 2 CDs.

B.254. Koor Van de Brt Bruxelles, Groot Omroepkoor & Radio Symfonie Orkest Hilversum, Reinbert de Leeuw, conductor. Yvonne Loriod, piano. Liner notes. Montaigne MO 782040, 1994, 2 CDs.

VIII. ELECTRONIC

Fête des belles eaux

B.255. *Œuvres pour Ondes Martenot by Olivier Messiaen.* Antoine Tisne; Akira Tamba; Susumu Yoshida; Sextuor Jeanne Loriod. REM 1997.

B.256. Ensemble d'ondes de Montréal. Daniel Toussaint; Tristan Murail; Jean Lesage; Serge Provost; Claude Vivier; Lise Daoust. SNE, 1992.

Timbres-Durées

B.257. *IDEAMA target collection by Olivier Messiaen.* Zentrum für Kunst und Medientechnologie Karlsruhe, Radiodiffusion française, Groupe de recherche de musique concrète, Radiodiffusion-Télévision française, Groupe de recherche de musique concrète. Pierre Boulez; Pierre Henry. ZKM/Mediathek-Audiothek LDC 36434, 1996.

Quatre Inédits *(for Ondes Martenot and Piano)*

B.258. *Olivier Messiaen: Inédits.* Jeanne Loriod, Ondes Martenot; Yvonne Loriod-Messiaen, piano. Jade 7432167411–2, 1999.

Index of Names

Numbers in **bold** refer to authors.

Index of Musical Works by Olivier Messiaen

17875191R00195

Printed in Great Britain
by Amazon